AMERICAN CURTISS HAWK BIPLANES
VS.
JAPANESE ZERO FIGHTERS

Here are incredible combat stories of America's "can do" pilots, flying obsolete planes against the Japanese Zero—one of the great fighter planes of World War II. Here are the exploits of Tommy Walker and Colonel Bob Scott (*God Is My Co-Pilot*) in the days when America was being pushed back all over the Pacific and only a few dedicated men stood between the Japanese and total victory. Here is the epic story of sky fighting soldiers of fortune in the sharkfaced planes of the Flying Tigers—in the early air war in the Pacific.

THE BANTAM WAR BOOK SERIES

This series of books is about a world on fire.

The carefully chosen volumes in the Bantam War Book Series cover the full dramatic sweep of World War II. Many are eyewitness accounts by the men who fought in a global conflict as the world's future hung in the balance. Fighter pilots, tank commanders and infantry captains, among many others, recount exploits of individual courage. They present vivid portraits of brave men, true stories of gallantry, moving sagas of survival and stark tragedies of untimely death.

In 1933 Nazi Germany marched to become an empire that was to last a thousand years. In only twelve years that empire was destroyed, and ever since, the country has been bisected by her conquerors. Italy relinquished her colonial lands, as did Japan. These were the losers. The winners also lost the empires they had so painfully seized over the centuries. And one, Russia, lost over twenty million dead.

Those wartime 1940s were a simple, even a hopeful time. Hats came in only two colors, white and black, and after an initial battering the Allied nations started on a long and laborious march toward victory. It was a time when sane men believed the world would evolve into a decent place, but, as with all futures, there was no one then who could really forecast the world that we know now.

There are many ways to think about that war. It has always been hard to understand the motivations and braveries of Axis soldiers fighting to enslave and dominate their neighbors. Yet it is impossible to know the hammer without the anvil, and to comprehend ourselves we must know the people we once fought against.

Through these books we can discover what it was like to take part in the war that was a final experience for nearly fifty million human beings. In so doing we may discover the strength to make a world as good as the one contained in those dreams and aspirations once believed by heroic men. We must understand our past as an honor to those dead who can no longer choose. They exchanged their lives in a hope for this future that we now inhabit. Though the fight took place many years ago, each of us remains as a living part of it.

QUANTITY PURCHASES

THE RAGGED, RUGGED WARRIORS

MARTIN CAIDIN

BANTAM BOOKS

TORONTO • NEW YORK • LONDON • SYDNEY • AUCKLAND

THE RAGGED, RUGGED WARRIORS

*A Bantam Book / published by arrangement with
Elsevier-Dutton Publishing Company, Inc.*

PRINTING HISTORY

Elsevier-Dutton edition published March 1966
1st printing ... February 1966
2nd printing ... July 1966

Bantam edition / July 1979
2nd printing ... May 1985

Drawings by Fred L. Wolff.
Maps by Alan McKnight.

ISBN 0-553-25062-0

Published simultaneously in the United States and Canada

PRINTED IN THE UNITED STATES OF AMERICA

H   11 10 9 8 7 6 5 4 3 2

ACKNOWLEDGMENTS

Grateful acknowledgment is made to the following for permission to reprint copyright material:

Brigadier General Robert L. Scott, Jr., USAF (Ret.) for excerpts from his book, *God Is My Co-Pilot*, with a Foreword by General Claire L. Chennault (New York: Charles Scribner's Sons, 1944). Copyright, 1943, by Robert L. Scott, Jr. This permission is granted in grateful tribute to the late General Claire L. Chennault, "who taught me all I knew about air war as it was then."

J. B. Lippincott Company for permission to reprint material from *The Mission*, by Martin Caidin and Edward Hymoff. Copyright ©, 1964 by Martin Caidin and Edward Hymoff. Published by J. B. Lippincott Company.

The Viking Press for excerpt from *The Flying Tigers*, by Russell Whelan.

Holt, Rinehart and Winston, Inc., for excerpt from *Thunderbolt!* by Robert S. Johnson with Martin Caidin. Reprinted by permission of Holt, Rinehart and Winston, Inc.

Vern Haugland and Harper & Row for excerpts from Mr. Haughland's book, *The AAF Against Japan*.

E. P. Dutton & Co., Inc., for excerpts from *The Lady and the Tiger,* by Olga S. Greenlaw. Copyright, 1943, by E. P. Dutton & Co., Inc. Reprinted by permission of the publishers.

E.P. Dutton & Co., Inc., for excerpts and maps from *Zero!* by Masatake Okumiya and Jiro Horikoshi with Martin Caidin. Copyright ©, 1956, by Martin Caidin. Reprinted by permission of the publishers.

E. P. Dutton & Co., Inc., for excerpts from *Samurai!* by Saburo Sakai with Martin Caidin and Fred Saito. Copyright, ©, 1958, by Martin Caidin. Reprinted by permission of the publishers.

THIS BOOK IS FOR

Ed Keyes

WHO FLEW ONE LOW AND SLOW

CONTENTS

PREFACE

War has been described as the single greatest cooperative effort of mankind. A war that extends around the entire globe and that endures over a period of some eight years represents a colossal effort that defies accurate recording. This is especially true when there are involved in that war, and the spotty attempts at recording its details, several dozen languages, as many nations, and combat arenas that spread across and beneath the surface of the sea, on the land, and throughout the ever-shifting air mass that girdles the planet.

There is also the problem of personal viewpoints, of history distorted by anger, to say nothing of specific and deliberate propaganda, ignorance, and ego. Even the vantage of new perspective, provided by the passing of years and the calming of tempers, does not guarantee either accuracy or objectivity in recording past events. Being able to see with 20-20 hindsight is virtually impossible in recording the manifold aspects of anything so stupendous as war in four dimensions—the fourth being the time scale of events.

Yet looking backwards into history is definitely an aid. Many of the incidents which once were seen only from a single viewpoint expand strangely into multidimensional pictures. What appeared to be black and white assumes shifting patterns of grayness. The passage of the years enables us to bring into new focus the attitudes, the convictions and the opinions, and the first-person involvement of participants who previously had failed to contribute to the archives that hold the records of past military, official, and personal events.

These many factors have the tendency to alter the accepted picture of historical events. The fabric of familiar history seems to ripple and to become distorted. There is an intrusion into the familiar that brings with it the disturbing realization that all is not, perhaps, as we have always believed.

This is the case with the time period of 1937 through most of 1942, when there was fought through Asia and the far reaches of the Pacific Ocean the aerial war of the ragged, rugged warriors. It is a period still largely hidden beneath the shimmering confusions of time and a thousand different points of view, each with its own degree of validity.

Much of the story of this aerial war has never been committed to the archives, or has been lost in privately printed and forgotten squadron histories. The fierce combat actions of entire groups, of hundreds of military aircraft and thousands of men, have sometimes escaped the attention of historians. Much of what our combat men performed in the line of duty was committed to paper, and then the records were lost forever through their destruction by bombing, fire, or other causes; the participants also were lost or, as happened often, simply drifted away along other paths.

From this period of historical chaos (when staying alive took priority over the urge to write about the events of the moment) writers seeking facts have in their frustration drawn the best possible conclusions from meager information. These conclusions have often suffered, as might be expected, from gross distortions, because there was so little valid data from which to pen the "final account."

This book is an attempt to set much of this record straight. Much has been written, of course, of the aerial combat of the period from 1937 through the first half of 1942, but these writings have been scattered, and have concentrated on specific areas—such as the combat record of the renowned Flying Tigers. There has never been an overall picture of the time period in which we are interested.

Even the definitive works, such as the Air Force Historical Office's official, seven-volume history, *The Army Air Forces in World War II,* contain glaring omissions. Nowhere in that series—nor in the official archives of the Air Force, for that matter—is there more than the barest mention of the 22nd Bomb Group, which operated out of Australia and New Guinea early in 1942. But this is the group that carried out the bulk of all medium bomber operations in the Southwest Pacific through the summer of 1942, and in this role it exerted a tremendous effect on the conduct of the war in that time. The author, working in partnership with Edward Hymoff, in 1964 completed an exhaustive survey of most survivors of that group, in order to assemble—for the first time—the story of a major phase of the war period when the term "ragged, rugged warriors" had very special meaning.

This book does not attempt an exhaustive survey of the years which hold our attention. Rather it is the author's hope to present an across-the-board study, to bring into one central focus the many scattered pieces—some of them written, others previously unrecorded—into a single volume.

In preparing this book, I have found it impossible not to make certain personal decisions as to content. It would be repetitious to place strong emphasis upon those battles and campaigns which already are intimately known, and which have received the treatment of many historians. It is not the purpose of this volume simply to repeat what is readily available elsewhere, but rather to weave a mixture of the unknown, the little-known, and the fragmentary with the salient and identified episodes of the time we are examining, in order to create a new perspective of that combat period.

Out of this effort, it is hoped, there will emerge a fresh and different picture of the air war, about which so little has been presented in terms of over-all continuity and integration of so many different events and campaigns.

Our story is not one of the ultimate victory we know so well, but of that time when victory belonged to some distant and unknown future, and the present was filled with raw and naked survival against terrible odds.

Much of the material for this book has been obtained through personal interviews, and through personal recollections kindly made available to the author by participants in the events described. That material has been integrated throughout the book, of course, but it appears worth our while to review some of the notes taken and the letters received, if only as a sample of the diversity of the experiences, words, and thoughts of these participants. They illustrate also the great variety of sources employed to weave the fabric of this story. For this book is not so much along the lines of the many "official histories," but rather a tapestry of material assembled from many, many different people and never-before-used notes and semi-official diaries.

From Carl W. Shrader of Amarillo, Texas:

"Our squadron was based at Wheeler Field on December 7, 1941. I awoke that Sunday morning to the rattle of a machine gun and looked out to see a Japanese torpedo bomber fly low across the field. . . . I believe this was the plane that torpedoed the *California*. I moved to the door of the tent and looked up to see several dive bombers in stepped-up formation. The first just released a bomb at that moment. The bomb hit the refueling site. The remaining bombs hit hangars and barracks along the flight line. Our squadron moved out to the golf course at Schofield Barracks, utilizing the course as a landing field for a brief period. We were subsequently stationed at Moruleia on the Dillingham Ranch, Barbers Point, Bellows Field, and back at Wheeler. . . ."

Al Abramson of Chicago, Illinois, reported on a different part of the world:

"The 11th and 22nd Bomb Squadrons (M), 341st Bomb Group, arrived in Karachi, India in July, 1942. B-25 aircraft arrived shortly thereafter and were flown to China. Major James Leland [flight leader] was killed when his lead plane and some others hit a mountain while trying to cross the Hump. . . .

"The 7th Bomb Group was partly in the Philippines when things started to happen. Some of the bunch headed for Australia; some made it, a lot of them didn't. Some of the rest were sent to India. . . .

"Master Sergeant Norton G. Stubblefield [armorer-gunner] of the 341st Bomb Group . . . received recognition from Chennault during 1942 as the most effective top-turret gunner. He also developed a 'wobble-gun' in the tail of the B-25. Some of the early B-25 models had tail gunners, and some didn't, because tail gunners so rarely lived through any action when they were equipped with only a 30-caliber gun. Stubblefield's 'wobble gun' was mounted on a jeep spring and carried a higher-than-average percentage of tracer ammunition. Its principal effect was psychological— to keep the Zeros clear of the B-25's blind spot, if possible. It worked fairly well.

"Most of our [the 341st's] losses in 1942 were due to the weather in India. One plane, for instance, disintegrated in a thunderhead. The co-pilot lived through the ordeal, but did not remember whether he bailed out or was blown out of the airplane. The right engine and the empennage had left the plane before he did. . . .

"In late 1942, because of losing the Leland flight, there were only six B-25s in the India-Burma theater, and usually only two of these were operational because of worn-out tires, getting shot up by ground fire, or similar reasons. At one point, *one* B-25 was flying five and six reconnaissance sorties per day over Burma (usually up and down the Irrawaddy River) with a total crew of two men—the pilot and a gunner. We were short of aircrews as well as planes.

"For a few days in September of 1942 we had over four hundred ground personnel, and one operational airplane with a crew of two who were 1,600 miles forward of the ground crews. Planes destined for us were continually diverted to North Africa and to Italy. So were our food and supplies for a while. . . ."

And from Robert E. Heath of St. Ann, Missouri:

"I was in the Navy, stationed on the *Langley* for several months before the war, until it was sunk about one month after the war started. We left Cavite about twenty-four hours before it was bombed, made our way south through the East Indies, sinking a submarine on the way, and reloading at Soerabaja, then to Darwin, Australia.

"Upon leaving Darwin we started north with a load of P-40s to the East Indies and to evacuate a group of people. But about one hundred miles out we were disabled by high-altitude bombers, which caused leaks in the hull sufficient to short out the engines.

"We were rescued by destroyers, which fired two torpedoes into the *Langley* to sink her. We were then transferred to the oil tanker *Pecos* at Christmas Island, and started south to Australia. About twenty-four hours later dive bombers sank the *Pecos* and we were again picked up—by the same destroyers as before. This time we were taken to Perth, Australia. . . ."

William Fent of Celina, Ohio, provided a lead to the use of aircraft which have "disappeared" into the blank spots of history:

"I was with the 54th Materiel Squadron, later in the 80th Depot Repair Group. I left the United States on the first convoy after Pearl Harbor and finally settled in Karachi, India. While there we assembled or processed all planes for the China-Burma-India theater during the first two years of the war. The P-40, P-66, P-43, and A-24 were among some of the early ones. . . ."

The final source to be quoted now we leave (by request) anonymous:

"The 20th was noted as one of the foremost 'moonlight requisitioning' outfits in New Guinea after we had been there for a few weeks. It wasn't long until the Fifth Air Force Provost Marshal visited us first when something large was missing. Our greatest coup was borrowing a complete mess-hall building in one night (metal roof, 2x4's, 2x6's screen wire) and getting it flown over the razorback hump to our advance echelon in Nadzab, New Guinea, the next morning. When the owners came back to load it on their LST's they couldn't find any mess hall or even the slightest evidence of where the hell the thing had gone.

"At one time we had fourteen extra jeeps until two drivers with identical serial numbers on their jeeps went through the same MP checkpoint at the same time. By the next morning we had more crew chiefs that had been reduced to the grade of private than any other squadron in New Guinea.

"We had a tech sergeant and a lieutenant assigned full duty to drive their jeep around the island to spot items worthy of 'borrowing.' When they found some good prospects they would come home for a detail of men and trucks. We didn't have a single man that ever got the Purple Heart for accomplishment of these 'vital missions.'

"We had a singular attitude to what we were doing. We were there to fight the Japs, we needed stuff to fight with, and a good part of the time we couldn't get what we needed. So we just went out and took it. To hell with the consequences—there was a war going on!"

They were ragged . . . and they were rugged. This is their story.

BOOK ONE

BOOK ONE

BOOK ONE

1

PROLOGUE OF BATTLE

The skies that mantle the earth are universal in nature. They are uncaring as to what takes place below or above, or even in their domain. The skies provide the battlegrounds for those who wish to wage war in the thin arena above the distant rock and soil. But when the last echo of stuttering guns and the scream of flame dies away, when the last whisper is no louder than a wisp of cloud shredded by wind, all is the same as it was before the conflict.

There are no markers, no battleground emblems, no plaques or statues to commemorate the spilling of blood and the tearing of metal. The skies are uncluttered by the debris of contesting men and their wings.

War in the air was formerly governed by unwritten law. That law, as in all martial conflict, evolved from the nature of the men engaged in the contest. Sometimes there were strong nationalistic factors involved. Men deeply steeped in traditions of soldiering carried those traditions with them into the skies. Where traditions were lacking, new ones were born overnight and, strangely enough, professional soldiers of differing nationality by and large came to agree on the same standards for their conduct while attempting to inflict defeat and death upon their opponents.

Thus in World War I, men of both sides considered it unsporting to turn their guns on another man who had taken to a parachute for survival, as did the observers in highly explosive and inflammable balloons to save their lives. The pilot who suffered the loss of his engine in battle, and whose wings sighed helplessly during the glide earthward, was considered to be beyond further attack. The goal had been met: the enemy was vanquished, and his death was unimportant against his defeat.

3

During that first great air war aviators were revered for bravery and regarded with wonder. Historians of World War I who should have known better perpetuated the fallacy that combat in the air was *the* way to fight and, if necessary, the finest way to die. The aerial gentlemen were painted as daring sportsmen who lived and died by special rules of conduct. In these grandiose chronicles of military valor and *esprit*, there seemed to be something unreal.

There was, to be sure, the final salute of the victor to his defeated opponent as that hapless worthy tumbled and flip-flopped in ungainly fashion toward the hard and resisting earth. But behind that final salute there lay the horror of being cremated while one was yet alive and healthy. No one appeared willing to write that the man who was being burned alive, jerking and twitching in the wind-whipped bed of flames, really didn't wish to die, least of all in this grotesque manner. And if one wished to avoid this terrifying end to life, in which valor and tradition seem to vanish with the first caress of fire against naked flesh, there was only the alternative of diving away from the blazing wreckage—a long and gut-wrenching plunge that ended against the earth.

Tradition and rules of conduct in the air varied with circumstances. Much depended upon the nature of the conflict. Customs observed in one part of the world were unknown in other parts.

Many of the unwritten laws of aerial combat were handed down from the mythology and the stories of derring-do arising from World War I. These carried over into the first large-scale aerial battles to follow that war— the battles waged over Spain and through the skies of China. These conflicts were fought for years before World War II. They are largely unknown to most Americans. From each of these battle arenas, however, came patterns of conduct in air fighting that carried over into the larger conflicts arising from global war.

It should be noted that despite the fact that these laws were uncommitted to parchment, they were very real, they were observed, and the adherence to them at times was savage in its discipline.

Such was the case in the early days of the aerial jousting over the ravaged hills and villages of Spain, when that hapless land writhed under the cruelties so specific to its civil war.

Luis Muñoz was a Loyalist fighter pilot, flying a snub-nosed Russian fighter plane along the Madrid battlefront. His Rata, speedy, maneuverable, heavily gunned, gave him a tremendous advantage in its performance against the Fiats and Heinkels used by the Nationalists in the life-and-death aerial struggle over Spain. Muñoz used his Russian fighter well in battle. In one of his first engagements he tore a Franco fighter plane to ribbons. His bullets sawtoothed the enemy into wreckage, and he splashed incendiary ammunition through its tanks. The Nationalist pilot with understandable haste hurled himself free of his blazing machine and tumbled through the air. Seconds later a touch of white blinked against blue sky. The white streamered out thin and long, and immediately changed shape into a billowing canopy of life-saving silk. Beneath the canopy hung the Franco pilot, grateful to have survived both the guns of his enemy and the funeral pyre of his own flaming machine.

As we said, Luis Muñoz was a pilot who used his fighter well in battle. And, immediately afterward, he used it very unwisely.

No one remembers what Muñoz was like personally, or what truly motivated his thoughts and his actions in combat. Perhaps at heart he was a killer, like so many other fighter pilots. Or he might have been a kid wild with the excitement of battle and the flush of his own victory. Maybe he hated all Franco pilots, for reasons best known to him.

Whatever his motivation, he brought his stubby fighter plane around in a tight turn, and he headed directly for his vanquished enemy floating in soft helplessness toward the earth. Muñoz squinted into his gunsights, and the small figure of the enemy in his harness grew larger and larger until, finally, Muñoz was satisfied. He squeezed a finger, and four heavy guns in the nose and wings of his airplane coughed and stammered loudly. The small figure in the harness twitched and jerked in a spasmodic writhing. There was a brief, strawberry-colored spray through the air, and the guns went silent.

Beneath the bullet-shredded parachute, clumping together in the form of a streaming, useless rag, the dead pilot fell uncaring to the ground. Even before his limp form thudded into the rocky earth, Insurgent troops ran to the scene. High above, the Loyalist planes wheeled and turned away, spreading their wings for home.

The Franco troops returned the bullet-shattered body of the fighter pilot to its home field, where the friends and the fellow pilots of the dead man could see for themselves the work of the eager Luis Muñoz and his four machine guns. The Nationalist pilots swore their revenge.

One week later they found the opportunity to demonstrate their disgust for the Loyalist pilot who had shot and killed a man helpless in his parachute. Another Loyalist pilot took a long burst into his engine; the propeller jerked around and then ground to a halt. The pilot picked out a flat area on the ground and nosed down to a dead-stick landing. As he stopped rolling he thrust his hands high above his cockpit in surrender. Rough hands dragged him from the airplane, shoved him into a truck, and then the pilot was driven at a furious pace to the airfield where men waited grimly for him.

The day following a German bomber eased its way beneath clouds and glided past the Loyalist airdrome at Huete. From the ground, pilots and ground crews watched a large and heavy box tumble from the bomber. The Heinkel disappeared in the distance as a parachute blossomed from the box, lowering it to a field near the airdrome. Men dragged the box back to the operations shack.

There the box was pried open. Several men became sick on the spot. Others walked away first, to stand hidden behind hangar walls where they could vomit alone.

Inside the box were the remains of the Loyalist pilot, victim of retribution. The unwritten laws had been violated, and this was payment. Both arms and legs had been torn off the torso. Then the head of the living pilot had been twisted around until the straining flesh tore and bones snapped and the head finally was wrenched completely from the neck. The signs of gross mutilation were unmistakable. The severed limbs and the face with horror etched into its lifelessness were dumped into the box with the torso, and then the box delivered to the Loyalist pilots.

No one could accept what had happened to the helpless

pilot who had surrendered. No one could, at the same time, justify the actions of Luis Muñoz.

It was a major war in the skies, but not so big that men were unable to give such matters their personal attention. This incident, in more or less the same details, was repeated several times, until the expression "gentleman's war in the air" became a travesty. The unwritten laws became something to remember; they became grist for the writer of aerial heroics, who chose to perpetuate them despite the growing similarities of air conflict and hand-to-hand combat on the ground, when the sole purpose of the combat came to be the slaughter of the enemy.

To be sure, there were exceptions to this rule. Not even the heat of battle could drive certain pilots from their religious adherence to what they considered inviolable rules for meeting their opponents in the air. Perhaps the outstanding example of this code was provided in late August, 1937, when the outstanding American pilot flying for the Loyalists fought a man-to-man aerial duel that was conducted according to the finest traditions of World War I—and fed new fuel to the legend of the "glory" of air combat as sustained by the writers of air fiction.

The occasion was literally a duel, between Captain Derek D. Dickinson of the Loyalists and Bruno Mussolini (son of the Italian dictator), who commanded a powerful force of fighter planes stationed at Palma de Majorca.

One evening, Bruno dispatched a message over the radio net of Insurgent headquarters. He issued a challenge to the Loyalists, stating that he, Bruno Mussolini, would alone meet any five fighter planes the enemy dared to send against him. Bruno Mussolini's bombast, however, contained more than sheer bravado. He was an experienced pilot and an aerobatic artist of great skill. He had many long months of successful air combat behind him. To these assets he also added the superb performance of Italy's newest fighter plane, a Fiat Romeo with a Hispano-Suiza engine of 1,300 horsepower—the most powerful and fastest fighter then in Spanish skies. This power advantage meant speed and rate of climb which, coupled with Mussolini's own skill and experience, gave him a decided edge over any opponent or opponents he might encounter in the air.

Colonel de los Reyes brought the "insulting message" from Bruno Mussolini to Captain Dickinson, who at the time was captain and leader of the famous Red Wings (Esquadrilla Alas Rojas), stationed at Castellon de la Plana. For nearly 18 months Dickinson had flown for the Loyalists; his last ten months had been spent in command of the Red Wings. He was familiar with Bruno Mussolini; the Italian led a strong force of enemy planes, and the two opposing forces had many times locked wings in stiff battle.

Captain Dickinson burst out angrily after reading the challenge from Mussolini. He implored his colonel to accept the dare, but on condition that he—Dickinson—should meet the Italian alone. For weeks afterward the Italians ignored the messages from the Loyalists, until finally the latter's insults became lurid, and 30 days after the original response, Mussolini took the bait.

The agreement was for the two men to meet at 15,000 feet, midway between the two airfields, and engage in combat, with no other aircraft interfering—no matter what might happen during the fight. Each pilot would bring with him two observation aircraft that were to remain well away from the battle and to maintain an altitude of no less than 16,000 feet.

During the duel, should either pilot decide he wanted to quit because of wounds, gun stoppages, or any other reason, he would throw over the side of his cockpit a heavy gauntlet to which would be attached a long silken scarf—six feet in length and three feet wide. Fluttering behind the heavy glove, it would be an unmistakable admission of defeat.

Against Bruno Mussolini in his new Fiat Romeo, Dickinson flew a Mosca, a Russian fighter with four guns in the nose plus another two guns in the wings—formidable armament for the Spanish air war. The Mosca had excellent maneuverability and until the arrival of the Fiat Romeo had been among the fastest airplanes at the front. Against the new Italian fighter, Dickinson knew he would have his work cut out for him.

At the appointed rendezvous in the sky, both fighters circled wide and then hauled up in Immelmanns, soaring up and over in loops, but breaking the loop at the top of the arc and half-rolling to normal flight. Then they rushed at one another, guns hammering.

The fight almost ended then and there as the Fiat's guns sent a stream of lead crashing into the Mosca. Mussolini may have been a braggart, but he could support his words with superb skill and gunnery in the air. In his first pass he stitched holes through the wings and the fuselage of Dickinson's airplane.

For 22 minutes the two pilots fought a spectacular man-to-man duel. Dickinson was regarded as one of the finest pilots ever to fly in Spain; he knew every aerobatic trick in the book and he invented others on the spot as the need demanded. For every stunt that he pulled, Mussolini matched him, and also took full advantage of the extra power and speed that his new fighter gave him. After 15 minutes of wild, steady fighting, the battle worked its way down to 8,000 feet. High above, the four observation planes circled and watched, remaining out of the fight.

It appeared to end with shocking suddenness. A long burst from the Fiat sent slugs tearing through Dickinson's arm and blood spurted from his left hand. Instinctively, Dickinson rammed the throttle forward for full power and kicked over in a dive. Against the faster Fiat, it was an error that almost ended the battle with the death of the American pilot. Mussolini anticipated the move and roared in to the tail of the Mosca, hammering out accurate bursts that steadily chewed up the Russian fighter.

Dickinson saved his life with a time-honored maneuver. He chopped power, banged the stick over to the left, and kicked hard right rudder. The Mosca presented itself almost sideways to the air and seemed to come to a stop. Mussolini shot past Dickinson and gave the American a rare opportunity for a long and accurate burst. The Fiat seemed to stumble in the air as the stream of bullets crashed home, but then it was back under control and Mussolini was clawing around to continue the attack.

Seven more minutes passed. Dickinson saw the instrument panel erupt before him even as glass showered into his face. Desperately he pulled back on the stick to start a fast loop; far below, Mussolini began to pull up tighter, intent on cutting inside the loop and catching the Mosca broadside in his guns.

Dickinson made his move. Still early in the loop, he stalled the airplane, whipped around to one side, half-rolling as the nose fell through the horizon. The Mosca came out of the hammerhead stall on its back, accelerating rapidly, and there, big as life, swollen in the sights, was the Fiat. Dickinson was just starting to squeeze the guns into roaring life when a hand was flung up in the cockpit of the enemy fighter. An object hurtled over the side, and white silk fluttered brightly against blue sky.

Bruno Mussolini had quit—with less than a second to live. Dickinson rolled out into level flight as the Fiat Romeo pulled alongside. The Italian pilot waved his arm, dropped the Fiat's nose in salute, and broke away for his home field.

On the ground at Castellon de la Plana, a shaken Derek Dickinson counted 326 bullet holes in his airplane.

The air war in Spain wasn't fought with all new fighters and bombers, although these were the aircraft that sparked the admiring paragraphs of reporters on the

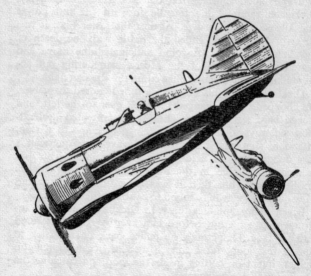

Russian-built Mosca fighter flown by Dickinson
in air duel against Mussolini.

scene, and helped in building up news dispatches into glowing descriptions of combat between heroes. The Alas Rojas squadron, operating on the Huesca front, sometimes flew offensive patrols in Nieuports left over from World War I! The pilots of these ancient and shaking machines considered themselves wonderfully fortunate when they failed to sight any of the black wingtips that marked the Insurgent planes.

As the length of the war grew, so did the number of planes hurled into the fray by the Italians, Germans, and Russians. One battle, described as "typical in numbers" by an American soldier of fortune flying for the Loyalists, saw a dozen Russian fighters diving on 20 Italian Fiats. The moment the battle was joined, 36 Heinkels streaked out of the sun to drop onto the Loyalists, catching them in the sandwich maneuver so favored in World War I.

As the war progressed, the Italians sent in large numbers of their latest fighters. The Germans threw Heinkel He-112 fighters into the fray, and then used Spain as a battleground for early combat models of their Messerschmitt Me-109, which they were to employ as their fighter mainstay in the Battle of Britain. The Russians sent not only airplanes, but squadrons of crack fighter pilots as well. France responded to the call of the Loyalists and shipped various types of fighters and bombers to the battleground. By war's end, the air battles were being fought with a bewildering variety of airplanes from all over the world.

But what had promised to become a carefully measured testing ground for future air campaigns failed to evolve. The air war over Spain became a scramble, with the diversity in aircraft matched by the moods and the means of the pilots and aircrews. Many men fought with great daring and bravery; others spat upon the aims and goals of the conflict and wasted no time in extricating themselves from difficult or lethal circumstances.

There were no real victors in the skies of Spain. The nations contributing numbers of fighters and bombers did so only to meet their own requirements of combat experience for their aircrews and to have a testing ground for equipment. As quickly as these aims were realized, large aerial forces were swiftly moved out of the fray. Sometimes they were replaced with new units testing experimental aircraft or modified equipment; just as often the needs of the combatants—Loyalists and Nationalists alike—were subordinated to the whims of the nations who employed Spain to suit their many conveniences.

As the Nationalists ground their enemies underfoot, support for the Loyalists in the air trickled away into a morass of ineffectiveness. Resistance on the ground crumbled, and with it went any pretense at an air arm that might decide the course of events far below. The pilots of the Loyalists scrambled for their lives, rushing to safety in any direction where they might escape the harsh hand of Nationalist retribution. In this fashion did the aerial conflict of Spain draw to its conclusion—marked by its inconclusiveness.

The nature of the aerial fighting in Spain was to mislead many Americans. There were few firm lessons to be found in the months of bloody fighting, a condition not surprising when one considers the nature of Spain as a "testing ground" for different nations and air forces. Attacks against enemy bastions and cities produced their grisly effects in terms of torn and bloodied human flesh and appalling casualties, but the military strategist was hard put to interpret meaningful results. Tactics changed as often as the wind. Commanders succeeding their fallen predecessors were wont to change the application of airpower as their moods saw fit. Out of the carnage there came the appalling silence of a nation licking its brutal wounds, and little else to show for the long months of lethal struggle.

What had happened in the air eluded strategists and historians alike. At the same time, there were lessons to be learned from that wild and mad fight. There were technical lessons, first of all: lessons as to the need for more guns for fighters, for better defenses built into bombers, for armor plating, and for coordinated tactics on the part of large fighter formations.

The pilot in Spain could not help but benefit from what took place in the skies over that country.

The aerial war of Spain ended on a note of preparedness for other wars, for which the first skirmishes were already being fought. Only a blind man could fail to see the swelling strength of Japanese airpower in the Far East. Only a blind man and a fool could fail to understand that the major aerial combatants in Spain—the Italians, Germans, and Russians—had satisfied their needs, and were hastily adjusting their own equipment and tactics to conform to what they had gleaned from their Spanish experience.

The United States, unfortunately, had more than its share of fools and blind men. And a disproportionate share of these men occupied the desks at our War Department, which chose, largely, to ignore the lessons carried to them in the experience of Americans who had fought—and successfully—in Spain. One such pilot, for example, was James L. H. Peck, a free-lance aerial soldier of fortune. Jim Peck had become the first American since World War I to shoot down a German plane in aerial combat. He had become an ace in Spanish skies with the destruction before his guns of two German and three Italian warplanes.

Jim Peck came home, his experiences fresh in his mind, and went to the War Department, to speak with officers of the Army Air Corps, to offer his services and the benefit of his experience. But Jim Peck failed in his mission. The War Department cared little for what had happened in Spanish skies, and they cared less for Jim Peck. His status as a seasoned combat flier and an ace mattered little against the fact that he was a Negro.

Official myopia even in the light of facts from Spain was much the same on the other side of the world, where the Japanese were systematically preparing for their major war—against the United States. Before they could be committed to the ultimate struggle, however, the Japanese were in desperate need of experience and time. They needed time in which to build up their military strength, and yet more time in which to test the mettle of their men and the effectiveness of their equipment.

The Japanese engaged in a great aerial conflict that lasted for several years. They fought against the Chinese, and against a mongrel assemblage of airmen and planes brought together by the Chinese in an ill-fated Foreign Legion of the Air. They fought, also, against a powerful Soviet air armada, sent to China specifically to test the cutting edge of Japanese airpower and to verify the needs of Soviet air strength.

Just as Americans had fought in Spain, so Americans joined the struggle in the skies of China. The leading proponent of Chinese—and American—airpower in that struggle was no obscure soldier of fortune. Captain Claire

Lee Chennault had spent his service life as a pilot in the United States Army. Fiery, abrupt, and often outspoken in his criticism of superiors (a trait that endeared him little to those superiors), he was nonetheless held in great respect for his brilliant flying skill, his tremendous drive and dedication to his service, and his successes as a tactician.

Chennault and a small band of like-minded men were distressingly frustrated in their roles as modern Paul Reveres. They shouted their warnings; they supported their statements with unquestionable proof. They were not only ignored, but they discovered, later, that both their warnings and their proof had been deliberately hidden and even destroyed.

So the great air war of the Asian mainland and the vast reaches of the Pacific ground toward its inevitable outbreak.

It was an air war in which the Japanese were left free to utilize their years of preparedness, in the form of brilliant piloting skill, developed tactics, and superior machinery. It was a strange war, deadly in its immediate results to us. It was a war locked within a twisting fog of havoc and confusion, many times created deliberately so as to disguise the unpleasant truths of that war—in which Americans were slaughtered because of unpreparedness and false beliefs that could not be eliminated prior to the battle.

Pearl Harbor, which received the greatest publicity, was the least of it. Pearl Harbor on December 7, 1941, was but a natural result of the preceding years, in which Japanese airpower was built to carry out a deliberate mission of conquest.

It was a "crazy kind of a war," throughout its preparatory stages. American volunteers fought with the Chinese, and were treated to the spectacle of Japanese pilots flying airplanes purchased from the United States, and being used in combat against Chinese and Russian air units. It was a war in which German technicians helped Chinese aircrews to fly German airplanes—against the Japanese—while other German technicians aided their Japanese counterparts in assembling German warplanes in Japan. It was a war in which flamboyant Italian officers roared in sleek limousines through the streets of Chinese cities, flying at odd times against the Japanese, while Italian politicians planned for the political-military alliance of Italy, Germany, and Japan.

It was the *war of preparedness* waged by the Japanese for their eventual mass strike against American and British military bastions throughout Asia and the Pacific—a strike that tore our defenses to shreds and inflicted staggering casualties among our own forces and those of our Allies.

When that war got under way, we were beaten back along every front on which we fought the Japanese. We found it a bitter pill to swallow. The "it" included almost everything about the Japanese. Their pilots we discovered to be highly disciplined and of great skill at their tasks. Their fighters were the greatest shock of all, because the Zero fighter proved superior to anything we could put up against the enemy. And badly as we were beaten in those first months of the war in the Pacific and in Asia, our Allies took a worse beating. It was a Japanese show almost all the way.

There still remain, after all these many years, gross misconceptions about that time and the events that occurred then. There is still the feeling that Japan for years hoarded her airplanes until she built up a huge majority of warplanes, and then descended upon us in an overwhelming, locustlike swarm of numerical superiority. The truth is that we outnumbered the Japanese, on December 7, 1941, almost two-to-one in military aircraft on the first day of war. Before that day was over, swift Japanese attacks decimated our forces and drastically changed the odds. The United States lost two-thirds of all its aircraft in the Pacific theater.

The Japanese onslaught against Pearl Harbor reached its greatest effectiveness in eliminating Hawaii as a source of immediate reinforcement for the Philippines. On those beleaguered islands, Japanese attacks rapidly smashed our remaining air strength until the best we could do, despite great courage on the part of our men, was temporarily to annoy the enemy.

What of the famed Flying Tigers—the American Volunteer Group? These men, who fought so hard and against overwhelming odds, appear to be forgotten in our review of the long period of Japanese preparations for her war against the United States. But this is not the case. The great majority of Americans who believe that the Flying

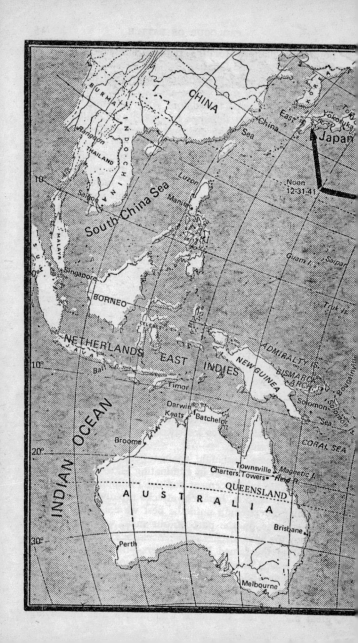

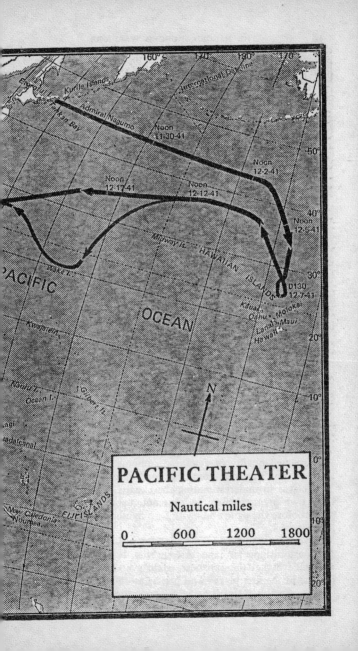

Tigers fought a lonely war against the enemy, long before America as a nation was committed to the battle, are in error. For the truth is that the Flying Tigers never entered combat against the Japanese until December 20, 1941—13 days after the attack against Pearl Harbor and the Philippines. Strange as it may seem, they were actually latecomers to the opening phases of the war.

In swift order Japan toppled her enemies and swept over the opposition that was so often bravely, but pitifully, presented against her military strength. As the war against the United States and her Allies burst across the Pacific, Japan controlled as much of the vast China mainland as she desired. The French had capitulated without a shot. Japanese forces took Guam and Wake. We were dispossessed in the Netherlands East Indies. Singapore tumbled with humiliating defeat into the Japanese net, and brilliantly executed Japanese tactics almost entirely eliminated the British as combatants. Within a few months anxiety and outright fear gripped much of Australia; some of its northern cities were brought under air attack and many of them abandoned. Japanese planes swarmed almost uncontested against northern New Guinea, New Ireland, the Admiralties, New Britain, and the Solomons. The occupation by the Japanese of Kavieng, Rabaul, and Bougainville threatened greater disasters; not only did these takeovers threaten the precarious supply lines from the United States, but they were being expanded into potential springboards for the invasion of Australia itself.

The long and dreary months after Pearl Harbor were a combination of disaster, humility, and astonishment. We were astonished—and too often with fatal results—at the unexpected quality of Japanese equipment. We had committed not one but countless errors, and the worst of these was in underestimating the enemy. We had believed our own press releases, and our antiquated planes fell like flies before the agile and swift Zero fighters of the Japanese Navy.

We must pause for a moment for a further word about this astonishing airplane. Astonishing, because we refused to believe that the Japanese could ever build such a machine in the first place. And just as astonishing because the Zero effectively swept aside *all* opposition. In this fighter aircraft the Japanese made the most of both qualitative and quantitative superiority. They used the former swiftly to achieve the latter.

The Japanese fighter was faster than any opposing plane. It outmaneuvered anything the Allies had in the air. It outclimbed and could fight at greater heights than any plane in all Asia and the Pacific. It had more than twice the standard combat range of our standard fighter, the P-40, and it featured the heavy punch of cannon. Zero pilots had cut their combat teeth in China and pushed to the utmost this clear advantage over our own men. Many of the Allied pilots who contested in their own inferior planes this hallmark of Japanese airpower literally flew suicide missions.

During these early and dark months the black night of defeat was sometimes lighted with bright sparks of heroism—and momentary success—on the part of the defenders. It was enough, at times, temporarily to check the sweeping advance of the enemy. But only temporarily.

We were fighting a dirty, crude, overwhelming, stinking war in the air. The conditions were primitive and rugged beyond belief. Men lived like animals, but fought—and died—like men. The picture of the American airman, as most people back home thought of him, was a grim joke. Our men lived in tents, and just as often slept on the open ground, scraping together food and personal belongings for day-to-day living. They flew combat mission after mission, until some of them fell asleep in their airplanes the moment their machines rolled to a stop—too weary to climb out of their seats. Their eyes were gaunt and their tempers frayed, and defeat did nothing to bolster their morale. But still they fought, striking those sparks of heroism and brief victory in the black night. They were, in every sense of the word, the ragged warriors of our nation.

Our story is of that opening period of the war in the Pacific and in Asia. It is the story of men who had no choice but to enter battle in machines that, back in the United States, would immediately have been condemned as unfit for a brief flight around an airport. Yet it was with this decrepit, weary, and outmoded equipment, patched together by unsung mechanics for whom the world became a blur of maintenance around the clock, that they fought America's war, a war for *time*.

We are aware, of course, that theirs was, in the end, a struggle of unquestioned success. Despite their smashing military triumphs, within one year of the opening strike of the war the Japanese had had the offensive in the Pacific wrested from their hands. The overwhelming numerical superiority which they had gained—largely through destruction of our forces with relative impunity—had become a cherished dream of the past. By the spring of 1943 the American steamroller had clearly shifted the balance of strength. The Japanese were undeniably powerful, unquestionably capable of fierce and dangerous action. But just as undeniable was the fact of new American strength. We enjoyed not only a huge increase in the number of weapons, but astounding advances in the quality of those weapons.

That was enough to put the Japanese on the defensive—and the handwriting of death and defeat on the wall.

But it all had to be bought—bought with time, sacrifice, and a savage war conducted largely in the air.

The Americans—along with the British, Australian, Canadian, New Zealand, Dutch, Filipino, and other combatants of the air war—learned something about that aerial conflict that the Chinese had known for a long time. The unwritten rules of war in the air, handed down from World War I, sustained to some degree in Spain and in shadow form over the early battlegrounds of Europe and Africa, didn't apply in the conflict with the Japanese.

Earlier in these pages I wrote: "Tradition and rules of conduct in the air varied with circumstances. Much depended upon the nature of the conflict. Customs observed in one part of the world were unknown in other parts."

We learned—to our dismay and outrage—that the Japanese pilot, almost to a man, considered the unwritten laws of chivalry of aerial war in European skies as indescribably stupid.

The entire concept of Japanese aerial operations was built around a single word: *Attack*. This was their code, their operational concept, the reality of their conduct in the air. Defensive air operations were not in their plans. They flew not as fanatics, but with a fanatical code of battle. *Attack*.

They were grimly unrelenting in this attitude. Fighter airplanes were offensive weapons. They could only be used as such. The purpose of an offensive weapon was to kill the enemy, to render him incapable of fighting any longer.

The man who bailed out of an enemy fighter *was fair game for Japanese guns*. It was not a matter of being cruel, of gunning down a helpless victim. That such sentiments are to us so real as to constitute a way of life should not blind us to the Japanese way of thinking— that the man in a parachute can live to fight again, and should be destroyed while the opportunity is at hand. It could not matter less if that man were still in his airplane, or floating to safety in a parachute, or even if he were adrift on the ocean surface in a life raft. *Kill the enemy*—that was the only way to fight for Japan.

By the spring of 1942 this was a well-established fact of life with American and Allied airmen. If a Japanese pilot caught a man drifting earthward beneath his silken canopy, the odds were that the pilot would attack—using his guns or his propeller to kill the American pilot and, all else failing, trying to make a high-speed pass directly over the parachute so that the wind would collapse the canopy.

Not all Japanese pilots pursued this "death to the enemy under all conditions" philosophy; no more so than all American and Allied pilots followed the covenant of *not* shooting a man helpless in his parachute or gunning him to death while he drifted in a life raft or a boat.

The hard pursuit of the Allied airman, no matter what his circumstance, brought into existence bizarre and often ridiculous beliefs about Japanese pilots. Quick to believe anything that might downgrade the Japanese as a civilized man, we spread the story that the Japanese cared little for their pilots' lives, that the pilots were forbidden to wear parachutes, and other such arrant nonsense.

Saburo Sakai, Japan's greatest ace (64 confirmed kills) to survive the war, sets the record straight:

"In 1942 none of our fighter planes carried pilot armor, nor did the Zeros have self-sealing tanks, as did the American planes. As the enemy pilots soon discovered, a burst of their 50-caliber bullets into the fuel tanks of a Zero caused it to explode violently in flames. Despite this, in those days not one of our pilots flew with parachutes. This has been misinterpreted in the West as proof that our leaders were disdainful of our lives, that all Japanese pilots were expendable and regarded as pawns instead of human beings. This was far from the truth. Every man was assigned a parachute; the decision to fly without them was our own and not the result of any orders from higher headquarters. Actually, we were urged, although not ordered, to wear the parachutes in combat. At some fields the base commander insisted that chutes be worn, and those men had no choice but to place the bulky seat packs in their planes. Often, however, they never fastened the straps, and used the chutes only as seat cushions.

"We had little use for these parachutes, for the only purpose they served for us was to hamstring our cockpit movements in a battle. It was difficult to move our arms and legs quickly when encumbered by chute straps. There was another, and equally compelling, reason for not carrying the chutes into combat. The majority of our battles were fought with enemy fighters over their own fields. It was out of the question to bail out over enemy-held territory, for such a move meant a willingness to be captured, and nowhere in the Japanese military code or in the traditional *Bushido* (Samurai code) could one find the distasteful words, 'Prisoner of War.' *There were no prisoners.* A man who did not return from a flight was dead. No fighter pilot of any courage would ever permit himself to be captured by the enemy. It was completely unthinkable."[1]

And there were times when our own fighter pilots, many of whom would never cut down a man in a parachute, grazed the dividing line of the unwritten code of fighter pilot conduct—as in this case, related by Major Robert S. Johnson, Thunderbolt pilot of the famed 56th Fighter Group, which flew in Europe during World War II. In this incident Major Johnson, who shot down 28 German fighters in aerial duels, describes one air battle:

". . . To get any strikes on me the Kraut first had to turn inside me, and then haul his nose up steeply to place his bullets ahead of me. The Focke-Wulf just didn't have it. At 8,000 feet he stalled out while the Thunderbolt roared smoothly; I kicked over into a roll and locked onto his tail.

"He was coming *at* me! I had slipped into firing position when he whipped around in a 180-degree turn; I've never seen a tighter or quicker turn in a fighter—*any* fighter—in my life. That man was *good!* He didn't even turn, I thought, just suddenly reversed his flight and ran at me. Several times we rushed at each other, and then I started firing inside bursts as he weaved toward the land. It worked. Twice he ran into a stream of my bullets. The Focke-Wulf snapped over in a steep turn and ran for the coastline.

"I didn't want this boy to reach home. The canopy leaped into the air as the pilot jerked the release; *I pulled around tight to get my bullets into him before he could get out of the airplane. He had one leg outside the cockpit when the slugs smashed him back inside.* [Italics added.] That's one man who would never sight again on our planes; if I hadn't gotten him, then he certainly would have shot down several of our fighters or bombers. He was as good as I'd ever met.

"Number Twenty-three!"[2]

Of all the incidents that reveal what men will do under the trying circumstances of war, none better suits our purpose than a brief study of the Battle of the Bismarck Sea, carried out from March 1 to 3, 1943. Every fighter and bomber that could be flown by the Fifth Air Force, and elements of the Australian air units in the area—137 planes in all—hammered at the Japanese fleet of 17 vessels carrying 5,000 troops of the 51st Division.,

When the day-and-night battering of the Japanese convoy ended, every one of eight transports, as well as a service vessel, and four of eight destroyers had gone to the bottom. Commander Masatake Okumiya noted of the battle that: "Desperately needed supplies littered the Bismarck Sea, and some three thousand corpses floated in the oily, bloody waters. . . . Our losses for this single battle were fantastic. Not during the entire savage fighting at Guadalcanal did we suffer a single comparable blow."[3]

The crippling loss of life—among Japanese reinforcements needed so badly on New Guinea—was acclaimed throughout the United States. The Fifth Air Force, along with Australian twin-engine Beaufighters, had blasted their way to a sensational victory over the enemy.

But the newspapers did not tell how the waters of the Bismarck Sea came to be littered with so many bodies—many more than could be expected to be killed during the bomb and strafing attacks against the Japanese ships. The truth—as it came out much later—is that we threw out the nearest window the "accepted" rules of conduct by which we fought, and did everything we could to slaughter the Japanese survivors in the water.

During March 4, our planes searched far and wide for any surviving vessels. Douglas A-20 Havoc light bombers and the heavily gunned Beaufighters (four cannon and six machine guns each) were given the roughest job of all.

The American and Australian planes swept up and down the Bismarck Sea, shooting at any sign of life. Cannon shells and streams of bullets tore into Japanese on life rafts, floating in the water, and huddled together in lifeboats. The water was whipped and churned into a bloody froth, the blood mixing with chunks of flesh and the oil from the sunken ships. When nothing was seen to move in the seas, the repeated strafing runs ended.

Oh, it's all there in the official record—described by Major Edward F. Hoover, assistant operations officer of the 5th Bomber Command:

"This was the dirty part of the job. We sent out A-20s and Beaufighters to strafe lifeboats. It was rather a sloppy job, and some of the boys got sick. But that is something you have to learn. The enemy is out to kill you and you are out to kill the enemy. You can't be sporting in a war."

2

BACKGROUND TO DISASTER

The heavy bombing strikes of Japanese bombers and fighters against Nanking and other Chinese cities in 1937 and 1938 received attention throughout the world. Horrific newspaper stories emerged from the smoke and dust that spread over the cities, and there were flashes of interest in newsreel scenes. This level of spectator involvement invoked discussion, but little else. Sated with reports of the war in Spain, with the flexing of German muscle in Europe, and with the everyday problems of a world first sensing the possibility of a massive conflict igniting in Europe and Africa, the average citizen didn't afford China and its internal hells much more than a passing glance.

Thus few people understood the magnitude of the punishment meted out from the air to the cities of China. There were formations of bombers with fighter escorts that numbered well over one hundred planes on a single strike. Attacks of this size became common rather than rare, and the Chinese came to hate the sight of the perfectly held formations in the sky. The Japanese droned overhead with flight-school precision in their maneuvers, V upon V, dropping their explosive missiles with a casual accuracy that was frightening to behold. On odd occasions the formations split, the pilots sliding the planes down into long dives, striking out at airfields and other targets, and giving their impatient gunners the opportunity to cut loose with their own weapons.

In the initial phases of the attack the Chinese, under the impatient tutelage of Claire L. Chennault, struck with stunning effectiveness against the Japanese raiders. In the air war in China prior to December 7, 1941, such incidents were, for the Chinese, great moments to remember

against a series of uncontested poundings from the enemy.

Through these years, the Japanese were doing much more than attacking the Chinese. They were, in fact, honing the fine edge of their airpower. China was to them a vast training ground, and the experimental station in which to discover faults and weaknesses, and to replace these weak links in their airpower chain with the equipment and the tactics required to make Japanese airpower second to none. In this endeavor they were unquestionably successful.

The twin-engine bombers came over gleaming in the sun, their massed engines droning out a sonorous beat that to the Chinese far below became as easily recognizable as the arrival each morning of the sun. No one on the ground who watched those formations and the superb manner in which the Japanese sustained their flights, through Chinese flak and fighters, could for a moment doubt that Japanese pilot and aircrew training was of the highest caliber.

In the first few days and weeks the Chinese rose to do battle, and they cut Japanese formations to ribbons, inflicting devastating losses. These losses the Japanese accepted philosophically; this was the only way to learn. The mettle of their airpower could be tested only in this fashion, and the Chinese discovered that the Japanese were swift to learn. The sight of large formations of Japanese fighters providing escort was proof—as was the sudden crippling toll of the defending Chinese fighter airplanes. In every battle where the air defense was given, the Japanese fighter pilots swooped eagerly to accept the challenge. They seemed to rush with all possible speed in order to come to grips with the enemy.

The Chinese learned, also, that the Japanese fighter pilots were the very best of all the enemy airmen. Their individual skill, their discipline, and their implicit faith in their fighter aircraft added up to a terrible combination. Once the Japanese fighters were on the scene, China's swift successes of the opening days ceased. Only when the Chinese pilots could elude the Japanese fighters and strike swiftly at the bombers, then dive away for safety, could China hope for success in the air. For to come to grips with the Japanese fighters was to accept the naked possibility of disaster, and all too often this was the result. Finally, the bombing raids settled into a new pattern.

Most of the strikes were carried out without interference
by Chinese interceptors. High over the land, the bombers
droned steadily, while above them were the fighters in
their slow S-turns, weaving back and forth, hungry preda-
tors waiting impatiently for the bombers to complete
their missions. It was then that the Mitsubishis, denied
their taste of battle in the sky, were unleashed.

Entire cities lay naked before them. Chinese antiaircraft defenses were sometimes heavy, but rarely effective,
and the Japanese fighter pilots quickly accepted the challenge by racing low over the cities, skimming rooftops,
and almost flying down broad streets and avenues. They
cut down anything in their sights as they shot low over
alleys, shooting up people, cars, stores, buildings, animals
—anything. Incendiary bullets started new fires to add to
those of the bombers—and it was the fires that especially
attracted the fighters. Fire in a Chinese city meant a swift
spreading of the flames; it meant panic, and people rushing into the streets to escape the leaping flames. The fires
therefore provided the Japanese fighters with targets—and
the Mitsubishis raced up and down the streets and alleys,
sending bullets into the people as they fled the burning
structures. The effect, as described by witnesses, was like
watching winged boomerangs flashing back and forth,
slashing and cutting up human beings wherever they could
be found.

Nanking was the first to be struck, and if the records
from that war are true, it was the most heavily bombed
of the Chinese cities. Like all big metropolitan centers of
China, each day it exuded the sounds, smells, and hectic
activity of teeming life. It seemed almost as if the Chinese
were trying to cram as much living as possible into the
hours before the Japanese came. The cessation of that
activity came with shocking suddenness, and always with
the same introductory note—the moaning cry of sirens
and the shrill cacophony of bells, gongs, and other noise-
making devices being beaten with fearful anxiety.

In that instant the city was plunged from one world
into another, preparing for the tidal wave of sound, the
bass thunder from over the horizon that presaged the arrival of the tearing explosions and the flames that inevitably followed. The already fast-paced activity of the city
took on a frenzied beat. People rushed for shelters, clutching children, pets, and valuables close to them; they

poured into doorways in a squeezing, shouting mass. Store fronts slammed shut with a clanging finality as shopkeepers bolted their doors and covered windows. Vehicles jerked to a stop alongside curbs or were simply abandoned in the streets as the frightened occupants sought shelter. Streetcars and busses were emptied within seconds. Like millions of rats abandoning a sinking ship —which, to these people, the exposed space of Nanking was to become—they scurried under cover to escape the inevitable rain of bombs and bullets.

Not all, however. Along the ragged edges of the city there was a different kind of exodus. The outskirts of Nanking were filled with ramshackle buildings that offered little protection against the enemy, and the people sought their safety in flight. The streets and alleys, the roads and paths and country lanes were filled quickly with flowing tendrils. Closer examination revealed the flowing mass and its spreading tributaries to be thousands upon thousands of Chinese, rushing to the safety of open country.

Such safety was an illusion. When the bombs were spent and the twin-engined Mitsubishis had turned for home, the fighters were unleashed. To the Japanese pilots the masses of people densely packed along the narrow roads were prime targets, juicy pulps to be burst open with hosing streams of machine-gun fire. The fighters flashed sunlight off their wings as the pilots half-rolled and plunged from the sky, the roar of engines blending with the growing cry of the wind, until both became a keening shriek that was unmistakable to all below.

To a pilot, people running on the ground are figures in the slowest of motions. A nudge of a rudder can sweep a path measured by the width of hundreds of human beings. Caught in the murderous crossfire of Japanese fighters sweeping in from opposite sides of the roads, the Chinese dashed hysterically off those roads and into the open fields, the marshy soil and the paddies bordering the thoroughfares. There they stumbled and floundered as stuttering sounds spat from the sky, and the sprays of bullets churned the water into rows of small white fountains stained with red. The toll from the strafing attacks reached into the hundreds, and then climbed into the thousands. . . .

The Chinese during the growth of Japanese airpower had not remained idle in their critical need to defend their land in the air. Unable to build their own defenses in the form of fighter aircraft, pilots, and operational systems, they turned to other nations. Thus foreign missions and advisers were an old tale to China. The country's desperation exposed it to the greed of hundreds of foreigners who flocked from around the world to commit financial rape as Chiang Kai-shek made desperate attempts to build fighting strength for China.

In July of 1936, William McDonald and Luke Williams, military air advisors to China, conferred with Madame Chiang Kai-shek; the Generalissimo's wife functioned as the acting chief of the Chinese Air Force. In their meeting the two Americans prevailed upon Madame Chiang to retain Claire L. Chennault as an advisor to the country. They emphasized not only Chennault's tremendous personal piloting skill and his extensive experience in leadership and tactics, but also the fact that there were a sufficient number of Americans then in China, whose value could be greatly enhanced behind the strong leadership of Chennault.

By the spring of 1937, the ex-captain of the Army Air Corps was on his way to the Asiatic land. Traveling by way of Japan, Chennault arrived finally in Shanghai, where he was met by Roy Holbrook, like Chennault also a former Air Corps pilot, but a man who had already spent sufficient years in China to know the political byways of the strange country. Holbrook wasted no time, and within several days Chennault was fully aware of why his services were so critically needed.

The basis of it was the very corruptness of China and the great majority of its officials, from the small-town politician to the major figureheads who wielded influence for personal gain—and the nation be hanged. The Chinese Air Force itself was a travesty. Its officers to a large extent were infected by the corruption that had so effectively diseased the other branches of government, with so few truly patriotic Chinese among them that attempts to create a modern airpower force were doomed to failure. Rivalry among ranking officers was both bitter and vicious. Individual capability counted for little, if anything, in the selection of officer personnel; the essential requirements were political connections, an influential family, and the key lubricant of Chinese politics—negotiable currency.

These men in uniform carried on a cutthroat battle to

gain power in the form of controlling large blocs of men and aircraft, and in this struggle the Japanese as the enemy remained far down on the list of priorities.

Men who carried the rank of officers and the status of pilots bore their personal animosities with them into their cockpits. Their flying, instead of being developed into team concepts and combat tactics, remained for the most part a free-wheeling adventure in which the leaders disdained the needs of the Chinese Air Force and flew with their personal retinues, who would follow them anywhere. Men returning from battle were far more likely to spin outrageous lies as to their deeds than they were to provide an honest assessment of their conflicts with the enemy. Thus it proved impossible to ascertain with any degree of validity whether or not the existing Chinese air units could be the basis of future effective defenses against the Japanese.

Chennault and a small, picked group spent several months in a flying survey of Chinese bases, training camps, remote outposts, supply and communications system, and other elements typical of any operational air force. What Chennault encountered, as he and his team traversed much of China in Douglas biplanes, left him scant reason for reassurance. The majority of Chinese pilots not only pursued activities guaranteed to further their own careers— at due cost to their air force—but were desperately in need of advanced training to qualify them as safe pilots, let alone men suited for combat.

As Chennault gathered his information, the threat of major Japanese military activity within China loomed greater on the horizon, until it brooded over the nation like a tremendous thunderstorm. The Japanese in their actions had become almost disdainful of the Chinese, and daily flaunted their military strength in acts that would have outraged and provoked any other nation into immediate steps for war.

Such was not, at this time, the temper of China. Many Chinese, including among their number a preponderance of wealthy and influential citizens, simply refused to accept Japan as the common enemy. Their own interests appeared to dictate otherwise, and concerted action had long been sabotaged by the nature of expediency that constituted much of the Chinese government. Powerful Chinese were quick to point fingers of accusation for military unrest not at the Japanese (who thoroughly exploited this internal division of interests), but at neighboring warlords.

The leaders of local provinces ruled their own areas with iron hands. Subordinate to none, their influence limited only by their own strength, they were loath to accept a common government which could only have diluted their own powers. Disdainful of central government politics, secure within their own spheres, they supported their local, absolute dictatorships with powerful military forces, forming, as it were, a group of bristling fortresses within the vast Chinese land.

The warlords were quick to work with any outside interest as long as their own desires were uncompromised and they judged the cooperation would benefit them. Thus they were willing, even eager, to work with the Japanese, rather than to resist the spreading influence of Japan within China. They were willing to work with any nation that would pay their price in goods including anything from raw materials to spices to young virgins. This exploitation of China and its masses beggars belief, and it should be stated as a matter of record that the plundering of the land owed as much, if not more, to internal greed than to foreign avarice.

The one authority that the separate warlords refused to recognize—unless their own interests were first met— was the central Chinese government. Chiang Kai-shek watched in helpless fury as the Japanese government, with great cunning, exploited the almost frantic desire of the divided Chinese factions to gain power. The Japanese spared no effort in providing economic, political, and even extensive military assistance to these satraps, fully aware that the growth of their localized power would inevitably prevent a national strength from arising.

In due time the various warlords built up strong military forces loyal only to the individual Chinese leader of the particular province. Anxious to sustain this division of Chinese strength, the Japanese in the early and mid-thirties trained Chinese soldiers; fitted them out with personal arms, mortars, and machine guns; supplied ammunition; and then, for the final blow to unity among the Chinese, supplied individual warlords with their own air forces! This included aircraft, fuel, weapons, ammunition, supplies, and even training for the pilots, crews, and mechanics.

The governor of Kwangsi Province, for example, ruled with a stern hand that brooked no nonsense from anyone. Absolute master of his area, he sustained his position with a crack army and a substantial air force of fighters and bombers. Attempts of the central Chinese government to overcome these islands of military might were frustrated by the very strength of the warlords. The situation in Kwangsi was repeated in Kwangtung, Yunnan, and several other major provinces.

Against this disheartening background, Chiang Kai-shek accomplished what American observers on the scene regarded as one of the greatest personal and political miracles of the century; slowly but with increasing effectiveness he began to wean the warlords away from a political life dedicated solely to their own interests, and to entice them with the picture of a China united in its political and military strength against the Japanese invader. In his struggle to accomplish this goal, Chiang Kai-shek wisely emphasized the realities of life rather than basing his appeal on open patriotism. The warlords worshiped personal power, Chiang realized. But they were not stupid men; each had risen to his position of prominence through daring, cunning, and a no-nonsense appraisal of the situation about him.

And not even the most secure of the rulers of the different provinces could ignore reality. The assistance of the Japanese to the separate warlords receiving Japanese aid was a bubble that could burst—with devastating effect, and virtually at any time that the Japanese so dictated. When it suited the convenience of the Emperor of Japan and his agents, any one warlord could be toppled from his position. Each warlord involved with the Japanese existed largely on Japanese assistance; the inflow of military strength could be halted at once, and Japanese military power in China was sufficient to isolate any one province and raze it to the ground.

On July 7, 1937, Japanese troops and military forces of the central China government clashed in a minor skirmish, at the Marco Polo Bridge near Peking. The action touched off the savage and bloody conflict to which the Japanese government applied the euphemistic name

"Sino-Japanese Incident," but which the rest of a shocked world knew as the Sino-Japanese War. Its outbreak was the turning point, the fulcrum on which history was to pivot. From this moment on, the tide of events could not be halted or even diverted. War between the vast but loosely organized land of China and the armed forces of Japan was about to erupt into full-scale military operations involving a major part of the national industrial and economic strength of each combatant.

The sudden alliance of China from within—a meeting of intent upon the part of the many different and opposing factions—came as a surprise even to Chiang Kaishek. It was as though this vast nation, bleeding slowly in so many places, had simply had enough. Provocation had aroused the dragon. In a moment all too rare in the history of China, the warlords appeared to accept the slogan of the students being chanted in the streets: *"It is better to be broken jade than whole tile!"*

Loyalty was sworn to the great land of China. Solidarity was the cement of the Chinese political structure, and never in all that country's history had there existed so tangible and meaningful a marshaling of forces to strike back against a common foe.

This rare and precious feeling was not to be sustained. The house of China, as had been its misfortune for decades, was again to suffer its weaknesses from within. It had required nothing less than a massive and unprecedented internal upheaval to bring together so many of the dissident factors of Chinese military and economic strength into a united front against the Japanese. But the Chinese Communists, now firmly established in Shensi and Shansi Provinces, dominated northwestern China, and their armies operated in guerrilla fashion as far east as Hopeh and Shantung.

Free of the internal dissension that had for so long hampered Chiang's struggle to build up central power, the Communists steadily increased their military strength and expanded their area of military operations within China proper. Behind their powerful moves lay massive Russian assistance, given freely and in vast quantities. Once again, alien interests were slashing the strength of the land. Russian assistance came with specific goals in mind: (1) consolidating the Communist grip on China from within, and (2) creating additional military problems and logistic nightmares for the Japanese, who were knifing deeply into the cities and strategic centers of China. Even as the central government and the Communists professedly put aside their long-standing mutual enmity to concentrate on fighting the Japanese, deep distrust soured their relationships and the specter of renewed civil war on a wider scale than ever darkened the future of China. The nation hoped finally to triumph in the war against Japan, which was to rage for several years prior to the entry of the United States into the conflict. But already there were omens, evident only to the discerning, of the distant future of China as a Communist land. Disaster lay in the soil, the air, and the politics of the great and unhappy land.

It was against this background that the airpower crucibles for the war across all Asia and the Pacific were being formed. . . .

Following the invasion by the Japanese of Manchuria in 1932, Chiang had made his first major attempts to build up Chinese airpower. His overtures for the establishment of a British mission to advise and build a Chinese air force had been rebuffed because of Japanese pressure against the British. Chiang was more successful, however, in negotiations with the American government, which in 1932 permitted an "unofficial mission" to journey to China.

Recently retired from the Air Corps as a Colonel, John H. Jouett was considered a pioneer in air tactics, and was also regarded as one of the stronger disciples of General Billy Mitchell. Among the group of Army pilots who arrived with Jouett in China was Harvey Greenlaw, who would in succeeding years become second-in-command of the American Volunteer Group (the Flying Tigers).

Jouett patterned the fledgling Chinese Air Force after the flight schools and organization of the U.S. Army Air Corps. He adopted the Army's schools, training methods, and programs, and tried to adapt American tactics to Chinese needs. Under Jouett, running the show for the unofficial mission, was a team of twenty Army reserve officers, including, as well as Greenlaw, the influential Roy Holbrook.

The initial use of this newly created airpower was not—as might be expected—against the Japanese, but against dissident Chinese who had refused to accept central authority. A sudden rebellion in Fukien Province prompted a powerful government reaction. Pioneering in aerial warfare within the country, a Chinese air general led a formation of seven ancient biplanes against the massive walls of the ramparts protecting the forces of the rebels. Flying at minimum speed, the ramshackle biplanes managed to hurl their bombs directly into the thick old walls of the insurgents' fortress. With the walls breached, troops of Chiang Kai-shek poured into the fortress and carried out a wholesale massacre of the occupants.

Ironically, Jouett and Holbrook, despite the success of the attack, where thrown by this episode into great disfavor with the Chinese government. Hired as advisors, rather than as mercenaries, they had refused Chiang's demands to utilize their military knowledge by actually leading the attack against the rebels. With a sensational and swift victory in his grasp, Chiang cursed the Americans for refusing their help in the battle, and condemned them for accepting money from China without providing their unrestricted support. Overnight, from a position of great favor with the ruling Chinese, the Americans came to be regarded with suspicion and hostility. The Japanese government also brought pressure to bear on Chiang against Jouett and his team. They were disbanded and left China in December, 1934.

During the three years from 1934 to 1937, the leadership of Chinese airpower rose and fell on the particular personal talents and idiosyncrasies of different foreign advisors to China. The ping-pong effect of advisors with American, Russian, Italian, British, and French backgrounds and convictions wrecked China's ability to sustain itself in the air, and threatened to keep the skies of China a playground for swarms of Japanese fighters and bombers.

Chiang Kai-shek's intensive search for a single, dominant leader to rescue the sagging remnants of Chinese airpower—a search that was carried out on an international scale—led the Chinese leader to Claire L. Chennault, an ex-captain of the United States Army Air Corps, who had retired from his career as a fighter pilot and tactician, a retirement directed to some extent by partial deafness resulting from years of exposure to thundering engines and the windblast of open-cockpit fighters.

The need for a single airpower leader in the spring of 1937 was more critical than ever before. Japanese forces had dug into their positions in Manchuria, and their strength within China proper was mounting with alarming speed. It was not excessive to state that Chinese airpower, in terms of men, machines, logistics, and organization, was on the verge of absolute collapse.

Chennault, living in retirement in the small town of Waterproof, Louisiana, seemed to be a perfect selection. A leather-faced veteran of the cockpit, he was also well known for his revolutionary ideas in the classroom, where he had railed against accepted theories of air combat. In addition to his blunt words to his superiors, which endeared him little to those gentlemen in a peacetime air force, he had carried his ideas one step further to the publishing of a book that caused a furor among airpower disciples; *The Role of Pursuit Aviation* had as its dominant theme Chennault's conviction that fighter planes used effectively could smash any attacking bomber force. To Chiang, whose cities lay naked before Japanese bombs, Chennault appeared as the most likely prospect to re-create Chinese airpower.

Particularly appealing to the Chinese leader was the fact that Chennault supported his claims in print with outstanding performance in the air. He was famed among military pilots as a superb aerobatic artist, and at one time, on tour throughout the United States along with two other Army fliers, had been regarded as a nine days' wonder. The three men, billing themselves as "Three Men on a Flying Trapeze," flew their three biplane fighters in whirling aerobatics—*while all three were tied together with short lengths of rope!*

Chennault was 47 years of age at his retirement, and to him the demands of China, and her needs in the sky, were a heaven-sent opportunity. He left almost at once for Asia and the employ of Chiang Kai-shek—and was on the road to lasting fame as one of the greatest airpower tacticians and strategists of all time.

Angered with Jouett, Chiang Kai-shek had turned to Italy for assistance in building up his air force. Delighted at the prospect of legal plunder in the disorganized land of China, the Italian government responded with a large mission led by a superbly attired, bombastic, and luxury-seeking General Scaroni. The good general brought with him from Italy no fewer than 150 pilots, mechanics, and engineers, all or most of whom wasted no time in turning their stay in China into a veritable junket. Their quarters were the finest, the food unexcelled, their hours of their own liking, and young virgins available of any age to suit the particular tastes of each man.

General Scaroni dearly loved public displays, and his long black limousine was often seen by the populace scurrying to escape its thundering passage as it roared through the narrow streets with complete disregard for Chinese lives and limbs.

In addition to the pursuit of the good things in life, the Italians managed to carry out every possible activity that would bring smiles to the governmental auditors back home. Under the orders of the Italian mission, Chinese laborers erected assembly and factory buildings. Charged "fantastic prices" for these structures, the Chinese learned also that they were to be used for the assembly and servicing of Italian Fiat fighters, lauded by the Italians but held in disrepute by fighter pilots of other nationalities.

There were loud hoots and cries of derision from the Italians when Chiang Kai-shek refused to renew the contract of Jouett and the "unofficial mission" to China. The Italians laughed at the sight of the departing Americans, and found it convenient to ignore the few Americans remaining in China, who were under contract as instructors at the Hangchow flight school. Through some oversight on the part of the Italians, perhaps, this school had escaped coming under the control of the Italian mission, and remained a separate entity of the Chinese government.

During his aerial survey of Chinese airpower facilities, Claire Chennault could not avoid, of course, running headlong into the debris strewn by the Italians through the Chinese Air Force. On his return he submitted a scathing condemnation of the Italians to the Generalissimo. Chennault pointed out that the graduates of Italian flight schools were killing themselves in a brutal progression. They were wrecking millions of dollars' worth of airplanes, and tearing down the structure of Chinese military airpower before it had much of an opportunity to take shape. The worst of it all was that the Italians graduated *every* Chinese student in their midst. Surviving a minimum number of weeks in training was tantamount to completion of the Italian course. The Italians turned pilots loose to man fighter planes when they were scarcely fit to fly trainers.

Chiang did not easily accept Chennault's report. No matter how convincing the credentials of this man, there had still been—to the Chinese leader—the distasteful episode of Americans refusing their services in a time of Chinese need. But Chennault was not asking Chiang to take his word on a mere matter of opinion. There were statistics, and these would not lie, nor could they be dismissed by Italian bombast. The long and short of it was that the Generalissimo had been told, and he believed, that he had 500 combat-ready warplanes ready to fight for him. The Italians had simply neglected to remove from the roster of service aircraft any machine that crashed. Thus the total number of 500 planes included all those—an aggregate—that had ever gone into service.

In actual fact, China had exactly 91 combat aircraft ready for service—less than a fifth of the number which Chiang Kai-shek had counted upon to support his bid for a central military authority for the country. And though these 91 combat aircraft were serviceable, they were by no means fitted by performance to meet the opposition now looming on the horizon.

This, then, was the sordid state of affairs when, on July 7, 1937, Japanese troops struck near Peking, precipitating the storm that had long darkened the sky. The incident at the Marco Polo Bridge was a deliberate Japanese military operation that presaged catastrophe for China.

Grateful for Chennault's honesty, and deeply impressed by the American officer, Chiang Kai-shek asked Chennault if he would take over direct command of the Chinese Air Force. The ex-captain agreed to the request, but with the proviso that a selected group of close friends and associates (Smith, Williamson, Folmer, Watson and several others), in whom he had absolute confidence, be made members of his immediate staff. Chiang agreed. And with authority vested in Chennault, the Generalissimo turned to other matters.

The overwhelming task faced by Chennault was to extricate the Chinese Air Force from the tangled mess into which it had been snarled by the Italians. At the same time, he had to operate on a crash basis to build a semblance of combat strength into the remains. Both were tasks considered impossible in the limited time available, but Chennault had always looked upon the impossible as a problem to be eliminated by intense labor.

Among his requirements—and he considered this critical—was the need for new fighter aircraft. Most of the 90-odd combat planes on the service list were Italian Fiats, and the American observers had immediately condemned these as firetraps for the Chinese pilots.

Chennault's problems were, of course, only a fraction of the huge load that China carried so shakily under the desperate leadership of Chiang Kai-shek. While the American captain struggled to build Chinese airpower, the Generalissimo buckled down to the task of meeting the Japanese on the ground. Chiang had one trump card above all to play—among his ground forces was one crack Army of 80,000 men, whipped into shape by a *German* military team.

Against this background of international legerdemain within China, the air legions of Japan prepared to make *their* move.

MITSUBISHI WHIRLWIND

By August 13, 1937, the fighting between Japanese forces and the troops directly under Chiang Kai-shek had spread across the land to Shanghai itself. Although most military observers, from the very outset of the conflict, conceded Japan a heavy advantage in the war in China, the Japanese themselves were suffering grave doubts about the safety of their field forces. Especially alarming were intelligence reports received from Japanese agents. According to Commander Masatake Okumiya, Imperial Japanese Navy, the reports stated:

". . . the Japanese garrison in that city [Shanghai] was completely encircled by a strong Chinese force, supported by three hundred planes based in the Nanking area. Additional reports revealed that a concerted Chinese attack could in a few days wipe out to the last man the Japanese marines who were isolated in Shanghai. The marine garrison faced overwhelming numbers of Chinese troops; since no airfield within Shanghai was usable, our men were denied local air coverage. . . . On August 14, following a series of sharp land battles, the Chinese planes opened bombing attacks against our forces in and around Shanghai."[1]

The Japanese could not know at the time that their intelligence estimate of 300 Chinese combat aircraft constituted a huge overestimate, and that Chiang actually had less than one-third that number of military planes available for combat operations. Neither did the Japanese realize the critical weaknesses of the Chinese, which the latter were soon to demonstrate in a parody of aerial maneuvers. If the initial Chinese air attacks were any indication of what was to come, then the Japanese might

Northrup 2E light bombers of the type used by
the Chinese to attack Japanese shipping.
They were fairly effective if the Japanese did not
mount any fighter defenses.

have done well indeed to *encourage* the Chinese in their tactics.

Curtiss Hawk dive bombers, well-worn biplanes purchased from the United States, were dispatched to attack Japanese cruisers in the Shanghai area. As the biplanes struck at the other enemy fleet units, Northrop light bombers (also purchased from the United States) were to concentrate their attack on the Japanese command center for the Shanghai operations—the cruiser *Idzumo*. This warship rode at anchor in the Whangpo near the Japanese consulate in Shanghai. Close to the *Idzumo* spread the International Settlement of the city.

Heavy clouds blanketed the skies over the Japanese warship. Other pilots would prudently have returned to base, or else struck at targets of opportunity where weather conditions were better. But not the Chinese, to whom loss of face seemed worse than being lost on their mission. Not to have at least tried to bomb the *Idzumo* was to them the same as quitting, and they bulled their way through the heavy cloud cover, then dove toward where they *thought* the *Idzumo* lay ripe for their bombs.

The planes screamed downward in a swift, shallow-angle diving attack, and at 1,500 feet they broke out of the clouds and shot for their target. But these were men poorly trained in the refinements of such attack, and the pilots neglected completely the new variables in their bombing runs—such as altered speed, angle, and height.

The result of this neglect was appalling—a devastating bomb strike directly in the center of the International Settlement. *One* bomb, exploding on Nanking Road (often described as the busiest and most densely packed thoroughfare in the world), killed nearly a thousand people outright, and caused serious injuries to another 1,150 human beings.

Adding insult to injury was the fact that the *Idzumo* never suffered so much as a scratch in its shiny paint, while the blast wave from the exploding bombs shattered glass throughout the United States cruiser *Augusta*.

On the morning of August 15, the day after this introductory debacle of Chinese bombing, a powerful cruiser raced under full steam down the Yangtze River, its decks brilliant with flame as all guns fired freely at Chinese bombers that pursued the warship. The Chinese pilots finally had snared a target; they threw themselves furiously at the vessel. High overhead, Chennault in a Hawk fighter plane studied the scene beneath him. His own aircraft rocked sharply as bullets spanged through the wings, and Chennault pounded his fist in the cockpit in helpless frustration.

The warship under violent attack was the British cruiser *Cumberland*. . . .

Even the long series of aerial combats which were soon to flare through China on a massive scale began in odd fashion. The only fighting in the air to mark the outbreak of the full-scale Sino-Japanese War took place when a slow seaplane from the *Idzumo* shot down a Chinese fighter.

On the evening of August 14, the Japanese struck their first heavy blow from the air. Mitsubishi Type 96 twin-engine bombers* of the Kanoya Air Corps made military

---

*During World War II, these bombers received the identification code of *Nell*.

history when they flew a mission that totaled 1,250 miles range; they took off from Taipei (Formosa) to strike at Chinese positions in the Shanghai area and returned non-stop to their home fields. The next day additional bombers of this type from the Kisarazu Air Corps lifted from Oh-mura Base on Kyushu Island to add their weight to the attacks. Beginning on the third day of the strikes—August 16—carrier-based fighters and bombers also struck at the Chinese.

No one could have forseen the devastating effect of

Mitsubishi Type 96 Nell bombers carried out
a major load of the attack against Chinese cities;
same type of plane was used extensively throughout
early years of World War II.

Chennault's hand prior to these heavy Japanese air attacks. Thanks to the hard-driving leadership of the American Army captain and his dedicated staff, a selected group of Chinese fighter pilots had been whipped into a semblance of a combat interceptor force. Playing his strength cautiously—with absolute command over the Chinese fighters vested in him—Chennault rocked the Japanese back on their heels, and stunned the Chinese themselves with the murderous effect of his tactics.

The Japanese made their initial bombing strike against Nanking without any interference from Chinese fighter planes. Indeed, not a single Chinese interceptor was to be seen in the skies; only a select group were aware that this constituted part of Chennault's defensive plan. The twin-engined bombers slid into their bombing runs over the city at a height of 5,000 feet. Having dropped their bombs with precision, and with the skies empty of the enemy, the Japanese pilots whooped with the excitement of battle and pushed their sleek airplanes into long, swift dives toward open targets. The gunners aboard the Mitsubishis trained their machineguns on buildings, vehicles, trains, and any hapless Chinese exposed to their sights. Back and forth thundered the Japanese planes, incendiaries spitting into the city and starting numerous small fires. Finally, their ammunition expended and their spirits soaring, the Japanese pilots rose toward the clouds and slipped into the white mists, beginning the slow climb to where they would emerge above the clouds and re-form into position for the flight home.

This was the precise moment Chennault had been waiting for—when the Japanese were relaxed, overconfident, and either short of ammunition or out of it entirely. At 10,000 feet a pack of Chinese fighters circled slowly, conserving fuel, poised on the brink of steep dives . . . poised until the command to attack came from far below the swirling white clouds. The bombers broke upward through the rolling cloud tops; one moment there was only white to be seen, and then sunlight glistened brilliantly from silver wings and flashing propellers.

Shouting into the wind of their open cockpits, the Chinese pilots pushed their control sticks forward and eased rudder pedals to bring their fighters around in curving dives. Like a swarm of maddened hornets they plunged into the midst of the Japanese formations with totally unexpected—and spectacular—effect. The Japanese planes were ripe for the aerial onslaught, and streams of bullets ripped open and exploded fuel tanks, smashed pilots into bleeding hulks over their control columns, and tore the Mitsubishis into wreckage. Within the space of several minutes the Japanese formation had been shredded—and of the 18 bombers, no less than eight plunged blazing from the sky.

Chennault and his team had performed the impossible. By teaching the poorly trained Chinese fighter pilots to fly in a combat element of pairs—no matter what might ensue in the battles—they whipped their students into ef-

fective combat teams. Whenever a pilot found himself
alone, he was immediately to "latch on" to the nearest
two-man team in the sky, and act as a seesawing tail
cover for the other two pilots.

Whatever had happened that day over Nanking, the results were no less than incredible. Nearly half of the entire attacking force had literally been blasted from the air.
And this was only the beginning, as the incredulous Japanese learned to their sorrow. Chennault was a hero in
Chinese government circles as his students three times in
succession demonstrated in bloody, slashing fashion the
value of his instruction. In three heavy raids carried out
over a period of only five days, the Japanese suffered
crippling losses.

The records kept by the American advisors in China at
the time show that Chinese fighter planes intercepting the
enemy in these first three daylight raids *shot down 54
Japanese bombers,* with the loss of all their crews. The
Chinese pilots, who had never expected anything remotely
like these results, almost went mad in their joy.

The effect of the Chinese defense system has been held
up to serious question in the years following. The claims
of 54 Japanese bombers shot down with virtually no losses
to the Chinese appear to beggar credulity. But there is no
question of what happened in Chinese skies over Shanghai, Nanking, Hangchow, and other cities, for the Japanese
themselves have provided us with full confirmation of the
aerial debacle as the air war opened in China.

The primary lesson learned by the Japanese, in the
words of an official study of the serious losses in the early
China fighting, was that "bombers are no match for enemy
fighter planes. Japan lost many men as this lesson was
administered, including Lieutenant Commander Nitta, Air
Group Commander, Lieutenant (JG) Umebayashi, and
Ensign Yamanouchi of the land-based attack-bomber
groups, and other pilots . . ."

Commander Masatake Okumiya, who at the time was
in the command staff headquarters of the Japanese Navy,
sheds more light on the strategic lessons learned in such
painful manner at the hands of the Chinese defenders:

"The planes of the aircraft carrier *Kaga* suffered disastrously. The twelve Type 89 carrier-based attack bombers, led by Group Commander Lieutenant Commander
Iwai, left the *Kaga* on August 17 for a raid against

Hangchow. Bad weather prevented a rendezvous with an expected fighter escort, and near their target the bombers were attacked by a group of Chinese fighter planes. Eleven bombers, including the commander's, were shot down. Lieutenant (JG) Tanaka managed to bring his bullet-riddled and crippled bomber back to the carrier; otherwise, the fate of the attacking group would never have been known, and another bomber formation might have suffered a similar fate. Tanaka's report astonished the officers of the fleet, and immediate warnings were issued to all bomber groups to take special precautions against the defending Chinese fighters.

"We discovered that when our fighter planes provided escort to, over, and from the target such incidents did not occur. Comparing the shattered unescorted bomber groups with the relatively unharmed formations which were protected by fighters, the Navy reacted quickly. The *Kaga* was ordered to return immediately to Sasebo and to receive a full complement of the new Type 96* carrier-based fighters."[2]

The Japanese—reputed to be slow in understanding the strategy of such situations—reacted with a swift vengeance.

While Navy headquarters in Japan rushed to get fighter planes into China, the theater commander ordered the end of unescorted daylight attacks against Nanking. For three days the Japanese remained absent from the city. Then, with a full moon bathing the Chinese countryside, a trickle of raiders appeared over the city. There were no mass formations, no spectacular V-upon-V waves of the twin-engine bombers. Sometimes the Mitsubishis came in alone, sometimes in pairs. But they came, all through the night, and the moon-washed city rocked for nearly eight hours with bombs spilling into its innards. The bombardiers took their time; their pilots set up bombing runs with perfection. There was no rush, for there were no fighters to interfere with their operations.

Once again, Chennault had lulled the Japanese into a sense of confidence. What the Japanese did not realize was that Claire Chennault was putting into practice in China the tactics he had developed for years as a tactician with the U.S. Army Air Corps. He had ordered the searchlights

---

*The Mitsubishi Type 96 Claude single-engine fighter.

normally concentrated on the edges of Nanking removed, and set up in a grid pattern throughout the city. On the second night of the attacks, the searchlights locked onto a bomber and remained with that bomber until, with the slant range increasing, another searchlight in the grid could pick up the aircraft and keep tracking it with a brilliant light beam.

A Chinese fighter pilot slid into one of the beams, keeping the Japanese bomber crew of one plane blind to his steeply climbing fighter. At pointblank range the Chinese pilot squeezed out a long burst into the vitals of the Mitsubishi; then, working with all the speed at his control, the fighter pilot rolled onto his back and sucked the control stick into his stomach, arcing away beneath the bomber. Behind and above him, flames blossomed in the sky, marking the effectiveness of the attack.

On the third night of bombing a swarm of Chinese fighters rose to do battle. The same pilot who had scored the night before blew another two bombers out of the darkened skies, and the other pilots managed to shoot down five more planes.

Once again the tactics of Chennault had paid tremendous dividends for the Chinese, and a staggering blow to the Japanese.

But the brief victories of the Chinese had come to their end, and now they were to reap the whirlwind of the Mitsubishis. In early September of 1937 the Japanese began their grimly determined effort to wipe Chinese air opposition clear out of the skies, and they began their campaign with the Second Combined Air Flotilla, equipped with the deadly new Type 96 fighters. Among the factors on which the Japanese relied was the quality of their pilot leadership—Lieutenant Commanders Okamura and Genda, and Lieutenants Nomura and Nango, famous through the Japanese Navy as men of superb skill.

On September 18 the Japanese struck at Nanking. Flushed with their victories of previous weeks, the Chinese fighter pilots rose with a shout to meet the invaders. The cries of battle changed all too quickly into the sounds of blood bubbling from dying lips. The Japanese had come to kill—and they went at their task with a terrible efficiency.

The pilots of the Chinese fighters—Boeing P-26 monoplanes and Curtiss Hawk II, Curtiss Hawk III, and Italian

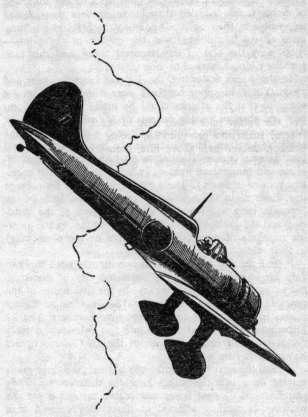

Mitsubishi Type 96 Claude was the first monoplane
fighter introduced by Japanese to air fighting in
China—and devastated the opposition.

Fiat biplanes—found themselves almost helpless before the slashing performance of the new Mitsubishi Type 96 fighters. The Japanese pilots flew a lithe killer that was faster in level flight, could outclimb the Chinese collection of fighters, and whirled through maneuvers that seemed impossible in their agility. Added to the brilliant performance of the Mitsubishis was the caliber of the pilots—these were the best of the Imperial Navy, and this fact, too, the Chinese learned to their dismay.

In the weeks following, the Japanese struck again and again. The twin-engine bombers were withdrawn from the scene so that the attacks could be made with dive bombers and their protecting swarms of Mitsubishi fighters. In desperate straits, the Chinese gathered every fighter plane available to them. They added to the Boeing, Curtiss, and Fiat fighters Gloster Gladiators (British) and Russian biplane and monoplane fighters (which had seen such excellent service in Spain). The Japanese could not have cared less. Each night the briefing rooms and mess halls of the Japanese rang with shouted announcements of the victories, and the grouped pilots laughingly added up the growing numbers of aces (pilots with five or more air kills) in their midst.

It took the Japanese less than two months not simply to gain air superiority over the contested city of Nanking, but to assert absolute supremacy. In the first battle of the renewed air war—on September 18—16 Chinese fighter planes had gone aloft to intercept nine bombers. The 27 Mitsubishi fighters that ripped into the defenders quickly decimated their ranks—11 out of the 16 Chinese fighter planes fell in flames.

During the next two months the Mitsubishi fighter pilots carried on a beat-the-bushes hunt for their enemy. They searched out Chinese bases and roared up and down the runways in strafing attacks; at times they cruised high overhead, taunting the Chinese with their presence to come up and fight. Japanese bombers stopped at nothing to attack targets, and the fighters trailed along, hoping that the bombings would rouse the depleted ranks of the enemy to combat.

The campaign was not simply to assure that the Japanese Navy could carry out its assigned attack missions against the enemy. It was a deliberate move to wipe out the remaining elements of Chinese airpower, and the

Curtiss Hawk biplane fighters, effective against
earlier-type Japanese planes, were slashed to ribbons
and shot out of the air by Type 96 Claude fighters.

Japanese left nothing undone to achieve this goal. It appeared incredible then—and no less so today—that in many respects the Chinese helped them to achieve their hopes.

The needs of the country notwithstanding, the political guile and backbiting in attempts to scramble up the power ladder seemed to go on unabated. Opportunities to seize political-military control received priority over combating the enemy, and those Chinese in high authority went to gruesome lengths to sustain their power—including shooting front-line fighter pilots who had deliberately, casually, or even inadvertently disobeyed orders. Because no Chinese pilot wished to be regarded as less than highly skilled and of unquestionable courage, these men often carried to the extreme attempts to save aircraft that were badly crippled or even on fire. More than one fighter or bomber lurched back to its home field, the crew grimly determined to save their plane, when common sense (to say nothing of the flames) dictated bailing out. The loss of an aircraft was nowhere as important as saving the crew so that the men could return to the combat zone in the sky. But there were dozens of crews who came home, successful in saving face, only to lose their lives in explosions and holocausts as they crashed their shattered planes.

In a desperate numerical position in July and August of 1937, the Chinese Air Force had received a steady inflow of replacement fighters and bombers; these the Japanese pilots just as steadily reduced in numbers. But while there were new planes to be purchased for dollars, only time in training could produce combat-worthy aircrews. Neither the aggressive Japanese nor the exasperating Chinese were ready, from their divergent positions, to provide that time.

Shanghai was to live with a ceaseless screen of Japanese airpower either overhead or always at the gates to the city; one or more Japanese aircraft carriers maintained its station for this purpose by cruising with impunity off the mouth of the Yangtze River just beyond the city. With a fighter squadron always on alert, around the clock, the Japanese were never more than a few minutes' time from throwing a powerful fighter force into the air to meet any tactical situation.

Japanese troops and naval units occupied the offshore islands, Chusan, Woosung, and Point. Engineers turned the air into clouds of dust as they pounded out runways. Never a people to be concerned with the creature comforts, Japanese mechanics and aircrews lived a spartan existence on the islands—and carried out a devastating assault against the Chinese on the mainland. The islands were some 15 minutes' flying time from major Chinese centers, and the short distances to and from targets meant that full bomb loads could be carried, and several missions flown in a single day.

Under the driving whip of Chennault—a whip cracked sporadically within the morass of Chinese temperament and inscrutable politics—the Chinese Air Force made desperate attempts to strike back at their enemy. Chennault controlled a small but powerful force of Northrop light bombers which he assigned to airfields in the Canton area. The American-built planes staged out of Canton to attack Japanese merchantmen and warships that steamed close off the coast in complete disdain of the Chinese. That the latter could fly and fight hard when their training was adequate and their leadership up to the task, the Chinese demonstrated in bloody fashion by sinking several cargo vessels and defending destroyers. These attacks were carried out in the face of severe antiaircraft fire (Japanese warship crews even then were outstanding at their duties) and not without heavy losses at times.

But once again, the attacks could be maintained only to that moment when the Japanese made their decision to wipe out the enemy forces. After one particularly heavy raid against their shipping, the Japanese met the successive bombing strike with a milling swarm of Mitsubishi fighters. Twelve Northrops dove against the Japanese ships. The Mitsubishis intercepted them long before they could reach their bombing position, and in the swift slaughter that ensued 11 bombers tumbled in flames. One light bomber escaped to stagger back to Hankow.

It seemed almost that Japanese fighters were biding their time to finish off this sole survivor. Several days later the pilot took his repaired Northrop into the air; almost at once the scream of a diving fighter split the air, and the Northrop was torn into blazing fragments.

On December 2, over the broken city of Nanking, the Japanese ran down the curtain. At the start of the battle the Chinese had nearly 90 fighter planes to resist their enemy, plus different types of bombers the exact number of which is difficult to ascertain; there appeared to have been from fifty to a hundred planes. On December 2, the Chinese unexpectedly put up a heavy force of Russian-built fighter planes over Nanking, hoping to catch the Japanese unaware. But the pilots in the Type 96 fighters were in prime form; they were as taut and ready for battle as any fighter pilots could be, and they responded with aggressive attacks against the late-model Russian planes. Led by Lieutenant Nango, the Mitsubishis tore the enemy formations into shambles, and then proceeded to chew up the individual fighters remaining. Ten Russian planes fell from the skies; only two escaped. That night the Japanese celebrated their one-sided victory—not a single Mitsubishi had been lost.

Thus ended the first major phase of the air war in China. Elated by a few initial victories, the exultant Chinese were taught quickly that Japanese airpower represented a formidable force not to be dismissed lightly. Not only was Japanese equipment superior to any that it encountered, but the air elements thrown into the battle by Japan had great staying power. Initial losses could be absorbed within the structure of the Japanese air forces, for the Japanese learned their lessons swiftly and took prompt remedial action that eliminated continued prohibitive losses.

With control of the air securely in their hands, the Japanese pressed even harder on the ground. Not even desperate resistance, enhanced by cooperation among the different Chinese factions who could no longer ignore the threat of disaster from the powerful Japanese, could stem the tide. The long Chinese withdrawal into the interior of the vast China mainland began—a march that became a bloody and battered retreat, with rearguard actions to hold off the thrusts of advance Japanese elements while the main body of the army, and the centers of government, rushed to place distance between themselves and the enemy. It was a staggering withdrawal . . . more than 2,000 terrible miles up the Yangtze.

There were two separate military aspects to this retreat. Chinese air-base facilities were carried to areas beyond the flight range of the aggressive Mitsubishi fighters. This was necessary not only to save the remaining Chinese air force from total extinction in combat, but to provide the bases and the means to institute new training, and to bring in as many additional fighters and bombers from foreign sources as the Chinese could purchase.

Simultaneously, the government prepared a last-ditch stand at Hankow to cover the mass retreat into the Szechwan Basin. Protected by towering mountains, Chinese forces could put the rugged terrain to good defensive use, adding to their regrouped strength the logistic problems of the Japanese, who were stretching their supply lines to the breaking point. If the Japanese were held back long enough, Chiang Kai-shek could realize the establishment of a new political and military government headquarters in the city of Chungking, well within the mountainous area of Szechwan.

No one had anticipated that the Japanese would so

quickly develop a complete grasp of airpower needs in the China war. Their concept of combat in the air was a development of the single word *attack*, and they had little intention of allowing the Chinese to remain free of their fighters and bombers so that they could build up their strength.

As quickly as the Chinese set up new air force headquarters at Nanching in Central China, some 335 air miles southwest of Shanghai, the Japanese moved to counter that advantage for their adversaries. The advantage was, to be sure, strictly a limited one—the new air force headquarters lay beyond the striking range of the Mitsubishi Type 96 fighter planes. This deficiency the Japanese intended to correct—and at once.

Lieutenant Commander Genda (who played a major role in the attack against Pearl Harbor) had an intrinsic grasp of airpower needs. As the air staff officer of the 2nd Combined Air Flotilla, he recommended that the Japanese Navy establish a series of forward air bases, no more than primitive outposts, between Shanghai and the new retreats of the enemy. In this fashion the Mitsubishi fighters could stage close to the Chinese positions and join the Japanese bombers as they flew to attack their targets; the indispensable fighter escort could thus be maintained, despite the extreme ranges faced by the fighter planes.

Commander Okumiya provides us with an official study of airpower in these early months of the war in China:

"Employing Type 95 land-based attack bombers as emergency transport planes, the Navy flew fuel and mechanics for the fighters into Kuangte Air Field. Although occupied by the Japanese Army, the airfield was partially isolated, since the enemy still controlled the supply lines. Our fighter planes landed at Kuangte for refueling, then resumed their flights for the Nanching area. Those planes with sufficient fuel to return directly to Shanghai flew nonstop from the target area; the remainder with short fuel reserves made another stop at Kuangte.

"The novelty of the new tactics proved completely successful, as repeatedly our fighters made disastrous surprise raids against the unsuspecting Chinese. . . . The demands of battle forced the naval planes into unexpected situations for which they had not been trained. Carrier-based dive bombers, attack bombers, and Type 95 [biplane] carrier-based fighters repeatedly reconnoitered, bombed, and machine-gunned enemy forces in direct co-operation with our army units, which were advancing steadily westward from the Shanghai area to Nanking. Although lacking in training and in experience, the naval pilots performed these missions so successfully that they received the greatest praise of the ground units, who benefited materially from their supporting attacks.

"These special operations were discontinued after three months of fighting, marked by the fall of Nanking. Many lessons were gained in the way of new tactics and operations from the campaign, especially (1) that air groups and combat planes trained at sea for sea duty can serve successfully without special training in any air campaign over land, and (2) that the key to success in any land or sea operation depends upon command of the air.

"The outstanding combat successes of the Type 96 [Claude] fighter planes ended a long-standing controversy in Japan, destroying once and for all the validity of the arguments of those who insisted upon retaining biplane-type fighters. Even with due consideration for its exceptional maneuverability, the short range and slow speed of the Type 95 carrier-based fighter doomed it to extinction. It required the final test of combat to determine which of these two fighter types would be the most effective in war.

"The China air battles vindicated completely the Navy's insistence upon the strictest training for all pilots and air crews. Although the naval pilots were trained specifically for operations against enemy surface fleets, their quality enabled them to perform with an efficiency superior to that exhibited by our Army pilots. Conversely, it was also determined that pilots trained specifically for maneuvers over land experienced great difficulty in overwater operations, even in merely flying long distances over the ocean.

"We discovered that the extended range of our Navy bombers opened new vistas of aerial warfare and that with these far-flying aircraft we could attack enemy positions far behind the front lines or while several hundred miles at sea. Most important of all, perhaps, we learned that certain types of air campaigns could not be strictly defined as either strictly 'land' or 'sea' battles, but required of the pilots the ability to fight under any conditions."[3]

For a brief time—a distressingly brief period—it appeared that the fighting in China might come to a swift end—not through unquestioned military victory but through negotiation. With the occupation of Nanking in December of 1937, military operations in middle China ground to an indecisive halt, while political meetings to come to a mutual agreement to halt the war were instituted.

The negotiations failed almost as quickly as they started. The continuance of the fighting was laid directly at the doorstep of the powerful hierarchy that ruled the Japanese Army—and their decision, states Okumiya, was abetted by "the desire of influential Chinese parties to see the war continued."

Whatever the complications and the political thievery behind the scenes, the war paused only a heartbeat, and flamed again with renewed fury. A month after the pause Japanese army units pounded Chinese defenses into rubble to conclude the Hankow operation triumphantly. A little more than one year later they were the undisputed rulers of Hainan Island and brought operations in the Shansi campaign to a position of strength, and consolidated all planned gains in enemy territory. In the interim the air war entered a fierce new stage, complicated by additional foreign elements in China, long-range Japanese attacks, and a brief interlude wherein a powerful Russian air force was sent to China to test its mettle against the old enemy of Russia—the Japanese military.

4

CHAOS

As the defenses of Nanking, during the autumn of 1937, crumbled beneath the mounting fury of the Japanese attacks, and as the fall of the city became imminent, Chiang Kai-shek directed Chennault to set up a network of air defenses and training centers well removed from the reach of the Japanese.

It was a time of devastation and mounting horror for the Chinese. Nanking after its fall in December, 1937, suffered explosive and incendiary damage and terrible destruction directly at the hands of Japanese soldiers "turned loose" by their commanders. In the weeks ensuing, one Chinese center after the other collapsed into Japanese hands. The aerial defenses of the Chinese had become a thin ghost; the Mitsubishis proved virtually invincible in the air. Wherever they reached their guns slashed and flamed Chinese aircraft.

As a matter of survival, the Chinese pilots learned to make one pass at their enemy—*if* they could penetrate the screen of Mitsubishis protecting the bombers—and then dive away at full throttle. Opposition in the air to the Japanese had degenerated into these hit-and-run tactics. Chinese fighters skulked at high altitude, waiting for a break in the aerial armor of the protecting fighter screens. They were expected, if nothing more could be done, at least to carry out this minimum defense against the enemy's bombers. There was sense in this procedure; to come to grips with the Mitsubishis in a protracted dogfight promised only destruction.

But they were expected to fight—no matter how carefully they might have to choose the moment. One Chinese fighter pilot, when attacked, immediately dove away from the fray, leaving his fellow pilots to fend as best they could. This the Chinese considered to be overstepping the bounds of caution, and to be outright cowardice. The pilot was shot to death by a firing squad.

The gaunt skeleton of the Chinese Air Force, which could not be filled out without an entirely new training program, months of time, and replacement aircraft (in which crews had to be trained), demanded emergency stopgap measures against the Japanese. Could foreign pilots be recruited in numbers sufficient at least to stem the tide until strength might be rebuilt? It had been done in Spain; why not use the same technique in China?

Claire Chennault reportedly was against the idea of an assortment of foreign pilots. He argued that stopgap measures did not win wars, and that the only means of rebuilding the Chinese Air Force was through a large and sustained training and re-equipping program. Chiang Kai-shek took a different view. He wanted a powerful Chinese Air Force as much as Chennault did, but in the meantime, for lack of crews and planes, the skies were naked to the enemy and Chinese were dying. Anything in the air would help, and a foreign legion of paid mercenaries appeared to be the only solution to China's immediate and critical needs.

The Chinese government was in dire need of replacements for its force of Northrop light bombers which had been destroyed by the Japanese. China had purchased 150 of the Northrop 2E bombers (export models of the Northrop XA-13 designed for the U.S. Army) and had lost every plane. Available to the Chinese as a replacement was the Vultee V11GB attack bomber, a single-engine raider that was fast, carried four guns firing forward as well as a single dorsal and belly gun, and could haul a heavy bomb load over ranges up to 2,000 miles. It was an airplane vital to the immediate requirements of the air war, and 30 of the bombers were rushed to Chinese air units. Other American warplanes also were purchased, among them export models of the U.S. Army's Martin B-10 bomber. The Martin 139, as the export version was known, had a top speed of 260 miles per hour and carried a heavy bomb load; nine were bought.

The Generalissimo's personal pilots, Royal Leonard and Julius Barr, were given the task of selecting from a "ragged and somewhat motley mob" the pilots who would form the complement of the International Squadron. After contacts were made, in late 1937 and early 1938, around the world, the Chinese contracted for the services of three Americans, one Dutchman, one German, and four Frenchmen. They hoped to fill out a combat group by adding the six best Chinese bomber pilots to the foreigners. These men in turn would soon be able to lead additional pilots and crews into battle as fast as new planes were made available.

Almost from the start the International Squadron ran into trouble, although their initial series of misfortunes was not of their own making. Chinese pilots selected to fly with the International Squadron considered the hiring of the "foreign dogs" to be a stinging rebuke to their own capabilities, and the pilots stormed off the airfield in a rage, refusing to have anything to do with Claire Chennault or his alien fliers. In full sympathy with their pilots, a group of Chinese bombardiers rose en masse and also trooped off. No matter that China was dying; no matter that the Japanese were striking out in all directions with terrifying success—loss of face could not be incurred by following the foreigners. It was a pure and simple case of "to hell with you and to hell with the war."

It was the sort of incident that brought American advisors to China to pound their heads slowly against the nearest wall. . . .

Left standing around with sheepish grins on their faces were the aerial gunners assigned to the International Squadron. In strange contrast to their fellows, the gunners didn't care with whom they flew and fought, just as long as they could get into airplanes to bomb the Japanese. Their spirit was commendable, but to a man they suffered one grievous fault—they couldn't shoot worth a damn. It took weeks of crash-priority training to bring these men around to where they knew how to hold, maintain, and fire a machine gun in such a manner that they might be expected to protect their own airplanes. In the interim the pilots for the International Squadron would be brought to China.

Through the years since those days of ragged combat in China, the conviction has grown that these foreign pilots were simply drunken louts who existed largely on whiskey and bombast, and that they came to China only to soak up easy money. In the cases of a few of these men perhaps the conviction is valid; of the majority it is not. Certainly these men were paid for flying for China and risking their necks for China—so was Claire Chennault and every member of the American Volunteer Group (the Flying Tigers), who came on the scene some years after the international group of pilots.

Curtiss Hawk fighter of the type flown by
George Weigel, who shot down four Japanese
bombers in a single engagement.

Included in the International Squadron were men of brilliant piloting capability. The American pilots included Jim Allison, who was considered the prize of the group; he was a hardened and experienced combat veteran from the Spanish Civil War. Another American was a veteran pilot named Gibson who had worn the uniform and wings of the Army Air Corps. George Weigel came to

China without a smidgen of military experience in terms
of combat, but he brought with him a fabulous feel for
flying and the rough-and-stumble school of pasture and
barnstorming flight.

The initial record of the International Squadron undoubtedly fell considerably short of what the Generalissimo had expected (though it did better than some others
had predicted), but all China was to come to know the
name of George Weigel. It flashed brilliantly and then,
almost as swiftly, was lost in the horror enveloping the
land.

Weigel's star shone during the murderous battering of
Chungking by Japanese raids that were carried out on
what amounted to a non-stop basis. The Japanese were
putting the city deliberately to the torch; the casualties
were appalling, and day by day sections of Chungking
were burned to the ground. The city lay helplessly exposed to the enemy.

Then there came that single bright flash of light in the
darkness of the slaughter. A Japanese raid during one
night had caused more than 10,000 Chinese to be burned
to death. Smoke drifted in a ghastly, sweetish-sick stench
from roasted flesh over the city the next day, when another wave of bombers thundered overhead.

A single Hawk fighter rose swiftly from a field on the
outskirts of the city. The airplane gleamed in the sun as
its pilot, George Weigel, hammered the throttle against
its stop to gain altitude as quickly as possible. His airplane was a modified Hawk 75M, with a heavy cannon
fitted beneath each wing.

Weigel streaked above the Japanese formation; then
suddenly his Hawk wheeled about sharply and fell upon
the broad sweep of bombers. Those men who knew him
say the touch of madness was upon Weigel; he had become violently ill at the sight of hundreds of women and
children burned alive the night before. The smell of the
charnel house hung in the air over the city as the silver
Hawk shot into the midst of the Japanese bombers.

The man seemed to be untouchable. He twisted and
dove and streaked in impossible maneuvers through the
Japanese planes, forcing formations to shred. Tracers from
the bombers strung glowing pearls about his plane, but
above the massed thunder of the Japanese engines there
could be heard clearly the snarling whine of the Hawk's

powerful engine and the coughing bursts of the heavy cannon.

Alone in the air against the enemy swarm, George Weigel smashed four of the Japanese bombers into flaming wreckage. Then, his guns and cannon empty, his airplane a sieve, he drifted in for a landing.

The next day *mechanical failure* crippled his fighter, sending him to his death.

One of the wildest of the international pilots was a hard-as-nails youngster, Herbert M. C. Walker, known to his friends simply as Tommy. Walker was a brilliant aerobatic pilot who learned his flying on the wing—in the second seat of a barnstorming biplane. He was also a daredevil stuntman, famous for his incredible feats of leaping from plane to plane in flight *without* a parachute, transferring from a plane to a speeding boat or a car, and back again. His wing-walking antics brought in huge crowds at county fairs the country over. After all this— enough for any man—it seems that Walker should have had enough. But he was famous among the barnstormers for his wild parachuting drops as well, including bailing out at 10,000 feet, and blowing a bugle wildly all the way down to the last possible moment of hauling on his D-ring to snap open his canopy. Walker was a Hollywood-version-come-true of the pilot who would try anything and fly anything; he added to his legendary feats by learning to smash airplanes into poles, houses, and anything else —for a fee high enough.

Wild in the air, he was remarkably even-tempered on the ground and bubbling over with warm friendship. His friends knew him as extraordinarily difficult, almost impossible, to rouse to personal anger. Yet Walker had been a deadly brawler in the ring, veteran of CCC camps, tank-town arenas, and other unsporting sports centers where a knee to the groin in a clinch was as much to be expected as a gloved thumb twisted in the eye. Walker had behind him more than 60 such professional fights—and he had won *every* match with a pulverizing knockout of his opponent. Tommy Walker's story as it related to the International Squadron in late 1937 and 1938 is a behind-the-scenes, intimate look into the affairs of that luckless organization. Walker's activities in the few years preceding his volunteering to fight for China also provide us with a view of what kind of man is likely to lay his life on the line. Dollars alone weren't an incentive that great—*not* when you realized what the Japanese would do to you if you were ever to fall into their hands. ...

Cloudbuster

In late 1933 the barnstorming act with which Tommy Walker flew and jumped ran out of cash customers in Texas. For several months the group of men had lived and flown gloriously, but the depression was just too rough to sustain the many gypsy flying acts beating their way around the rural areas of the country. After two miserable weeks of collecting nickels and dimes—all their customers had to offer them—the men decided to break up the team and call it quits.

A fellow pilot called Walker aside to explain the details of a smuggling deal that demanded sharp flying under conditions fit to make a brave pilot blanch. Walker knew the barnstorming troupe was through, and he jumped at the chance. It was flying; it was also a bundle of money in a short time for a fairly brief number of flights. His friend didn't know what his contraband cargo was, and Walker didn't want even a hint of what they would carry. He asked no questions, received no information voluntarily, but ran his winged delivery service as agreed. From Houston, Texas, Walker and the other pilot flew to a farmer's pasture just outside of El Paso del Norte, in Mexico, where their contact delivered the cargo and delivery instructions to them.

It was a good life; their contract paid them $500 in hard cash before each flight, and awaited them on their return with another $500. One thousand dollars for less than two hours of straight flying was the kind of business that Walker and his friend enjoyed.

It didn't take much longer for the ground to cave in beneath them. The Mexican *Rurales* had worked themselves into a towering rage at the will-o'-the-wisp antics of the old Fleet biplane that Walker pushed back and forth across the border. Neither Tommy nor his pilot friend paid much attention to the rumors circulating about plans of the *Rurales* to catch the smugglers; after all, a horse simply doesn't fly very high and it just can't catch a plane—even an old Fleet. But there was a difference between Walker and the other pilot, a difference that would bring them down without their cherished airplane. Walker lived it up on the ground, but in the air he was an old daredevil, and you do not gain age in that business by being lucky. Good fortune runs out very quickly; Walker in the air was as sober and industrious as any justice on the bench.

Not so the owner of the biplane; *he* stayed drunk most of the time, and it mattered little whether they were in the air or on the ground. His playful disposition, added to his contempt for the Mexican border patrol, brought them to grief.

On a night with the moon washing coldly over the rough desert terrain, they hedgehopped across the brush, rising and falling with the swells of the land. Behind Tommy Walker his compatriot warbled happily, taking occasional swigs from a flask and shouting into the wind streaming past the open cockpits. Under that full moon, he caught sight of a mounted Mexican border patrol—searching for the smugglers—and immediately grabbed the controls away from Walker.

Fun is fun, but Walker found the next several minutes too much even for him. At their low altitude he didn't dare wrestle for the controls, and he had to sit helpless in the cockpit as his friend dove at full speed directly for the mounted patrol. The Fleet screamed low over the startled Mexicans, several of whom leaped headfirst from their horses to escape the slashing propeller. Laughing uproariously, the pilot turned sharply and thundered back for another pass to scatter the rest of the horsemen.

The Mexicans had regained their wits, and the airplane was a clear target in the moonlit sky. More than a dozen rapid-fire rifles banged away at the swiftly approaching biplane. The odds were a thousand-to-one against their being hurt—but the odds caught up with them.

A bullet spanged through a control cable, snapping it in two. Tommy Walker had just enough time to horse back on the stick to jerk the plane upward into a climb; at the top of the sudden ascent the Fleet slewed around wildly and whipped off into a tight spin. Before it completed the first turn both Walker and his friend—expert jumpers —were out of their seats and cracking silk. They barely sneaked back across the border.

By 1934 Walker was the feature attraction at the Chicago World Fair's Motordrome—especially its Wall of

Death. For a month he rode a motorcycle at breakneck speed within a giant barrel, crushing centrifugal force glueing the wheels to the side of a vertical wall. With other riders, he crisscrossed in stunts that kept the on-lookers gaping, with Walker always a split-second away from disaster in those tight, roaring confines.

The Fair ended and the open road beckoned. Walker kept check on air shows, and wherever the remaining barnstormers showed up, he was on hand to fly, wing-walk, or jump—he didn't care what he did so long as there was money in it. The depression, however, clung like a smothering blanket to the remaining barnstorming troupes, and weeks would slip by without a nickel coming in.

Walker turned to his fists to eat. He bummed rides and rode the rails from Louisville to Memphis, then to New Orleans, stopping off in small towns to slug it out with vicious, experienced local fighters in smoke-filled arenas. He had come to be a deadly veteran in the ring, with his natural balance, swift reaction time, and steel-hard build. In a few weeks he slammed and pounded his way through one fight after the other; a natural south-paw, his powerhouse left crushed consciousness out of 26 opponents. Nine others were simply battered into limbo, or were saved from bloody punishment when even those hardened referees grabbed Walker's arms to save his op-ponents.

His life settled down into a rugged pattern as an itinerant flying stunt man, daredevil parachutist, and brawling club fighter who had never known defeat. An air show in San Diego hit it lucky, and for a solid month Walker jumped, stunted, and flew wild aerobatics. The money was rolling in again, but weeks of a lean belly had taught Walker his lesson. Three times a week, at the San Diego exposition, he climbed into the ring (always betting his purse on himself) to smash other fighters into oblivion.

Money bulged fat and crisp in his pockets. He had it made, and there seemed no limit to the suddenly bright horizon of flying, jumping, fighting—and a steadily grow-ing pile of greenbacks.

It was the summer of 1937 and all-out war flamed in China. Whatever his reasons—and Walker won't try to recall them today—he turned away from the best money-making deal he had ever known, and walked into the office of the Chinese consul to offer his services as a fighter pilot. Walker's visit came shortly after Chiang Kai-shek had made his decision to form the International Squadron. The Chinese offered him papers to sign, and said he would be called within 30 days. But in the meantime, they told him (*after* he had signed the papers) his life was in danger.

"This building," explained the consul to Walker, "is under the constant surveillance of Japanese intelligence agents. I assure you that you have been watched and that before the day is out they will know your name and a great deal about you. *Be careful*. Where will you be staying?"

Walker explained that he would await his call in Seattle.

"If you remain in that city until we call you," the consul went on, "it would be, ah, wise to avoid—shall we say—too many dark corners?"

Walker grinned at the warnings. He was immune to such advice; there had been too many narrow escapes as a parachutist and a stuntman, too many fights. To him the entire affair sounded exactly like a Hollywood thriller about the mysterious Orient.

Three weeks later Walker had his first brush with the Japanese—and he learned, almost to his sorrow, that the Chinese consul had not overstated his case. With a close friend, Dutch Wendt, the two men were in one of the many Japanese restaurants of Seattle for dinner. Walker was to discover (weeks later) that the restaurant doubled in brass as a center of operations for Japanese intelligence in the northwestern United States; that same night, however, he learned that the Japanese truly did have the Indian Sign on him. Trying to get service at the counter, he and Wendt were steadfastly ignored—while several Japanese moved in to tables directly behind them. Dutch Wendt gave vent to what Walker describes as "his usual explosive temper" and shouted at the nearest Japanese waiter. That worthy responded with a burst of saliva directly into Wendt's face.

Both Walker and Wendt were sensitive to trouble when it was about to erupt about them; however, it must be noted that Dutch Wendt reacted in splendid fashion. His hand flashed across the counter and a massive fist twisted the waiter's shirt. Abruptly the Japanese found himself in an unusual position—dangling in the air. But only for a moment, until Wendt's other fist thudded with terrible impact directly into his face. Bones splintered and blood gushed; the waiter was unconscious before Wendt dropped him to the floor.

For the next ten minutes both Walker and Wendt had the time of their lives. Japanese came at them from all sides, and instinctively they went back-to-back as they slugged it out with the "clientele" and an astonishing number of waiters for such a small restaurant. Walker was unbelievably swift with his fists, and Wendt was of the old roughhouse school, and a man of great physical bulk as well. The Japanese got in a few blows that drew blood, but the pistonlike effect of Walker's fists and the hammering blows of his friend began to pile Japanese up on the floor around them. Sirens screaming just outside the restaurant ended the battle royal; the two men went out the back windows as police poured in through the door.

Two weeks later Dutch Wendt departed for the East Coast, and Tommy Walker began his career as a soldier of fortune for the Chinese. The pay didn't make him unhappy; under an alias, he went to the Orient with a monthly pay of $500 in gold (less than what he made a week as a stuntman), but with a bonus awaiting him in different forms. He was to receive $1,000 in gold for every enemy plane destroyed and confirmed, as well as additional bonuses for missions completed successfully against ground targets.

The Chinese gave him a loaded .38 revolver and a shoulder holster, and they warned him—grimly—to stay very alert and always to be armed. He had been marked by the Japanese for death; those men battered and beaten in the restaurant had lost face with their superiors, and the word had gotten around that they wanted nothing so much as to toss Walker's mangled corpse into the nearest sewer. Tommy listened carefully; and he stayed "very alert and very well armed."

The next morning a new passport was in his hands. Tommy noted that he was going to Australia "for his health." He was also a captain in the Chinese Air Force, and on his way to join the International Squadron then being formed in China.

Weeks later, the ocean liner nosed into its dock in Hong Kong. There agents of the Chinese Air Force picked up Walker, and brought him to a meeting with three European pilots also joining the squadron. Later that same day they were on a train for Canton, where they checked in at the New Asia Hotel.

The sight at Hankow airfield—after Chinese descriptions of the planes they would fly—evoked bitter laughter from the new pilots. The sprawling field displayed a sickly assortment of fighters, bombers, and trainers parked about at random. Mixed in with the different planes were a dozen Russian fighters. Tommy stared at Curtiss Hawk II and III biplane fighters, several of the new Vultee attack bombers, and a half-dozen Martin 139 twin-engined bombers. He stared in wonder at a decrepit Savoia-Marchetti tri-motored bomber left over from the days of General Scaroni, and he looked with envy at six spanking new Gloster Gladiator biplane fighters from England. They belonged to a well-known Chinese fighter group, the Gypsy Squadron, which had started out life with 50 of the new British fighters. Less than a year later the squadron was down to seven planes, and it reached its end in a roaring clash over Hankow. Seven Gladiators and 35 Russian fighters went up to stop 100 Japanese fighters and bombers. Six of the seven Gladiators were shot down, and half the Russian force was shattered by the wild-flying Japanese pilots.

For three weeks Walker and the other pilots languished on the ground. The International Squadron was still being formed, and for some obscure reason the Chinese refused to let Walker or the other men take up any planes on the field. Without airplanes to fly, they had little urge to watch other pilots in the air, and they set up camp in the largest bar in the city, where the whiskey flowed freely and females flocked to their sides.

At the start of the fourth week the Chinese assigned Walker to the Fifth Pursuit Group of the Chinese Air Force. It was here that he struck up a close friendship with Claire Chennault. The two fliers hit it off perfectly; Walker's background as a stunt flier found a responsive chord in Chennault. It was a close and a personal war then; the days of the Flying Tigers and the bold newspaper headlines were years in the future.

The Chinese gave Walker a weatherbeaten Hawk III,

Gloster Gladiator, British-made biplane fighter,
fought in limited numbers in China.
Heavy odds and attrition wiped out the force.

a weary biplane fighter with two machine guns, of .30
and .50 caliber, each firing through the propeller. With a
750 horsepower Cyclone engine (which ground like a
coffee machine, Walker recalls) the Hawk III could barely
top 210 miles per hour. But she could maneuver and
twist like a frightened angel, and to Walker that more
than made up for old age and slow speed.

Walker flew missions with three other Hawk fighters
on four-plane patrol flights. Every other day he flew one
or two missions, except when special strikes or intercepts
were ordered. Up to now his adventures had been anything but a war for him, but with succeeding missions
the face of China began to change both his impressions
and his attitude toward what he was doing in the battered
country. He could see the brown tides of thousands of
troops locked in battle. On every point of the horizon,
towns and villages cast their greasy smoke palls into the
sky.

The narrow roads were choked with trucks, armored vehicles, and long files of men grinding dust into the air behind them. They were Japanese columns; they were also the primary targets of the Hawk fighters.

Walker and his wingmen strafed trucks and troop columns. Day after day they poured low over the roads, pressing rudder gently so that their streams of lead would hose back and forth into the densely packed men. The Japanese fought back with the snarling thuds of bullets pumping into the old fighter planes; holes appeared magically in the fabric wings and bodies. Sometimes the Hawks faltered, and sometimes they smoked, but they brought the men back to their home fields without loss.

Japanese gunboats infested the rivers and canals, and these became the favorite hunting grounds of the fighter planes. Dozens of the gunboats, as well as troop barges, splintered and burned under the fire of Hawk fighters in trail, creating the effect of a long buzz saw within the vessels. The waters of the canals ran red and choked with bodies, and the fighters swung at treetop level, always seeking the advantage of such surprise, to strafe bivouac areas, observation balloons, gun positions—anything that was Japanese.

Tommy Walker changed one night. The other men watched in unspoken curiosity as he returned to his barracks, white-faced, nauseated. He had been well out in the country, his natural bent of curiosity prompting him to join a Chinese patrol that penetrated into the shadowy zone through which moved the patrols of both nations' forces. They stopped at a small Chinese village where the townspeople had just begun the grisly task of disposing of the bodies of more than one hundred women and young girls—including the children of the village—all of whom had been raped and tortured, and then murdered.

From that day on, Walker flew every time he had an airplane available. He took every opportunity, in between his assigned missions, to fly solo raids. He stayed low, away from the Japanese fighters, using hills and trees for concealment. He was up before dawn, waiting in the Hawk's cockpit for the first splinter of light on the distant horizon. The Japanese didn't expect attacks at that time of day, and Walker slid his fighter into the air, wound up the gear, and went off on what became a series of devastating lone-wolf missions.

Curtiss Hawk biplane fighter flown by
Tommy Walker in lone-wolf strafing attacks against
Japanese ground targets.

He went after the troops on the narrow roads moving
out on their early morning patrols, moving carelessly because no one ever struck from the air at such a time. He
searched especially for the troop barges that bulged with
men; catching them still half-asleep, he made his turns so
that the sun, low on the horizon, always loomed directly
behind him. In that savage early morning glare, he was
all but invisible to the men on the ground and in the boats
when his twin guns rattled in their mounts and the lead
hosed into the thickly packed bodies. Always the sun;
always that concealment of blinding light; always that
precious advantage of time in which to strike and be
gone before the massed guns on the ground could be
brought to bear against him.

His fellow pilots thought he was mad, and the Chinese
were convinced of it—and grateful.

The Fifth Pursuit Group maintained from six to ten
Hawk fighters on hot alert, ready to fly at a minute's
notice. They were considered virtually helpless against the
massive Japanese strikes in the air. The Japanese Navy

came over regularly in formations of 27 to 36 twin-engine bombers escorted by a like or a superior number of the Mitsubishi fighters. Most of the time the pilots of the International Squadron did not make even an attempt to fight these powerful striking forces.

Claire Chennault had little interest in dead heroes—which is what his men would be if ever they tried to slug it out with the superior enemy forces. Chennault's orders were specific: when an alert sounded, you were to run for safety. No heroics; Chennault explained acidly to his men that it would take only one or two major air battles for the Japanese to notch their guns in celebration of wiping out the remaining Chinese fighters.

The only exceptions to the rule came when the vast spotter network provided a long warning time. Under these conditions Chennault ordered the Hawks into the air, to climb as high as possible and try to put the sun between themselves and the approaching Japanese formations. They would take the weary biplanes as high as their laboring engines would permit, and circle above Hankow, waiting. If they saw the chance to slip past the screen of weaving fighters, then the Hawks were to "give 'em hell." This meant a screaming dive at full power directly into the bombers, one long burst at one target, and then run for it. Keep up full power, keep the nose down, and dive for your life.

The Hawks screeched and buffeted madly at 300 miles per hour, great speed for them but easily attainable in the sleek Japanese fighters. Thus their only chance was to pour their slugs into the vitals of a Japanese bomber—"go for the tanks and the engines; if you miss them, you'll still clobber the crew in the cockpit"—and escape before the swarm of fighters closed in on them. Walker flamed one bomber—but that was all.

"Most of the time we never made it to the bombers," he explained. "The Japs were a hell of a lot faster than we were, and we were usually outnumbered five or six to one. If we saw the fighters turning in toward us before we got to the bombers, our orders were to get out of that beartrap before we got mangled. So, we got.

"In a man-to-man fight, I could whip any Jap sonofa-bitch they had. Sure, the Mitsubishi was good, but in a brawl, that Hawk would do wonders. It was the export model of one of our best Navy carrier fighters, and it was a rugged machine. If you flew it right, it was light enough on its feet to take on the best the Japanese had. Now, those Jap pilots were good; make no mistake about it. But we were damned good, too. I had been barnstorming and flying square corners in the air before most of those Jap pilots ever got into training school."

The Japanese one day put Walker to the test. Cut off from a diving escape after making a futile stab at the bombers, he found himself boxed in by several fighters. Wisely, he didn't try to run for it—the faster Mitsubishis would have been on him in a flash. Instead he went into a tight turn, his wings vertical to the ground, sucking it in tighter and tighter. One Japanese fighter tried to cut it in short to slice into his turn; Walker held his turn steady. As he knew would happen, the Japanese fighter clawed into a high-speed stall, and its high wing snapped the ship over. Immediately Walker rolled swiftly, *not* at the tumbling fighter but at the next man in line. The maneuver was completely unexpected; his twin guns chewed up the pilot in his cockpit and set the Mitsubishi aflame. Before the other pilots could react, Walker was through the hole and rushing earthward in a vertical dive.

But he was also on the receiving end of punishment. Ten Mitsubishi pilots came out of the sun in the classical maneuver and bounced the four-ship formation in which Walker was flying. It was a slaughter. Two of the Hawks went down immediately with dead pilots at the controls. A third Hawk stumbled in the air and exploded in flames; the pilot had only a last moment and he used it to pour a burst into the cockpit of a Mitsubishi. Then the Hawk disappeared in a huge fireball.

That left only Walker. He twisted and weaved like a madman, but it didn't help. The Japanese fighters took their time, and they sawed his plane from one end to the other. The Hawk was coming apart under him as Walker snapped out bursts at the surprised Japanese pilots. Then two of them came up from underneath and the Hawk became a thundering ocean of flames. Walker stayed with the winged furnace as long as he could; over the Chinese lines his clothes were smoking. Then he went out, gripping the D-ring but not opening the chute. He fell so far the Japanese pilots thought he was dead and wheeled away. Six hundred feet up the expert parachutist yanked hard; the canopy cracked open, and two seconds later he was on the ground and running for cover—just in case.

Despite all their training, many of the Chinese bombardiers, as Walker put it, "couldn't hit the broad side of a barn from twenty feet." Chennault asked Walker to fly as pilot or lead bombardier on missions with the twin-engine Martins and the Vultees. When the weather was poor, Walker elected to fly. He led the formations in to their targets from heights of only 400 feet. The other crewmen and the Chinese screamed that it was suicide. The blast from the exploding bombs slammed with brutal force into the planes, and they were peppered with pieces of steel and debris from the uplifting targets.

Walker always answered their enraged shouts with one question: "Anybody get shot down by Japanese fighters?" He kept up the low-level raids as long as Chennault would let the planes take off.

"It was a wild war, real crazy," Walker explained. "For one thing, it was the most disorganized mess you ever saw. The flying was ragged as hell and it was just plain dangerous to fly with most of the men—some of the International Squadron people were nuts who never did know how to fly, and most of the Chinese just couldn't fly. In the air, the word discipline was a hollow joke. If Chennault could have seen those formations—I use the word loosely—over target, he would have wept. Everybody flew where the hell they pleased. It was worth your life to rely in battle upon a Chinese crew member. Most of them were brave enough, but they were always being insulted by some thing or another. The crazy bastards would sulk at their guns and refuse to fire at the Japanese whenever they thought somebody had insulted them."

Ten months after he started fighting in China, Tommy Walker returned to his home field in a Vultee that was more wreck than airplane. A vicious crossfire from Japanese ground positions had torn the airplane into a smoking shambles. One gunner was dead, sprawled like a bloody and broken doll over his weapons. The other lay helpless within the airplane, both legs shattered.

Streaking down the runway, the landing gear of the crippled bomber collapsed suddenly. The ship careened wildly. There was a scream from tearing metal and the Vultee started through a huge somersault, breaking up as

Vultee V11GB export attack bombers—
good airplanes but poorly used by the Chinese
and the International Squadron pilots.

it smashed back to the runway as jagged, burning wreckage. Chinese soldiers dragged Walker bodily from the flaming, exploding plane, his skin seared and his right knee ripped wide open to the bone. He was in the hospital for five weeks, and finally hobbled out on crutches.

He had behind him 70 missions in Hawk fighters, 12 in the Martins, and 35 more in the Vultees—as well as two confirmed kills. But he never flew again in China, for the International Squadron had disappeared; in fact, it was disbanded shortly after he entered the hospital.

The men had set themselves up in a "permanent roost" in Hankow, on a hell-for-leather thoroughfare known as Dump Street. It thrived with prostitutes, dope smugglers, perverts, unlimited supplies of excellent whiskey, and a sprinkling of Japanese agents. The latter cultivated the friendship of the foreign crews. Lax in discipline and with tongues loosened by liquor and females, the pilots, pure and simple, shot off their mouths. They were especially talkative about a major mission being planned.

The Japanese agents took it all in, and later that night their radios crackled with coded messages to Japanese airfields. The morning following, Chinese bombers were lined up neatly at the Hankow airfield. There was a deep thrumming drone in the sky and the long line of bombers on the ground disappeared in sheets of flame as Japanese bombs sliced neatly and accurately to the ground.

The International Squadron was sent packing.

American Warplanes in China

The Curtiss P-40B Tomahawks of the Flying Tigers, garishly painted with their shark's-mouth insignia (copied after the same design on German fighters being flown in Africa), became famous the world over after Pearl Harbor. But these fighter planes were latecomers to the China scene, where many hundreds of American airplanes had been sent in the air war against the Japanese. The large numbers of these aircraft provide an excellent indication of the size of that air war.

The Bellanca 28-90B Flash was a fast (280 miles per hour) single-engine, multi-purpose, bomber-fighter which promised excellent use in China. That promise was never realized. An undisclosed number of the airplanes were shipped to Shanghai, where they were destroyed, still in their shipping crates, by Japanese bombers.

The Northrop 2E, export version of the U.S. Army's XA-13, was an outmoded light bomber by the time it went into action with Chinese pilots. It could reach 200 miles per hour with a bomb load, but only for a brief period of flight, and cruised at a much lower speed. The Chinese received 150 of these planes; they achieved some success against Japanese merchant ships and light warships, sinking several of their targets. All the Northrop 2E bombers were finally lost in combat and training accidents.

Thirty of the Vultee V11GB attack bombers, export versions of the Army's A-19, were bought by China. Some of these planes were used with great success against Japanese army forces; finally all were lost. They proved so effective that the Chinese ordered 78 Vultee V12C and V12D bombers, improved models of the V11GB.

One of the strangest aircraft in China was the Spartan Executive, a five-place business airplane, which was converted to a two-place multipurpose military aircraft. Powered with a 400 horsepower engine, it carried three guns and up to 300 pounds of bombs. An unknown number were delivered to China.

Ungainly in the air and terrifyingly vulnerable to attack was the Curtiss BT-32, a bomber conversion of the Condor commercial airliner—in *biplane* configuration. It mounted five .30 caliber machine guns and carried nearly two tons of bombs. An unknown number were delivered.

The Martin 139 export version of the U.S. Army's B-10 bomber had a top speed of 260 miles per hour, and was considered a fine weapon for its day. By the time it became operational in China (nine were delivered) it was considered to be greatly outclassed by Japanese twin-engine bombers. Almost all the Martins were destroyed on the ground by Japanese bombs, or lost in training accidents.

The Boeing XP-925A was the export version of the Boeing Model 218 fighter (from the series that produced the famous P-12 biplane fighters of the U.S. Army). Only one was sent to China, where it was to be demonstrated before a large order was committed. It became the first American fighter to destroy an enemy plane in China when it shot down a Japanese fighter over Shanghai. Only this one model was known to have been delivered; the Boeing was lost in battle.

A sharp improvement over the American biplane fighters was the Boeing 281, export version of the stubby, monoplane P-26 fighter designed for the U.S. Army. A 600 horsepower engine gave the airplane a top speed of 235 miles per hour. Ten were purchased in 1937.

The Grumman SF-2, in an export version of a scout-fighter biplane designed for the U.S. Navy, was also purchased by China. The quantity is unknown.

Two of the best-known American fighters in China were the Curtiss Hawk II and Hawk III—different models of a biplane developed in export models from a Navy shipboard fighter design. Between 1932 and 1936 China purchased more than one hundred of these airplanes. Hawk III fighters were also built in that country under an export license agreement with the Curtiss company.

The Curtiss-Wright CW-21 was a very fast, highly maneuverable, and fast-climbing monoplane of modern design. Many of these were sold to the Netherlands East Indies; an unknown number were delivered to China, and

Most of the nine Martin 139 twin-engine bombers
sent to China were destroyed on
the ground in Japanese bombing attacks.

some of them are known to have engaged Japanese fighters
in battle.

Several other types of aircraft—Beechcraft light transports and Douglas DC-3 twin-engine airliners among them
—were sent to China. Apparently several aircraft types
were never identified publicly; there are references from
several reliable sources to "the arrival of some fifty North
American planes," for example, but further information
is unavailable.

The one airplane that represents the sorry state of airpower management in China in the period 1937–38, in a
fashion unapproached by any other, was the Curtiss Hawk
75. (None of this involves airpower shipments from other
countries besides the United States, such as 50 British
Gladiator fighters, unknown numbers of French fighters
and bombers, the hundreds of Italian fighters and bombers, and more than 400 warplanes from Russia delivered
to China in the period 1937–39—to name only *some* of

the quantities.) The Hawk 75 was the forerunner of the better-known Curtiss P-36 Mohawk designed for the U.S. Army. The export version of the Hawk was considered an outstanding machine for its time—and in most respects unquestionably superior to the Mitsubishi Type 96 (Claude).

The Hawk could reach a speed of 280 miles per hour at 10,700 feet and was armed with four machine guns. It became famous among the pilots of the many countries to which it was sold for its superb controllability (it was used against latest-model Messerschmitts early in World War II—*with* success). In tests against the early Spitfire Mk. I, Hawk fighters flown by British pilots had proven able at high speeds to outmaneuver the Spitfire. At high diving speeds the British fighter encountered heavy resistance to aileron movement, and could roll only in sluggish fashion. The Hawk, by comparison, remained extremely light on the controls even at high speeds.

A report of tests with the Hawk at England's Royal Aircraft Establishment (against the Spitfire Mk. I) showed the Hawk "as extremely easy to fly with exceptionally good handling characteristics and beautifully harmonized controls. At 400 miles per hour the Hawk proved far superior to the Spitfire in a diving attack . . . and in a dogfight at 250 miles per hour the American fighter again proved the superior machine. . . ." There were many advantages to the Spitfire, of course, which earned it its classical reputation the world over, but the British reports noted that the Hawk was "by far the better airplane for aerial combat in which maneuverability was of prime importance."

The Chinese government purchased the Curtiss demonstrator model in 1937 (for a reported $55,000) to be used as the personal fighter of Claire Chennault. Early in 1938 the Curtiss company had orders for 112 of these outstanding fighter planes; late that same year the Hawks were in China.

The soaring hopes for these machines, with which China might begin to wrest back air superiority from the Mitsubishi Type 96 fighters, were dashed to wreckage almost immediately.

First the planes experienced serious delays in getting to the combat zone. The Chinese cursed and accused Curtiss engineers of failing to assemble the airplanes in proper fashion, with the result that the Hawks suffered a rash of mechanical breakdowns and failures. Troubleshooters from the company rushed to China and finally cleared up the mechanical bottleneck, but not without outraged cries from the Americans that the fault lay not with the airplanes but in the stupendous mechanical ineptitude of the Chinese.

Late in 1938 the first Hawks were in the air with Chinese pilots. What ensued was enough to make strong men weep. One after the other, the Chinese fliers wiped out Hawk fighters in bizarre accidents, until the ranks of the pilots were decimated by these fatalities.

Initial combat training was held at Hengyang, where the airfield has been calmly described as a "hysterical madhouse." The Chinese students were forced to fly in the midst of Russian pilots sharing the field with them, and the Russians were wild, unpredictable, and totally without concern for the shattered nerves and battered bodies of their Chinese companions. During several days of the week, and often at night, the Japanese further reduced the numbers of the precious Curtiss fighters by pouring a continuous rain of bombs upon the airfield.

But no one could outdo the Chinese themselves. Because of the wild antics of the Russians and the distressing accuracy of Japanese bombardiers, training with the Hawk fighters was moved to a distant field.

There, on their first formation flight, six out of the 13 Chinese pilots involved destroyed their Hawk fighters while doing nothing more involved than trying to land.

RED STARS AND ZEROS

By the summer of 1939, two years after they first began to crumble resistance in Shanghai, the Japanese military machine looked back with satisfaction upon its accomplishments on the Asiatic mainland since the Marco Polo Bridge incident. There had been a towering slaughter of the Chinese—a bloodbath that the Japanese admitted was deliberately calculated to bend the Chinese through terror to their will. The Japanese had climaxed their two years of military operations with the virtual achievement of all their original goals. It was true that the Chinese still defended their land (a surprise to those in the Japanese hierarchy who looked upon the Chinese with contempt), and that at times the cost to Japan in men and materiel had been unexpectedly high.

Nevertheless, the price was acceptable. Vast portions of China lay in Japanese hands, and the plunder of that nation was following the same pattern as had taken place in Manchuria. The sea lanes were a Japanese thoroughfare, and merchant ships flying the Rising Sun sailed low in the water from holds bulging with materials desired in the Japanese islands.

From the Japanese point of view, there seemed to be little left in China in the way of meaningful resistance. Dozens of towns and villages had been wiped entirely off the map, cities had been gutted, and the fear-inspired discipline had brought many millions of Chinese laborers to perform for their conquerors. What industry the Japanese did not control had been shredded or destroyed; only a small fraction had escaped, carried under terrible hardship into the remote areas of China by her defenders.

After the occupation of Hankow, China's tottering forces were frantically dug in behind the natural defense barriers of the land. The Japanese had mauled the Chinese steadily, pushing them always back, until at long last the Chinese Army could begin to take advantage of its surface features. They entrenched themselves within mountains, at the far end of gorges and ravines; they dug in on the opposite sides of treacherous and wide mudbanks, rivers, and swamps. The Japanese Army took a long and hard look at the high and narrow mountain passes of Szechwan, they studied the tumbling might of the Yellow River, and they looked askance at the curving, deep gorges of the Yangtze. They looked; and they held their positions. Why risk the army and precious weapons when wings and bombs now could accomplish the same task of destruction, and at infinitely less cost?

The Japanese had their choice of selective war against the Chinese, and they chose the course of simplicity itself. Use the land forces in China proper and the Navy at sea to seal off the Chinese nation from help and supplies—and bomb the retreating defenders into submission. It would be a two-pronged campaign—starvation by blockade and destruction from the air.

As a start, the Japanese selected Chungking to become the object lesson for all China not yet in their hands. There was no question about their methods—the bombing of Chungking was openly a terror campaign. Well aware of the flammable nature of the city (as they were to learn of their own cities years later), the Japanese intended to burn the city, section by section, to ashes.

The first raid to hit Chungking came in early May of 1939 with a light force of 27 bombers. Yet the Japanese struck with telling fury, as the incendiary bombs scattered in a selected pattern and set off huge fires within the area struck. High winds whipped the flames into a holocaust; on the first night 10,000 people burned to death (the flames ran unchecked for three days and nights). It was the single deadliest raid to date in the war; the previous high toll had taken place in Nanking, when 4,000 Chinese in the huge air-raid tunnel perished as Japanese bombs struck, simultaneously, at opposite ends of the tunnel.

By late 1939, the Japanese had become so powerful in the air that they were carrying on in a manner no fiction writer would commit to paper. Japanese fighters cruised slowly up and down the flight lines of fields strewn with

Chinese and Russian planes, methodically shooting up aircraft, barracks, hangars, and anyone in sight.

According to reliable eyewitnesses to the scene, at one airfield several Japanese pilots *landed* on the main runway, taxiing swiftly to the flight line. Overhead there swung a cordon of other Japanese fighters, maintaining a lethal protective umbrella, and gunning down anyone unfortunate enough to emerge from cover. The Japanese pilots left their engines running, leaped from their cockpits, and ran to nearby Russian bombers. They set aflame rags, straw, anything that would burn, and hurled the flaming materials into the planes, setting aflame entire rows of vitally needed aircraft. While their friends kept up a steady machine-gun barrage from the air, the Japanese pilots returned to their planes and roared into the air.

While these events went on, the raids against Chungking mounted in brutal fury. The size of the Japanese formations increased until they were more than five times larger than the attacks at the beginning of the campaign to destroy the Chinese city. Up to 150 bombers in a single mass formation struck at Chungking, not sporadically, but almost every day, steadily grinding the city underneath a giant heel of flame until the scenes of gray ash spread farther and farther.

In the period of only one month, the Japanese poured 8,000 tons of bombs into Chungking. In the first six months of their attacks, hammering in day-and-night blows at the hapless, stunned city, they had dropped a total of *35,000 tons of bombs*. The appalling weight hurled into Chungking may be better appreciated when we compare it with the massive assaults carried out by our giant B-29 bombers in World War II. The *total* tonnage released over Japan came to 96,000 tons of bombs —on *all* the cities and targets of the Japanese islands. In six months, Chungking alone received more than one-third of all the bombs dropped on Japan for the entire war.

There were asides to the great conflict in China that still appear, so many years after that struggle, to defy understanding. Japanese soldiers and airmen in China constantly were amazed at the seeming insanity of their enemy. "The most startling aspect of the conflict, however," wrote one pilot, "was the savage internal struggle between Chiang's forces and those of the Communist Chinese. At every opportunity the latter would strike at Nationalist forces when they were retreating before our own troops."[1]

One Japanese provided the explanation that attempts by the Japanese military to occupy the tremendous land area of China "would have been absolutely impossible. Instead, our troops occupied key walled towns at strategic areas, cutting enemy communications, and then exacted tolls and taxes from the millions of Chinese peasants within the authority of the occupying Japanese forces.

"But outside the protection of these major walled towns violent death awaited all but the most powerful Japanese formations. Chiang's guerrillas, as well as those of the Chinese Communists, waited in savage ambush where they would do their utmost to annihilate those troops which fell into their hands. It also was obvious to our officers that those Chinese officials within the occupied cities, despite their fawning and seeming cooperation, remained in constant touch with agents of the guerrilla bands roaming the open countryside and the mountains. And, in many instances, to facilitate the problems of occupying enemy cities, such contacts were maintained with the direct acquiescence of the Japanese commanders!

"It was, indeed, a strange war.

"Many times I flew land-support missions and was astonished at the sights below me. I saw Chinese farmers tilling their farms, paying no attention to pitched hand-to-hand battles or blazing firefights between Chinese and Japanese troops less than a mile away. On several occasions I flew low over the streets of walled towns that were surrounded and under fierce bombardment from our artillery. On those streets rows of stores were operating under 'business as usual' conditions, although the blood of the defending Chinese garrison stained the streets red."[2]

Red Star in China

Of all the aspects of the kaleidoscopic air war in China, fewer seem to be stranger than the participation of the Soviet Union, with its tremendous support to China and the direct involvement of its own, independently operating combat air units.

Despite the growing strength of the Chinese Communist armies and political factions, the Russians remained remarkably clearheaded about the chaotic situation in China. They appeared to be convinced that the greatest opposition to the Japanese would be made through the forces commanded by Chiang Kai-shek; the need for supporting the Chinese Communists, while important to their long-range plans, took a back seat to the urgency of slowing down the Japanese war machine. The Chinese Communists were interested primarily in seizing control of China; Chiang Kai-shek had as his most critical need the stopping and possibly the defeat of the Japanese. With war looming in Europe, the Russians wanted no part of a great conflict along their borders with Japan. Accordingly, they exercised little restraint in presenting an aggressive military front wherever they encountered Japanese forces.

The extensive assistance rendered to Nationalist China can be understood more clearly through an awareness of this long-range attitude of the Russians. The Soviets had little liking for Chiang Kai-shek; relations had been strained ever since the Generalissimo's Central Government troops had massacred thousands of Chinese Communist soldiers at Shanghai and elsewhere in 1927.

Fighting the Japanese was nothing new to the Russians, of course. There had been the devastating defeat of the Russo-Japanese War in 1904–1905. The Russians had continued to clash with their perennial enemy in Siberia, and they grasped every opportunity to strike hard at the Japanese through the convenience of the Sino-Japanese Incident.

The extent of Russian aid to the Chinese is extremely difficult to specify from the remaining records; the logistics of that conflict seem to have escaped attention in other parts of the world, overshadowed as they were by the march of events in Europe. From the Soviet Union, China received nearly a quarter billion dollars in negotiable currency, with which to purchase an extensive variety of Russian military equipment. In addition to hundreds of new antiaircraft guns and mechanized equipment, the Chinese immediately ordered 400 modern fighters and bombers, along with the ground support equipment and the training necessary to convert this number of aircraft into an effective fighting force.

In addition to their cash-weapons-airplanes arrangements with the Chinese government, the Russians moved into China with a powerful air force of their own. This armada was made up of six full squadrons of the Russian Air Force, plus elements of an armored division which was used primarily to protect the perimeter and approaches of communications to the Russian fields.

The Russians maintained a sharp cleavage between the planes sold to China and the use of their own forces. Where their own crews were involved, the Soviets took orders from no one, yet might, on an unpredictable basis, listen to advice from Chennault or the Chinese commanders. More often than not they simply went their own way. They were willing to fight and to kill Japanese, but not for an instant would they countenance taking orders from Chiang Kai-shek or anyone else. All Soviet missions flown in China were carried out under the direct command of the leader of the Russian expeditionary force, General Asanov.

Americans in China who observed the Russians on the ground and in the air were quick to evaluate Soviet equipment as outstanding and the quality of the Russian pilots and their crews as nothing less than superb. They flew missions by day and by night; they went into the air willingly every time they were ordered to attack the enemy. They astonished the Chinese and the Americans with their willingness to fly at any time, no matter what the weather or how long they had been without rest. In summation, they had an immense confidence, they were brilliant in their piloting, aggressive in combat, rigidly disciplined, and "tough as hardened leather" as men and as pilots.

Olga S. Greenlaw, who spent several years in China before World War II, lived at the edge of Hengyang airfield, where the Russians based two bomber squadrons. As she described these planes:

"While they were flying for China, they were manned by regular Russian pilots and mechanics. With Russia officially at peace with Japan I never did figure how that had been worked out. The Russians were unique and amusing. The pilots, particularly, had a passion for wrist watches and wore three or four on one wrist at a time. They were paid, by Russian standards, big money by the Chinese Government and obviously spent most of it, saying it wouldn't be any good to them in Russia. Their doctor asked me confidentially to give him all the lowdown I possibly could on Mary Pickford. They were all

Hollywood-mad and sent us bottles of vodka in return for our copies of dog-eared motion picture fan magazines."[3]

Saburo Sakai, then a fighter pilot flying the Mitsubishi Type 96 fighter in China, describes the effect of a Russian bomber attack against his base outside Hankow:

"I remember the day with absolute clarity—October 3, 1939. I had just finished reading my mail, and was servicing the machine guns of my fighter plane. Everyone at the field was relaxed; what was there to worry about? We had whipped the Chinese and international pilots in almost every combat.

"Abruptly the silence was broken by frenzied shouts from the control tower. In the next instant, without any further warning, the world erupted into a series of shattering roars. The earth heaved and shook, and blast waves smashed at our startled ears. Someone bellowed—unnecessarily—'Air Raid!' and then the sirens shrieked a useless, belated warning.

"There was no time to try and run for the shelters. The blasting crescendo of exploding bombs was a constant thunder now; smoke rose over the field and I heard the shrill scream of bomb fragments cutting through the air. Several other pilots ran frantically with me from the machine shop for shelter. I crouched low to escape the whistling pieces of steel, and dove headlong onto the ground between two big water tanks. I was none too soon. A nearby machine-gun storage shed went up in a roaring blast of fire and smoke, and then a stick of bombs walked across the field, hammering at our ears, sending up great spouts of smoke and earth.

"A second's delay in diving for the ground would have meant my end. The nearby series of bomb explosions suddenly ended and I lifted my head to see what had happened. Above the steady *crump!* of bombs exploding all across the field I heard anguished cries and groans. The men lying all about me had been badly wounded, and I started to crawl toward the nearest pilot when I gasped from a knifelike pain in my thighs and buttocks. I reached down with my hand and felt the blood seeping through my trousers. The pain was bad, but, fortunately, the wounds were not deep.

"And then I lost my head. I was on my feet and running again, but this time I ran back toward the airstrip, glancing up at the sky as I moved down the runway. Overhead

I saw twelve bombers in formation, very high, wheeling about in a wide turn at a height of at least 20,000 feet. They were Russian SB twin-engined planes, the main bombers of the Chinese Air Force. And there was no denying the incredible effectiveness of their sudden surprise attack. We had been caught totally unprepared. Not a single man had any warning until the bombs were actually released from the Russian planes and shrieking in their descent. What I saw on the airfield itself was a shock.

"The majority of the 200 Navy and Army bombers and fighters parked wing to wing on the long runways were burning. Great sheets of flame burst outward from the exploding fuel tanks, sending billowing clouds of smoke into the air. Those planes still safe from the flames were leaking gasoline from shrapnel holes in their fuselages. The flames traveled from one plane to the other, fed upon the dripping gasoline, and, one by one, long rows of bombers and fighters mushroomed into blinding crimson. Bombers were exploding like firecrackers, and the fighters flared like matchboxes.

". . . the terrible destruction wrought by only twelve enemy planes was incredible. Almost all of our planes had been destroyed or wrecked. The commander of the base lost his left arm, and several of his lieutenants, as well as pilots and maintenance crews, were killed or maimed."[4]

Russian fighter pilots in combat were, to say the least, distinctive. They were wild with their airplanes—and they were also wildly unpredictable. No one who ever flew with or against the Russians could find any reason to doubt the courage of those skilled airmen, and the Japanese remembered occasions when a small group of Russian fighters would tear into a numerically superior Japanese formation. But at a given moment, for no particular reason one could fathom, they would decide abruptly to break off a fight, and Russian fighters would be seen screaming low over the countryside, engines howling under full power, and running from the battle. The next day the same number of planes would plunge into Japanese formations outnumbering the Red fighters three or four to one, and the Russians would stay locked in furious dogfights to their last bullet or drop of fuel.

The Japanese learned quickly to pay full attention to

the Russians, and they pursued their enemy with a special vengeance. Above all, they hoped to catch the Soviets unprepared on the ground—as the Japanese themselves had suffered in the devastating losses described by Saburo Sakai.

One entire Russian group was, in fact, caught in this fashion and virtually annihilated by a surprise Japanese bombing attack. With Russian fighters caught on the ground, the Japanese bombers droned back and forth slowly over the airfield, releasing their bombs with exquisite precision and timing. When the bombs were gone, fighters flashed across the field at low altitude to strafe any remaining aircraft. Virtually the entire Russian unit was destroyed.

In the air, the Russians were encountered in the I-16 (often referred to as the E-16 or N-16) monoplane fighter, the same stubby machine that had earned so excellent a reputation in Spain. The I-16, with its heavy firepower and big engine, was a rugged opponent, but it simply couldn't turn with the Mitsubishis in a free-for-all dogfight. To accept combat with the Japanese on these terms meant to give the Mitsubishi pilots a decided advantage. Yet the superior *pilot* could always turn the odds. Every so often one of the better Russian fliers would engage a Mitsubishi in a fierce plane-against-plane dogfight; epic battles were reported for such occasions, in much the same manner as in the fight between Dickinson and Mussolini in Spain (but without the gentlemen's agreement).

On one such occasion, a Russian combat leader and a Japanese pilot in a Mitsubishi Type 96 fought a spectacular duel over Nanking. Japanese pilots in the air circled well off to the side of the fight and did not interfere with the battle royal between two masters that lasted nearly 30 minutes. The dogfight ended only when both pilots finally exhausted their ammunition. The two fighters flew alongside briefly; the Russian rolled his airplane rapidly and then pulled up sharply in salute. He could see the Japanese pilot grinning in his open cockpit; the enemy waved his arm and turned for his home field.

One of the epic battles of the China air war had come in the spring of 1938 as a result of the Russians' accepting the advice of Chennault (to that pilot's open astonishment). Chennault recommended that the Russians and the

Chinese team up to bait a trap for an impending Japanese raid against Hankow.

The Japanese struck the city on April 29 in a formation of 15 bombers escorted by 24 Mitsubishi fighters. As they made their bombing runs against their target, 20 Chinese pilots in Russian fighters intercepted the Japanese planes. They shot down two bombers, but committed the fatal error of trying to slug it out in a free-for-all dogfight with the Mitsubishis. The Japanese scattered to the winds and before the Chinese could press their initial diving advantage, the red-balled fighter planes were clawing around in tight turns and hammering at their opponents. Without losing a single fighter, the Japanese pilots shot down 11 out of the 20 Chinese-manned airplanes.

Then the Japanese formation regrouped—as the surviving Chinese dove away for their lives—and set off for home. The trap was perfect, the Japanese pilots concluding that there would be no further defense activity after more than half the entire fighter force sent up against them had been destroyed. The Japanese had just settled down into the loose formations for the long flight back to their home bases when the Russians hit them like a two-pronged thunderbolt.

Forty Russian fighter planes, outnumbering the Mitsubishi fighters almost two to one, dove with tremendous speed from high altitude. They plunged in two wedges of 20 fighters each. The first wedge screamed in between the bombers and the protecting Mitsubishi Type 96 fighters. Again the Japanese revealed their superb response to attack; this time, following the hand signals of the leader, they kept their formation and wheeled in unison to hit the Russians. Recognizing the excellent discipline of their attackers—obvious to them as Russians—the Japanese formed a defense maneuver of massed guns.

And did exactly what the Russians hoped they would do—swung away from the bombers. Howling directly out of the sun came the second wedge of 20 fighter planes. Wisely, they *ignored* the bombers, and hit the Japanese fighter formation with terrible effect. In that first devastating pass, half the Japanese planes went down in flames. The fury of the blow blew apart the tight formation, and the diving fighters came wheeling up and around to make their second pass. Half the Japanese pilots responded to this threat, while the others seemed indecisive as to whom they should fight—the first Russian force or the second wedge that had struck. In that turmoil and indecision, the Russians swarmed all over their enemy.

Every Japanese fighter went down. In the brief interval before their destruction the Japanese pilots managed to shoot down two Russian fighters, and then it was all over. At this point the Russian formation discipline vanished, and 38 fighter pilots went roaring for the 13 bombers in the air. The slaughter continued—only three of the twin-engine bombers escaped.

It was the single worst loss of the entire China air war for the Japanese naval air forces. Twenty-four fighters and 12 bombers had gone down with all their crews, and the enemy had lost but 13 planes (11 Chinese and two Russian pilots).

Against the Japanese Navy directly, this was the rarest of victories. The close-knit organization and operations of the Japanese helped them enormously in fighting the polyglot array of forces hurled against them. Their maintenance problems were far simpler than those faced by the Chinese, who were flying with aircraft utilizing parts from the United States, Germany, England, France, Italy, and several other countries. Control of airpower in Chinese hands was a nebulous affair, and information received by the Japanese, through their agents, confirmed that the many hundreds of airplanes received by the Chinese suffered disastrous losses in training and because of pilot ineptitude.

By late 1938 the Japanese controlled the Hankow air base, and moved in heavy aircraft forces usually assigned to duties aboard aircraft carriers at sea. The Japanese Army was desperate for effective close-in support for their ground forces, and the Navy was ordered to fill the gap. There were also powerful surface forces of the Japanese Navy on duty in China (antiaircraft, heavy weapons, and base-defense troops formed the majority of these forces), and the Navy looked with some misgivings on the ability of Japanese Army airpower to defend their operational centers in China.

Among the air units moved into China were groups of Type 97 (Kate) attack bombers; designed expressly for torpedo bombing attacks, this airplane was unusually fast and maneuverable, and proved excellent in torpedo, level, and dive-bombing strikes. Along with these planes came

Aichi Type 99 (Val) dive bombers. Much slower than the torpedo planes, the Vals nevertheless proved a deadly weapon against heavily defended enemy positions, being able to dive vertically at reduced speed with a heavy bomb load—factors contributing to great accuracy against even small targets. Additional forces of the twin-engine Mitsubishi Type 96 (Nell) bombers were sent to China, along with greater numbers of the Type 96 (Claude) fixed-gear fighter planes.

Beginning in May, 1939, the Japanese Navy launched a major aerial offensive against the Chinese. Chungking, Chengtu, and Lanchow became major strategic targets. For six months Japanese bombers and fighters pounded and hammered their opponents in raids that went on by day and by night.

Inexplicably, after the Chinese Air Force had been battered into a weak and almost completely ineffectual force, the Japanese "within another six months noticed definite signs of recovery." The Navy accelerated the tempo of its attacks, striking with great effectiveness against Chinese targets. And yet the Chinese, absorbing cruel and ceaseless punishment, continued their strange increase in airpower strength.

While these aerial campaigns were being waged, another, wholly separate—and exceptionally fierce—air war flared suddenly on the Asiatic mainland. This was well to the north of the fighting, along a geographical strip of rugged land already well stained with blood and littered with the debris of many past battles.

In May, 1939, savage fighting erupted along the Russo-Manchurian border. This time the Russians and the Japanese hacked at each other in a wild, no-holds-barred melee that ran for some four months. It was strictly a conflict between the Japanese and the Russians, and in the air the latter struck with terrible fury at their enemy.

Throughout the air fighting in China, the Japanese Navy scored far and away the greatest number of successes against the Chinese. Yet the bulk of Japanese airpower in China was made up of Army planes. Many of them lacked the performance of their contemporaries, and were assigned to missions that concentrated on direct support of ground troops and mechanized units in the field.

When the fighting broke out along the Russo-Manchurian border, the task of meeting the Russians in the air fell to the Japanese Army. The fine line of distinction that separates a successful airpower force from one that is likely to be shredded at the hands of the enemy was nowhere more evident than in this conflict with the rugged Soviet airmen. The remoteness of that struggle has unfortunately clouded many of the details, especially what must have been monumental fights in the air.

Most of the aerial fighting was carried on at low altitude, since the Russian air force, designed from the outset to protect and support the Red Army on the ground, stuck with dogged determination to its mission. The Japanese Army air units, in turn, struck at the Russians to break up their support of Red ground forces. In the struggles that ensued, the Russian pilots essentially whipped the Japanese at almost every turn.

The Japanese Army hurled into the battles virtually *all* its strength assigned to the Manchurian sector—500 fighters and bombers. Before the fighting ended in September, 1939, four months after its inception, *the Japanese lost those 500 warplanes,* as well as 150 pilots, and an unknown number of aircrew members. No one appears able to pinpoint the losses suffered by the Russians, but the evidence available indicates that the Japanese suffered the worst of it. And there is no question but that the Japanese Army air forces in that combat *were wiped out.*

As the Russo-Manchurian fighting still boiled, World War II became a reality with the dissection of Poland. With the advent of open war on the European continent, both the Russians and the Japanese (the latter staggering under their losses) withdrew from continued direct combat.

In China proper, however, the air war flamed to new heights in the ensuing months as the Japanese Navy, with increasing participation by the Army, made its bid to destroy the resurgent Chinese airpower and to continue the primary mission of defeating the Chinese on the ground. From mid-May to early September of 1940 raids against major Chinese centers increased in fury; during this four-month period an aggregate of 3,717 twin-engine Japanese Navy bombers appeared over the city of Chungking. Army bombers on a number of missions joined the Mitsubishi Type 96 (Nell) bombers, pouring heavier and heavier bomb loads into the wrecked city.

The Japanese consider their losses during this period to

have been heavy. Once again the old pattern of air war was being repeated. The Type 96 (Claude) fighters were unable to escort the long-range bombers to their city targets, and the Chinese husbanded their fighter strength for just those moments when the escorting Mitsubishis had to turn back. It was then that the Chinese struck with every airplane they had, bringing the Japanese to conclude the "definite signs of recovery" of their enemy.

Yet the losses suffered were nowhere as prohibitive as those endured in the opening days and weeks of the Sino-Japanese Incident. The Japanese records show that of their twin-engine bombers sent over target in the four-month period mentioned (for a total of 182 day-and-night raids), the Chinese destroyed nine, and inflicted major damage on another 297. A new element had come into the fighting—half the losses and damage were the direct result of a greatly increased number of antiaircraft guns.

Nevertheless, the specter of disasters occurring once again, at the guns of Chinese fighters attacking the unescorted Japanese formations, unnerved Tokyo. "We could alleviate this unsatisfactory situation," concluded Commander Okumiya, "only by securing command of the air over the targets."[5]

Once again the Japanese were proving quick to learn the basic lessons of airpower. Air superiority—command of the air over the territory of the enemy—could be gained only through a superior fighter airplane, available in numbers sufficient to sweep the enemy from the skies.

And there was such a superior fighter airplane: the Zero was called upon to make its combat debut.

Enter the Zero

The Japanese pilots who in the summer of 1940 first received the new Mitsubishi Zero fighters for combat against the Chinese were as excited about their new machines as their opponents were dismayed. Saburo Sakai, who flew the Zero as few other pilots could, recorded his first impressions of the sleek fighter:

"At Kaohsiung I was in for a tremendous surprise. On the airfield I saw strange new fighter planes, as different from the familiar Type 96 Claudes as night from day. These were the new Mitsubishi Zero fighters, sleek and modern. The Zero excited me as nothing else had ever done before. Even on the ground it had the cleanest lines I had ever seen in an airplane. We now had enclosed cockpits, a powerful engine, and retractable landing gear. Instead of only two light machine guns, we were armed with two machine guns and two heavy 20-mm. cannon, as well.

"The Zero had almost twice the speed and range of the [Type 96] Claude, and it was a dream to fly. The airplane was the most sensitive I had ever flown, and even slight finger pressure brought instant response. We could hardly wait to meet enemy planes in this remarkable new aircraft."[6]

In combat at Pearl Harbor, and throughout other theaters on and after December 7, 1941, the Zero fighter carried with it an aura of mystery. This airplane was, in fact, regarded as "Japan's secret fighter" when it burst with such explosive impact amidst the Allied air forces. The legend was then perpetuated, and it has been nourished ever since, that the Japanese produced the Zero and then went to tremendous lengths to hide it from the eyes of the world.

This is all arrant nonsense, despite what historical studies may say and the reader may have been led to believe. For the truth is that the Zero fighter airplane was a machine tested in battle under a great variety of conditions prior to its first attack against American and other Allied aircraft, and the only mystery surrounding the Zero is how we failed to understand its characteristics in great detail.

For certainly every attempt was made to give us the technical and performance aspects of this excellent and deadly fighter aircraft. Long before the Japanese struck at American installations in the Pacific and Asia, Claire L. Chennault had sent to Washington (and the British had sent to Australia and to England) an exhaustive report on the Zero fighters encountered in China. With that report went a frank appraisal of the Zero's capabilities as a weapon, and a grim warning that this airplane would raise havoc when it was finally let loose among our airmen. The response to this report was unbelievable.

Despite *photographs* and dozens of combat encounters provided in every small detail, military officers in the War

Department of the United States concluded that no airplane could perform as the new Japanese fighter was alleged to—and that the report on the Zero was a deliberately contrived fake! The report was not only ignored, it failed even to make the War Department's files, and apparently was tossed into the nearest wastebasket.

Thus the tremendous impact of the Zero—largely because its outstanding performance *did* come as a devastating (and lethal) surprise to Allied airmen—owed more to the acute myopia of high military officials than to any Japanese attempt at secrecy.

The first combat mission flown by the Zero fighter took place approximately *16 months before the attack on Pearl Harbor.*

On August 19, 1940, Lieutenant Tamotsu Yokoyama led an escort formation of 12 Zeros, weaving high over a force of 50 bombers, during a strike against Chungking. The day following another 12 Zeros, protecting the same number of bombers, were led by Lieutenant Saburo Shindo against the same target. Chinese fighters offered no resistance to the heavy bombing raids. Yet the Japanese were more than satisfied with the two missions, for the Zeros on those two flights had initiated a revolution in fighter combat—each force had flown a round trip of more than 1,150 miles nonstop. This was performance considered in the Allied camps to be impossible.

Again on September 12 an escort formation of 12 Zero fighters failed to stir opposition from the Chinese during a raid against Chungking. Despite the fact that the Zeros swooped down from their high perch to strafe airfields and ground installations, the Chinese remained absent from the air. The next day 13 Zeros appeared again over the city; this time the Japanese pilots were determined to rouse the Chinese to battle.

With the bombing runs completed and the twin-engine raiders with their escort out of sight over the horizon, a Japanese reconnaissance plane cruised at very high altitude over Chungking. Shortly after the Japanese planes disappeared from sight, the reconnaissance plane flashed the word that Chinese fighters had appeared over the city and were descending to land. Immediately the Zeros turned back for Chungking, climbing steadily for higher altitude. They reached the target with the sun behind

The Mitsubishi Zero fighter—described by
the U.S. Government after the Pearl Harbor strike
as a "mystery" Japanese fighter—saw extensive combat in
China sixteen months before the December 7, 1941,
attack against the Hawaiian Islands.

them, and the 13 fighters plummeted from the sky in a
sudden attack that caught the Chinese completely by surprise. Bursting out of the brilliant light of the sun, the
Zeros scattered 27 Russian-built fighters flown by Chinese
pilots, a mixture of I-15 biplane and I-16 monoplane aircraft.

The wild fight lasted for almost 30 minutes, during
which the surprised and startled Chinese pilots were cut
to pieces by the new Japanese fighter planes. The battle
ended with every Zero in the air, and the skies marked
with the thin smoke plumes of the enemy aircraft. Every
one of the 27 fighters had been lost, a testimonial both
to the skill of the Japanese and to the performance of their
new fighter—and the wild confusion and helplessness of
their opponents.

Fighter Officer Koshiro Yamashita became a national
hero in Japan by blasting five enemy fighters from the air,
reaching the coveted ace status in the swirling battle. The
Chinese cut down their own odds when two of the Rus-

In first major engagement against Russian-built
fighters in China, on September 13, 1940,
thirteen Zeros shot down or destroyed a total of
twenty-seven planes, including many of these I-15 biplane
fighters, without loss to the Japanese.

sian-built fighters collided in the wild melee and smashed
into a mountainside. Three other Chinese pilots startled
the Japanese when they hastily bailed out of airplanes
that had never been touched by the Zeros.

The smashing victory over Chungking—along with the
destruction of most of the enemy fighters known to be in
the air—encouraged the Japanese to throw to the winds
the caution they had exercised for so many months in
their raids into the Chinese interior. Hewing to the old
adage of striking while the iron is hot, that same afternoon a powerful force of Val dive bombers—*without*
fighter escort—staged out of Ichang air base to strike
against Chungking. Japanese reconnaissance reported the
interceptor defense of the city was broken by the Zeros,
and they were right. Not a single Chinese fighter rose to
oppose the slow dive bombers. Two days later, on September 15, Kate attack bombers created tremendous damage in the city. Again, the skies remained free of defending Chinese fighters. On the 16th the marauding Zeros

failed to flush any fighters, but they caught a luckless Chinese bomber and blew it out of the sky.

The Japanese remained true to their concept of *"attack the enemy wherever he can be found."* On October 4 eight Zero fighters escorted 27 twin-engine bombers in a very long-range strike against Chengtu in Szechwan Province, pursuing the Chinese to their airpower redoubt. No fighters rose to intercept. The Zero pilots made a wide swing around the target, descended through broken clouds, and burst upon unsuspecting Chinese pilots flying at Taipingssu airfield. Before the Chinese could scatter, five Russian-built fighters and one Russian-built bomber were shot down, again without loss to the Japanese. The aerial victory soared to more meaningful proportions when a reconnaissance plane took pictures of 19 burned hulks on the Chinese field—which had been strafed by the Zero fighters.

This was the pattern that followed wherever the Zero fighters made their appearance in China. There would be a brief and furious encounter with the startling new Japanese airplane, brutal losses sustained by the Chinese, and the immediate confirmation of Japanese air superiority. Writing of the October strikes with Zeros, Commander Okumiya noted that as a "consequence of these attacks, the backbone of Chinese air strength in the Chungking and Chengtu areas was broken. For weeks afterward the skies over these two cities were conspicuously free of enemy planes."[7]

By the end of 1940 the Japanese, in the combat debut of the Zero fighter, had placed an aggregate of 153 of the new planes over enemy targets. Fifty-nine Chinese planes were shot down and another 42 destroyed in strafing attacks. Zeros lost: *none.*

Through the early months of 1941 a small force of Zero fighters carried the brunt of offensive air operations against the Chinese. The general pattern of aerial combat remained unchanged. The Chinese slowly built up their strength by remaining out of the skies, and then hurled a large force of fighter planes at the Japanese. Still the pattern went unbroken: the Japanese pilots responded to the enemy's sudden stiff opposition by shredding the Chinese formations and shooting down large numbers of the defenders. On March 14, 1941, 24 Chinese fighters fell from the skies over Chengtu, without loss to the Zero pilots.

Not until May 20, 1941, did the Japanese lose their first Zero, and then the victory went to a fierce antiaircraft barrage rather than the guns of any Chinese fighter plane. A force of Zeros strafing Taipingssu and Shuanglin airfields in the Chengtu area ran into unexpectedly heavy fire from the ground which succeeded in setting afire the Zero flown by Chief Flight Petty Officer Kimura. More than a month later, on a low-altitude flight between Lanchow and Yuncheng, the second—and last—Zero to be lost in combat prior to World War II went down under a withering antiaircraft defense.

The total battle engagements for the Zero fighter in China make ridiculous the contention that the Japanese had been keeping their star aerial weapon hidden from Allied eyes prior to the opening gun of war across the Pacific. There were American, Russian, British, and other Allied observers in China. The Zeros carried out 70 separate missions, including bomber escort, fighter sweeps, and on-the-deck strafing attacks. The Japanese put an aggregate of 529 of their new fighters directly over Chinese cities, on missions that sometimes ranged nearly 1,200 miles. They shot down 99 Chinese fighters confirmed, in addition to damaging many more.

While the Japanese never lost a Zero to Chinese fighters, two of the Mitsubishis, as we have seen, were shot down by ground fire, and it is known that the wreckage, much of it only lightly damaged, fell into Chinese hands.

The impact of the Zero fighter on the Chinese air war was overwhelming. Commander Okumiya provides the summary:

"In late August and early September of 1941, their missions accomplished, the China-based bombers reported to new stations in both Japan and Formosa. During their second combat tour of four months, we placed twenty-six hundred bombers over enemy targets. Of this number, we lost only one bomber, and that airplane fell to enemy antiaircraft fire. In the dozens of raids which the bombers carried out, they encountered only ten Chinese fighter planes which managed to slip past the escorting Zero fighters. Even so, the enemy fighter planes failed to destroy any of our planes.

"These facts clearly demonstrate the Zero's effectiveness in the China campaign. Where once we had reached the point of prohibitive bomber losses to enemy fighters and antiaircraft, the arrival of the Zeros destroyed the enemy planes' effectiveness as interceptors. In summation: *the Zero gave us undisputed command of the air over both our own territory and that of the enemy.*"[8]

The Japanese were ready to set aflame the Pacific battlefront.

BOOK TWO

BOOK TWO

6

"NIITAKA YAMA NOBORE"

"December 7, 1941 . . . will live as the date of one of the most brilliant military performances of all time. Superbly planned and superbly executed . . ."

"On December 7, 1941, he [the Japanese] achieved complete surprise. He struck swiftly, boldly, accurately. . . . He made full capital of the paralyzing effect of his initial assault."

"The attack achieved perfect tactical surprise. . . . From the standpoint of air employment alone, his first stroke was masterful."

These are strong statements. At first glance one might attribute them to a zealous Japanese historian preparing an "objective record" of the opening phase of the great Pacific war which exploded into being on the morning of December 7, 1941, with the swift and stunning assault of the Japanese Navy against our installations at Pearl Harbor. Certainly the statements are a ringing tribute to the overwhelming success enjoyed by the Japanese in their pulverizing air strike of that Sunday morning.

But they were never written by any Japanese historian. Instead, they are excerpts—only a few among many like them—from official United States military documents. Three dozen years is a time long enough to dull the emotional response to the scene and permit a dispassionate appraisal of the manner with which we were plunged into all-out war. The years soften the emotions, and also cloud the memory of the debacle that committed this nation to 1,351 days of combat. Even today it requires a sharp jogging of memory to recall the extent of the severe losses we endured on the Hawaiian island of Oahu.

In her two-pronged, devastating aerial attack with 353 carrier-based warplanes, Japan's pilots either sank or rendered useless for a long time to come the battleships *Arizona, California, Oklahoma, Nevada,* and *West Virginia;* three destroyers; the target ship *Utah;* the minelayer *Oglala;* and a large floating drydock.

The battleships *Maryland, Pennsylvania,* and *Tennessee* sustained heavy damage and loss of life, as did the three cruisers *Helena, Honolulu,* and *Raleigh,* the seaplane tender *Curtiss,* and the repair ship *Vestal.*

There were a total of 301 American naval aircraft of different types in the Oahu area on the morning of December 7. Japanese bombs and guns destroyed or severely damaged more than half this force.

Another 11 U.S. Navy aircraft were destroyed during the raging Pearl Harbor battle. The carrier *Enterprise* was 200 miles distant from the Hawaiian islands when it launched a group of planes, all of which were armed and carrying live ammunition. Several of these aircraft blundered into the heavy antiaircraft barrages that studded Hawaiian skies. Most of the planes, however, were shot down by Japanese fighters that attacked the American carrier aircraft immediately upon encountering them in the air. Of the 11 crews, nine were lost. *Not one of these U.S. Navy aircraft fired so much as a single shot in defense against the marauding Japanese planes!*

During the investigation into the circumstances leading up to the staggering blow dealt against Pearl Harbor, a review board queried a Pacific Fleet intelligence officer on his opinion as to what might have happened had the carriers *Enterprise* and *Lexington,* in the Hawaiian Islands area, attacked the Japanese task force. The response was not encouraging: "I think the American forces would have taken the licking of their life. The American people were not psychologically prepared for war. I am referring to the American Navy as part of the American people. American carrier planes were attacked by Japanese fighters, and it is to be observed that these planes were armed with machine-gun ammunition and their machine guns *were ready to fire.* I can find no record of any of these carrier planes firing one single shot at any Jap plane."

The Japanese study of their own Pearl Harbor strike

notes an essential law of airpower doctrine: "The fundamental rule of any air battle is to gain immediate control of the local air by eliminating the defensive activities of enemy fighter planes. This precept was rigidly adhered to in the Pearl Harbor attack."[1]

Japanese bombs and guns swiftly eliminated 37 bombers and 104 fighter planes of the Army Air Forces in the opening phase of the strike. During this process they shattered and set aflame hangars, storage shops and warehouses, barracks, fuel and ammunition storage dumps, and other vital installations. The official report of the attack notes, regarding the blows delivered against Wheeler Field: "Almost all of the bombs, released at altitudes of 200 to 250 feet, struck with deadly accuracy along the hangar line. They destroyed forty-three airplanes by fire and twenty-nine by other means."

The plan was simple: wipe out the air defenses of the Americans, and achieve, as quickly as possible, maximum air superiority so that the dive, level, and attack bombers might carry out their missions with minimum interference from the enemy.

Lieutenant Akira Sakamoto led 25 Val dive bombers of the first attacking wave in a shrieking assault against Hoiler Air Base. Japanese intelligence had pinpointed Hoiler as the main center of American fighter-plane operations in Hawaii; Sakamoto's mission was to eliminate this fighter opposition before the planes, reportedly kept under alert status, could get off the ground.

Hard on the heels of the Sakamoto attack came 26 more dive bombers led by Lieutenant Commander Kakuichi Takahashi. The second attacking wave swarmed over Hickam Air Field, spotted as the center of American heavy-bomber operations. Destroying these planes and the base facilities would prevent a long-range bomber pursuit of the Nagumo Task Force of six aircraft carriers and 17 supporting ships. The Japanese formation split into two wedges; one struck at the bomber base, while the other force rushed against Ford Island, where the Japanese believed a strong force of American Navy fighters were based. Complete surprise was achieved—and the dive bombers smothered the opposition.

"While a few enemy planes managed to get off the ground," noted the Japanese study of the Nagumo Task

Force mission, "our attacking aerial forces were relatively free from enemy fighter opposition, and our fleet was now protected from an American aerial counterattack."[2]

The opening phase of the battle went in classic style—as dictated by the Japanese.

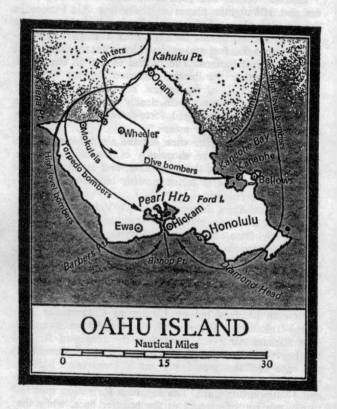

OAHU ISLAND
Nautical Miles
0   15   30

We suffered disastrously in human lives lost. A total of 2,844 men from the military forces on Oahu died. Enemy fire wounded and maimed another 1,178 Americans.

Despite the tremendous victory gained, Japan escaped with only trifling losses—far less than the Japanese themselves expected. So successful was the surprise attack, and so effectively did the follow-up waves of planes carry out their missions, that the entire assault cost the Japanese only 29 aircraft shot down and 55 men lost. Not one Japanese vessel sustained so much as a scratch.

For this insignificant price, Japan destroyed more than 300 American aircraft, wiped out military airpower in the Hawaiian area, rendered impotent all but the carriers of the Pacific battle fleet, shattered island installations, eliminated Hawaii as a source of major reinforcements for the rest of the Pacific area, and killed and wounded more than 4,000 Americans. Its extraordinarily light losses also left the Japanese task force free to hurl its strength at other objectives in the Pacific.

During the many years since that crushing defeat, the events that occurred at Pearl Harbor and during the preceding weeks have undergone the scrutiny of hundreds of investigations and studies. Literally millions of words have accumulated as to who was to blame for the debacle, and what were the shadowy conditions that permitted the Japanese to strike so decisively a blow at the most powerful American bastion in the Pacific. Political considerations throughout many of the investigations have transcended the straightforward recital of military events (which at best are still beset with confusion arising from honest differences of opinion), and the attempts to conclude the unhappy affair with firm answers remain burdened with accusations, countercharges, and dark hints.

The official studies as they relate to the participation of the Army Air Forces note that the "attack achieved perfect tactical surprise: neither the exact day nor the location of the initial Japanese blow had been correctly estimated." There is also what the author regards as the most conclusive argument in understanding what lay behind the stunning success of the Japanese at Pearl Harbor: "Nothing in the record indicates that the story would have been substantially better had airmen been in full control of their own forces, whatever minor differences that might have meant. Wherever the fault lay, the AAF in Hawaii, and the fleet whose defense was its chief mission, suffered an overwhelming defeat."

There is a hard fact about the Pearl Harbor attack that gains little attention: our military strength in the Territory of Hawaii was far from the ineffectual force it has been made to seem. The United States had more than sufficient strength in warships, carriers near the islands, and land-based aircraft to have dealt the Japanese crushing losses. It should be understood clearly that it was not military weakness in numbers which committed to death nearly 3,000 men on Oahu Island. Rather, it was the combination of perfect tactical surprise on the part of the Japanese, and the ineffectual manner in which we responded to that attack, that gained for the enemy their signal success.

"If the American air force had detected in advance the approach of the Japanese fighters and bombers and had thrown up an air defense of fighter planes," concluded Commander Okumiya in the Japanese critique of the mission, "our accomplishments would surely have been lessened and our losses increased. It is conceivable that, had Pearl Harbor been protected by air defenses, the assault against Hawaii could have lost much of its effectiveness, and the nature of the Pacific War proportionally altered."

The events leading up to the Japanese air strike seem more bizarre with the passage of time. Not once, but five times, we received warning through movement of Japanese forces of the attack that was about to take place.

We ignored the sinking of a Japanese submarine by an American destroyer off Pearl Harbor, *before* the attack.

No one appeared to be galvanized into action, or at least into sounding a warning, by the shooting down, and death, of an American Navy pilot by Japanese fighter planes, *before* the attack.

We ignored the sighting by radar of a Zero floatplane fighter, catapulted off the cruiser *Chikuma,* which reconnoitered Pearl Harbor *before* the first attacking wave reached its targets.

We ignored both the first and the second warnings of radar operator T/3 Joe Lockard, who detected on his radar screen, and reported, the lead wave of Japanese bombers even then on their way to bomb Oahu.

And it is documented fact that an American seaman watched 25 Japanese bombers circling, unmolested, over Pearl Harbor—while the bombers *waited* for a second force to catch up with them before commencing their dive-bombing runs!

For the full telling of the story, we must return to November 28, 1941, and turn back the clock. . . .

By the afternoon of November 28, the military and naval commanders in Hawaii had read the contents of a secret message which had been received less than 24 hours previously from the War Department in Washington, D.C. The message carried a warning unmistakable to any military official: there appeared every indication of an impending break in relations between the United States and the Japanese Empire. Diplomatic negotiations to halt the ugly trend of events in the Pacific and Asia were foundering; the situation, which seemed to worsen with every day and almost with every hour, carried within it the implicit threat of exploding into military action on the part of the Japanese. There could be little question as to this possibility, for the message included, among other points of emphasis, this warning:

Japanese future action unpredictable, but hostile action possible at any moment.

Ten days before the first bomb fell against Pearl Harbor, the direct threat of such action had been posted to the military commanders who carried the responsibility of defending the Hawaiian Islands against such an attack. In Hawaii proper, the Army and Navy opened their secret files and set into motion the alert conditions preplanned for such a contingency as was implied in the warning from Washington. In accordance with its own local estimate of possible enemy action, the Army instituted its Number One Alert. This was the condition that called for defensive preparations especially against sabotage, and against uprisings by Japanese agents believed to be on the Islands in a number great enough to cause serious damage to Army installations. (Not a single authenticated instance of any such act of sabotage has ever been established.) The Number One Alert, unfortunately, precluded defense activity against any attack from outside the Territory of Hawaii, such as might be carried out by enemy warships and aircraft.

By definition of its alert status, the Navy was to be ready to open fire with some secondary antiaircraft batteries and gun positions to repel a surprise attack. On the paper that spelled out the alert status, this promised a commendable state of vigilance; in reality it was nothing of the sort. Only a minor fraction of the firepower potential from the fleet resting quietly in harbor would be kept ready to open fire upon any hostile aircraft which might *suddenly* appear overhead.

By the first days of December, another crack in the defensive wall of Hawaii had been closed. Unfortunately, however, while a potentially valuable new defense system was installed, its actual usefulness was limited. This was not the fault of the mechanisms involved, but rather of the attitude of the men who commanded the defense systems when the Japanese finally did commit themselves to the strike.

The Army placed in operation six new radar detection stations. These had been installed specifically to provide warning in the event of an *early morning carrier attack*. It was this type of assault which the military commanders at Pearl Harbor and outlying installations considered to be the most likely move of the Japanese. Somewhere, somehow, the chain of command must certainly have become inextricably entangled. The Army's Number One Alert, which had been placed in effect, completely ignored (emphasizing protection against sabotage as it did) the possibility of a carrier-launched air strike. Further evidence of the clash of opinions could be found in the operation of the radar stations; they remained active, with personnel on duty, only from four to seven o'clock in the morning, a total of three hours per day.

There was in the Hawaiian Islands by December an AAF strength of 754 officers and 6,706 enlisted men, the majority of them concentrated on Oahu. The AAF stood ready to meet all situations with a total force of 231 military aircraft, of which the men considered no more than 115 planes to be generously listed as up-to-date models.

These combat-quality machines included 12 B-17D Flying Fortress bombers; these were the last models of the four-engine bombers to be built without power turrets and without any tail-gun protection of any kind. Twelve A-20A Boston twin-engine attack bombers represented modern bombing strength, and there were also a total of 99 P-40 fighters, of different types. Supplementing these "first-line" aircraft was the secondary force. This consisted of 33 lumbering, helpless B-18A medium bombers, 39 P-36A Mohawk fighters (well outclassed by the

Zero), and 14 ancient P-26 fighters which with great kindness might be listed as merely decrepit.

The AAF's 18th Bombardment Wing was headquartered at Hickam Field and the 14th Pursuit Wing at Wheeler Field. Units of the two forces were further deployed at Bellows Field and at Haleiwa. In addition to these major bases, foresight was evident in a string of emergency and auxiliary fields scattered on the islands of Kauai, Lanai, Hawaii, Maui, and Molokai.

To conform to the requirements of the Army's alert status, the AAF parked 57 bombers at Hickam Field, which was to prove unfortunate, since this air base adjoined Pearl Harbor proper. Since the order of the day for the ten days preceding the Japanese strike had called for defense against possible acts of sabotage, the AAF unknowingly played directly into the hands of the Japanese. Mechanics packed the bombers as tightly together as it was possible to move them. There they stood, wingtip to wingtip, ripe and juicy for the bombs and streams of bullets from the Japanese, who, of course, found all their targets neatly set up for them in the most ideal position for destruction.

At Hickam Field mechanics virtually stuffed and jammed planes into hangars (which were hit with bull's-eye accuracy by Japanese pilots, or clustered them together in inviting targets. At Bellows Field, 17 miles away on the eastern side of the island of Oahu, another 20 aircraft had been pushed together into another plump target.

At Wheeler Field, 12 miles inland from Hickam, the AAF continued its invitation-to-disaster arrangement of its military aircraft. No less than 151 planes were aligned with beautiful precision along the field, wings almost brushing, in the juiciest plum of all for the enemy. Included in this splendid sight were no less than 75 new P-40 fighters. (What 75 airborne P-40s could have done to the Japanese force may be left to the imagination; airborne and in a position to intercept, they could—as Commander Okumiya has noted—easily have changed the entire course of the war.)

The disparity between the oncoming attack, already being launched by the Japanese, and possible enemy action contemplated by the Army was nowhere more evident than at Wheeler Field. So all-important did the threat of sabotage loom in the minds of the commanding officers of the area, as they considered the possibilities of enemy action, that *the fighters had been emptied of all their fuel and ammunition, to make them less flammable, and then their guns were dismantled.*

Even had the warning of attack been sounded an hour in advance of the first bomb, these precious fighters would have remained useless hulks chained to the ground.

The aircraft of the Navy likewise stood naked to assault from the skies. At Ewa, the Marines repeated the ostrich stand of the AAF, and 49 modern fighters and bombers, and some auxiliary planes, were lined up in that vulnerable wingtip-to-wingtip position. Most of the PBY Catalina patrol bombers at the Navy Seaplane Base at Kaneohe Bay either were lined up together or parked tightly within hangars. At the Naval Air Station on Ford Island, headquarters for Navy Patrol Wing 2, an additional 70 aircraft huddled together in an open invitation to destruction.

It was almost as if the concept of aircraft dispersal had never existed. Never in their wildest optimism did the Japanese ever hope to find everything so neatly stacked in their favor.

And the main objective of the Japanese air attack, the warships of the Pacific battle fleet of the United States Navy, awaited their savage mauling. Fully two-thirds of the 102 Navy combat vessels in the entire Pacific lay waiting at anchor, in drydock, or tied to their piers. Ripe for splitting by Japanese bombs and torpedoes were the eight battleships, nine cruisers, 28 destroyers, five submarines, and auxiliary vessels.

Fate gave the United States one unexpected—and incalculable—favor. None of the six fleet aircraft carriers was then in port or would be exposed to the Japanese when the attack came on the morning of December 7. This great stroke of fortune prevented the very backbone of strength of the Navy from being damaged so badly that the enemy successes subsequent to the Pearl Harbor strike would have been far more extensive.

The Japanese Move Out

The enemy began his move of major fleet units against Pearl Harbor nearly a full month before the task force was in position to commit Japan to its fateful clash with the United States. On the morning of November 10, the first units of the Nagumo Force sortied from Kure naval base on Honshu Island. During the next eight days the remainder of the fleet slipped anchor and eased away from their harbors.

The Japanese executed every move with the most meticulous care and precaution against any leak in security. All ships maintained strict radio silence. To prevent American naval intelligence from discovering the initial departure out of Kure, the vessels remaining at the naval base kept up a steady stream of radio communications which were to compensate for the sudden lack of messages from ships of the Nagumo Force, which had put to sea. Unquestionably the maneuver was carried out with splendid success; neither the American nor the British monitors tracking Japanese radio traffic assumed that there had been any sudden or major changes in the known disposition of the Japanese naval forces.

Not even the most stringent security measures are foolproof, and the Japanese *did* commit one fatal error. Or it *should* have been a fatal error; that it was not so was due to the continued American belief—ingrained in almost all high-ranking officers—that the Japanese could not possibly outwit the United States.

The Pacific Fleet intelligence officer, scrupulously studying the Japanese fleet's radio traffic, was alerted by the sudden absence from this traffic of the call letters for two aircraft carriers assigned at the time to Kure. At once this officer flashed a priority message to Pearl Harbor. Admiral Kimmel considered that since this was the only reported change in the radio communications of the Japanese, the matter was unimportant. His conclusions proved disastrous.

Thus the first vital clue to the movement of the Japanese battle fleet, scanty though it might have been at first glance, went unheeded.

From Kure the Japanese fleet units moved to their assembly point at Tankan Bay (Hitokappu Wan) on Etorofu, the largest of the Kurile Islands.

Six days later, the Japanese were ready to begin their final move in the phase that would hurl all the Pacific and Asia into war. On November 26 the Nagumo Force slipped away from its isolated rendezvous point in the Kuriles and began what the Japanese pompously, but with

deep conviction, termed their "divine mission." Doubtless
the Americans on the receiving end of the Japanese attack
would have been somewhat surprised to consider the enemy assault even remotely of a divine nature, but to the
Japanese officers and seamen, they were embarked upon a
modern-age crusade in the name of the Empire.

Whatever their convictions, of the efficiency of the Japanese striking force there could be no question. Commanded by brilliant (if somewhat cautious) Vice-Admiral
Chuichi Nagumo, the men aboard the fleet of only 23
vessels were trained to razor sharpness. Size notwithstanding, at the moment they eased their way onto the high
seas they were undoubtedly the finest and most powerful
naval air striking force the world had ever known.

The crews to man the planes of the First Air Fleet
had been picked with meticulous care from the ranks of
the entire naval air arm. *Every* pilot had a *minimum* of
800 hours flight time and many of them were veterans
with thousands of hours at the controls of their planes. Of
the pilots who were to lead different elements into battle,
the fury of combat and the coughing roar of guns were
not at all strange to them; they had cut their combat
teeth in China. Among the fighter pilots there were men
who had already fought Chinese, Russians, and Americans,
and who were ranked as aces.

The Zero fighter was the best in the Pacific. The torpedo bombers of the Nagumo Force were the fastest in the
world and the dive bombers and their crews had per-
fected their techniques for years on the Asiatic mainland.

By December 2 the Nagumo Force was well at sea, but
the going proved rough for the Japanese. So violent
were the swells marching across the sea that on several
occasions men were washed overboard. Secrecy and timing were imperative—the ships did not bother to slow
down for them. The danger of collision in the ship formations was considered by the Japanese to be "alarming";
the wind ripped signal flags to shreds, and thick fog banks
hampered formation discipline in a fleet which did not
dare to violate its strict radio silence.

On this same morning, December 2, Tokyo flashed its
final orders to Admiral Nagumo. His radio operator
rushed to him the coded message from the headquarters
of Admiral Isoroku Yamamoto:

"Niitaka Yama Nobore."

Those were the words—*Climb Mount Niitaka*—to open World War II on a global basis. The die was cast. The Nagumo Force, with the carriers *Akagi* and *Kaga* of the 1st Carrier Division, *Soryu* and *Hiryu* of the 2nd Carrier Division, *Zuikaku* and *Shokaku* of the 5th Carrier Division; the battleships *Hiei* and *Kirishima;* the two heavy cruisers *Tone* and *Chikuma;* one light cruiser, nine destroyers, and three supporting vessels, turned to the south and increased speed.

Under the Seas

The Nagumo Force was not the only Japanese striking group in the Pacific bearing down on Pearl Harbor. An advance expeditionary force of 20 submarines had sortied to the east to probe the seas ahead of the main surface fleet.

Sixteen of these submarines were of the long-range I type, each 320 feet in length and displacing 1,955 tons surfaced. Eleven I-type submarines carried small floatplanes with folding wings which were accommodated in watertight compartments aft of the conning towers. These small aircraft extended tremendously the scouting capabilities of the submarines.

The other five I-type submarines carried armament of a drastically altered nature. These were midget submarines which were towed by heavy clamps behind the mother sub. Into each of the suicidal weapons were crammed two men and two torpedoes.

The Advance Expeditionary Force departed from Kure and Yokosuka during the three days of November 18–20. Their first stop was Kwajalein, where they took on fuel and supplies, and received final confirmation of their orders. Then they moved out to take up their scouting positions, ranging from some nine miles to 100 miles from Pearl Harbor. By December 5 all the submarines involved were on their patrol stations.

On the night of December 6–7, the mother submarines cast off their five midgets, and the Japanese began to probe into the defenses of the American naval bastion.

The attack was under way.

The Final Hours

It is 42 minutes past three o'clock the morning of December 7. . . .

Aboard the converted minesweeper USS *Condor,* on patrol two miles outside the naval base of Pearl Harbor, Ensign R. C. McCloy, USN, stares hard across the water —and becomes the first American to make contact with the enemy in the war which has not yet flared openly. Across the darkened surface, spray glistens on steel—the conning tower of a Japanese midget submarine. McCloy acts instantly and sounds the alarm; moments later blinker lights flash in the darkness as the *Condor* passes the word to the destroyer *Ward.*

Immediately the destroyer bursts into life as general quarters clamors through the warship and the destroyer increases power, commencing her "guns hot" sweep for the enemy undersea raider. But for the next several hours the Japanese aboard the midget submarine draw tight around them the cloak of darkness and water, and the search proves frustratingly empty. Then a third American ship is brought into action. Unknown to its crew, however, the repair ship *Antares* has already been involved, for the Japanese have been scurrying along in the wake of the ship, hoping to be able to slip into Pearl Harbor when the anti-submarine nets open to permit safe entry of the American vessel. The search remains an elusive cat-and-mouse hunt; while the submarine trails *Antares,* the American crew searches fruitlessly for the Japanese raider.

It is six o'clock the morning of December 7. . . .

Aboard His Imperial Majesty's heavy cruisers *Tone* and *Chikuma* the Japanese crews wave and shout lustily to the two pilots on each warship who sit in the cockpits of their float-equipped Zero fighters. Their orders are to proceed directly to the American naval base at Oahu and to make a reconnaissance flight over Ford Island. If the American ships are still at anchor—or if they have moved out—word is to be sent immediately to the fleet.

The deck officers aboard *Tone* and *Chikuma* brace

Floatplane Zero fighters of the type catapulted from
the Japanese cruisers *Tone* and *Chikuma*, and
which surveyed Pearl Harbor from the air
prior to the main Japanese attack.

themselves, raise their arms, then bring them down sharply. There are four sudden *CRAAACKS!* and four Zero
fighters slash into the air.

Even as the floatplanes bank and wheel for Pearl Harbor, the Japanese carriers, far behind the cruisers which
have forged ahead, swarm with activity. The Nagumo
Force is now some 200 miles from Pearl Harbor. The
hour of destiny is at hand; it is time to launch the first
attacking wave.

At 0600 hours it is still dark. A fresh northeast wind
and moderate running seas make the carrier decks pitch
badly; this is a trifling problem—no carrier pilots have
ever been so well trained, are so fit for the mission at
hand. A heavy overcast at 6,000 feet hides the sky, but
nothing can dampen the spirits of the Japanese aboard
their warships.

One by one the planes thunder down the decks to
slide into the air. Thunder growls louder and louder until
a storm of roaring sound tumbles and swirls away from
each ship; the cry of power rises and falls as the warplanes rush ahead, lift from the decks, and swing through
the choppy air to assemble in their formations. Soon all
the aircraft assigned to the initial attack to smash the

Americans are in the air and circling in formation—40 torpedo bombers, 50 level bombers, 50 dive bombers, and their escort of 50 Zero fighters—190 crack warplanes in all, waiting for the signal from the floatplanes scouting far ahead that all is well, that the American fleet remains ripe for destruction.

Far below the wheeling formations, thousands of Japanese sailors line the carrier decks. Emotion wells high in their breasts; it is the hour of destiny! The Orientals are about to strike, to assert the supremacy of the Empire, and the wind carries the shrill *Banzais!* screamed into the teeth of the dawn.

It is 15 minutes before seven o'clock the morning of December 7 . . . .

Aboard the destroyer *Ward* a gunnery officer squints through the new light of day and stares hard across the water. Several minutes before, a lumbering Catalina flying boat had dropped smoke bombs to mark the location of the Japanese midget submarine for which the ships *Ward*, *Condor*, and *Antares* have been searching since ten minutes to four.

Then—there it is! The officer cries out *"Fire!"* Flame and smoke erupt from the Number One gun; a high-explosive shell screeches through the wet air at the enemy submersible.

This is the first shot fired in the war which has not yet begun. . . .

The shell howls harmlessly through the air, missing the conning tower of the submarine by scant inches. Even as it ricochets from the water with a high-pitched whine another shell bursts from the destroyer's gun position. The flame and smoke barely have time to erupt from the muzzle when hell breaks loose across the water. The second shell smashes with a terrifying belch of bright red flame and exploding metal directly against Japanese steel. First blood has been drawn.

Another shell follows, and yet another, as the gun crew pumps the explosive missiles swiftly into their weapon. Even as steel and fire crash into the submarine (hopelessly wrecked with the first hit), *Ward* heels hard over, her screws churning madly. Puffs of smoke blossom with hissing sounds on the aft deck, and in pairs the depth charges waddle through the air, splash into the ocean. Seconds later crushing shock waves rip through the water just below the surface. Water boils and leaps into the air.

The crushed and broken Japanese submarine clutches her two-man crew and drags them down to a watery grave.

At 0651 hours *Ward* gets off a message to Pearl Harbor: "We have dropped depth charges on sub operating in defensive area."

Perhaps the message is not strong enough. Two minutes later, exactly at 0653 hours, a second message crackles to Pearl: "We have attacked, fired upon and dropped depth charges on sub operating in defensive area."

The operator at Bishop's Point acknowledges the receipt of both messages.

Nothing comes of that flash signal. . . .

It seems that there is little indeed at Pearl Harbor this fateful morning that can function properly or create a desired response. Since ten minutes before four o'clock, when the three American warships searched for the enemy submarine, a radio naval station has listened to all the conversations which pass between the ships.

The men then on duty at the radio sets made absolutely no move to report this information to the duty officer!

Not until *Ward* dispatches specific messages of armed contact with the unknown submarine is action first taken.

But again there are bungled operations—and again the priceless opportunity goes by the board. A yeoman, described subsequently in official investigations as "not very bright," delays in decoding the flash messages received from the destroyer. Not until 12 minutes past seven o'clock do the messages reach the duty officer. This man, at least (and at last!) wastes no time; immediately naval headquarters orders the destroyer *Monaghan* to move out and render assistance to *Ward*.

During this period the staff duty officer encounters difficulty in trying to reach Admiral Kimmel. It still seems difficult to believe, but alert planning is so poor that there is no direct line to the Admiral's quarters. The commander of the naval forces is completely out of touch with his warships, aircraft, shore installations, and men. The local switchboard is so congested that it is 25 minutes past seven before the Admiral receives word that an enemy submarine had been sighted three hours and 42 minutes previously, and that this same submarine has been attacked and is presumed sunk—35 minutes before Admiral Kimmel is finally informed of this fact.

By the time the Admiral receives the information, dresses, rushes to his office, and reviews the reports waiting for him, it is too late.

It is 15 minutes before seven o'clock the morning of December 7....

The aircraft carrier *Enterprise* steams at high speed toward Pearl Harbor. Shortly after dawn, 200 miles from the naval base (the same distance from the naval base as the six carriers of the Nagumo Force, but on a different bearing), the carrier launches several flights of planes which at this moment are flying on to Ford Island.

At 0645 hours the ship is quiet. In the radio room the operators handle routine messages. Suddenly:

"Don't shoot! This is an American plane!"

The anguished scream which bursts so unexpectedly from the radio is torn from the throat of Ensign Manuel Gonzalez, of *Enterprise*'s Bombing Squadron Six. On his way to Ford Island, Gonzalez flies within sight of the Japanese bombers and their prowling fighter escorts, at that very moment racing in toward Pearl Harbor. But Gonzalez does not live very much longer; the Zero fighter pilots are swift and sure.

Ensign Manuel Gonzalez, USN, is the first American to die in the war which has not yet begun.

No alarms, no alerts are sounded. It is bitter irony, but Gonzalez truly dies in vain.

It is 15 minutes before seven o'clock the morning of December 7....

Two men sit in the darkened interior of an Army mobile radar station at Opana on Kahuku Point, Oahu. The radar station has been active since four o'clock; in another 15 minutes the two men will shut down the power systems, lock the station, and go off duty.

One of the men stares into the glowing radar screen. There is disbelief in his eyes. There appears a single small blip on the screen; it is an aircraft, unidentified, bearing at high speed toward Oahu.

There should be no blip—not in *this* position. At once the senior operator, T/3 Joe Lockard, picks up the telephone and notifies his immediate superior that an unidentified aircraft, possibly hostile, is approaching the island.

A soldier on duty has provided evidence of being alert, of using his equipment properly, *of providing the first radar warning of the coming strike.*

But fate is yet to smile grimly. The reaction to Lockard's report is not one of action. It is, in fact, dismissed with annoyance. Lockard is reprimanded lightly and is ordered to quit having the "jitters." After all, it is a beautiful Sunday morning and the officer on duty does not like to be disturbed by excitable enlisted men who disrupt his routine with panicky calls about unidentified aircraft.

This is the United States Army. When you are an enlisted man and you have been "read off" by your superior, you do *not* argue with that officer. And so the man who tracks on radar the first of the Japanese planes approaching Oahu, and *follows that enemy aircraft for 15 minutes* on his glowing screen, can do nothing else but to say, "Yes, sir," and replace the telephone on its cradle.

It is now seven o'clock. Each of the six radar stations maintained by the Army for the specific purpose of scanning the approaches to Oahu for hostile aircraft has reached the prescribed limit of its required morning alert time. The men are now free to close down the stations and return to their barracks for morning mess.

Five stations close down; one remains open. The sixth station is the same radar site at Opana which earlier picked up on its scope the advance Japanese floatplane. T/3 Joe Lockard, the same man who shortly before has been told to get rid of his "jitters," prepares to disengage the radar set, power down the installation, and secure the truck.

But he delays. Private George Elliot, Lockard's assistant, asks for additional instruction in operating the new radar equipment. Since the truck which is to carry the two men to their mess hall is late, Lockard agrees.

It is now two minutes past seven o'clock—two minutes after the radar station was to have been closed down. Once again fate intercedes, and once again the United States is given an incalculable reprieve from the devastation even at that moment rushing toward the American fleet and our land-based aircraft. Once again the United States seems strangely impelled to ignore all the warning signs and leave itself naked to the imminent enemy assault.

The warning comes again on that same radar screen. This time there is no single airplane. This time the strange shadow which appears on the radar scope grows into glowing pips which can only be airplanes—many, many airplanes—moving in formation.

The two operators stare at the screen, first with disbelief, then the thought that something has gone wrong with the set. There simply *can't* be that many airplanes in the air!

But the new electronic equipment functions perfectly. And those *are* airplanes, at approximately 132 miles' distance from Oahu. Their bearing is three degrees east of north and they move inexorably toward Oahu with a ground speed estimated at 150 miles per hour.

Elliot plots the mass swarm of aircraft *for 15 minutes* until he is absolutely certain of the flight track. There is no longer any doubt whatsoever of what the two men see, and in alarm they watch the glowing mass on the screen paint its electronic picture of the great formation which every moment slashes time and distance between itself and Pearl Harbor.

Lockard reaches for the phone; then he hesitates. He had called in once before and had not only been ignored, but had been mildly reprimanded by his superior. Should they call in again? Of course! There is no question but that they must flash the alarm at once, inform their superior of what is happening. Out there on the ocean is a mass of airplanes, and they can only be enemy airplanes. All hell itself is winging toward them. They *must* warn Pearl Harbor!

Lockard picks up the telephone for the second time at exactly 17 minutes past seven o'clock. Destiny squeezes out the remaining minutes and seconds—the Japanese air armada is only 38 minutes away from the precise instant that the first bomb will be released from its shackles.

Three minutes pass. Lockard finally speaks to the watch officer at the information center of the Hawaiian Interceptor Command at Fort Shafter. *This is the critical moment.* Joe Lockard is the one man with knowledge of the onrushing enemy attack who is in the position to warn

Oahu. With his warning, fighters can be sent into the air to intercept the enemy force well out to sea. American carriers can dispatch their fighting airplanes. Ships can go to full air defense status, and the entire sprawling installation can come to some measurable semblance of bristling guns. The more helpless planes—bombers, scouts, and auxiliaries—can be dispersed. Warships not only can protect themselves and the base with their weapons, but they can get under way quickly and increase tremendously the difficulties of the Japanese in attacking the moving, gun-firing targets. If Lockard's warning is acted upon, the debacle then rushing like an avalanche at Pearl Harbor at its worst can do no more damage, at best may have the strength of its blow shunted and diluted.

The watch officer is Lieutenant Kermit A. Tyler. He listens to Lockard's report, which is given with some excitement. But Lieutenant Tyler is not impressed; indeed, Tyler is not even the regular duty officer. He is an Air Corps officer present at Fort Shafter "solely for training and observation." He is green and inexperienced, he is not eager to "rock the boat" so early in the morning—and it is this forced calmness that destroys the last opportunity of salvation for Pearl Harbor and nearly 3,000 men who will die.

Tyler dismisses the threat of an approaching enemy air fleet. The concept of a mass Japanese attack is ridiculous to him. He knows, also, that a formation of B-17 bombers is expected from California, scheduled to land at Oahu for fuel before staging on to the Philippines. Tyler knows, also, that some additional aircraft are expected momentarily from the carrier *Enterprise*. Most likely there are also the regular Navy search planes in the air.

So many probables are enough to keep Tyler very calm indeed. The information, the precious information telling where the Japanese air fleet is located, what bearing it follows, what speed it is making, and when it will arrive— all this Tyler dismisses, without any further checking, as "unimportant." In his ill-advised opinion the information is not worth acting upon.

"Okay; it's okay. That's all."

In that curt dismissal to Joe Lockard the fate of Pearl Harbor is sealed. Lieutenant Tyler dismisses the report of the radar station and turns his mind to other thoughts.

(Later, when the angry investigators begin to sift

through the factual debris strewn in the wake of the Japanese strike, Joe Lockard is not to be forgotten. He is to win an officer's commission and the Distinguished Service Medal for "exceptionally meritorious and distinguished service in a position of great responsibility.")

It is 30 minutes past seven o'clock the morning of December 7. . . .

Time is running out fast for Pearl Harbor. In only 25 more minutes the first bomb will fall. Back at the Opana radar station, Lockard and Elliot remain at the glowing scope. They continue to plot the incoming formations until the unidentified aircraft are only 22 miles away. At this distance the two men lose the incoming aircraft on the permanent "echo" of their electronic equipment. Brakes squeal outside; Lockard and Elliot board the truck that will take them to breakfast.

Even as they bounce over the road, Fate steps in for one final attempt at least to minimize the disaster about to overwhelm our military bastion. It is a last chance, watered down by the passage of time, but still a last chance.

We do not take advantage of it. . . .

In Pearl Harbor, Boatswain's Mate Milligan is on the deck of the destroyer *Allen*. Milligan is a man with excellent eyesight, and as he looks into the clear morning sky he can see 20 to 25 planes orbiting slowly at about 5,000 feet. Their formation is a splendid sight to behold as the sun glistens off the wings of the turning planes.

It is calamitous that Milligan does not have binoculars through which to view the wheeling about of that impressive formation. If so, then he could easily have noticed that the aircraft circling so leisurely at 5,000 feet bear the red ball of Japan on their wings and fuselages.

Incredible though it is, the planes which Milligan studies are Aichi 99 dive bombers. They arrived at Pearl Harbor before the heavily laden torpedo bombers, and here, for many long minutes, the dive bombers wait. In complete safety, unopposed, they circle over the most powerful American naval bastion in the world. It is almost too much to believe—but it is true.

It is also unfortunate that this particular man, Milligan, has not been informed of the change in training operations at Pearl Harbor. For the six weeks prior to December 7 at the naval base, there were held at Oahu regular Sunday morning antiaircraft exercises, in which crews took field positions for defense against simulated attack by carrier-based planes!

But on this morning, December 7, the carriers are at sea and the antiaircraft training exercises *have been canceled*. Milligan, however, knows only that there have been frequent air attack drills of late, and the thought that the planes he sees circling for so many precious minutes could possibly be Japanese never enters his mind.

It is 55 minutes past seven o'clock the morning of December 7. . . .

Time has run out.

7

AIR FIGHT OVER PEARL

JAPANESE

Captain Y. Watanabe, Imperial Japanese Navy:

In Japanese tactics we are told that when we have two enemies—one in front and one in back—first we must cut in front with our sword. Only cut and not kill—but make it hard. Then we attack the back enemy and kill him, and then return to the front enemy and kill him. We aimed not to capture but to cripple Pearl Harbor. We might have returned for the capture later.

The order to destroy the targets of the enemy at Pearl Harbor was issued exactly at 3:23 A.M. (Tokyo time) on December 8, 1941, when Commander Mitsuo Fuchida of carrier *Akagi*, supreme air commander of the Pearl Harbor Attack Air Groups, radioed all his pilots in the air over or approaching the naval bastion:

"All aircraft immediately attack enemy positions."

Moments later Fuchida dispatched his second radio message, this time to Admiral Nagumo, awaiting word with the task force:

"We have succeeded in the surprise attack."

"These two wireless messages," recorded Commander Masatake Okumiya in a study of Japanese airpower in World War II, "were the signals for raising the curtain of war all across the Pacific and the Indian Oceans. Immediately thereafter Japanese air fleets launched their attacks against enemy installations over a front of thousands of miles."[1]

The first bomb that started that war screamed away from an Aichi 99 dive bomber flown by Lieutenant Akira

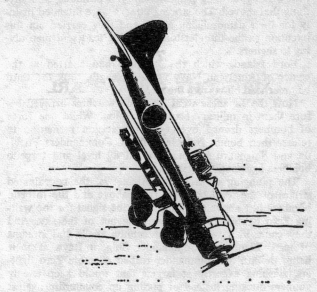

"The first bomb that started that war
screamed away from an Aichi 99 dive bomber
flown by Lieutenant Akira Sakamoto. . . ."

Sakamoto. Immediately behind Sakamoto's aircraft,
splitting up into wedges to strike at separate targets, came
another two dozen raiders, plunging from the sky at different angles and screeching around in precision formation turns so as to come into their targets from different
points of the compass. The maneuvers, so carefully
planned, came off beautifully as the bombers arrowed in
along different courses, hurling their bombs with extraordinary accuracy into the aircraft and installations scattered throughout the American base area.

Hard on the heels of Sakamoto's group, but veering off
to strike swiftly against Hickam Air Field, rushed 26
more dive bombers led by Lieutenant Commander Kakuichi Takahashi. Before the startled defenders knew what
had hit them, the bombers were coming back for repeated
passes, tearing through the flames and smoke of their

own making, strafing planes, men, gun positions, and anything that moved. The strafing attacks were intended mainly for their demoralizing effect, and they carried out this intention as the thunderstorm of flying lead sent men diving to shelters.

Ford Island, which the Japanese had charted as the center of American Navy fighter strength, took the third hammerhead blow from the air.

Now the Japanese went after the warships arrayed before them in military textbook fashion. While one force of bombers droned overhead in precision formation to release their bombs from level flight, Commanders Fuchida and Shigeharu Murata directed 89 level and torpedo bombers against the warships.

The plunging dives of the Aichi 99s, the coordinated strikes of the level bombers from above and the torpedo bombers just above the water, was the signal for the waiting Zero fighters to come barreling out of the sky. And they came in a whirlwind of cannon shells and streams of lead, Lieutenant Commander Shigeru Itaya at their helm. Behind the commander rushed 42 more Zero fighters, slashing expertly at targets that would keep enemy gunners ducking instead of putting up counterfire against the many bombers. The Mitsubishis cut in at minimum altitude, pilots snapping hot bursts against antiaircraft emplacements, aircraft, gun positions against warships, and any ground targets that appeared prime for their massed cannon and machine guns.

The pilots had been warned to expect very intense fighter opposition from the Americans. Not a Japanese pilot dreamed that most of the American planes would be lined up wingtip-to-wingtip, naked of their guns and fuel, and incapable of roaring into the air. Only four American fighters were encountered by the Japanese, and the Americans, despite their courage at rushing against the mass of Japanese planes in the air, were simply overwhelmed almost at once. Four Zero pilots claimed definite kills on their return to their carriers.

Exactly one hour and 15 minutes after Lieutenant Sakamoto tripped the bomb release of his dive bomber, the second attacking wave reached its attack position over Oahu. The Japanese crews under the command of Lieutenant Commander Shigekazu Shimazaki of carrier *Zuikaku* looked down upon a scene of wild devastation.

They reported flames in sight in almost every direction and smoke boiling thickly into the sky. The Americans by now were fighting back wildly, even if their defenses had been caught completely by surprise. Antiaircraft bursts splotched the sky in a pockmarked pattern.

Shimazaki led a force of 170 bombers and fighters. With the same crisp precision that marked the initial wave, 54 level bombers sailed overhead in formation, bombs spilling in long rows into the American positions far below. The Japanese move once again was to cut the effectiveness of the defenses. Even as the bombs arrowed toward their targets, the thunder and roar shaking Pearl Harbor was split by a new sound—the shrill scream of 80 dive bombers plummeting for the kill against the American warships. Lieutenant Commander Takashige Egusa took his planes in to pointblank range, howling earthward to release their bombs. Swooping up like white hawks, the dive bombers raced perilously low over the American vessels, clearing the way for the other planes behind them.

Lieutenant Saburo Shindo, longtime veteran of air war in China, brought 36 Zero fighters through the crackling roar and violent air of the battle. Shindo ordered his men to minimum height so that the American gunners would have their attention diverted between the level bombers up high, the dive bombers plunging in steep dives, and the Zero fighters caroming in after them from all points of the compass at mast-high levels.

Approximately two hours after the first explosion the battle was over.

The torpedo-bombing attack has been vividly described by one participant, Chief Flight Petty Officer Juzo Mori of the carrier *Soryu*:

"The assigned objectives of the *Soryu* torpedo bombers were the American battleships which we expected to find anchored along the wharf of the Oahu Naval Arsenal. We dropped in for our attack at high speed and low altitude and, when I was almost in position to release my own torpedo, I realized that the enemy warship toward which I was headed was not a battleship at all, but a cruiser. My flight position was directly behind Lieutenant Tsuyoshi Nagai, and we flew directly over Oahu Island before descending for our attack.

"Lieutenant Nagai continued his torpedo run against the cruiser, despite our original plan to attack the enemy

battleships. However, I did not expect to survive this attack, since I and all the other pilots anticipated heavy
enemy resistance. If I were going to die, I thought, I
wanted to know that I had torpedoed at least an American
battleship.

"The attack of the *Soryu's* planes was met with intense antiaircraft fire from the enemy fleet, since the
bombing waves from the *Akagi* and the *Kaga* had already
passed over. My bomber shook and vibrated from the impact of enemy machine-gun bullets and shrapnel. Despite
my intention of swinging away from the cruiser, now
dead ahead of my plane, and attacking the group of battleships anchored near Ford Island, I was forced to fly
directly forward into a murderous rain of antiaircraft
fire.

"Because of this and the surrounding topography, I flew
directly over the enemy battleships along Ford Island,
and then banked into a wide left turn. The antiaircraft
fire did not seem to affect the plane's performance, and I
chose as my new objective a battleship anchored some
distance from the main group of vessels which were at the
moment undergoing torpedo attack from the *Soryu's*
planes. The warship separated from the main enemy
group appeared to be the only battleship yet undamaged.

"I swung low and put my plane into satisfactory tor-
pedoing condition. It was imperative that my bombing approach be absolutely correct, as I had been warned that
the harbor depth was no more than thirty-four feet. The
slightest deviation in speed or height would send the released torpedo plunging into the sea bottom, or jumping
above the water, and all our effort would go for nought.

"By this time I was hardly conscious of what I was
doing. I was reacting from habit instilled by long training,
moving like an automaton.

"Three thousand feet! Twenty-five hundred feet! Two
thousand feet!

"Suddenly the battleship appeared to have leaped forward directly in front of my speeding plane; it towered
ahead of the bomber like a great mountain peak.

"Prepare for release. . . . Stand by!

"*Release torpedo!*

"All this time I was oblivious of the enemy's antiaircraft fire and the distracting thunder of my plane's motor.
I concentrated on nothing but the approach and the torpe-

do release. At the right moment I pulled back on the release with all my strength. The plane lurched and faltered as antiaircraft struck the wings and fuselage; my head snapped back and I felt as though a heavy beam had struck against my head.

"But . . . I've got it! A perfect release!

"And the plane is still flying! The torpedo will surely hit its target; the release was exact. At that instant I seemed to come to my senses and became aware of my position and of the flashing tracers and shells of the enemy's defensive batteries.

"After launching the torpedo, I flew directly over the enemy battleship and again swung into a wide, circling turn. I crossed over the southern tip of Ford Island.

"To conceal the position of our carrier, as we had been instructed to do, I turned again and took a course due south, directly opposite the *Soryu*'s true position, and pushed the plane to its maximum speed. Now that the attack was over, I was acutely conscious that the enemy antiaircraft fire was bracketing and smashing into my bomber. The enemy shells appeared to be coming from

Kate torpedo bomber on its attack run at Pearl Harbor; this was the aircraft type flown by Chief Flight Petty Officer Juzo Mori of the carrier *Soryu*.

all directions, and I was so frightened that before I left the target area my clothes were soaking with perspiration.

"In another few moments the air was clear. The enemy shells had stopped. Thinking that now I had safely es-

caped, and could return to the carrier, I began to turn to
head back to the *Soryu*. Suddenly there was an enemy
plane directly in front of me!

"As my plane, the Type 97 carrier-based attack bomber, was armed only with a single rearward-firing 7.7-mm.
machine gun, it was almost helpless in aerial combat. I
thought that surely *this* time my end had come.

"As long as I was going to die, I reasoned, I would take
the enemy plane with me to my death. I swung the bomber over hard and headed directly for the enemy aircraft, the pilot of which appeared startled at my maneuver, and fled! Is this, really, I questioned, what is called
war?"[2]

Before the savage strike against Pearl Harbor ended,
the Japanese counted their losses as five torpedo and 15
dive bombers. Along with these aircraft, another nine
planes were lost—the first Zero fighters to be shot down
in combat since the airplane's combat debut 16 months
earlier in China.

Among the casualties was Lieutenant Fusata Iida, the
squadron leader of Zero fighters from carrier *Soryu*. Iida
led the 3rd Covering Fighters Squadron of nine fighters,
which struck in the second wave of the assault. Near
the Kaneohe Air Field the Zeros mixed it up in a brawl
with defending American fighters, resulting in swift losses
for the defense. With the sky clear the Zeros rushed
earthward to strafe the field. Lieutenant (JG) Iyozo Fuji-
ta, second section leader in the formation, relates the
events that caused the loss of Iida:

"When our planes machine-gunned the airfield at Kaneohe, I looked for but failed to see any antiaircraft guns
on the field. Later, however, when all the fighters assembled their formations over the field I noticed a white
spray of gasoline shooting out from Lieutenant Iida's
plane. There appeared to be no other damage to his fighter, and I assumed he would be able to return to the
carrier.

"Such was not the case, however. Lieutenant Iida circled over the Kaneohe Air Field until he was sure that all
our fighters were assembled in formation. Then, and only
then, he closed his cockpit canopy and began to descend
toward the airfield. Suddenly the Zero whipped over into
an inverted position and dove vertically for the enemy
positions below.

"Thinking that he was going to make another strafing run on the field, I immediately began a wingover to follow his plane down. I realized abruptly, however, that Lieutenant Iida was flying in a most unusual manner, quite different from his usual tactics. I watched his plane as it dove in its vertical, inverted position until it exploded on the ground between the Kaneohe airfield hangars."[3]

AMERICAN

The exact sequence of events as air combat took place over Pearl Harbor, and in the airspace surrounding the stricken naval bastion, remains forever locked within the chaos and confusion of that day. While it is true that the Japanese scored a stunning victory over our air and naval units, and that the Japanese were for the most part little bothered with aerial opposition, it is true also that those pilots who did get into the air did well by themselves and their nation. The fighting was sparse, it was wildly and widely scattered; nonetheless, it was lethal, and it resulted in the loss in the air of both Japanese and American aircraft.

In the light of what happened that day, with the lightning-swift effectiveness of the Japanese strikes, the performance of the AAF's fighter pilots is all the more commendable. The Navy crews who were shot down by Zero fighters on December 7 were hit with all the devastating effectiveness of skilled and experienced Japanese pilots who rushed to the kill. Defensive action had to be instantaneous or it was worthless; as the record has indicated, there is no evidence that even a single shot was fired by the destroyed Navy aircraft as they were gunned from the skies.

The AAF pilots had time in their favor, even if that time could be measured on some occasions in bare minutes. And that is exactly what the crews in the Navy aircraft lacked—the precious moments in which to react to a situation that was totally unexpected.

There were dozens of Army pilots who fairly screamed at their mechanics to ready their planes for immediate takeoff. Urgency and desire are no substitute, however, for the minimum four hours' notice that was required to rearm and to fuel the fighter planes that had been so disastrously bunched together and rendered helpless for flight. There were plenty of pilots, most of whom suffered from lack of airplanes to carry the fight into the air.

The few men who did manage to become airborne engaged in a hazardous adventure simply to take their fighters off the ground. Some of these pilots went up several times, and among them they managed to fly a total of approximately 25 sorties against the Japanese. The most effective defense was carried out by a group of pilots of the 47th Squadron, 15th Pursuit Group, who by good fortune had spent the entire night engaged in a poker game; thus they were awake and together when the Japanese struck the area.

The five men—Lieutenants Harry M. Brown, Robert J. Rogers, Kenneth A. Taylor, John J. Webster, and George S. Welch—were still at their poker party at Wheeler Field when the Japanese arrived. The room in which they were playing filled with the roar of 30 Japanese dive bombers passing directly overhead; soon afterward the earth heaved with the bellowing crump of exploding bombs.

Eight miles from Wheeler was the small field of Haleiwa, which escaped the heavy lash of the Japanese strikes. The men called the training field, ordering whatever airplanes were available to be made ready for takeoff immediately on their arrival. They piled into the first automobile outside their poker room and survived a mad, careening dash to their training field. On their arrival they found two P-40 fighters ready and waiting, the engines warmed up and propellers spinning. Each fighter had operative only four .30-caliber machine guns; George Welch and Kenneth Taylor clambered swiftly into the Tomahawk fighters. Twenty minutes after the first bomb exploded, the two fighters were racing down the runway.

Welch and Taylor climbed swiftly, and they found combat waiting for them even as they pulled their fighters up to the altitude of the enemy planes. They cut over Barber's Point and then rushed at 12 dive bombers circling Ewa Marine air base; the Japanese planes were carrying out a leisurely pattern of strafing, pulling up and wheeling around, and diving again to strafe the field.

The Tomahawks tore into the rear of the Japanese planes. On their first pass, Welch poured his fire into the fuel tanks of an Aichi bomber; the plane burst into flames and spun wildly into the ground. Almost immediately afterward another explosion rattled the sky as Taylor's guns poured bullets into a second dive bomber and shot apart the fuel tanks.

The two fighters turned sharply to come back in again for a second pass at the Japanese; on the turn Taylor saw an Aichi heading out to sea. Taylor wracked around in a steep bank and dove under full power at the fleeing bomber, his bullets streamed into the plane and it tumbled crazily to explode in the surf. Behind him, George Welch hammered at his second target. The Japanese bomber made it two each destroyed for the American pilots when it disappeared in a roaring blast.

Things began to fall apart swiftly for Welch at that moment. One of his four guns jammed, and bullets rained against the airplane. The next instant an incendiary bullet slammed into the cockpit; Welch hauled back on the stick and shot upward into the relatively calm air above the clouds. He paused only long enough to assess the damage, and dove headlong back into the fight. He saw Taylor riddling one bomber until it veered sharply in the air and faltered; even as Taylor swung from that plane to attack another in its strafing run, Welch joined him by rushing against another bomber.

Both pilots scored again. Welch's target flipped through the air and exploded on impact with the ground. The plane attacked by Taylor dove away from the fight and headed out to sea, trailing a thin plume of smoke.

By now they were out of ammunition and running low on fuel. The Tomahawks weaved through the thickening barrage of their own antiaircraft fire and thumped down to landings at Wheeler. They shouted at the mechanics for more ammunition and fuel. Immediately two men dashed into the midst of a huge blaze in a hangar, staggering out again with cartridge belts and ammunition boxes. Other mechanics poured fuel into their tanks.

Officers on the scene advised Welch and Taylor against going up again; Japanese planes were thick and black in the sky. But there were also 15 dive bombers headed directly for Wheeler, and the only way to save the two precious fighters was to get them off the ground before the Japanese struck.

The takeoff proved to be both harrowing and almost fatal. Welch gunned his fighter and thundered down the runway, straight into the teeth of the diving enemy formation. Three Japanese planes picked him out for their special target and wove a glistening web of tracers into and about the Tomahawk. Welch banged rudder and stick violently, sailed through the worst of the enemy fire, and broke into the clear. He swerved sharply to observe Taylor fighting desperately for altitude; the Tomahawk was still low and slow and, at this point in takeoff, vulnerable to attack. A Japanese plane was glued to Taylor's fighter, pouring lead steadily into the airplane. Welch came around in a screaming dive and picked off the Japanese ship; it burst into flames and immediately smashed into the ground, disappearing in a rolling blast.

But the Japanese also had scored. With a bullet wound in his arm, Taylor staggered around the field in his riddled airplane. He brought the Tomahawk in for a safe landing, but was out of the fight.

Welch had taken several direct hits from the rear gunner of the dive bomber he had shot off Taylor's fighter. Japanese bullets had pounded into the propeller, the engine, and the cowling of Welch's Tomahawk. Despite the damage, the airplane responded well to the controls, and Welch went grimly off in search of more Japanese. He didn't have far to look; near Ewa Field he ran into an enemy plane that turned sharply away from him and dashed out to sea. Welch caught up with the Japanese five miles offshore, closed in to short range, and sent the enemy plane tumbling into the ocean.

Welch returned from this engagement to Haleiwa; he had now flown two sorties and had shot down four enemy planes. As quickly as his fighter could be rearmed and refueled, he streaked down the runway for a third crack at the Japanese. Flying with him as wingman in a Curtiss P-36 Mohawk fighter was Lieutenant John L. Dains. This was also Dains' third sortie for the morning; he had been up previously once in another P-36 and once in a P-40, and had damaged several enemy aircraft.

The third time into the air for the two pilots was ill fated—but not because of the Japanese. By now the antiaircraft was both extremely heavy and, especially, wildly indiscriminate. Gunners were shooting at anything they saw in the sky, making little attempt in the flaming bedlam and explosions that rocked the area to separate friend from foe. A burst of antiaircraft fire tore apart the P-36 fighter in which Dains flew; his airplane cartwheeled crazily from the sky, carrying Dains to his death (he was the only pilot of the six men taking off from Haleiwa that day to be killed).

Welch managed to evade the deadly barrage that had killed Dains; no sooner had he fled the bursting shells than another storm of antiaircraft fire from Pearl Harbor bracketed his fighter, spattering it with steel. Welch ran for his life, dropped down low, and managed (through a storm of antiaircraft) to work his way back to a landing at Wheeler.

(For their "extraordinary heroism" on the first day of war, Welch and Taylor each received the Distinguished Service Cross. Welch's four kills were confirmed; for a time Taylor was listed as having shot down two enemy

Obsolescent and outperformed by Zero fighters,
Curtiss P-36 Mohawks nevertheless put up
a strong fight at Pearl Harbor. Several kills against
enemy planes were confirmed to P-36 pilots.

aircraft confirmed, with two probables, but later confirmation of the second two kills was made. The two pilots together had accounted for eight of the enemy destroyed.)

At 8:50 A.M. five pilots of the 46th Squadron, 15th Pursuit Group, shot down the runway of Wheeler Field in P-36 Mohawk fighters. The danger of being shot down by their own antiaircraft fire was considered "extreme," and the pilots were warned not to attempt the gauntlet of the heavy barrages over Pearl Harbor. Notwithstanding the warnings and the danger, the pilots climbed out through heavy smoke, reaching 8,000 feet in the area of Diamond Head. Here they encountered their first enemy aircraft—nine Zero fighters.

The P-36s rushed into the Zero formation, catching the Japanese pilots off balance. Almost as quickly as the fight started, Lieutenants Lewis M. Sanders and Philip M. Rasmussen each flamed a Zero.

Lieutenant Gordon H. Sterling, Jr., latched onto the tail of another Zero fighter, twisting and maneuvering wildly to keep his bullets pouring into the evading enemy plane. He scored direct hits (his fellow pilots claimed the Zero as destroyed; the official records show it only as damaged), but almost at the same time a Zero looped sharply, came around on his tail, and shot down Sterling in a mass of flames.

Lieutenant John M. Thacker fought with the Japanese until his plane was riddled from nose to tail with cannon fire, and his guns jammed. Helpless against the Zeros, he rammed the nose of the Mohawk down and dove for his life, returning safely to his field. The last engagement was fought by Lieutenant Malcolm A. Moore who pursued a Zero, damaging the enemy fighter, until it slipped into clouds over Kaena Point.

At Bellows Field enlisted men on duty or in their barracks responded quickly to the Japanese air strikes. Crewmen of the 86th Observation Squadron rushed to action without waiting for orders; they grabbed machine guns, ran out to the flight line where O-47 observation planes were grounded on the field, and mounted the guns in the cockpits. From these positions they fired directly at Japanese planes as they rushed low over the field.

Other men ran to P-40 fighters of the 44th Squadron, 18th Pursuit Group (on detached service at Bellows Field for gunnery training). The mechanics fueled the Tomahawks while armorers loaded the planes with ammunition.

Almost as soon as the P-40s were ready, Japanese Zeros came in fast and low in a strafing run. Three pilots made an ill-fated attempt to slug it out with the Japanese.

Lieutenant Hans C. Christiansen was killed almost immediately. (There are two versions of Christiansen's death; one report claims he was killed "while getting into his plane." According to Vern Haugland, in *The AAF Against Japan*, the Japanese Zeros "machine-gunned Lieutenant Hans C. Christiansen just as he got his P-40 under way. It plunged into underbrush at the end of the runway, its pilot dead.")

Lieutenant George A. Whiteman made it into the air —directly into the guns of six Zero fighters who ran at him in a pack. He barely got into the air when his Tomahawk smashed back into the ground in a tumbling ball of flame and wreckage.

Lieutenant Samuel W. Bishop lasted only moments longer. He brought his Tomahawk off the ground into a steep climbing turn to bring his guns to bear against the Zeros. The Japanese wasted no time in hacking the P-40 into shreds, and wounding Bishop severely in a leg. Fighting every foot of the way, he ditched the battered airplane into the water off Oahu and, despite his bleeding leg, swam ashore.

Vern Haugland compiled a report on other aerial activities of that confused morning—all of it distressingly one-sided:

"Some of the airplanes which met the enemy over Oahu were unable to engage in combat. A few airborne civilian craft made for safe landing fields as promptly as possible. At the height of the raid, fourteen unarmed B-17s arrived from the United States on the first leg of a proposed six thousand-mile flight to the Philippines. The tremendous fuel load required that the 2,392-mile water hop from Hamilton Field, California, be made without the weight of guns and ammunition.

"By means of skillful maneuvering, all pilots managed to land at scattered points on Oahu. Japanese strafers inflicted some crew casualties and damaged several Flying Fortresses.

"Captain Richard H. Carmichael led a group of six planes from the 88th Reconnaissance Squadron, 7th Bomb Group, which arrived over Oahu about eight A.M. Other pilots in the group were Lieutenants Frank P. Bostrom, Harry N. Brandon, Robert E. Thacker, David G. Rawls and Harold N. Chaffin.

"Lieutenant Bostrom, who three months later flew Douglas MacArthur out of the Philippines to Australia, was driven away from the island by antiaircraft fire on his original approach. He flew around for fifteen minutes, then asked permission to land at Hickam but was told to stay away. Six Japanese fighters attacked him as he circled, pursued him almost all the way around the island and shot out two of his engines.

"Eluding the attackers, Bostrom brought the new B-17 down on a golf course with only a few minutes' supply of gasoline remaining.

"Lieutenants Brandon, Thacker and Rawls braved the furious antiaircraft fire and Japanese attacks, and landed successfully at Hickam Field. Hedge-hopping Japanese fighters strafed crew members as they ran from their planes to shelter.

"Captain Carmichael and Lieutenant Chaffin, unable to land at Hickam or Wheeler because of fires on the airdromes, brought their planes down safely on the 1,200-foot Haleiwa fighter strip.

"A formation from the 38th Reconnaissance Squadron, led by Major Truman H. Landon, landed without difficulty at Hickam and Wheeler Fields. Enemy attacks shot out the ailerons of the plane piloted by Lieutenant Robert H. Richards and seriously wounded two crew members. Richards landed downwind on the 2,600-foot fighter strip without further injury to the crew.

"Although none of the new Flying Forts had been able to put up any resistance to the Japanese, most of them soon were armed and ready for use by the Hawaiian Air Force. . . ."[4]

In the U.S. Air Force History Office's official history, *The Army Air Forces in World War II*, is found the notation that the "enemy's victory had been perfect as few military operations are. Its early consequences were to follow closely enough Japanese hopes."[5]

The Japanese made their move against the Philippines.

BOOK THREE

8

DEFEAT IN THE PHILIPPINES

On the first day of the war in the Pacific, Japanese military forces—

Struck a severe blow with a large formation of bombers against Wake Island. . . .

Attacked the island of Guam with 18 bombers and set in motion the invasion fleet which would overrun the poorly defended American base within three days. . . .

Smashed American air strength on the island of Luzon in the Philippines by wiping out a major force of fighters, bombers, and other aircraft, and devastating air defense and ground facilities. . . .

Struck with heavy bomber formations against British defenses on the islands of Nauru and Ocean, lying between the Solomon and Gilbert island chains. . . .

Bombed Hong Kong Island, and dispatched a strong force of troops against Kowloon on the mainland opposite Hong Kong to wreck carefully prepared defense plans. . . .

Swept through the International Settlement at Shanghai, and captured the crew of HMS *Petrel* (but not before they sank their ship). . . .

Rushed aboard the American gunboat *Wake* and *while the crew slept*, captured the warship intact; the Japanese, with a fine sense of irony, recommissioned the *Wake* in the Japanese Navy as the *Tataru*. . . .

Sortied an invasion fleet along the east coast of Malaya; troops poured ashore from six transports and two destroyers at Singora and Patani. Other troops were rushed across the Kra Isthmus. . . .

Sent large bodies of troops across the borders of French Indo-China (already occupied by the Japanese through agreements with the French), into Thailand (Siam); resistance was light and sporadic. . . .

Attacked Singapore with powerful formations of dive
and attack bombers and escorting Zero fighters from aircraft carriers cruising offshore. . . .

In the face of sudden British resistance with bombers
(of which the Japanese shot down four), invaded British
defenses at Kota Bahru, Malaya. Preceding the invasion
was a powerful barrage from an invasion fleet of heavy
warships; 40 dive bombers also shattered installations at
the Kota Bahru airfield to destroy most of the British
air power in the immediate area. . . .

The Japanese also sank a crippling percentage of Allied
merchantmen discovered by their aircraft and fleet units,
including three American, 41 British, one Greek, and
seven Panamanian cargo vessels (200,000 tons of shipping slipped away from the Philippines to escape the Japanese). . . .

And, as the initial blow, the Japanese eliminated the
Hawaiian Islands as a source of danger or interference to
Japanese operations elsewhere in the Pacific and in Asia.

On the opening day of the Pacific War, the Far East
Air Force in the Philippine Islands counted its military air
strength at approximately 150 assorted fighters, bombers,
and miscellaneous types of aircraft.

Seventeen Boeing B-17 Flying Fortress bombers (of the
early B-17C and B-17D models, which lacked tail guns
and power turrets) were based at Clark Field, on Luzon,
northwest of Manila.

At Iba airfield, on the west coast of Luzon almost due
west of Clark, was the 3rd Pursuit Squadron with 18 Curtiss P-40E Kittyhawk fighters. (Greatly improved over
the P-40B Tomahawk, the P-40E was more powerful,
faster, and mounted six .50-caliber machine guns in its
wings.) The 17th Pursuit Squadron and 21st Pursuit
Squadron, based at Nichols Field, southeast of Manila,
each had 18 of the new Kittyhawk fighters. Sharing Clark
Field with the force of heavy bombers was the 20th Pursuit Squadron with 18 of the older P-40B Tomahawks.
Approximately a dozen Seversky P-35 fighters, old, slow,
and seriously underarmed, operated with the 34th Pursuit
Squadron from Del Carmen, 15 miles southwest of Clark
Field. Completing the fighter strength was a rickety force
of 12 Boeing P-26s (open cockpits and fixed landing

PHILIPPINE ISLANDS

Nautical miles

0 30 60 90 120   180

Aparri
Tuguegarao
Vigan
LUZON
Lingayen Gulf
Baguio
ZAMBALES
Rosales
Tarlac
Cabanatuan
Clark
Del Carmen
Iba
San Fernando
San Marcelino
Olongapo
Del Monte
Subic Bay
Manila
Nielson
Cavite
San Miguel Bay
Bataan
Mariveles
Nichols
Corregidor
Lipa
Cabcaben
Batangas
Legaspi
Bataan Field
Hermosa
Mindoro
Waterous
San Jose
Masbate
Samar
N
Panay
Negros
Cebu
Bohol
Cagayan
MINDANAO
Davao

gear) flown by the Philippines Air Force from Batangas, on the south coast of Luzon.

The airpower defense of the Philippines was completed with a miscellaneous assortment of 21 other aircraft, some of which were fabric-covered biplanes and considered useless for combat.

Against this defensive array the Japanese mounted a modern striking force that operated from five bases on Formosa (Kaohsung, Tainan, Taichung, Chiai, and Tungkan). Assembled at these five fields were a total of 184 Zero fighters, 192 twin-engine bombers, and 24 long-range flying boats. Not all of these aircraft were able to operate over the long distances to and from the Philippines; the Japanese considered their effective strike force to consist of 108 Zeros and 144 twin-engine bombers, plus the flying boats for long-range reconnaissance at sea.

Until two weeks before combat operations got under way, the Japanese judged their striking force to be seriously deficient, as their best intelligence estimates placed American airpower in the Philippines at some 900 military aircraft. The extensive use of twin-engine reconnaissance planes operating at heights up to 30,000 feet, however, enabled the Japanese drastically to reduce this estimate to some 300 machines, a force they considered well within their means to eliminate.

Monday morning, December 8, local Philippines time, military installations went on combat alert. It was then three o'clock in the morning in the Philippines (8:30 A.M. Hawaiian time), and the first warnings of imminent attack came not through military channels, but from commercial stations that broke into their regular scheduled broadcasts with news flashes of the attack against Pearl Harbor. Despite a lack of official confirmation of this news, its consequences were potentially so great that the Philippines command alerted all units to be ready for immediate takeoff.

Within 30 minutes of the alert, the Iba radar station, halfway up the west coast of Luzon, reported unidentified aircraft approaching the islands, with their present positions some 75 miles offshore. Several minutes later they were reported on a bearing that would take them directly over Corregidor.

Several P-40 fighters of the 3rd Pursuit Squadron

scrambled from their runway and roared into the darkness, climbing rapidly under ground radar control. For a while it appeared that the first air battle over the Philippines was about to be joined; the P-40 pilots, however, passed well beneath the unidentified aircraft and never sighted their quarry in the darkness. (The aircraft were Japanese Mitsubishi Type 96 Nell bombers on reconnaissance; they broke off to the west, unaware of the American fighters attempting the intercept.)

Later that morning, at approximately 9:00 A.M., the "delayed" opening of active hostilities caught up swiftly with the Philippines. Spotters and radar stations flashed warnings that enemy aircraft were over Lingayen Gulf, bearing south toward the city of Manila. Immediately all the B-17 Flying Fortresses stationed at Clark Field were ordered into the air (*sans* bombs) to prevent their being destroyed on the ground, and also to carry out long-distance reconnaissance flights against an expected Japanese invasion fleet. As the bombers sped out to sea, the Tomahawks of the 20th Pursuit Squadron climbed under full throttle to intercept the oncoming enemy.

By 0910 hours, there were 54 American planes in the air, with 36 fighters being maintained on instant reserve to join in interceptions. Still there was no contact with the Japanese.

Then at 0923 hours, Colonel Harold H. George flashed the alert that there were "approximately twenty-four bi-motored enemy bombers near Tuguegarao and seventeen near Baguio. . . ."

Approximately seven minutes later men on the ground heard for the first time a sound that would become terrifyingly familiar to them—the increasing shriek of Japanese bombs spilling from high altitude, arrowing toward their targets with an accuracy that was to become both hated and feared. The first bombing strike, without interference to the Japanese formations, tore up military installations at Baguio, the summer capital in the mountains lying to the north of Manila. Air fields south of Baguio, at Cabanatuan, also received a major attack.

Two hours later the radar stations flashed the word of a second attack on its way, with the enemy formations approaching from over the China Sea. Still at Iba, the 3rd Pursuit Squadron scrambled all operational Kittyhawk fighters to intercept the Japanese. At Nichols, cursing and sweating mechanics were still trying to refuel the fighters of the 17th Pursuit Squadron; with the aircraft still not fully fueled, the pilots were ordered into the air immediately to set up patrols over the Bataan Peninsula. The 34th Pursuit Squadron, almost at the same time, received its assignment to set up aerial cover over the city of Manila.

At Clark Field were the P-40s of the 20th Pursuit Squadron and the B-17 bombers of the 28th and 30th Bombardment Squadrons. One Flying Fortress was still in the air at the tail end of a reconnaissance flight, and armorers were preparing those planes on the ground for a strike against the Japanese airfields on Formosa.

Then, in the traditional sense of the phrase, all hell broke loose. The Kittyhawks of the 3rd Pursuit Squadron were circling the Iba airfield, preparing to swing into their landing patterns; the fighters were low on fuel and the pilots angry and frustrated with their failing to come to grips with the enemy. At that moment the Japanese caught the Americans with a shattering surprise attack. Once again that day the air seemed to split with the growing scream of the Japanese bombs hurtling earthward.

The P-40E pilots slammed home throttles and climbed desperately to turn into the enemy, but they could hardly have been caught at a greater disadvantage. Zero fighters swarmed into the American formations with deadly effect. Lieutenant Jack Donalson threw his fighter into the midst of the Japanese planes, and not even the agile Zeros could catch the wildly flying American pilot long enough to shoot him out of the sky. Donalson poured bullets into aged), providing the main resistance to the Japanese. The Mitsubishi pilots made the most of their superior advantages of altitude and diving speed; before the one-sided dead pilots. Three other P-40Es were forced to crashland on nearby beaches when the pilots exhausted their fuel. two fighters (and claimed—correctly—two aircraft damfight ended, five Kittyhawks went down in flames or with

The Kittyhawks, while failing to down any of their opponents, had actually achieved a precious advantage for Iba. By turning into the diving Japanese fighters, they forced the enemy into a swirling battle, and prevented them from carrying out a slow and methodical strafing of the airfield, upon which the Japanese were counting heavily.

Clark Field failed to receive this reprieve. The wheezing, obsolete Seversky P-35s of the 21st Pursuit Squadron were ordered into the air from Del Carmen to protect Clark Field (where bombers and fighters were still being refueled); unfortunately, thick dust at Del Carmen so obscured the runways that the fighters were delayed in their takeoff rolls. By 12:15 P.M. the delays had become so serious in establishing air cover over Clark that the pilots of the 20th Pursuit Squadron—their planes still not fully fueled—were rushed into the air to protect their own field.

Once again the Japanese struck with superb—and unplanned—timing. Four Tomahawks had barely made it into the air when the first barrage of hundreds of bombs from 60 twin-engine bombers began chewing up the runways and airfield installations. Flame geysered through the swiftly thickening dust and smoke in a terrifying procession of bombs; the Japanese wheeled slowly over Clark, contemptuous in their precision formations, raining bombs for 15 minutes upon the American field.

Fires were raging fiercely from hangars and buildings when the last bomb struck. Men on the ground rushed to combat the flames and attend to the wounded, but this was the moment on which the Japanese counted to deliver the second blow of the attack—and which the pilots of the 3rd Pursuit Squadron had prevented at Iba. As the stunned defenders at Clark set about to halt the flames, a new sound was heard. The men had barely looked up when a swarm of Zero fighters streaked through the billowing smoke, the noses and wings of the Japanese planes sparkling bright red from their firing guns and cannon.

A devastating strafing attack—usually carried out by fighters in minutes—had begun. And the Japanese were to keep up their firing passes, coming down again and again against the airfield, for more than an hour!

The men of the 20th had fought desperately to get their fighters into the air, but this struggle was lost even as it began. Five Tomahawks were flung crazily from the runway by exploding Japanese bombs as the American pilots defied almost certain death to engage the enemy in battle. The strafing Zeros accounted for the destruction of another five Tomahawks. Despite the bombs and the

Japanese fighters that followed immediately afterward, Lieutenant Joseph H. Moore, Squadron Commander, managed to lead three fighters into the smoking skies.

Lieutenant Randall B. Keator became the first American to destroy an enemy aircraft in the air battle for the Philippines. Immediately after his kill, Lieutenant Moore displayed great courage and spectacular flying skill by rushing into the mass of Zero fighters, shooting two of the Mitsubishis into flaming wreckage.

Other air battles were in the meantime being fought. The P-35 fighters from Del Carmen managed finally to become airborne. They reached a height sufficient to give them an advantage over the Japanese pilots by diving against the Zeros. At that moment the American pilots were given their first exhibition of the superb performance of their enemy; with "ridiculous ease" the Zeros flashed around in tight turns and scattered the Severskys. To the surprise of the Japanese, the slow P-35 fighters recovered and snarled back into the fight. But where the American pilots had the courage to fight, their planes lacked the

Seversky P-35—"museum piece fighter" of
American air defense of Philippines.

performance to make that courage pay off. The Zeros shot the P-35s to ribbons; miraculously none of the American planes was shot down, although several were described on their landings as "flying wrecks."

Of the attack against Clark Field, correspondent Vern Haugland (who spent more time in the Pacific than any other newsman and who came to know the Japanese on face-to-face combat terms) wrote:

"For ninety minutes the Japanese bombed and strafed almost at will, taking their choice of targets and attacking as vigorously and recklessly as they had at Pearl Harbor. At one blow they wiped out most of the hangars and installations and airplanes at this most important American air base in the Far East. Some planes also attacked Nichols Field, Fort Stotsenburg and other scattered points.

"At least fifty-five men were killed, and 110 wounded. Of the twenty-two B-17s and ten P-40s on the field, only seven B-17s escaped complete destruction, and only two or three of the seven could be repaired. In one day, the Japanese had succeeded in wiping out half the heavy-bomber force and one-third of the pursuit strength of the Far East Air Force."[1]

The Attackers

The Japanese had much more than their own preparations working for them—Fate also played a hand in favor of the attackers. The effectiveness of the Japanese bombing and strafing attacks against the Americans could hardly be denied—our combat ability had virtually been wrecked in terms of effective numbers. But the exact timing of the Japanese strikes could not have been better had the Americans cooperated in their own destruction. What did happen was that the weather, unknown to the Americans, had dealt them a fatal blow.

The Japanese had planned a concerted strike against American and British installations throughout the Pacific, with the opening blow carried out against Pearl Harbor. Immediately upon confirmation of that attack, the Philippines were to be hit with everything the Japanese could throw at the defenders. This inevitable timetable was immediately obvious to the Far East Air Force, which, upon receiving word of the bombings in the Hawaiian Islands, had not only placed its forces on alert, but also dispatched fighters into the air to intercept the Japanese long before they reached their targets.

Had the Japanese been able to keep to their carefully planned schedule, they would have run directly into the hornets' nest of American fighter planes *which they expected to encounter in the air.* And this is where the Fates stepped in. . . .

As the Japanese reported the events of the day:

"Early in the morning of December 8, 1941, thick fog rolled in from the sea completely to shroud our air bases on Formosa. On the very first day of the war, when a coordinated effort was of the utmost importance, our planes could not leave their fields. We cursed and fumed, for even as we paced helplessly in the swirling gloom the Nagumo task force planes turned Pearl Harbor into a shambles. If the enemy in the Philippines had the opportunity to counterattack quickly, he could disrupt completely our carefully laid plans. Finally the initial reports of the Pearl Harbor raid reached us through Tokyo; still the fog did not lift.

"After long hours of chaining us to the ground, the fog dispersed before the morning sun. We wasted no time and, as quickly as their engines could be warmed, the fighters and bombers thundered from the field and headed southward. As the gods of war would have it, the crippling fog proved to be a tremendous asset in our attack against the American air bases. Our planes reached Luzon Island at 1:30 P.M., Tokyo time, several hours later than we had originally scheduled. By this quirk of circumstances, we caught the American fighters completely off guard. Receiving the reports of the Pearl Harbor attacks, the fighters took to the air in anticipation of a forthcoming raid. After waiting in vain for several hours for our planes, *which were then sitting helplessly on the ground* [author's italics], the enemy planes, their fuel exhausted, returned to their fields. Almost immediately afterward our fighters and bombers swept in to attack."[2]

The commander of the 23rd Air Flotilla, which was attached to the 11th Air Fleet of the Japanese Navy at Takao, Formosa, provides a second viewpoint in a statement quoted by the United States Strategic Bombing Survey:

"We greatly feared an American raid, and when heavy fog kept us on the ground we became very nervous about it.

"Our fears increased at eight A.M. when we intercepted American radio transmissions indicating that B-17s were heading toward Formosa.

"At 10:10 A.M. a Japanese pilot erroneously reported the approach of B-17s. We expected the worst, and put on gas masks in preparation for an immediate attack.

"Immediately thereafter, the fog having lifted somewhat, all planes took off for the Philippines. *We were amazed to find the American planes lined up on Clark Field.*"

Through the night on Formosa, Japanese pilots and crews stood by their fighters and bombers; orderlies brought hot breakfasts to the men on the runways. The Japanese airmen were told that they would begin their takeoffs at four A.M. so that they would be in a position to strike at "the propitious moment." Then at three A.M. the unexpected happened with the fog that rolled over the airfields, which within an hour "reduced visibility to only five yards."

By seven o'clock the Japanese were experiencing a mixture of emotions—fear at being caught on the ground by American bombers, and frustration at being unable to take off to strike their distant targets. Saburo Sakai, one of the Zero fighter pilots on Formosa that morning, describes the moment when loudspeakers crackled the news of the carrier-force assault against Pearl Harbor:

"A wild, surging roar went up in the darkness. Pilots danced and slapped their friends on the back, but the shouts were not entirely those of exultation. Many of the fliers were releasing their pent-up anger at being chained to the ground while our other planes were smashing at the enemy.

"The attack created a factor which we must consider. The Americans were now warned of our attack plan, and it was incredible that they would not be waiting for us in strength in the Philippines. The tension increased as the morning approached. The fog had crippled our plans; worse yet, it would allow the Americans to send their bombers from Luzon and catch our planes on the ground the moment the fog lifted. We manned our defense installations. Machine gunners slipped live rounds into their weapons, and every man on the field strained for the sound of enemy bombers.

"Miraculously, the attack never came! At nine in the morning the fog began to lift and the welcome sound of the loudspeakers told us that we would take off in only one hour. Every pilot and bomber crewman on the field climbed into his plane without awaiting further orders.

"Exactly at ten the signal lights flickered through the last wisps of fog. One after the other the bombers rolled down the long runway. One, two, three, then six planes were in the air, climbing steadily. The seventh plane was racing down the runway, 1,200 feet from its starting point, when suddenly the right landing gear collapsed. With a great screeching roar the plane spun along the ground on its belly, flames enveloping the entire fuselage. In the harsh glare of the fire we saw the crew struggle through their hatches and jump onto the ground, then run furiously away from their plane. The next instant a tremendous blast rocked the field as the bomb load blew up. None of the crew survived the explosion.

"Repair crews were on the runway in seconds, and the men proceeded frantically to drag away the twisted pieces of metal. Dozens of men raced against time to fill the smoking crater; in less than fifteen minutes the signal was given for the next bomber to resume its takeoff. By 10:45 all planes were airborne, fifty-three bombers and forty-five Zero fighters.

"The fighters broke up into two groups, one staying with the bombers as escorts, while the other flew ahead to tackle the interceptors, which, we felt certain, after the long delay in our attack, would be awaiting us in great strength."[8]

Mystery

As the continuity of events indicates clearly, the United States lost a precious advantage, in failing to blunt, and perhaps even wreck, the carefully planned strike of the Japanese against the Philippines from their Formosa bases.

We were fully aware of the location of those bases; for approximately two weeks prior to December 7, PBY Catalina flying boats of the United States Navy had flown reconnaissance missions over the island of Formosa, playing a cat-and-mouse game with Japanese fighters through clouds. None of the lumbering flying boats had been downed; the Japanese were convinced that the Americans had gained complete details of the locations of their bases. The existence of the Flying Fortress bombers at Luzon was considered an extremely dangerous threat to the success of the Japanese plans; the unexpected fog that chained the Mitsubishi fighters and bombers to their fields was considered, as well, to be potentially disastrous.

Why, then, were the long-range B-17s, with their heavy bomb loads and excellent accuracy, not dispatched to attack these fields? The heavy concentrations of Japanese bombers and fighters on the ground, filled with ammunition, bombs, and fuel, provided a prime situation for a devastating holocaust that could have broken the back of the Japanese airpower elements assigned to the Philippines campaign.

The bombing strike that could have altered the entire face of the war in the Pacific by preventing the "little Pearl Harbor" of Clark Field and other Philippines installations was never made—but the reasons *why* that attack failed to materialize apparently will forever be the subject of bitter controversy among the men who were present at the scene.

General L. H. Brereton in his diary stated explicitly that the need for such an aerial attack was glaringly obvious and, accordingly, he had requested of Lieutenant General Richard K. Sutherland (chief of staff for General Douglas MacArthur) permission to launch the bombing strike. Sutherland, wrote Brereton, delayed so long that the vital moment of bombing the enemy on his home bases vanished with the passing minutes, and finally went up in smoke and flames when Japanese bombs rained down upon Clark Field.

Some time after Brereton's charges, General MacArthur clouded the issue with a statement (made in Tokyo) that attacked Brereton and denied that such a bombing attack strike ever had been requested. General MacArthur stated:

"In order that there may be no mistake as to all facts

in the case, I wish to state that General Brereton never recommended an attack on Formosa to me and I know nothing of such a recommendation having been made . . . ; that he never has spoken of the matter to me either before or after the Clark Field attack; that an attack on Formosa with its heavy air concentrations by his small bomber force without fighter support which, because of the great distance involved, was impossible, would have had no chance of success; that in the short interval of time involved it is doubtful that an attack could have been set up and mounted before the enemy's arrival.

"That the enemy's bombers from Formosa had fighter protection available in their attack on Clark Field from their air carriers, an entirely different condition than our own; that I had given orders several days before to withdraw the heavy bombers to Mindanao, out of range of enemy land-based air; that half the bombers, eighteen, had already been so withdrawn when war broke; that General Brereton was fully alerted on the morning of December 8 and his fighters took to the air to protect Clark Field, but failed to intercept the enemy; that tactical handling of his own air force, including all measures for its protection against air attack of his planes on the ground, was entirely in his own hands; that the over-all strategic mission was to defend the Philippines, not to initiate an outside attack.

"Our air forces in the Philippines . . . were hardly more than a token force . . . They were hopelessly outnumbered and never had a chance of winning . . . They did everything possible within their limited resources. I attach no blame to General Brereton or other members of the command for the incidents of battle. Nothing could have saved the day for them."[4]

The conflict between the statements of General Brereton and MacArthur (in which Sutherland remains conspicuously silent) may be solved by no man. But there are some remarkable phrases in the special statement issued by General MacArthur which reflect not only a conflict with conclusions drawn by other military officials *but also a complete disregard of the facts!* General MacArthur, in short, alludes to facts and circumstances which simply did not stand up.

General MacArthur refers to a fighter-escort mission between the Philippines and Formosa, "because of the great distance involved," as "impossible." American air commanders in the Philippines also drew this conclusion and simply did not expect any fighter attack against Luzon. General MacArthur, however, employs lack of knowledge of Japanese fighter performance to draw firm conclusions which are entirely at fault, i.e., that the Japanese obtained their fighter escort cover *from their aircraft carriers*—when, in fact, not a single aircraft carrier was employed throughout the entire Philippines campaign in 1941–42!

Commander Masatake Okumiya, discussing the effectiveness of the Zero fighter as a combat weapon, sheds light on MacArthur's conclusions:

"After the beginning of the war, we learned that, although the Zero fighter had appeared in battle in China more than a year prior to December of 1941, the Allies professed astonishment at the sight of our new fighter and were caught completely unaware by the Zero's performance. Months after the Philippines campaign, the Allies still did not realize the true flight capabilities of the Zero. When Zeros raided Port Darwin, Australia, early in 1942, the enemy accepted without question the fact that the Zeros must have flown from our carriers, when in reality they flew from our newly captured land bases on Timor Island. . . .

"We can judge the effectiveness of our Zero fighters by observing that in all our operations in the first months of the war, the Zero fighters of our land- and carrier-based air forces destroyed 65 percent of all the enemy planes lost. This accomplishment contributed directly to the success of our operations in many respects other than the destruction of the enemy aircraft; without control of the air, our bombers and torpedo planes could not possibly have eliminated enemy resistance so thoroughly.

". . . at Pearl Harbor, as well as in the Philippines and Dutch East Indies, we could not possibly have achieved our sea, land, and air victories with a fighter plane of lesser performance than the Zero. Our entire strategy depended upon the success of this aircraft."[5]

General MacArthur further refers to the Far East Air Forces as being "hopelessly outnumbered." Once again this statement is in conflict with the facts. Defending Philippines positions were 54 P-40E Kittyhawk fighters (officially considered to be superior to the Zero fighter),

18 P-40B Tomahawks (used so effectively by Clair Chennault with the Flying Tigers), and from 12 to 18 obsolescent Seversky P-35 fighters. This gave the defenders a total of from 80 to 90 fighter planes (not counting the virtually useless 12 Boeing P-26s of the Philippines Air Force), plus 33 B-17 bombers and an odd assortment of 21 other planes unfit for combat.

The Japanese had available for operations over the long distance to the Philippines from Formosa a total of 144 twin-engine bombers and 108 Zero fighters. On the opening strikes they employed all these bombers and 84 Zero fighters—hardly numbers that rendered the Far East Air Forces "hopelessly outnumbered."

Had the Tomahawks and Kittyhawks been in a position to strike they could not only have completely disrupted the attack of the bombers, but might well have decimated their ranks.

There is one final point that requires mention. General MacArthur makes it clear that the defense of the Philippines was to be carried out without "outside attack," i.e., a strike against the Formosa bases of the Japanese. Air Force tacticians could only fume helplessly at such reasoning—two dozen or more Flying Fortresses, catching the Japanese on the ground as the fog cleared from the Formosa fields, could have altered the course of the Pacific War.

The Tenth of December

December 10, 1941, went into the history books of the Pacific War for a number of reasons—two among them being the destruction of a myth at the expense of the British, and the creation of a myth from amidst the shock that had swept the United States. The British paid the price of losing two of the greatest battleships in existence to land-based Japanese airpower, drawing the curtain once and for all on the fable that the battlewagon was still the ruler of the seas. The United States, desperate for a measure of success against the rampaging Japanese, sought for—and created—a fable of heroism. Strangely enough, the fable could not match the truth of which our people back home knew nothing.

In the case of the British, the debacle about to befall them centered upon the mighty battleship *Prince of Wales* and the fast and deadly battle cruiser *Repulse*. The Japanese considered the unexpected appearance of the powerful British warships in the Singapore area as seriously endangering their plans for the invasion of Malaya and surrounding territories. Japanese intelligence made it clear to their fleet commanders that the British dreadnaughts were better gunned and far more dangerous than even the fast battleships *Haruna* and *Kongo*, at the time under the flag of Vice-Admiral Nobutake Kondo, Commander in Chief of the Second Fleet, and operating off the Malayan coast. Despite the heavy concentration of Japanese seapower against the British—the Japanese mounted two battleships, seven heavy cruisers, two light cruisers, and 14 destroyers in the area—Admiral Isoroku Yamamoto was so concerned about *Prince of Wales* and *Repulse* that he ordered a major land-based air fleet into position to attack the British vessels. Yamamoto's concern was not that the Japanese surface fleet could not handle the British, but that if the British warships ever broke loose amidst the Japanese landing forces, they could swiftly wreck many or most of the transports, with terrible loss of life among the invasion troops.

Even the attack at Pearl Harbor and the carnage spread along Battleship Row had not decided the issue of the battleship's supremacy on the high seas. It was one thing to destroy warships tied up helplessly in a harbor, and something else again to sink such dreadnaughts when they were moving swiftly on the ocean, with all guns firing in their own defense. The Japanese were about to settle the matter. . . .

At 12:20 P.M. the Japanese bombers searching the seas off the Malayan coast for the British warships received a flash alert from a single reconnaissance plane: *"Sighted two enemy battleships. Seventy nautical miles southeast of Kuantan. Course south-southeast. 1145."*

The first torpedo slammed into one of the British warships (the *Prince of Wales* and the *Repulse* were escorted by three destroyers, and were accompanied by a single merchant ship) at 12:45 P.M., just 25 minutes after they were tracked by the reconnaissance aircraft. Shortly after one P.M. a second major bomber force arrived on the scene. Lieutenant Sadao Takai, a squadron leader of the Genzan Air Corps, who participated in the preattack sea patrol and, later, in the sea battle off Malaya, kept detailed notes of his activities. Excerpts from those notes reveal in intimate detail the events of the day:

"... At exactly 1:03 P.M. a black spot directly beneath the cloud ahead of us was sighted. It appeared to be the enemy vessels, about twenty-five miles away. Yes—it was the enemy! Soon we could distinguish the ships. The fleet was composed of two battleships, escorted by three destroyers, and one small merchant vessel. The battleships were the long-awaited *Prince of Wales* and the *Repulse!*

"The 1st Squadron picked up speed and moved ahead of my squadron. Lieutenant Commander Nakanishi ordered: *'Form assault formation!'* A little later: *'Go in!'*

"The enemy fleet was now about eight miles away. We were still flying at eighty-three hundred feet and were in the ideal position to attack. As we had planned, Nakanishi's bomber increased its speed and began to drop toward the enemy fleet. He was headed to the right and a little ahead of the warships. Trying to maintain the same distance and not be left behind, the bombers of my squadron also increased their speed as I started a gradual dive. I headed toward the left flank of the enemy formation.

"... Coordinating my movements with those of the 1st Squadron, I led my squadron to the attack so that the enemy ships would be torpedoed from both flanks. The 1st Squadron was circling about four miles to the left and forward of the enemy ships and was about ready to begin its torpedo run. Antiaircraft shells were exploding all around the circling bombers. The planes could be seen between the flashing patches of white smoke as the shells exploded. ...

"We began the attack at an altitude of 1,000 feet and about a mile and a half from the enemy. No sooner had we emerged from the protection of low clouds than the enemy gunners sighted our planes. The fleet opened up with a tremendous barrage of shells, trying to disrupt our attack before we could release our torpedoes. The sky was filled with bursting shells which made my plane reel and shake.

"The second battleship had already started evasive action and was making a hard turn to the right. The target angle was becoming smaller and smaller as the bow of the vessel swung gradually in my direction, making it difficult for me to release a torpedo against the ship. It was expected that the lead torpedo bomber would be compelled to attack from the most unfavorable position. This was anticipated, and it enabled the other planes following me to torpedo the target under the best of conditions.

"The air was filled with white smoke, bursting shells, and the tracers of antiaircraft guns and machine guns. As if pushed down by the fierce barrage thrown up by the enemy, I descended to just above the water's surface. The airspeed indicator registered more than two hundred knots. I do not remember at all how I was flying the airplane, how I was aiming, and what distance we were from the ship when I dropped the torpedo. In the excitement of the attack I pulled back on the torpedo release. I acted almost subconsciously, my long months of daily training taking over my actions.

"A giant battleship suddenly loomed before the plane. Passing very close to the towering stern I swung into a hard turn and sped away from the warship. I began a wide circling turn in a clockwise direction, hastily easing the complaining bomber out of its steep climbing turn.

"Not many shells appeared to be bursting about us. The engines were still roaring loudly and only moderate damage had been inflicted upon my airplane. I pulled up again in a steep climb and leveled off, once we were within the clouds. I took a deep breath, and forced my taut muscles to relax.

"Suddenly my observer came stumbling forward through the narrow passageway, crying, 'Sir! Sir! A terrible thing has happened!' When I looked at him in surprise, he shouted, 'The torpedo failed to release!'

"I felt as though cold water had been dashed over my head and entire body. We were still carrying the torpedo! I forced myself to be calm and reversed our course at once. I passed on my new orders to the men. 'We will go in again at once.'

"I began to lower our altitude as we flew through the clouds. The second torpedo run on the battleship would be very dangerous; the enemy gunners would be fully alert and would be waiting for us. I did not like the idea of flying once again through a storm of antiaircraft fire which would be even worse than before.

"We dropped below cloud level. We were on the side

of the enemy battleship, which was just swinging into a wide turn. Our luck was good—no better chance would come!

"I pushed the throttles forward to reach maximum speed and flew just above the water. This time I yanked hard on the torpedo release. Over the thudding impact of bullets and shrapnel smashing into the airplane, I felt the strong shock through the bomber as the torpedo dropped free and plummeted into the water. It was inexcusable that we did not notice the absence of this shock during the first torpedo run. . . .

"I waited for the bombers of my squadron to assemble.

"All through the attack we had concentrated only on scoring direct hits on the enemy vessels. We had ignored everything but the release of our torpedoes into the British battleships. We had even forgotten to worry about our own safety. Once we had released the torpedoes, however, we were able to study the situation around us. Tracer bullets and antiaircraft shells filled the sky all about the airplanes, and we could feel the thud and shock vibrating all through the fuselage and wings as bullets and shrapnel ripped through the plane metal. It seemed to each of us that all the guns were aimed at our own plane. We became afraid of losing our own lives."

Describing the situation as the Japanese bombers completed their runs, Takai continues his account:

"By now the *Repulse* was a shattered hulk. It was still moving, but slowly, and was gradually losing speed. It had completely lost all fighting power and was no longer considered a worth-while target. It was only a matter of minutes before the battle cruiser went down.

"To all appearances, the *Prince of Wales* was intact, and defending herself furiously with an intense antiaircraft barrage. She was selected as the next bombing target. Fourteen 1,100-pound bombs were dropped; several scored direct hits on the enemy warship. The bombs struck directly in the center of the battleship. . . .

"Ensign Hoashi's plane caught the dramatic last moments of the two battleships. Minute by minute, as he circled above the stricken warships, he radioed back a vivid report of what was happening far below him. Twenty minutes after being hit by torpedoes, the *Repulse* began to sink beneath the waves. By 2:20 P.M. the great ship was gone.

"A few minutes later a tremendous explosion ripped through the *Prince of Wales*. Twenty minutes after the *Repulse* had sunk, the *Prince of Wales* started her last plunge and disappeared quickly. . . ."[6]

More than 26 torpedoes and three heavy bombs completed the mission upon which the Japanese had set out. It enabled the Japanese to draw the conclusion that it was a "mistake leading to the most serious consequences that the British failed to . . . provide air protection for their prized battleships. . . . It was completely incredible that the two warships should be left naked to attack from the skies. Interception of our level and torpedo bombers by British fighter aircraft might have seriously disrupted our attack and perhaps permitted the two warships to escape destruction. The battle of Malaya illustrated in the most forcible manner that a surface fleet without fighter protection was helpless under enemy air attack. The battleship, long the ruler of the seas, had been toppled from its dominant position and was now just another warship to be destroyed by aerial assault."[7]

The Last Few Flying Fortresses

Despite the staggering blows inflicted by the Japanese against our air forces in the Philippines, American bomber crews strained to fly reconnaissance missions *and* bombing strikes. The invasion of the Philippines was considered to be only a matter of hours, perhaps a few days at the most, and the transports moving southward into the islands would be packed with troops and equipment. Several sharp attacks delivered quickly could influence tremendously the fighting that would rage on the ground.

Complicating the attempts at reconnaissance and bombing, however, were the frequent, continuing attacks of the Japanese. Often the bombers were forced into the air, in darkness and in daylight, simply to escape destruction on the ground from Japanese bombers and fighters heading for their fields.

Further complications arose from the confusion that attended much of the activities during those early days of the war. *The Army Air Forces in World War II* notes of this period that "reports both from the warning net and from patrol planes revealed principally the confused and nervous state into which our defenses had been thrown by the enemy. As Admiral Hart later reported, 'an extraordinary crop of incorrect enemy information' came over the warning net, and there were reports of 'enemy sightings when nothing was actually sighted and when a vessel was really seen she was usually reported in one of two categories: irrespective of size, she was either a Transport or a Battleship.' "[8]

On the night of December 9–10, however, there could no longer be any doubt but that the Japanese were making their move. Factual confirmation of a Japanese invasion force moving against the Philippines was received (these were elements of the Japanese Third Fleet), and the Japanese opened the 10th with a powerhouse assault against remaining American defenses.

Nichols Field and the naval base at Cavite were literally wiped out as military installations. Japanese bombers flew with impunity—guaranteed them by the maneuvers of the Zero fighters that smashed all attempts to break up the bomber formations—and pounded their targets. The official evaluation of "completely ruined" was made of the power plant, industrial facilities, and supply depots at Cavite. Many naval craft suffered heavy damage, and the submarine *Sea Lion* was ripped open and sent to the bottom.

December 10 was also the date of the first offensive strike by our bombers against the enemy—and the birth of the myth which saw the destruction of the Japanese battleship *Haruna*, sunk as a result of a suicide dive in a B-17 flown by Captain Colin P. Kelly, Jr. There were many other aspects to the myth of this incident, among them the belief (that persists to this day) that Kelly was awarded the Congressional Medal of Honor (he wasn't). But that is part of our story. . . .

During the 9th of December, the AAF was staging its few B-17 bombers into the Philippines to join those already there, to prepare attacks against the warships and transports of the Japanese Third Fleet. Included in the northward transfer was a Boeing B-17D piloted by Colin P. Kelly, Jr.; he flew with six other bombers from the field at Del Monte in Hawaii to the combat-area base at San Marcelino.

Units of the Japanese Third Fleet had sortied from their ports in Formosa, and were landing troops and equipment at Aparri in the extreme northern section of Luzon, and at Vigan on the northwest coast. These attacks tied up the defending forces and enabled the Japanese to carry out their preparations for the major invasion yet to come—which would be at Lingayen Gulf. The Japanese fleet thus spread out into three task forces. These included the Aparri and Vigan invasion groups, while the third, consisting of warships, stood by to provide general firepower support as the situation might warrant.

At 0600 hours on the 10th (while the Japanese themselves were getting their own air strike forces in position to attack the Philippines), five Flying Fortresses, led by Major Cecil Combs, took off from the shambles of Clark Field. Each bomber carried 20 demolition bombs of 100 pounds each, and raced forward to attack the Japanese forces at Vigan. As they climbed for altitude they rendezvoused with other bombers of the 17th Squadron.

Over Vigan the bombers struck from different altitudes at the Japanese ships, which already were unloading supplies to support the invasion. The Fortresses made their bombing runs not in a solid pattern, but at altitudes extending from 7,000 to 12,500 feet, releasing long strings of their small missiles.

As the Fortresses made their strikes, another force roared in against the Japanese. These were the Curtiss P-40E Kittyhawks of the 17th Pursuit Squadron and the obsolescent Seversky P-35s of the 34th Pursuit Squadron. Immediately upon their arrival at the battle scene the fighters swept in to strafe the flak guns on the ships, hoping to draw the heavy antiaircraft fire away from the Fortresses.

When the brief strike ended, one Japanese transport had exploded and rolled over, sinking immediately in the shallow water. Three of our fighters also had been lost in the fierce battle, among them the P-35 of Squadron Leader Lieutenant Samuel H. Marret. Marret had screamed in low against a transport for a deck-high strafing run when the vessel exploded; the thundering blast caught Marret unawares and flipped his plane entirely out of control. The fighter was destroyed and Marret killed—one of three fighters lost in the battle.

Another bombing mission had been scheduled that morning to coincide with the strike against the Japanese forces at Vigan. The second mission was delayed when

Boeing B-17D Flying Fortress . . . undergunned,
obsolescent models of our main heavy bombers
were in the Philippines during Japanese air attacks,
proved ineffective in hitting Japanese invasion forces.

Major Emmett O'Donnell's 14th Squadron was forced to
stage northward from San Marcelino to Clark Field so that
the planes could refuel and bomb up before departing on
their missions. Colin Kelly was the pilot of one Fortress
in this squadron.

Clark Field was a smoking, gutted shambles when the
big Flying Fortresses slid from the sky for their landings.
Japanese attacks had ripped the runways into pitted and
gouged strips so badly mangled they were considered "impossible for use" with four-engine heavy bombers. Nevertheless, men working feverishly had managed to scrape
clear a tiny strip no longer than 2,000 feet in length
which could be used by the B-17s. Leaving this short
clear area the Fortresses taxied in weaving paths to remain clear of craters and the charred skeletons of dozens
of our planes. Farther out from the runway, buildings
had collapsed into blackened ruins, and aircraft hangars
loomed starkly as gutted shells.

Preparing the mission was a task demanding super-
human efforts on the part of the ground personnel at
Clark—since many of the men assigned to the air base
had bolted in terror for the hills when the first shriek of
falling Japanese bombs split the air. Dozens of men had

dashed away for their lives, openly terrified by the shattering roar of the Japanese bombs and the strafing runs of the Zero fighters. By the time the Fortresses staged in to Clark for their missions the air base was still critically shorthanded. Many of the men working on the airplanes were wounded and in need of hospital rest; nevertheless they refused to leave the airplanes until they were ready for takeoff.

O'Donnell's big airplanes slid into the runway at Clark two and three at a time, staging in low and cautiously to avoid the attention of any Zero fighters that might be prowling for exactly such a kill. It took better than expert piloting by the men at the yokes of the Fortresses to bring their heavy airplanes down on the tiny runway, and it is a tribute to their skill that every B-17 made it down without damage.

As quickly as the bombers rolled to the sides of the runway, mechanics dragged them off to dispersal areas where they could be refueled and loaded with bombs. The pilots, meanwhile, assembled for their orders and a briefing given them by Colonel Eugene L. Eubank, commanding officer of the 19th Bombardment Group.

Several of the bombers had been fully fueled and loaded with bombs, but most of the Fortresses were still undergoing this servicing when the air base received warning of large enemy formations on the way. To protect the B-17s, they were ordered into the air at once. The effectiveness of the Zero as a strafer still burned brightly in the minds of the survivors, and it was all too easy to imagine the new bombers on the field being chopped to ribbons in the firing passes of the Mitsubishis. Five B-17Ds took off individually, and the first three airplanes that made it aloft headed for the Japanese beachhead at Vigan. These were piloted by Major O'Donnell, Captain E. L. Parsel, and Lieutenant G. R. Montgomery.

O'Donnell reached the invasion area ahead of the other two bombers, and immediately went into his bombing runs from the high altitude of 25,000 feet. From five miles above the ocean his crew excitedly pointed at—and rushed to attack—what they thought was the prize target of all, an enemy aircraft carrier. (As was noted earlier, the crews had reported consistently all their targets as warships or transports; the belief that the Zeros could *only* have come from aircraft carriers made it all too easy to "see" such a target when in reality the Japanese had deployed all their carriers elsewhere.)

O'Donnell and his crew went through one of the most frustrating "immediate attacks" experienced by any bomber crew. For 45 minutes Japanese antiaircraft blazed away at them, upsetting the aim of the bombardier and forcing new runs over the invasion force. The Fortress would roar in steady as a rock for another run, and faulty bomb release mechanisms would leave the men spitting curses as the bombs hung up in their racks. For 45 minutes (during which the "enemy aircraft carrier" mysteriously failed to send up defending fighters) O'Donnell returned doggedly to the attack, but the combination of Japanese flak and faulty equipment defeated him—none of his eight 600-pound bombs struck an enemy vessel.

Parsel tried his luck at half the altitude; he roared in at 12,500 feet against a warship which, from this lower height, his crew judged to be either a destroyer or a cruiser. Four 300-pound bombs slicing down from the Fortress produced only spuming columns of water instead of smoke as their target went unscathed. Parsel came back in for a second run and this time his crew shouted at a strike against a transport (the Japanese later denied any such hits, stating only that one transport had suffered a bomb exploding near the ship).

Montgomery in the third Fortress arrived on the scene with only one 600-pound bomb in his bays. The bomb fell harmlessly in the water near the transports.

The two remaining Fortresses got into the air from Clark Field at 0930 hours; Lieutenant G. E. Schaetzel headed for the Japanese invasion force unloading troops and supplies at Aparri. From five miles up, the airplane released its bombs carefully against a cluster of transports; the crew reported the bombs striking smack in the midst of the assembled vessels. They claimed several damaging hits, but again the attackers were in error, for no ships sustained damage. The attack this time brought added opposition from the Japanese. Zero fighters staging down from Formosa to cover the invasion forces intercepted vigorously, chopping up the Fortress in flanking attacks. The high altitude aided the B-17D in escaping its pursuers; Zero performance fell off at five miles while the turbosuperchargers of the American bomber enabled it to "come into its own." Schaetzel managed to escape, and returned to San Marcelino.

The fifth bomber departing that morning from Clark Field was piloted by Colin Kelly. He had been instructed by Colonel Eubank to seek out and to attack a Japanese aircraft carrier (another!) that was reported to be steaming at high speed off Luzon's northern coast. Kelly, with three 600-pound bombs aboard the Fortress, completed his search pattern, but without making any contact with the "reported carrier." Finally an enemy vessel was sighted; his navigator, Lieutenant Joe M. Bean, sighted a "concentration of enemy ships"—*officially* reported as consisting of a 29,000-ton battleship of the *Kongo* class, six cruisers, ten destroyers, and 15 to 20 transports.

From this report emerged probably the most confused battle "documentation" in our military history; there was no battleship beneath Kelly's Fortress, and the number of Japanese ships was grossly exaggerated. Official Japanese records of the campaign show clearly that there was in the Philippines area *one light cruiser* of the *Nagara* class, six destroyers, and four transports—a total of seven warships and four transports, not 17 warships and 20 transports.

Kelly swung his big bomber around into his attack run at 22,000 feet over the "battleship." Only one bombing run was made, and Sergeant Meyer S. Levin released in train the three 600-pound bombs carried by the Fortress. Later the crew was to claim that two bombs had straddled their target, and that one bomb struck dead-center— "right down the stack," as many newspapers wrote with enthusiasm. In their postmission briefings, the crew stated also that the "battleship" had been slammed to a stop dead in the water, that it trailed oil and was burning.

Actually, the light cruiser had not even been scratched by a bomb! During the run over the target, Kelly's plane was unmolested by antiaircraft fire or fighters—indeed, the Japanese were unaware of the Fortress overhead until the bombs were whistling down to explode harmlessly in the sea.

So chaotic were conditions at air force headquarters that the official communiqués of the events involving Kelly's bomber (false to begin with) were distorted and swiftly expanded into a major victory for the United States. On December 10, datelined Manila, an Army communiqué claimed:

"One of our bombers late yesterday attacked a Japanese battleship of the *Hiranuma* 29,000-ton class, a capital ship, ten miles north of Luzon, and scored three direct hits and two very close alongside. When the bomber left the battleship was blazing fiercely."

Note the claim that five bombs were dropped when Kelly's Fortress actually carried only three. Note also the *official claim* that three hits were scored, instead of the one direct hit reported by the surviving crew members of Kelly's bomber. How it was determined that the battleship was blazing fiercely is a mystery, since the light cruiser had never been struck at any time. Further compounding the confusion is the report of the battleship as being of the *Hiranuma* class; no such vessel as the *Hiranuma* ever existed in the Japanese fleet.

However, people in the United States were electrified with the news. Headlines screamed that a battleship had been bombed, set afire, and sunk.

The next day another Manila-datelined communiqué was issued:

"The Commanding General, Far Eastern Command, confirms the sinking of a 29,000-ton battleship yesterday by the American Army Air Forces, north of Luzon. This battleship is believed to be the 29,000-ton *Haruna*, or a vessel of the *Haruna* class."

This was sweet news to a people whose sense of superiority had been so rudely shattered by the sweeping successes of the Japanese. It was a straw of hope and pride in an otherwise turbulent sea of crushing and humiliating defeat, and we made the most of it. Everyone took up Colin Kelly's name; he was the national hero who had saved our honor and our pride, and in the process had smashed a capital ship of the enemy.

As the celebrations went on, the 29,330-ton *Haruna* (of the *Kongo* class) was steaming unharmed off Malaya, where it remained until December 18.

The derision and scorn in Tokyo rose to new heights the day following when the United States Navy reported that one of its lumbering PBY Catalina flying boats had attacked and bombed successfully another *Kongo* class battleship. The Navy claimed that the battleship was left flaming and stopped dead in the water. The Catalina pilot stated that he felt it was impossible for the warship to remain afloat another 24 hours. The Navy, "cautious" in its claim because no one had actually *seen* the ship go down, listed the vessel as "severely damaged and probably sunk."

The ship under attack was actually the heavy cruiser *Ashigara*, then the flagship of the Japanese Third Fleet operating off Luzon. The vessel's staff officer, Captain Kawakita Ishihara, made it painfully clear that the Catalina had never so much as scratched the paint on the *Ashigara*, let alone leaving it in flames.

As reports of the new "sinking" came in, Americans mushroomed Kelly's exploit to fantastic proportions. Most people believed then, as they still do today, that Kelly had made a suicide dive into the "battleship." The exact origin of this fable is difficult to place, but it might well have stemmed from the death of Lieutenant Marret, the pilot whose P-35 fighter was destroyed by the exploding Japanese transport earlier that day.

Marret's death was not announced in the United States until December 20, when details were released to the effect that Marret had *deliberately flown into the side of the enemy vessel*. This was not the case, of course, but people at home were desperate to believe anything that reflected courage, sacrifice, and defeat inflicted upon the Japanese. Lieutenant Marret had exhibited the highest courage when he flew his old fighter plane, without self-sealing tanks, directly into the flashing gun muzzles of the Japanese. He gave up his life in combat for his country. It is regrettable, therefore, that he was erroneously reported as having made a "suicide dive."

In the confusion that reigned in those early weeks of war and defeat, it is readily understandable that the public fused the meager details of the deaths of Colin Kelly and Sam Marret. For Marret was at the time the only pilot specifically reported as having sacrificed himself in a suicide crash. This appears to be the source of the legend of Kelly's suicide dive.

Kelly's death came from attack by Zero fighters. Early on the morning of December 10, 27 Zeros left their Tainan base on Formosa for a mission to cover the Philippines invasion. The fighters circled Clark Field, found no worthwhile targets remaining at the shattered American base, and swung over the coast to fly cover for the Vigan invasion force.

The fighters circled slowly at 18,000 feet when several pilots noticed three large water rings on the ocean surface —the marks of bomb explosions. From their height the Japanese pilots failed to see water geysers or columns, but the rings were unmistakable. The Japanese were astounded. The enemy had attacked and not a single Zero pilot had sighted a bomber! When finally the Fortress was seen it was far off, several thousand feet above the fighters and fleeing at high speed.

Three Zeros remained as invasion fleet cover, while two dozen fighters raced at full throttle after the American bomber. Among the pilots was Saburo Sakai; he and several other pilots drew within firing range of the Fortress when the bomber was about 60 miles from Clark Field. Suddenly, three Zeros (from the Kaohsiung Wing which earlier that day had destroyed Nichols Field) sped against the American plane in a head-on attack, but without noticeable effect.

Seven fighters of the Tainan Wing, including Sakai's plane, then rushed at the Fortress. Each pilot peeled off from a loose formation and made a diving firing pass from above and behind. By the time the ten fighters had completed their runs the bomber was almost over Clark Field. The Japanese pilots found it hard to believe what they saw—they had poured bullets and cannon shells into the Fortress, and apparently without effect. By now it should have been flaming wreckage, but the big airplane flew on, seemingly unperturbed by its attackers.

The Fortress slipped into a shallow dive, picking up speed as it raced for safety within a thick overcast. While the other fighters milled around far behind the bomber, Sakai, followed by two Zeros, pushed over into full power dives. Sakai slipped beneath the Fortress and then raced in from underneath and to the rear.

Unknown to the Japanese pilot, the B-17's radioman had left his gun position within the bathtub beneath the Fortress; Sakai's approach went unnoticed by the crew. The Americans' first warning came with the shuddering impact and explosions of bullets and cannon shells within the fuselage. Kelly slammed rudder back and forth to fishtail the big airplane and give his waist gunners a crack at the Japanese fighter, but it was too late. Sakai watched big chunks of metal explode off the right wing, and then a thin white film trailed behind the plane. The Zero bored in, firing short bursts, and then, suddenly, flame licked within the fuselage.

His ammunition exhausted, Sakai rolled away to one side to permit another fighter to close against the target. But the effort was wasted; the big airplane was doomed. The flames spread swiftly and the second Zero pulled up in a steep climb, the pilot half-rolling to watch the diving Fortress.

Sakai followed the burning airplane as it rushed earthward, amazed to see the wings remain on an even keel. Abruptly three dark objects sailed into view—crewmen bailing out, their chutes opening almost immediately. The next moment the burning airplane flashed out of sight within the heavy clouds.

Reports which were later circulated in this country to the effect that the Zero fighters had machine-gunned the parachuting crew members proved no more valid than the claim that a warship believed to be the *Haruna* had been sunk through Kelly's "suicide dive." Only three men went out of the Fortress while it was still above the clouds, and they fell quickly within the rolling gray masses. Sakai was the only Zero pilot near the bomber when the men bailed out, and he had exhausted his ammunition. No Japanese fighter went *beneath* the clouds at this time of the day—as we shall see.

During the morning takeoffs from Clark Field, Lieutenant Colonel Frank Kurtz was present when Colonel Eubank briefed Colin Kelly on his mission. Kurtz remembered Kelly as being unusually tired. His clothes were grimy and grease-stained; apparently he had assisted his crew in preparing the Fortress for flight. He had flown all night to reach Clark Field, and without any interval for rest was preparing for the combat mission. Kurtz was in the Clark Field tower to handle the signal gun lights when the bombers of O'Donnell's 14th Squadron took to the air.

Shortly past twelve noon, Kurtz heard the sudden engine roar of a B-17. From the sound, the bomber was approaching swiftly, perhaps even in a dive. For several seconds, however, Kurtz (a highly skilled Fortress pilot himself) could see nothing above him but the thick overcast.

Suddenly, off in the distance, Kurtz saw the white silk of a parachute blossom into an open canopy, just below the cloud layer. Several more chutes appeared against the dark gray clouds, one after the other.

Then, farther out, a dark object streaked from the clouds and plunged into the ground.

Kurtz did not discover until much later that day that it was Kelly's Fortress that had crashed. This was the only B-17 lost on December 10. (This established beyond question that Sakai was in fact the Zero pilot who set afire Kelly's bomber. Only one Fortress was lost, and only one Japanese pilot claimed a probable kill—and over Clark Field. The pieces slid together neatly.)

More than ten years after the war, Frank Kurtz and Saburo Sakai met in Tokyo, where they conferred on the events that had transpired at Clark Field so many years before. . . .

Now we return to the Flying Fortress immediately after its bombing strike against the Japanese warship. Inside the airplane as it sped from the scene, the gunners remained at their weapons; an attack by fighters could come at any moment.

We know already the details of the firing passes made by the seven fighters of the Tainan Wing and the three Zeros of the Kaohsiung Wing; these did little harm to the Fortress.

The last firing pass was followed by a lull in the battle. The milling Zeros fell far behind the bomber as Kelly approached Clark Field. It was at this moment that the radio operator, who manned the single gun in the bathtub position, left his post. He returned to the radio compartment to receive landing instructions from the Clark Field tower.

And just then Sakai struck from below and to the rear, unnoticed by the bomber crew until he opened fire with his two machine guns and two 20-mm. cannon.

Streams of tracer bullets and exploding cannon shells ripped through the Fortress. The lead and steel raked the Fortress viciously from nose to tail; Sakai was an excellent marksman and made the most of his ammunition. The instrument panel before the two pilots erupted in a deadly spray of shattered glass and metal. Bullets drummed along the thin skin like hail, and the heavy bomber shuddered as the cannon shells gouged big tears in the fuselage and wings. Just above and behind the cockpit the fuselage skin was ripped to twisted shreds, and the gunnery commander's Plexiglas dome shattered, the pieces whipping away in the howling wind. Then a thin film, either smoke or spraying fuel, leaped into existence from the right wing.

The Zero fighter closed in to pointblank range. Again the staccato, hammering bursts ripped into the fuselage and, at the left waist gun position, Tech Sergeant William J. Delehanty spun wildly away from his machine gun. Blood pulsed darkly from his body, draining his life swiftly from multiple wounds. A booming explosion tore through the bomber. A cannon shell had exploded the low-pressure oxygen tanks in the radio compartment; within moments the empty bomb bay was the scene of crackling flames.

Sheets of fire spread rapidly from the ruptured oxygen tanks. Acrid fumes swirled thickly through the airplane; it might be only seconds before the entire Fortress disappeared in a single flaming blast. Yet they were still under attack; abruptly, the shuddering blows from the Japanese fighter ended.

In the cockpit Colin Kelly had only one choice. He barked out the order on the intercom for the crew to bail out at once. Kelly personally faced a terrible decision. Flames curled and licked about his feet. Unless he blew open the escape hatch above him and got out—at once —he might be caught in the fiery explosion that threatened to engulf the diving Fortress. If that were to happen, he would be roasted in his seat like a moth in a flaming cocoon.

Kelly's decision was made even as he thought about it: the crew was his responsibility. So Kelly and his co-pilot, Lieutenant Donald D. Robins, remained at the controls to hold the airplane in steady flight. Once they abandoned the controls the Fortress might roll onto its back or whip into a spin; the men could easily be trapped.

Quickly the men abandoned their fiery craft. S/Sergeant James E. Hokyard, PFC Robert A. Altman, and PFC William L. Money scrambled out the rear compartment and tumbled through the air. Joe Bean and Meyer Levin popped the escape hatch in the nose and dropped into the sky. Delehanty slumped lifeless in the waist. As the five men leaped clear, Kelly and Robins remained alone in the airplane, as the flames climbed higher around them.

Now they made their move to break free of the blazing, winged coffin in which they rushed earthward. Choking smoke and fumes billowed thickly into the cockpit, stinging their eyes and tearing at their throats. The big airplane beneath their hands was a dying and flaming cripple. Chunks of metal broke loose and flipped crazily behind the Fortress, the sputum of flames and battle damage. There rose a shrieking keen above the roar of the engines as the wind plucked greedily at torn and jagged metal. The controls were a shambles, and the once-responsive machine answered their demands strangely. Farther aft, the .50-caliber machine guns banged wildly as they flopped around on their abandoned mounts.

In the brief seconds during which the bomber plunged into the overcast, Kelly and Robins began their fight to live. They released the cockpit escape hatch and began to clamber upward from their seats. They never completed the attempt.

The fearful explosion came without warning; a terrific blast shattered the interior of the bomber and smashed the great airplane out of control. Robins remembers nothing but the sudden, shattering blast which hurled his helpless body clear of the flaming, plummeting Fortress. He had barely enough time as he fell through the air to yank desperately on the D-ring of his parachute. The silk blossomed out and snapped tight, jerking Robins to a halt in his harness.

But what of Kelly? It appears that he, too, cleared the airplane; most likely the funneling blast upward into the cockpit flung him away from the exploding airplane. What happened next will never be known.

Colin Kelly's parachute did not open. Perhaps the explosion stunned him, or hammered him unconscious, and he never made the attempt to jerk open his parachute. Perhaps, if this is so, he fell unconscious to his death. Or perhaps there was no time, and his body struck the ground with lethal impact before he could release the silken angel in its pack.

The body of Colin Kelly, with his parachute unopened, was found near the wreckage of his Flying Fortress.

On December 20, 1941, the Far Eastern Command announced awards of the Distinguished Service Cross to 13 officers and enlisted men.

Three of those awards were made posthumously.

One of them was for Colin P. Kelly, Jr.

He had sacrificed his life so that other men might live. And there is no legend in that.

The missions of December 10 were the last to be flown from Clark Field. So shattered was the air base that it could no longer be used even for staging bombers through on flights. Our fighters could not promise even a faint shadow of protection from Japanese air attacks, and without fighters, the bombers could not long survive.

The sighting of Japanese convoys sliding up the coasts of Luzon—at Zambales on the west and at Legaspi on the southeast—brought the Flying Fortresses quickly into the battle. Six B-17s operated out of Del Monte. On December 12 they flew two bombing missions against the Japanese forces at Vigan, planning to strike two days later at Legaspi.

On the first mission one Fortress failed to clear the runway when a tire exploded during the takeoff roll; the pilot managed to save the airplane and brought it back to the taxiway. Two others made it off the ground, but returned to the field because of serious engine trouble. The three other bombers hit the invasion fleet and ran for safety, but not before Zero fighters snared one of the Fortresses. They shot the B-17 to ribbons, blew into junk two of its four engines, but failed to keep the plane from crashlanding under control at Masbate. The crew— all of them miraculously still alive—scrambled from their bomber as Zeros strafed steadily and exploded the bomber in flames.

A Distinguished Service Cross went to Lieutenant Hewitt T. Wheless on this day. For 30 minutes a swarm of 18 Zero fighters snarled and chewed up his Fortress; the anger of the Japanese pilots at their own failure to down the big bomber seemed evident as they pressed their attacks to the point of almost ramming the airplane. Despite their failure to shoot the plane out of the skies, they shredded it so badly that they killed one gunner, wounded the other three, shot out one engine, destroyed the radio system, blew away the tail wheel, and sliced off seven out of 11 control cables. There was an estimated total of a thousand holes in the Fortress. Despite the severe damage, Wheless fought his plane out of the sky, and eased to a successful crashlanding in near-darkness in a small, barricaded field near Cagayan, Mindanao.

By December 14 Japanese formations of more than a hundred bombers and fighters picked remaining targets in the Philippines at their leisure, destroying their objectives in methodical fashion. The Fortresses were ordered out of the Philippines to new permanent bases in Australia. For a brief time they staged northward on long, exhausting flights to strike Japanese invasion forces in the Philippines. The missions were extremely hazardous, with the number of Japanese fighters seeming to grow every day, and the results achieved on the long-range strikes were judged as negligible.

The bombers—by order—abandoned their bases in the Philippines. Unhappily, the fighters were doing little better to stave off defeat.

9

LAST-DITCH STAND—
THE FIGHTERS

The weather, which had so disastrously worked against the American fighter forces on the opening day of the war in the Philippines, came to their aid on the second day. Except for a night raid with a small bomber force against Nichols Field, the Japanese were unable to utilize their strong airpower forces against the stunned American units on Luzon. Four P-40s that took off to intercept the enemy in the night attack failed to sight their quarry; the Japanese released their bombs, killed and wounded 18 men, destroyed a hangar and damaged several planes, then flew back to hazardous landings in storms at Formosa.

The Japanese managed, despite the torrential downpours, to get several dozen Zero fighters into the air. Unknown to the Americans on Luzon, the Zero formations actually reached the Philippines. Unnoticed from the ground, the Japanese pilots fought their way through storms, but could not press home any attacks. On the return flight to Formosa, the fury of the storms increased and broke up the big Zero formations. The Japanese pilots split up into V formations of three fighters each, scattered well apart, and dove for the ocean surface, racing over the wind-whipped waves at 50 to 100 feet in order to stay below the thick clouds. Several Zero fighters made emergency landings on isolated islands.

December 10, of course, precipitated heavy action on the part of both the Americans and the Japanese. In addition to the attacks made against Japanese transports and invasion forces, other fighters struggled desperately to halt the marauding attacks of the heavy Japanese formations. The morning of December 10 had been filled with escort missions and strafing attacks; the afternoon proved to be another of those helpless and infuriating days with the Zero fighters asserting their lethal superiority.

The Japanese struck in their first afternoon raid with a force of 27 bombers and approximately 100 fighters. (Many official reports claiming an escort of 150 Zero fighters are in error; the Japanese did not even have that number of Zero fighters available for missions into the Philippines from the Formosa bases.)

Fighters of the 17th, 21st, and 34th Pursuit Squadrons took off in force to intercept the Japanese, but found themselves blocked at almost every turn by the precision maneuvers of the Zero pilots. The official records of the interception state resignedly that our planes "were overwhelmed in their attempts to break up the enemy's bomber formations."

The experiences of the different fighter squadrons were unhappily similar. Ten P-40s of the 17th Squadron rushed in to attack a group of bombers protected by an estimated 40 Zeros, and the American pilots never were able to crack the aerial defenses. Every time the P-40s rushed in, "enemy fighters thwarted almost every effort," and the bombers continued on their way, unmolested, and methodical in their bombing attacks. During the engagement only *two* American pilots—Lieutenants Joseph H. Moore and William A. Sheppard—ever got near the Japanese bombers, and their penetrations proved ineffectual when Zeros cut them away from their targets.

Three P-40s went down from the ten airborne fighters of the 17th Squadron, without loss or even "apparent damage" to the enemy.

By the evening of December 10, the American fighter defense of the Philippines was considered to have had its back thoroughly broken. The Interceptor Command could count a total of 22 P-40 and eight P-35 fighters for the entire Philippines; a number of Boeing P-26 fighters were not even included in this count, and were regarded simply as "virtually useless."

General MacArthur's headquarters made the interpretation of fighter defense official when the orders came through that the remaining fighter planes were no longer to engage in interception or pursuit of enemy aircraft, no matter what the occasion. All fighters henceforth would be used for reconnaissance only. Thus by the 10th of

On December 13, 1941, Captain Jesus Villamor of the
Philippines led five other pilots in ancient P-26 fighters
against a Japanese force of more than 50 bombers . . .
an ineffective but nonetheless courageous attack.

December the Japanese had accomplished their primary
mission—eliminated *effective* American airpower from
the scene. The bombers had been pulled back to the Del
Monte Field on Mindanao, and the fighters were being
restricted officially to reconnaissance flights. This urge to
preserve the little airpower that was left gave the Japanese
a grateful respite—their landing operations could now
continue at leisure and without interference from the
Americans.

During December 12 and 13, Japanese formations of
more than one hundred fighters and bombers systematically destroyed whatever targets they could find in the
Philippines. They smashed ground facilities at Clark Field,
Batangas, Olongapo, Nielson, and Nichols Fields.

Both American and Filipino pilots found it impossible
to follow strictly the orders that forbade them to close

with the Japanese, and American fighters at various times struck at the enemy formations. On December 13, in a move of incredible courage, Captain Jesus Villamor dove with full throttle against a Japanese formation of more than 50 bombers. What made the interception incredible was that Villamor was at the head of six ancient P-26 fighters! The Filipino pilots in their museum fighter planes failed to down any Japanese planes, but they gnawed and worried so effectively that they minimized damage to the Filipino airfield at Batangas.

No man inflamed the spirit of the Americans more than Lieutenant Boyd D. (Buzz) Wagner, who proved a genius at the controls of his P-40 fighter, a man of extraordinary courage against superior odds, and "one hell of a fighter" in the eyes of his compatriots. Wagner commanded the 17th Pursuit Squadron, and on December 13 he flew a solo reconnaissance mission to Aparri. The lack of detailed records and the years intervening have clouded some of the pertinent moments of action that day, but there is no question of the effectiveness of Buzz Wagner.

He descended through heavy clouds over the invasion area at Aparri, and managed to break out of the clouds almost directly over two Japanese destroyers—which immediately opened fire with a heavy barrage. Wagner dove for the sea and ran from the destroyers on the deck at high speed.

He turned back in a wide circle for Aparri, and discovered that he had attracted the personal attention of two Japanese fighters. Immediately Wagner swung into a hard climbing turn directly into the sun. It would appear that the Japanese pilots concluded that Wagner was running for home; they turned and flew back to their own forces.

Wagner had other ideas. His P-40 came around swiftly and dropped down in the high-speed attack for which the P-40 was to become so well known. Before the Mitsubishi pilots knew just what had happened, Wagner had cut both fighters to ribbons and exploded their fuel tanks. Even as the enemy planes tumbled and flipped toward the sea, Wagner was into a strafing run over the Japanese planes that had moved into the Aparri airfield. He completed two strafing passes when three more fighters bounced him from above and behind.

Once again Wagner proved his mastery with the P-40

—two more Japanese fighters went down in flames. Buzz Wagner flew home very satisfied with his work for the day—four Japanese fighters shot down and three to five more fighters burning on the ground from his strafing runs.

Three days later, Wagner and two other pilots—Lieutenants Church and Strauss—took off for a dive-bombing and strafing attack against Japanese fighters and bombers at Vigan airfield. Remembering the fighters that had bounced him over Aparri several days before, Wagner ordered Strauss to remain on cover patrol, while he and Church started into their bombing runs. Church's fighter took several direct hits from heavy enemy flak, and burst into flames. Church remained in the dive, released his bombs and fired his guns in a blazing pass across the field —and went into the ground in a long, flaming streamer.

Wagner continued his attack, releasing his 30-pound fragmentation bombs with accuracy. Before ending five bombing and strafing passes, he had set several planes afire, ignited a fuel dump, and raised general havoc at the field. He was awarded the Distinguished Service Cross.

Several days later Wagner downed his fifth enemy plane to become the first American ace of World War II.

The rare events of isolated victory in the air against the Japanese began to fade away almost entirely, and by December 23 the beginning of the end hove clearly into sight. A major Japanese invasion force struck at San Miguel Bay in southern Luzon. The 24th Pursuit Group threw every available plane into the action to slow down the Japanese, but the entire force amounted to only 12 P-40 and six P-35 fighters. Armorers loaded the airplanes with 30-pound fragmentation bombs which, effective though they were against troops, could hardly create serious damage to the transports and warships. The fighters struck with fury and managed to disrupt part of the invasion; nevertheless, the Japanese shrugged off the attacks and kept pouring ashore. Miraculously none of the American fighters went down before the vicious antiaircraft fire, although two P-35s were so badly damaged the pilots barely managed to crashland their planes.

Before two weeks passed, the Japanese locked their grip even more tightly on the Philippines. They poured fighters and tactical bombers into three separate airfields, and increased the weight of their attacks. The dive bombers especially tore apart what few airfield installations remained for the Americans and the Filipinos.

There is one invaluable document of that air fighting that provides an intimate and rare glimpse of what the events were like. Lieutenant David L. Obert, a flight leader in the 17th Squadron, 24th Pursuit Group, kept a diary of fighter operations. This is the story of how our fighter pilots fought their first campaign in World War II:

"By the fourth day of the war [December 12, local time, in the Philippines], the 24th Group, except for a few daily reconnaissance flights, had ceased operations and was attempting to reorganize. The 3rd Squadron, without aircraft, was sent south of Manila to supervise construction of a landing strip. The 21st was sent to the Hermosa vicinity to prepare a similar strip. The 34th was left at Del Carmen, and the remaining pilots of the 17th and 20th were pooled at Clark Field to fly away what remained of the P-40s.

"About noon December 24, air force personnel in the Manila area were ordered to embark at the port within six hours for Bataan Peninsula. The 17th Squadron, of which I was acting commanding officer, was ordered to set up servicing facilities at Pilar airstrip, under construction at Bataan.

"We decided to proceed to Bataan by truck. Air headquarters at Fort McKinley had disappeared by this time, and all units were pretty much on their own. Everyone was scurrying around collecting personal equipment and burning papers. At Nichols Field, the engineers were beginning to set fire to the gasoline stores and were placing demolition charges in the concrete runway. At 1900 hours [7 P.M.], the last of the 17th Squadron pulled away from Nichols Field, which was blazing and being shaken every few moments by explosions. We found several extra trucks, abandoned by units departing by boat, and loaded them with food and clothing from the quartermaster warehouses.

"Christmas morning our convoy started for Bataan. For two hours there was little traffic, but as we turned on the road leading from San Fernando to Bataan, we ran into an unbroken stream of trucks and cars. The

Japanese by destroying a few bridges or strafing along the highway could have completely disrupted the road movement.

"Pilar was really a dust strip over what a few days earlier had been rice paddies. The 20th, 34th and 3rd Squadrons went to campsites in the northern part of Bataan—to Mariveles, where the highway had been widened into an airstrip, to Cabcaben, another rice paddy airfield, and to Bataan Field, three miles north of Cabcaben.

"The 21st Squadron flew its planes from Lubao into Pilar Field December 29. During this movement Lieutenant Wyott of the 17th Squadron, flying a P-35, was shot down and killed by friendly antiaircraft. All the remaining fighters on Luzon now were located on Bataan and Pilar airfields. Two officers of the 17th Squadron, Lieutenant Majors and Lieutenant Charles Paige, assigned liaison duties with an antiaircraft unit in an attempt to prevent fire at friendly planes, were killed by the muzzle burst from an antiaircraft gun.

"We were told January 3 that a last fighter mission from Luzon would be flown, to bolster the morale of troops, and then all planes would be evacuated to Mindanao. We had nine P-40s left at Pilar, and nine at Bataan. Led by Lieutenant Edward Dyess, the planes would assemble over Del Carmen at 1100 hours January 4, go up to 20,000 feet, shoot down an entire formation of attacking bombers, then land, immediately refuel and take off for Del Monte, 520 miles to the south.

"The nine Pilar pilots circled Del Carmen for an hour January 4, then returned to find that the mission had been cancelled. At Pilar, they immediately refueled and took off for Del Monte, only to become separated by bad weather.

"I landed at Del Monte with the help of automobile lights and a dim line of runway lights. Four of the other pilots had preceded me there, and a fifth had landed his P-40 in a pineapple field near by. Lieutenant Wilcox crashed on Bohol Island and was killed. Lieutenant Cole landed on a barricaded airfield on Negros, was seriously injured, but later made his way to Del Monte by boat.

"At Del Monte, no one knew we were coming or why. We were received as outcasts. Brigadier General Sharp, who commanded the ground forces, went out of his way to be antagonistic, and Major Elsmore, the senior air officer, treated us more as truant schoolboys than as combat pilots.

"We spent the next fourteen days at Del Monte working on our planes and taking turns flying reconnaissance missions.

"General MacArthur's headquarters on Corregidor radioed January 18: 'Send four P-40s back to Bataan immediately.' General Sharp was shocked and we, the pilots, were shocked. The general was losing his, until now, seemingly unwelcome air force, and we were going on what seemed to be an uncalled-for, foolish mission. Our guess was, 'Bataan is falling and some Air Force brass hats want to get away.' There were now eight pilots available. We drew cards: Lieutenant Woolery, Lieutenant Ibold, Lieutenant Benson and I won the assignment from which everyone agreed there was no return. Actually, they were almost right. I was the only one to return, months later.

"We started back January 19. We were out over water when Benson's engine quit. He had ridden two planes safely into the water; but this time because of the solid overcast below him, he bailed out. Low on gas near Mindoro, we buzzed San José airfield and were surprised to see American troops come running out. A Lieutenant Baggett met us and said his detachment of sixty men had been out of touch with the rest of the world since early in the war when they had proceeded to Mindoro by boat on orders from some Air Force colonel.

"At Bataan, Colonel George, now the Air Force commander in the Philippines, said he did not ask for us and did not know we were coming until we were on our way. The Air Force there, by January 20, had all but disappeared except for the nine P-40 pilots forming the Bataan Field Flying Detachment. The field itself was a perfect example of what can be accomplished by painstaking camouflage and aircraft revetment. Although it was often bombed and strafed, no planes were damaged on the ground by enemy action.

"From January 4 to January 20, the Bataan planes made numerous reconnaissance flights. On January 20, Lieutenant Marshall J. Anderson bailed out of his damaged plane and the Japanese pilots began to shoot at him in the air, causing his parachute to collapse several thousand feet above the ground. We had our first taste of this Japanese tactic on the first day of the war, when Lieutenant George Elstrom of the 3rd Squadron was shot and killed after bailing out.

"All of the Bataan pilots were picked men, and Colonel George told us we could quit flying whenever we wished. Food was becoming very scarce. Everyone went around feeling hungry most of the time. Three of us flew to Mindoro February 3 to check a report that the Japs had captured Waterous Field, near San José. Finding no sign of enemy activity, Lieutenant Woolery, Lieutenant Hall and I landed at San José and had breakfast with Lieutenant Baggett. We each loaded a 100-pound sack of sugar into our P-40s to ferry back to Bataan, and since Woolery and Hall still had their bombs, they decided to bomb the Japs on the Bataan front line, on the way back, while I provided protection from enemy fighters.

"Over Manila, they started to dive for an attack. I took my eyes off them for a second to look for possible enemy fighters. When I looked back, I saw nothing at first, and then, off to one side, a large mid-air explosion. Woolery and Hall were never seen again, two of the best pilots in the Philippines. Lieutenant Woolery had received no decorations or awards, although few persons were more entitled to them. (Later awarded, posthumously, the Distinguished Flying Cross.)

"On the afternoon of February 3, while I was still bewildered from the events of the morning, General George said some pilot who knew the way to Mindanao would have to make an urgent courier flight to Del Monte. Lieutenant Earl Stone and I were the only two who had flown that mission, so again the cards were brought out. I drew first and won the ace of spades. General George told me, 'If you succeed, your mission will be of more value than if you shot down twenty bombers.'

"At Del Monte, General Sharp barked, 'What are you doing here? Did you steal one of the P-40s from Bataan and run away?' I fumbled in my cockpit and brought out the written orders, and after a few more questions, left hoping that the Japs would come over and give the general in his underground office a good bombing.

"On the return flight, I was given a sealed bag and told that it contained Allied codes, for Corregidor. 'If anything should happen that you can't get through, eat or destroy every bit of the contents,' the officer said. It would have made quite a large meal.

"I stopped overnight at Cebu and loaded up with Cognac, chocolate and candy from the quartermaster. There was a detachment of Filipino cadets at Cebu with three planes—two PT-13s with two wing-mounted .30 caliber machine guns, and a P-12 without guns. My return in the heavily overloaded P-40 marked the first of many resupply flights from the southern islands to Bataan—the maiden voyage of the much-famed 'Bamboo Fleet.'

"Big guns from the Cavite shore had been making life miserable on Corregidor. Jesus Villamor, a Filipino captain, went up in an old Filipino trainer to photograph the gun positions, and four of us went along in P-40s as escort. Eight Japanese fighters attacked. We shot down six of them; one P-40, piloted by Lieutenant Stone, was lost.

"The P-40s made a number of flights to drop supplies and ammunition to an isolated force northeast of Baguio. One day Corregidor ordered two P-40s to go out and search south and west of Corregidor for submerged friendly submarines. This seemed sort of a foolish mission, but General George said run it, he didn't know how we were going to find submerged submarines, much less identify them as friendly. We searched for two hours without finding any submerged friendly submarines.

"Late in February the 21st Squadron was withdrawn from its infantry role and placed at Bataan Field, and the 20th Squadron was placed at newly completed Marinoles Field. The 17th and 34th were left on the beaches as infantry.

"We flew reconaissance, interception, resupply, dive-bombing, and leaflet dropping missions to Luzon cities. By the end of February, we were getting only two meals a day. Everyone was weak and starved, and many had malaria. But rumor had it that P-38s and P-39s were on the way.

"In mid-March, Captain Dyess led the six remaining P-40s on a highly successful attack against shipping in Subic Bay. One plane, piloted by Lieutenant Crelle, was lost, and three cracked up on landing. This mission was flown without the approval of Corregidor headquarters, which became extremely unhappy over the loss of four planes until it was learned that several ships were sunk. Then all was forgiven.

"General George bade us all goodby one afternoon, and we later learned he had gone with General MacArthur to Australia. We felt like orphans after he left, but everyone said, 'He knows what we're up against. He will send help soon.'

"Lieutenant Hughes, Lieutenant White, and several mechanics of the 20th Squadron raised a Navy 'duck'— an amphibian plane—from the water near Mariveles, where it had been sunk early in the war, and after days of work, finally had it in operating condition. They figured on using it to escape if Bataan should fall. When the time came, however, they were left to the Japanese while higher ranking officers escaped in their plane.

"Several pilots escaped from Bataan at the last minute. Lieutenant Donaldson flew to Panay and crash-landed his P-40. Captain Lunde and Lieutenant Keator headed for Cebu in a P-35 and made a water landing near Samar. Lieutenant Raymond Gehrig and Captain Randolph escaped to Corregidor at night in PT-13s and later flew to Del Monte. Someone at Corregidor said they had taken off without permission, so they were both ordered to return to Corregidor the following night. Although it was thought to be an impossible flight, they made their way back to Corregidor and landed on a very short, narrow runway without lights. In a stormy session, they finally proved they had been ordered to make the previous flight by the ranking air force officer on Corregidor, so they were permitted to take off again for Del Monte, each with an important passenger and important records. The Japanese by that time had captured the intermediate refueling point at Santa Barbara, so the men had to land when they ran out of fuel, and finish their journey by boat.

"On April 12, four of us were ordered to destroy all fighters on the ground at Davao Airfield. We found only three Jap planes there, but destroyed them. On April 13, our P-40s covered the landings and takeoffs of B-25s which had arrived from Australia for a hit-run raid. It was the last fighter mission ordered by the 24th Pursuit Group. Lieutenant Burns was killed on takeoff.

"The bombers went back to Australia that night, and all of the men participating were decorated at Melbourne, some with the Silver Star. The fighter pilots, who felt that they had flown much more dangerous and difficult missions than the bombers on those two days, received no recognition. The crowning blow was that the bombers received credit for destroying the three airplanes knocked out by the P-40s at Davao.

"A few days later, Corregidor ordered a plane at Del Monte returned to Corregidor. All pilots physically able to fly cut cards for their mission back to what was almost certain capture, at best. Captain Bill Bradford, who had been flying the plane regularly between Del Monte and Bataan, drew the low card. Everyone later thought that he had stacked the cards and drew the low one purposely, because he was the most likely one to complete the flight successfully. He reached Corregidor, but crashed on takeoff to return to Del Monte.

"On April 23, a B-24 arrived at Del Monte. General George evidently had sent it, because at the top of the list of personnel to be returned to Australia were the names of the survivors of his Bataan Field Flying Detachment. In Australia, we joined the air force organization being taken over by General George. His death in an airplane accident a few days later was the saddest incident of the war for the pilots who had flown for him and who had been so close to him on Bataan.

"One point deeply impressed by the air war in the Philippines: Complete air superiority is extremely difficult if not impossible to achieve. Under the most adverse conditions and in the face of almost unlimited numbers of enemy aircraft, remnants of the 24th Fighter Group were able to operate on a limited scale and present a threat to the enemy almost indefinitely."[1]

The Americans in the Philippines were to fight to the last airplane and the last pilot. Scattered bombing missions sank some Japanese ships and damaged perhaps several dozen. Fighter missions carried out with the rapidly shrinking force of P-40s and a few P-35s contributed to the damage of invasion forces. But against the mass of Japanese military power, these were little more than gnat bites in the hide of a lumbering elephant.

The Philippines fell before the onrushing tide.

. . . . . .

10

THE TIGERS

There are few combat organizations that fought a war
with such devastating one-sided effect as the American
Volunteer Group—the Flying Tigers—and about which
there are so many misconceptions. The author has yet to
meet one person, be he average citizen or a man who
has worn the Air Force blue and has been a fighter pilot
for some 20 years or more, who knew *when* the Flying
Tigers embarked on their spectacular combat career.

With rare exception, the belief is held that the Flying
Tigers were locked in mortal combat with the Japanese for
a long time (usually estimated at "several years") prior
to the attack against Pearl Harbor and our entry into the
war. People are convinced that the AVG long constituted
the only bulwark of the United States against the Japanese, showing the American flag during a time when our
country was doing its best to stay *out* of war.

The truth is that the Flying Tigers fought their first
battle—a smashing victory—against a Japanese force attacking Kunming, China, on December 20, 1941, (13 days
after the strike against Oahu). Three days later the AVG's
P-40B Tomahawks flying out of Mingaladon, Burma, with
the Royal Air Force dove into a formation of Japanese
bombers raiding Rangoon, the Burmese capital. With those
two battles, each over a different nation but against the
same enemy, the American Volunteer Group was launched
on its brief but spectacular career.

The sporadic and largely inadequate reporting of combat events in China that reached the outside world lent
itself to the creation of certain "facts" contrary to the
true course of events. Thus there arose the conviction
that when the Tigers fought for China and devastated
their opposition, the Chinese for the first time were to

know the pleasures of one-sided victories in the air against the Japanese. While the record of the Tigers requires nothing in the way of excuses or explanations, it is simply not true that they were the first to create massive aerial victories in Chinese skies—as our preceding pages have established with specific incidents and facts.

Let us review the chain of events that brought the Flying Tigers into existence. . . .

The United States since early 1941 had evinced the closest interest in the requirements for military air operations in China; the sale for years of American aircraft to the Chinese government had certainly been carried out with the tacit consent of the Roosevelt administration. Lauchlin Currie, in the first months of 1941, was traveling throughout China as an adviser to President Franklin D. Roosevelt, accumulating much information on the economic requirements of China, and estimating its needs, in terms of American aid, for continuing to resist the military pressure of Japan. In the spring of 1941, Brigadier General Henry B. Clagett received orders to transfer from the Philippines to China, to function as an Army Air Corps representative who would determine military air requirements of the Chinese; Clagett was also to evaluate the true potentialities of major military air operations in China for containing the powerful Japanese air units operating in that country. American aid to China was already substantial, and the Burma Road was covered with an increasing number of American trucks and supplies. But the crying need of the battered Chinese nation was for the aircraft and the machinery that would establish a true airpower force that could achieve a steady success against the Japanese.

The needs of China, as finally recognized by the United States government, could hardly have come at a more inauspicious time. We were striving to build up our own Army and Navy air elements. Russia staggered before the massive assault of German armies, and American planes were needed desperately to stem the tidal wave of the victorious Wehrmacht. The British had flooded the American aircraft industry with huge backlog orders for fighters, bombers, transports, trainers, and other aircraft types.

Yet China—in terms of our own interests—could not be denied. The United States government concluded an arrangement wherein we agreed to provide China with

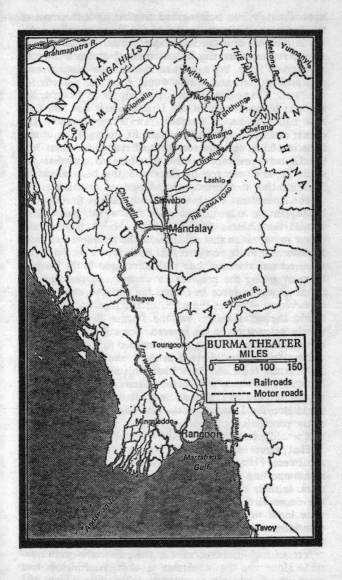

BURMA THEATER
MILES
0   50   100   150
——————— Railroads
------- Motor roads

approximately 300 training and combat aircraft (most of which were considered outmoded for the needs of the Army Air Forces and the Royal Air Force), as well as the means for transforming this numerical strength into an operational force. We agreed further to train pilots, crews, and ground personnel which would form the nucleus for the "new" Chinese Air Force. By October 1, 1941, training was to commence in the United States for 500 Chinese fighter pilots, 25 bomber crews (approximately 125 men), and 25 specialists in armament and radio. In direct support of this new program, Brigadier General John Magruder led a military mission to China to complete the study of airpower requirements and the best means of implementing the forthcoming American assistance.

The agreements concluded by both nations thus created a program on a long-range basis that would, specifically, rebuild the Chinese Air Force into a fairly modern airpower organization that could make the Japanese pay careful attention to its new strength. Such programs, however, require much time for their realization, and in the interval between getting the program under way and realizing the actual airpower force in China, the Chinese cities would be naked to attack at the whim of the Japanese. Not only would the cities suffer, but the Burma Road and vital supply arteries could be severed. Something in the way of an interim airpower force was needed to fill the gap.

That "something" arrived in the United States early in 1941 in the form of Claire Chennault and General P. T. Mow of the Chinese Air Force; Chennault and Mow came to this country to create an immediate organization that could stop the Japanese in the air. The long and short of many proposals and counterproposals was an agreement that would create the American Volunteer Group.

That agreement called for volunteer pilots—from the Air Force, Navy, and Marines—as well as ground crews and supporting personnel who also would serve as volunteers. Initially there was anything but a stampede to join the cause advanced by Chennault; the American pilots were loath to risk losing their commissioned status and especially seniority toward higher rank. Not even the attractions of combat flying and the financial rewards could overcome such disadvantages to the pilots who were queried. However, the confirmation that Washington had given its official—albeit under-the-table—blessings to the program persuaded many of the men to sign up with Chennault.

By early summer of 1941, Chennault had the signatures of the 100 pilots he required, as well as approximately 200 other men who would function to support the flight operations. Early in July the advance elements were on their way to China.

The manpower problem had been solved, but fighter airplanes were another—and vexing—matter. No one seemed willing to part with 100 modern fighters, especially in view of the combat situation with Germany. Finally the planes were acquired; 100 Curtiss P-40B Tomahawks, disdained by the British for fighting in Europe against German planes because of the Tomahawks' inferior performance, had been assigned to Sweden. The Swedish order was canceled, and Headquarters AAF officially placed its blessing on giving the order to China—the AAF was already replacing the P-40B with the newer (faster, higher-flying, more powerful, and more heavily armed) P-40E Kittyhawk model. The first contingent of Tomahawks arrived in Rangoon, Burma, barely in time to permit training operations to begin under Chennault's careful guidance. By September, 1941, training was under way.

To whip his volunteer pilots (who included bomber and transport pilots without any fighter experience) into shape, Chennault needed time and help from the British, who provided that assistance willingly. The Royal Air Force, itself sadly lacking in aircraft and manpower, shared with the AVG their Kyedaw training field at Toungoo, Burma, some 175 miles to the north of Rangoon. This gave the AVG a training camp well back of the reach of the Japanese fighters operating against Chinese targets. The AVG in its initial organization went through all the difficulties one might associate with such an endeavor, plus several that seemed particularly made for a difficult operation. Assembling the P-40B fighter planes was a technical nightmare unto itself. Living conditions for the crews were described simply as abominable. Equipment was lacking and spare parts from the very beginning were scarce and always remained that way.

Toungoo, as described by Olga Greenlaw (who kept an official war diary of the American Volunteer Group; her husband, Harvey Greenlaw, was second-in-command in the AVG to Claire Chennault), was filled with "all the bugs God created to fly through the air or crawl on the ground, floors, walls, ceilings, into your food, down your back, up your legs and in your hair—beetles, lice, spiders, flies and fleas, moths, mosquitos, centipedes, bedbugs, ticks and a lot more you never heard of. The place was an entomologist's paradise. . . ."[1]

Kyedaw was raw and primitive. British and native engineers had simply hacked a huge X out of the jungle to serve as two runways. They threw up one hangar and scattered some shacks around it, then began construction of barracks that were both dispersed from one another and removed from the field (and the Japanese bombs that were expected at some time in the near future). Kyedaw came with all the built-in unpleasantries one might imagine—an atmosphere fairly dripping with humidity, hordes of insects and animals, jungle growth, torrential downpours, and unquenchable fields of mud following the heavy rains.

Despite the unpleasant conditions, by November the AVG had a total of 174 pilots and ground personnel, all of them working hard to whip the group into a fighting force. The pilot ranks from the first were cut back from the expected figure—five pilots became disgusted with the primitive living conditions, the heat and the rain, the insects and the rats that chewed the buttons off their clothes at night; they were fed up with the waiting and the lack of flying, and they sullenly bid Chennault farewell and left for the United States. Overcoming its obstacles, the AVG had 20 Tomahawk fighters assembled for training the first pilots, with another ten at the docks. While the planes were ready for training, they were still an unhappy distance away from comprising a fighting force. There were some machine guns available for the airplanes, but not a single bullet for those guns. Getting around Burma and China proved a towering obstacle, which the AVG eased somewhat by borrowing a Beech transport from the Chinese.

The organization of the AVG was clearly defined in terms of its personnel. All the pilots (and ground personnel) were strictly volunteers, without an oath signed to either the nation of China or the American Volunteer Group. They were signed under commercial contracts, without military rank, and it was understood clearly from the beginning that no man could be compelled to remain with the group at any time he felt that he "had had it" and wanted out. Although Chennault established a "dishonorable discharge" from the AVG, events proved that those who walked out couldn't have cared less. It was a discharge of psychological value but little else.

The pilots were divided into Wingmen, Flight Leaders, Element Leaders, Deputy Squadron Leaders, and Squadron Leaders. The pay scale for all elements of the AVG was set up on a graduated basis. The lowliest clerks started the bottom of the ladder with $150 monthly (American dollars). Mechanics' pay increased until $400 per month, the highest for the ground personnel, was reached for line chiefs. The pilots' pay began at $600 monthly for wingmen and $675 monthly for flight leaders, and went up to $750 monthly for squadron leaders. What added incentive to the pay scale was the bonus paid by the Chinese—$500 for every enemy aircraft shot down and *confirmed* as shot down (confirmation coming only with examination of the wreckage on the ground by the Chinese).

Accidents under the operational conditions of the AVG during training were inevitable and, in fact, were rendered more frequent by the need for transition training for many pilots who had to step down from what might have been a four-engine heavy bomber into the cockpit of a fighter known for its tricky handling characteristics. But the P-40B could prove to be a handful even for the experienced fighter pilot.

On September 6, Sandy Sandell cracked up one Tomahawk, but fortunately emerged from the wreckage without injury. Two days later the AVG suffered its first fatality. John Armstrong and Gil Bright collided in midair during a mock dogfight; Bright got out of his smashed airplane and parachuted safely, but Armstrong was killed.

Frank Schiel was mixing it up with other pilots in a practice dogfight when his P-40B whirled into an outside spin. Frantic efforts on Schiel's part to bring the airplane out of its deadly maneuver proved useless, and Schiel barely managed to get out of the spinning fighter. His efforts saved his life at the cost of minor injuries.

Max Hamer was killed in another training accident. Then Pete Atkinson took a Tomahawk up to high altitude to test the fighter in a screaming power dive. At

5,000 feet the tail suddenly ripped off the airplane. At tremendous speed, the fighter tumbled so violently it went through an explosive disintegration, killing Atkinson.

The men struggled with and cursed at their equipment. Radio sets, so vital to coordinated combat tactics, often proved to be defective and, just as often, entirely useless. The suffocating, humid heat rotted tires on the airplanes. Vital thrust bearings were found to be faulty and needing replacement—when replacements were so scarce as to be almost unavailable.

On December 8 (December 7, Pearl Harbor dateline), when Japan ignited the fires of open war throughout the Pacific and Asia, her military forces enjoyed a thorough position of strength on the Asiatic mainland. The Japanese Army occupied the largest cities of China, and maintained a tight grip on the key areas of 11 provinces. Much more to the point, the Japanese controlled some 95 percent of the modern industry of China. Japanese soldiers ruled over one-fourth the Chinese mainland—and controlled the destiny of half the huge Chinese population.

The airpower position of the Chinese, British, and Americans combined could only be described as perilous. The British had assembled (from English, Australian, and New Zealand forces) a total of 255 planes in Malaya and another 29 assigned to Rangoon. The Chinese Air Force was largely destitute, and the AVG was never to have more than 50 to 60 planes at one time ready to fight.

Against this force, with many of its planes obsolescent and the pilots untried in combat, the Japanese arrayed powerful airpower elements. In southern Indo-China alone they spread a total of 600 Army and 200 Navy craft, with the crews well blooded in combat against the Chinese and the Russians. Within 800 miles of Rangoon the Japanese operated from nearly three dozen major airfields and auxiliary strips.

War came to lower Asia with thundering fury. Swarms of Japanese attack bombers, dive bombers, and fighters ripped into Hong Kong the dawn of December 8, 1941. The major airfield at Hong Kong was left a shambles. Even as the field burned, Japanese troops raced against Kowloon, across from Hong Kong on the mainland, and battered the opposition rushed against them; 17 days later Hong Kong was firmly in Japanese hands.

Japanese fighters and bombers from aircraft carriers pounded Singapore on the morning of December 8; as quickly as advance landing fields were secured, Army bombers and fighters took up the campaign to smash British defenses. Everywhere the Japanese struck, they scored stunning victories. They rolled from Thailand into the British Malay States, sliced into the Malay Peninsula to isolate British airfields, and began their steam-roller push toward Singapore itself. Early in December Japanese soldiers burst out of Thailand and knifed into lower Burma—and decided the pattern of battle for the Flying Tigers.

At the request of the British, Chennault assigned the AVG 3rd Pursuit Squadron (Hell's Angels), led by Arvid Olson, Jr., to reinforce the Royal Air Force at Rangoon. Twenty-one P-40B Tomahawks were to assist the Brewster Buffaloes and Hawker Hurricanes of the British forces.

The 1st Squadron (Adam and Eve) and 2nd Squadron (Panda) transferred en masse to Kunming.

On December 15, the Tigers lost another Tomahawk fighter when a pilot crashed into a rice paddy and wiped off the airplane; the pilot escaped without injury.

Still battle had not been joined, and still the Tigers sheared down their operational strength with the inevitable accidents. On December 18, one P-40B nosed in at the end of the runway after a faulty takeoff. Moments later a second fighter plunged into a parked car. Viewing the scene, Chennault snarled, "Christ from Vicksburg!" and stalked off.

Then came December 20, and first blood for the Tigers. Sandy Sandell described it to Olga Greenlaw for the war diary of the AVG:

"Jack Newkirk took off first, and his flight was to protect Kunming from the enemy planes by circling the field at 18,000 feet. My squadron was to act as assault echelon and fly to 15,000 feet, patrol the line from Iliang and Chenkiang and intercept the Japs if they came that way, that is, if they got away from Jack's flight. Well, we were cruising around 16,000 feet seventy-five miles northeast of the field, when we saw ten enemy two-engined bombers, single tail, aluminum construction—and that red sun on the wing tips. There was no mistake, they were the Japs. Two flights of four attacked from beam out of the sun, after overtaking them from the rear; one flight plus two

weavers remained above as reserve. Then our flight split
into pairs, and singly after the first two or three runs,
then we went on with coordinated attacks from all directions, that is, above and below, except dead ahead.

"After fifteen minutes of combat, reserve flight and
weavers came into attack, and the pilots with jammed
guns fell to the rear or turned back to the home base.
Every enemy ship seemed to be smoking badly when we
broke away to the field. At this time, we were about 175
miles southeast of the field. The enemy flew extremely
good formation under heaviest of fire—a shallow V formation. They used the second ship from the left of the V
formation as a decoy, flying about 300 yards ahead and
a little above the squadron. The two end planes were shot
down, and later the second from the right. I saw three go
down for sure but I don't think more than six of them
got back to their base."

Sandell underestimated the Tigers' claw on their first
mission; four of the Japanese bombers got home, leaving
six planes out of the ten as wreckage far below.

All the Tigers came back to their field.

An unexpected loss struck the AVG particularly hard.
China had received several new Curtiss-Wright CW-21
Demon fighters—lithe and lightweight interceptors that
could outclimb even the Japanese Zero. Three AVG pilots
were assigned to ferry the Demons from Toungoo to
Lashio, about 280 miles to the northeast. But the engines
ran badly on the ferry mission, the fuel proved to be
filled with water, and all three pilots had to make forced
landings. One of the pilots was killed when his fighter
exploded on landing.

Three days after the first bloodletting in China skies,
the Hell's Angels squadron in Burma went up with the
British to stop a large Japanese formation of fighters and
bombers. As Olga Greenlaw filed her AVG war-diary report:

"No air raid alarm signal was given at Mingaladon. All
ships were suddenly ordered off airdrome. No information
of enemy prior to take-off was known. Three minutes
after the take-off radio orders were given: 'ENEMY APPROACHING FROM EAST.' No co-operation was given
by anti-aircraft guns—pilots report that it was practically
nil and very inaccurate. Fourteen P-40's and sixteen

Brewsters (R.A.F.) joined the fight. There was no friendly support from nearby airdromes. There were two formations of enemy bombers. The second formation, about twenty-seven ships, was about ten miles behind the first, and about 3,000 feet above. The enemy flew a very close formation—large V of V's. They were attacked by the P-40's and Brewsters before they dropped their bombs. The enemy formation did not change its course or formation until after the bombs were dropped. When individual enemy bombers were shot down, the remaining bombers quickly filled in the key positions by means of fast executed cross-overs. Bombers put out a strong cross-fire from top of turrets, and air was filled with white tracers. The enemy aircraft is camouflaged brown and green on upper surfaces, and a light grayish green on the undersides. The red circles are painted on upper and lower wing tips."

The Tigers shot down six enemy planes (confirmed) in the battle, and the British pilots chopped another four out of the sky. Two of the Tomahawks went down before Japanese guns, but the pilots came home, and that was cause for wild celebration that night. The AVG reports shows that the Brewster Buffaloes were so badly mangled that several crashed on landing.

(Aerial battles such as this particular incident provide nightmares for air-war historians. The AVG records as kept by Olga Greenlaw at AVG headquarters show that two Tomahawks were shot down and that the pilots survived; that the British lost several planes but no pilots. Other records—which much later received official scrutiny and confirmation—show that the AVG lost two Tomahawks *and* their pilots, as well as having two other Tomahawks "demolished." Hank Gilbert and Neil G. Martin were shot down and killed in the battle. Paul Greene was shot down, but survived a bail-out and an attack from Japanese fighters while hanging in his parachute. The records list George McMillan's fighter as being "demolished," but do not state how. The final study of the first fight in Burma shows four Tomahawks shot down and two AVG pilots killed. Most difficult of all to understand is the report at AVG headquarters that shows only that several Brewsters were lost on landing. The Royal Air Force confirmed that they lost five fighters and five pilots killed. Thus the tally for the first engagement with the enemy over Burma comes to ten Japanese planes destroyed for the loss of five British and four American fighters—about as even as you can get.)

In the next Burma conflict, the Tigers sharpened their claws. Twelve shark-nosed Tomahawks dove into the midst of 78 Japanese fighters and bombers. It was Christmas Day, but there was precious little good will for the occasion. Once again, two Tomahawks went down—but only two, and both pilots returned to their home field. Initial reports showed that the Japanese had lost 17 planes; soon afterward, Olson amended the first reports with the following telegram to AVG headquarters:

"ALL PILOTS RETURNED AFTER BATTLE DECEMBER 25 SHOT DOWN TEN FIGHTERS NINE BOMBERS STOP BRITISH ACCOUNTED FOR SIX STOP LIKE SHOOTING DUCKS STOP WOULD PUT ENTIRE JAP FORCE OUT OF COMMISSION WITH GROUP HERE STOP HAVE ELEVEN PLANES LEFT STOP OLSON"

But that was only the beginning for the day. Before Christmas was gone, another Japanese bomber force rushed against Rangoon. For the day, the Japanese hurled 108 fighters and bombers against the city. The Royal Air Force fighters shot down eight Japanese planes for five of their own lost in battle. The Flying Tigers were able to notch 28 Japanese kills on the AVG scorecard—with only two planes shot down and no pilots killed. It was quite a day!

The men of the AGV were a cross representation of the American military services, with the exception that they were under no compulsory discipline. Like pilots everywhere, the majority of these men were dedicated to the cause for which they fought. Some of the pilots unquestionably were in the deal for the money; others found their reward in the heady excitement of wrestling with death in the air. And there were some—only a very few— who should never have come. One pilot, who remains nameless in these pages, was reported by the other men to have run away during a fight. As he fled, two Japanese fighters whipped onto his tail. Immediately one of the AVG pilots bounced the enemy planes, shooting down both. For his pains, the second AVG pilot was himself shot to ribbons. He came very close to being killed in his parachute when the Japanese tried to turn him into chopped meat with their guns as he drifted earthward. The pilot who had "run out" on his mates in the air did not fly combat with them again.

Before the Tigers and the British finally moved out of the Rangoon area (the Tigers went back to China), the city of Rangoon seemed to go entirely mad. Every man who witnessed the activities in the city insists that nothing could really describe what went on. The whites fled as quickly as they could. Indians in Rangoon were somewhat more stoic about the Japanese tidal wave rushing down on the city; they "just up and left, starting the long walk back to their own country," explained one pilot.

City officials released the lepers and the insane, who ran howling and shrieking through the streets and alleys. They rapidly turned the city into a house of horror. Thieves and muggers ran wild. Looters stripped every human corpse of anything they found to their liking. Whole blocks burned fiercely with no attempt to quench the flames. Natives ran amok through the streets, flashing knives and killing on sight anything that moved before their crazed eyes. No one dared to hazard the city at night. The police tried only to survive in the maelstrom of hate and terror that seethed all about them. The Tigers were more than glad to leave *that* behind them. . . .

Along with the smashing victories in the air, and the astonishingly low casualties suffered at the hands of the Japanese, went the sorrowful and inevitable accidents that claimed both planes and lives. Late in December two Tomahawks were lost when the pilots ran out of fuel in a thick overcast, and had to leave their planes. Then one P-40 ran wild on landing, careened out of control and smashed into a car. The crash demolished the airplane and wrecked the car . . . and killed an AVG pilot who had been asleep in the vehicle.

Through it all the aces were coming into being. Charley Older was one of the first to get five Japanese flags painted on the flanks of his shark-nosed fighter. Duke Hedman, in a day to be remembered, sent five enemy aircraft tumbling and flaming from the skies to achieve his coveted ace status in a rush.

The pilots had listened carefully to Chennault's admonitions to fight and run away and live to fight another day—and it showed in the astounding number of kills the pilots continued to mark up on the AVG scoreboard. Frank Lawlor recalled what happened to him on the 18th of January:

"At ten in the morning Rossi and I escorted six Blenheims on a mission from Mingaladon to Tavoy. We flew across the Gulf of Martaban to the opposite shore and turned south until we reached Tavoy. Rossi got lost, so I found myself the only escort of the Blenheims. The Blenheims were going over to evacuate people. Before taking off I was told that if a white cross was on the field, Tavoy was still in British hands. If not, the Japs had it. I looked down and saw no white cross. I looked up and saw six Jap fighters. No sight of the Blenheims. Evidently the Japs didn't see any Blenheims, either, so they concentrated on chasing me all over the sky. I shot one down and then proceeded to prove the theory that he who fights and runs away lives to fight another day."

By January 24th, 35 days after their initial bloodletting, the Tigers had hurt their Japanese enemy where it counted most—in destroyed airplanes and the loss of irreplaceable aircrews. The Tomahawks shot down 62 (confirmed) enemy planes in aerial combat, and added to this toll by destroying another 11 fighters and bombers on the ground in strafing attacks. In this same period the Flying Tigers lost three men killed in battle and another two men due to accidents. In the air, the combat ratio was already better than 20 to one.

Sometimes their Chinese allies acted in a manner that drove the Tigers to distraction. A formation of Tomahawks escorted 18 Russian SB-3 bombers with Chinese crews on a mission to strike Japanese airfields, and during that mission went wild trying to maintain some protection for the Chinese. As AVG headquarters recorded the events of the day in the war diary of the group, the Chinese refused to fly the single large formation that would have aided the Tigers in providing top cover. Instead, the Chinese pilots split up into two formations of nine bombers each, with the first formation leading the stragglers by a distance of a mile. The Tigers didn't know which formation to protect and were torn between covering one formation thoroughly and leaving the other open to a diving attack.

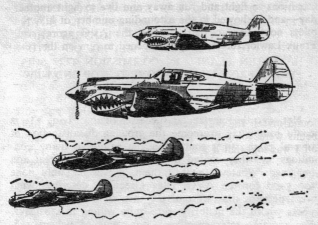

Tomahawks of the AVG escort Chinese
crews flying Russian SB-3 bombers on a mission
against enemy airfields.

After dropping their bombs (through clouds where the
Chinese judged the enemy field *should* be), the leader of
the first Chinese formation swung around in a tight turn
and rammed his throttles forward. Immediately his plane
pulled away from the rest of his formation. The other
pilots, trying to stay with their leader, soon were scattered
haphazardly over the China landscape. The Tigers, running low on fuel, had to run for their own base, leaving
the Chinese to fend for themselves.

A second escort mission several days after the first
exhibition didn't help matters any; it was a repetition
flight. (Later the Chinese *did* work out coordinated maneuvers, and on one particular raid destroyed 30 Japanese
bombers caught on the ground.)

The action in Burma continued apace. Newkirk replaced
Olson in the Rangoon campaign; one of his messages to
Chennault read:

"CHENNAULT: RAID ON 1030 SEVEN HEAVY
BOMBERS AND TWENTY-FIVE FIGHTERS STOP
SEVEN AVG AND TWO HURRICANES AND FOUR

BUFFALOES TOOK OFF STOP ENEMY INTER-
CEPTED STOP ALL ENEMY BOMBERS SHOT DOWN
IN FLAMES AT LEAST TEN FIGHTERS SHOT
DOWN STOP OUR LOSSES ALLIED OO* STOP
HAVE TEN PLANES IN COMMISSION TEN SUF-
FERING FROM LEAD POISONING STOP END NEW-
KIRK."

Not even the spectacular successes of the Flying Tigers
could completely overcome the growing dissatisfaction of
several pilots; they soured on the primitive living conditions and they chafed under grievances both real and
imagined. Whatever rubbed them, it was certainly none
too good for the AVG. Olga Greenlaw describes what
were perhaps the rarest of the men in the AVG—those
pilots whom the majority were quite willing to see leave.
Her remarks refer specifically to events of February 5,
1942:

"Wyke came into my office to show me a special order.
It was a dishonorable discharge for Larry Moore and Ken
Sanger. They couldn't take it. Sanger had been nervous
ever since he came back from Rangoon with Ole's squadron, and afraid he would be sent back there. Ole told me
he couldn't get Sanger to stay on the field or out of the
trenches. Sanger then was sent to Lotze—one of the
stations of the Net—but remained there only a week.
When he returned he told Harvey [Greenlaw] he had
promised Moore's mother he would take good care of
him. Harvey talked to the Colonel [Chennault] about it.
The Colonel shrugged his shoulders and said that it was a
problem, all right, and that it was better to get rid of
them. When the two boys put in their resignations, they
were gladly accepted, but they got dishonorable discharges just the same. Everyone said: 'Good riddance. We
don't want that kind of guys here with us.'

"However, their dishonorable discharges didn't seem to
do them any particular harm. They hastened back to the
States and sold a few hair-raising stories about their exploits with the ferocious Flying Tigers and then penned a
slightly fantastic but still very successful motion picture."

---

*That is, no British or American losses.

The war went on. The day following the incident of the
"dishonorable discharges" the fighter pilots of the AVG
shot down their 100th Japanese plane in the defense of
Rangoon. . . .

There were occasions when members of the AVG were
"treated" to spectacles that left them wondering about
the attitude of the Chinese toward human life—and the
inevitable comparison of how the Chinese and the Japanese sometimes treated those they considered to be their
enemies. One such occasion came about when several
Chinese were caught stealing telephone wire from AVG
buildings, and were sentenced to death *by torture.*

After announcement of the sentence, a shrieking, cack-
ling mob surged into the "death courtyard" to be witness
to the spectacle. It was a scene straight out of a madhouse, and with all the sound effects that one might have
dredged from a nightmare. There were the toothless of
both sexes, the cripples of all ages with their gnarled
limbs and open, running sores; there were the inevitable
children in rags with their lips and chins matted with
mucus; there were beggars, whores, pimps, thieves, and,
intermixed with the crowd, lepers with parts of their faces
and bodies eaten away, all come to shout encouragement
to the executioners and imprecations upon those about to
be mauled to their deaths.

The guards lashed together the wrists of the hapless
prisoners. Their arms were then pulled over their heads;
a stout rope was wound around their wrist bindings, and
at a signal other guards hauled the men off their feet until they dangled well above the ground. The position was
extremely painful, but only preparation for the next step.
Huge boulders were dragged to the scene to the accom-
paniment of clapping and shouts from the crowd. The
boulders were tied to the feet of the prisoners, and then
the men were hoisted up even higher so that the boulders
stretched their bodies. Loud snapping pops testified to
bones being pulled from their sockets; the prisoners
screamed in agony, setting off a reaction of shrieks and
cries from the onlookers.

Four guards appeared with leather and steel whips; the
sight of the torture instruments inflamed the crowd,
which howled with laughter, shrieked obscene comments,
and danced little jigs at the scene before them. Guards
ripped the trousers from the hanging men until they were

fully exposed. Then, methodically and slowly, with just the right amount of pressure to allow the torture to last as long as possible, the guards commenced to whip the prisoners to death.

They were artists at their work as the whips slashed flesh and sprayed blood in crimson showers through the air. They had done their tasks before; this much was evident as the whips curled around the bodies to slice pieces of flesh from the genitalia of the prisoners. After a while white bone was revealed through the gore.

The prisoners remained alive for more than an hour, until the slow dripping of blood into the dust beneath their feet marked the only signs of activity in the courtyard. That, and the vile curses and the sounds of the Chinese spitting on the corpses . . .

This, too, was China.

In the air, the Flying Tigers fought as few other men have fought. As the weeks and months passed, even the rugged Tomahawks began to fail under their constant use and the lack of spare parts and adequate maintenance facilities. Despite these problems, and an increasing number of missions against Japanese ground forces, with the attending heavy ground fire, the Tigers continued to reap their fearsome toll among the Japanese in the air.

With increasing maintenance problems, with the feeling that to a great extent they were the forgotten stepchildren of the United States, condemned to fight with only a trickle of resupplies, the Tigers found their tempers wearing thin. Several men fell out badly among themselves.

Bob Neale (who became the leading ace of the AVG) apparently rubbed Gregory Boyington pretty raw. The "explosion" came when Neale accused Boyington of reporting for night alert duty while he was drunk. Boyington quietly left, drove to the adjutant's office, and immediately turned in his resignation. Greg Boyington thus went on the AVG record books as receiving a dishonorable discharge from the AVG.

Yet this is the same Greg Boyington who had already shot six Japanese planes out of the air, and who was looked upon as a spectacular pilot and a killer in aerial combat. Boyington left the AVG to return to the Marines, where he went on to shoot down another 22 Japanese planes, running his score to 28 confirmed kills—and in the process receiving the Congressional Medal of Honor.

There was also a "little insurrection" among the pilots, which Olga Greenlaw records as being precipitated by orders from Chennault to fly an escort mission for RAF Blenheim bombers which were to attack a Japanese airfield. The AVG pilots balked; they declared they were being sent on a suicide mission. The Blenheims were slow, and often they never showed up on the missions to which the AVG pilots were assigned.

Five pilots from the AVG volunteered for the mission which Chennault had ordered—but 27 of the Flying Tigers said to hell with it, and submitted their resignations en masse, all their signatures penned to a single sheet of paper.

Chennault's reaction was: "If you want to show the white feather, you can all quit!"

His men were enraged at this remark. Fortunately, cooler heads prevailed and there was a meeting of the opposing forces (or the American Volunteer Group might have ended right then and there).

The five volunteers flew the mission—and the British bombers never showed up!

Some time afterward, the condition of the Tomahawk fighters had so deteriorated that even Bob Neale stopped short and refused to fly "suicide missions." He drew the heated anger of Chennault by flatly refusing to take the beaten-up and worn-out Tomahawks on missions of strafing and bombing Japanese troops in the face of murderous antiaircraft fire. Many Chinese commanders insisted upon AVG missions being flown over their areas to bolster the morale of the Chinese soldiers; but, as one AVG pilot remarked acidly, they hadn't come to China—and you didn't win wars—by flying for morale purposes.

Bob Neale stuck fast to his decision, and his men backed him up. They would fly all the defensive—interception—missions that came up, but they would not go out on the "suicidal" ground attack sorties.

As long as he was able to do so, Claire Chennault set up rotating assignments for his men. Kunming, by comparison, was an assignment where a man could catch his breath and shake off the bone-weariness that hugged the pilots flying in Burma; there the men existed under crude and primitive conditions, and their combat missions were frequent and exhausting. Lack of proper food, and jungle-like living quarters, did little to help keep the pilots in the kind of physical and mental shape needed to fight the Japanese fighter pilot in close aerial combat.

The system of rotating assignments also enabled the AVG to work with the Royal Air Force for as long as it was possible to sustain such liaison. In this manner Chennault could help to defend Rangoon (and, in fact, he provided the greater part of its effective aerial strength); he could keep his planes patrolling over a part of the Burma Road, and along the Salween River he could provide a measure of support to the hard-pressed Chinese ground forces.

Through the pilots of the American Volunteer Group, Chennault was able to establish beyond any question the solid validity of his tactics, and to sweep aside the last of the carpers and Doubting Thomases who had been so quick to dismiss Chennault as a man with no real grasp of tactical air situations. Chennault concentrated on the two-fighter element in hit-and-run tactics against the Japanese, and he made his rules for fighting the most effective of their kind in the world.

The P-40B Tomahawk had good speed in level fight. At low altitude it could run with the Zero, although it suffered a performance loss as it climbed (the Allison engines lacked superchargers). Since many of the Japanese fighters encountered by the Flying Tigers were the fixed-gear Claudes and Nates of both the Japanese Navy and Army, the Tomahawks on many occasions proved to be greatly superior in level-fight speed compared to the opposition.

But even against the Zero fighter the Tomahawk was spectacular in a dive. It was this diving speed, and the ruggedness of the P-40B, that enabled Chennault so effectively to utilize his hit-and-run tactics. Many times AVG pilots returned to their home fields with their airplanes shot to ribbons (but still flying), and it took only one glance at a pilot's armor plate, studded with Japanese bullets, to make him swear by his airplane. For without that rugged construction, without the heavy armor, many of the AVG pilots would never have survived their encounters with the agile Japanese fighters.

In maneuverability and in rate of climb, the Japanese fighters took a back seat to no one, and to get into a swirling dogfight with any of the Japanese fighter planes was to beg for disaster—which was invariably delivered.

Thus Chennault hammered into his men over and over again the admonition *not to fight on Japanese terms;* if they used the best advantages of their P-40B fighters by adapting them to specific tactics, they could—and they did—whip the Japanese in the air.

These tactics might not have proven effective on other types of missions—on long-range escort, it is obvious that you cannot whip an attacking enemy by diving out of the battle. But for the situation confronted by Chennault, against the overwhelming odds his men had to face, his tactics were brilliantly vindicated. Chennault's mission was to stop the Japanese—to break up their attacks by slicing into the enemy formations. For this purpose the attack in which a plane struck and dove away, and possibly climbed overhead for a second attack, was effective. His was a defensive mission. On other types of combat—such as long-range escort—the need of the escorting fighter was to stay with the bombers, to be able to maneuver with the enemy and slug it out. The fighter that dove away from an escort mission left the bombers unprotected. This, essentially, was not Chennault's concern.

For a while after the introduction of the AVG to battle, the Japanese made a determined effort specifically to wipe out the American force. And not even the lopsided victories of the AVG in the air could long stem the Japanese steam roller on the ground. Despite the AVG's kill superiority, which *The Army Air Forces in World War II* lists as an "almost incredible number,"[2] the tide of war clearly remained in favor of the Japanese.

By the end of February, Rangoon had become a nightmare of internal disintegration. Early in March the AVG was forced to abandon the city, and the men withdrew to Magwe. The Japanese lost no time in smashing at Magwe, and the AVG retreated once again, this time across the Chinese border to Loiwing. Less than seven weeks later the Burma campaign was almost concluded in terms of Japanese aims and requirements. As Japanese soldiers through the familiar routine of packing up and leaving. poured into and through their opposition, the AVG went Finally they were forced to make the move to Kunming, where the group at last fought—albeit with weary airplanes and wearier pilots—as a single entity. The Burma Road by then was useless, and the AVG turned its attentions and its operations to Hengyang and Kweilin.

"The AVG for all practical purposes," states *The Army Air Forces in World War II*, "had long since become a part of the armed forces of the United States, and plans had been made for its incorporation into the AAF. But the AVG was a volunteer group in fact as well as name. . . ."[3] The AAF historical archives state further that "the induction of the AVG, from the first a perplexing problem, proved disappointing in its results. . . ."[4]

The pilots were weary of combat, they were tired of overseas duty, and those who were ready to return to uniform wanted, at the least, a brief visit home before embarking on long combat tours with the AAF, the Navy, or the Marines. Many of the men were angered by the offhand manner with which they were treated by the AAF officers, and it was this action as much as any other that soured their ideas of joining up with the AAF. Other pilots wanted to return to their prior branches of service. Some of the men failed to pass the physical examinations to become pilots with the AAF! And some "preferred to take remunerative positions with the China National Airways and Hindustan Aircraft companies. . . ."[5]

There is always friction when it is necessary to dissolve an organization such as was created in the Flying Tigers. Rifts and arguments and disagreements there may have been, but the pilots grimly stuck to and defended their fellows. Several AAF officers could not have been more insulting in their conduct with the Tigers—such as one colonel (who commanded a fighter group with the 10th Air Force) who sneered at the AVG pilots as plain mercenaries. The good colonel also stated plainly that he could take on the best AVG pilot in a dogfight and whip him handily.

Whereupon there was a blur of hands and the appearance of $5,000 American on the table before the colonel —who was invited immediately to match the bet by flying against the *worst* pilot in the AVG. The colonel managed to "laughingly wriggle his way out" of what had suddenly become a damnably embarrassing situation.

The cumulative damage, however, had been done. Only five pilots elected to transfer from the AVG into the AAF (another 16 men served briefly during the transition of command; one of these pilots died in action), and no more than 15 ground crewmen accepted service with the

AAF. The transfer of fighting power en masse, upon which so many hopes had been placed, was not to be.

When the Flying Tigers closed the record books, in the first week of July, 1942, they could count a total of 286 Japanese fighters and bombers destroyed in aerial combat. This figure is important; it represents *only* those airplanes the Chinese government confirmed by discovering the wreckage on the ground. It does not include those Japanese airplanes that were *seen* crashing into deep water —for which confirmation (and the $500 bonus) was not granted. By conservative estimates, perhaps an equal number of Japanese aircraft—another 300 planes or so—had tumbled into the jungles, the waters and the mountains of Southeast Asia and parts of China without ever being confirmed as destroyed. Many times a Japanese fighter or bomber, its wings and fuselage riddled, its tanks trailing a thin plume of fuel, or smoking, would struggle away from a fight without confirmation of its loss. (Records available from the Japanese after the war established beyond question that many more airplanes were lost to the Flying Tigers than were claimed by the group; the AVG pilots carried out the strictest "confirmation required" process of any fighter-pilot organization known.)

To accomplish its officially confirmed score of 286 enemy planes shot down in combat, the AVG lost nine pilots in battle; another four missing in action were presumed to be dead, for a total of 13 men lost to Japanese guns. Two AVG pilots were killed on the ground by Japanese bombs. Nine other AVG pilots met death in training accidents or while ferrying airplanes.

One of the most remarkable sidelights on the AVG combat record is that never did the available combat strength of the group exceed a total of 55 fighters ready for battle at any one time.

Despite the formidable obstacles that confronted them, the AVG carved a niche in aviation's hall of fame. Bob Neale exceeded the triple ace status by shooting down 16 planes. David ("Tex") Hill racked up a score of 12; Bill Reed got 11; and George Burgard, Bill McGarry, Ken Jernstedt, John Newkirk, Bob Little, and Charles Older all were double aces with ten kills each, plus sharing other kills with fellow pilots. There were so many pilots who shot down five or more enemy planes in aerial combat

Before the AVG was disbanded, the pilots
received some replacements with a fighter markedly
superior to their Tomahawks—the P-40E Kittyhawk
with greater power, six .50-caliber machine guns,
and improved flight performance.

that the AVG might well have been described as the
Group of Aces.

On July 4, 1942, the American Volunteer Group was
phased out of existence, and the China Air Task Force,
under the helm of Claire Chennault, took over the job of
aerial war in China.

The story of the AVG was done, but their heritage of
battle will live forever.

11

THE RAGGED TENTH

They activated the Tenth Air Force in the United States on February 12, 1942, and shipped the first echelon off to Asia. Within a month of its activation the men were cursing the heat, insects, and other hells of India and Burma, and preparing to strike at the Japanese with a bomber and fighter force so ragged and short of supplies and parts that its existence seemed to—and in reality did —depend on the whims of the long and precarious supply line that stretched all the way to the United States.

The major targets of the Tenth—which flew its first combat mission on April 2, 1942—were enemy bases and shipping scattered across Burma, Thailand, and the Andaman Islands. The Tenth's fighters had the unenviable task of trying to stem, with a handful of planes, Japanese air raids against India. The 7th Bombardment Group, with its heavy bombers, was a battered force long before it ever arrived at its Indian airfields. The Flying Fortresses of the 7th B.G. were actually on their way to the Far East before the war began, and they were unfortunate enough to be caught at Pearl Harbor, trying to land their unarmed planes, just as the Japanese waves of fighters and bombers struck at Oahu. During the hurried reshuffling of our forces caught en route to overseas destinations at war's outbreak, the bomber crews received their assignment to the Tenth Air Force, with orders to expedite their movement. The ground echelons found themselves victims of a tortuous routing, through Brisbane, Melbourne, and Freemantle, then to Ceylon and finally arriving in India in March, 1942.

When the planes of the Tenth went into action in Burma, the crews were shorthanded. They were in dire need of fresh replacements even as they began their combat tours. Their first replacements, however, were already as weary as the men they joined. Some of the earliest were veterans of the AVG. Others were wandering about, waiting for reassignment after their original outfits had been scattered to the winds or destroyed in the opening battles of the war. And there was a touch of fiction about some pilots and crewmen—men who trickled in to the bases of the Tenth after completing their famed mission against the Japanese homeland in the raid led by James Doolittle from the aircraft carrier USS *Hornet*, on April 18, 1942.

The twin-engine medium (B-25 Mitchell) and four-engine heavy bombers (B-17 Fortresses and B-24 Liberators and LB-30 Liberators, the export version of the B-24) of the Tenth had to spread their operations across an area comparable to half the continental United States. The task eased somewhat when new B-24 replacements came into action, for these deep-bellied raiders had greater range and speed than their B-17 contemporaries.

No one will ever know what the Tenth really could have done in its combat operations against the Japanese— because the Tenth provided a source of ready replacements for combat theaters considered more critical than Burma. Just as operations would get up steam in Asia, orders would come through from Washington for men and planes to rush thousands of miles to a new front for "temporary combat duty."

Historians bemoan this fate, especially as regards the 7th Bombardment Group. In June, 1942, for example, *every* heavy bomber of the 7th B.G. was flown from India to the Mediterranean, where they were hurled into a round-the-clock interdiction campaign against the supply lines of the Germans, attacking targets of Tobruk, Benghazi, Suda Bay, and other logistics centers. Not until Rommel was contained and considered "no longer to be a danger" did the heavies leave North Africa and return to their own private war against the Japanese.

The 7th Bombardment Group flew its first combat mission on April 2, 1942, with a disastrous beginning. On a dual mission, the first strike, by two B-17s, was to be flown from Asansol in western Bengal against Rangoon. The first airplane crashed and exploded on takeoff, obliterating the Fortress and wiping out the entire crew. Shaken by the sight of their fellows' crash, the second crew managed to get into the air and started the long flight against the Japanese-held city. They never completed the mission; engine failure forced the plane to hobble back to its base at Asansol without sighting the target. The second part of the mission went off with somewhat more success. Two B-17s and one LB-30 went in very low (3,500 feet) against enemy shipping in the Andaman Islands to release 16,000 pounds of bombs. All three planes received heavy damage from antiaircraft fire, but returned safely to their base.

The day following—April 3—six heavy bombers managed to reach Rangoon; one Fortress went down. No one ever saw the plane leave the formation and it was never learned how the bomber was lost. After the "heavy raid" of the six bombers, the group settled back into the pattern that was to reflect its missions—putting the airplanes back into shape to go out again. For 13 days the bombers accepted the servicing of mechanics who patched and repaired with inadequate tools and spares. Finally on April 16, six heavy bombers took off again to hit Rangoon, and dumped a meaningful pattern of 42 bombs (250- and 300-pounders) against shipping clustered in the harbor.

Thirteen days again passed before another mission could be flown; on April 29 the Rangoon docks suffered very heavy damage from an effective strike with rows of 500-pound bombs.

During May the bombers divided their attention between shipping, dock facilities, and Japanese airfields. The Myitkyina air base, in northern Burma near the Chinese frontier, especially came in for special attention, and there was much to say for the accuracy of the 7th's bombardiers—a series of raids with the small bomber force completely neutralized the Japanese field by destroying every building in sight and chewing the runways into cratered mudpies. On May 25 five Fortresses reminded Rangoon that we were still in the war. For the next 11 days the Fortresses flew several other missions—and then abruptly ended their combat role in Asia.

First the monsoon season thundered in, drenching the fields, turning runways into quagmires, and making life miserable for all concerned. In one respect, however, the torrential rains were a blessing, for the mechanics could devote extra time to repairing the heavy bombers. Or so they thought. . . .

In mid-June the hopes for some extra maintenance time vanished with the urgent call to rush every bomber immediately to Africa.

In the spring of 1942 the Japanese swept virtually with impunity through northern Burma, while their fighters and bombers raised havoc with the defenders both on the ground and in the air. The Japanese were in a position to mete out devastating punishment, and they made the most of their advantage. In the air they harried our planes at every turn. It was a hard, slogging aerial fight in which our men fought desperately to change the one-sided odds. For the Burma campaign the Japanese were so disdainful of Allied airpower that they never assigned more than 200 fighter planes to the campaign at any one time. But they followed the pattern that, in that theater, proved so effective for them: they kept their aircraft where they were needed, and obtained excellent dispersal against attack by the Allies by basing their planes on many small fields scattered throughout the jungle country.

No better proof of the Japanese superiority was to be found than their program of using Burma as a training ground for green pilots. Replacements were sent to Burma to fight the Americans and the British and, when the new pilots were blooded and considered to have a minimum of combat experience, they were shifted to other theaters where the Japanese considered the opposition to be more demanding. Not until we began to build up numerical strength in the CBI (China-Burma-India) Theater did the Japanese react with what could be called "serious attention" to Allied airpower.

The history of the Tenth Air Force is one in which transport- and cargo-flying runs through every vein of activity. Some of the wildest flying done in any theater in the world was performed by the few transport aircraft—*and* the bombers—of the Tenth in the dark days of 1942. In March of that year, Burma was crumbling under the steady pounding of the Japanese. Defeat threatened, and it was recognized that we needed a twofold effort to stem the tide—military air operations combined with air transport of supplies into China. The cost would be staggering, but it would be far worse if supplies were not pushed across the towering mountain barriers into China. The day of flying the Hump, crossing the rugged mountain wall of the Himalayas, loaded with such quantities of supplies that records were broken daily, lay in the distant future. The fleets of transports that would defy weather, altitude, and the Japanese still had to be built. In the months of 1942 the tonnage was literally a thin trickle, and every pound that could be dragged across the mountains through skies ruled haughtily by the Japanese was precious beyond any monetary value.

The Tenth came into being in India in a surreptitious fashion. During the final days of February, 1942, Major General Lewis H. Brereton (then commander of the Far East Air Force) and a small group of officers were working their way to India. It was a flight of tremendous distance; the men flew in a B-17 and an LB-30 from Java to Ceylon, and staged on to Dumdum airfield near Calcutta, India. Their secret cargo, wrapped in a blanket, was $250,000 in cash, with which to purchase local labor and supplies to get the Tenth into action. Brereton was given the dubious honor of becoming the Commanding General of an Air Force in a country that boasted a total of ten airfields, not one of which was suited for military operations. Every thing was a matter of borrowing, buying, or simply stealing. The British made desk space available in their military center at New Delhi, India, for Brereton and his staff. The logistics problem for their fledgling air force would have made a strong man weep—the shortest distance to the United States (around Japanese bases) was 13,000 miles, and transit time was guaranteed to be at least two months.

The chief port of American entry for supplies was Karachi, which lay a thousand miles from the center of combat operations. The Indian railroads boasted a weird array of Toonerville trolleys as rolling stock, and *four different rail gauges*. There were some highways, but even the most hardened truck driver shuddered at the sight of their rough and narrow surfaces, which became impassable during the torrential rains of the country.

Thus the first task of the heavy bombers arriving in India was not to drop bombs, as one might suppose, but to transport supplies. From March 8 through 13, the initial force of seven B-17 Fortresses and the one LB-30 Liberator hauled 58,000 pounds of supplies, and a battalion of 465 native troops, from Asansol to Magwe, Burma. On the return flights, 423 frightened civilians clambered gratefully into the bombers for an unexpected evacuation.

Nearly three weeks after this emergency transport operation with bombers, on April 2, the Tenth flew its initial missions carrying bombs, as already described. The extent of American bombing operations, with this small and ill-equipped force, cannot escape comparison with the actions of the Japanese in the area. On two separate missions on April 4 and 9, Japanese carriers launched swarms of planes against British forces at Trincomalee and Colombo, Ceylon, and shattered British resistance in the attacks. Besides inflicting extensive damage on vital installations, the Japanese sank two British heavy cruisers and struck their most telling blow when Japanese bombers ripped the aircraft carrier *Hermes* into a blazing hulk and sent her to the bottom.

By April of 1942, Colonel Caleb V. Haynes (with the assistance of Colonel Robert L. Scott, Jr., who had flown with Haynes from the United States to eastern Assam), was trying to whip an aerial logistics force into being. His organization was impressive in title as the Assam-Burma-China Ferry Command—the ABC Ferry Command, as it became known—but as rudimentary in performance as were its initials. The ABC had great hopes and monumental goals, but it started out with the debilitating weaknesses of having insufficient airplanes, spare pilots, crews, and just about everything else needed to create a working ferry organization.

The transports consisted of several weary and battered C-47s, which after several weeks in operation might have been condemned in other theaters; in the CBI, however, the venerable Gooney Birds were kept in the air despite the abuse to which they had been subjected. Alongside the Army planes flew their civilian cousins, the commercial DC-3s, manned by American, Chinese, and Pan American Airways pilots. The promise of more airplanes was a bitter mockery, and the German hell-raising in Africa not only prevented the arrival of replacement aircraft for the ABC, but actually reduced our strength there. A Tenth Air Force officer noted in his diary: "Brereton assigned our most experienced ferry pilots to the transport of supplies to the Middle East and took twelve of our transport planes—fifty percent of our operational transport strength. We were months getting them back.

One was shot down by British fighters or antiaircraft near Cairo. We only got five planes back, finally."

When some of the Doolittle Raid survivors showed up in Assam, their plans for continuing back to the United States went up in smoke as the local command virtually "pressed them into service in the finest traditions of shanghaied seamen." Any ideas that the newcomers held that they might be participating in a massive supply operation to China disappeared when they saw the one airport at Dinjan from which the supply flights took off on their hazardous runs. Into this single airfield crowded the few C-47s and the mixture of Chinese and commercial DC-3s, some British transports, and the special fighter force assigned to protect the aerial trucks. The "special fighter force" was especially a bitter joke in the theater, since it consisted of two wheezing P-40B Tomahawks handed down from the AVG, and two Republic P-43 Lancers which suffered so badly from leaking fuel tanks that they were looked upon as flying firebombs, and were disdained even by the Chinese fighter pilots. The men crowded into wretched quarters, ignored military rank as a ridiculous leftover from a world they could remember only dimly, and worked 16 to 20 hours a day, while the pilots tried to thread their way through mountain passes, storms, and marauding Japanese fighters.

The crews operating out of Dinjan performed near-miracles in their operations. The Britsh and American forces defending Burma were retreating before the Japanese tide, and ferry plane pilots thundered low over jungle trees to drop food and supplies to the men hacking their way out of the thick growth—as the Japanese pounded along after them. The transports during the period from April 22 to June 15, 1942, managed to ferry 465 combat troops and 733 tons of supplies into Burma bases—and carry out 4,499 evacuees who had despaired of fleeing the Japanese. In this same period the British transport crews, working with the men of the ABC, dropped 55 tons of supplies to the jungle-surrounded troops, and evacuated 4,117 people from Burma.

There was also the mission of dragging supplies into China, and during the month of May the few transports hauled 160,000 pounds of equipment and supplies over the towering mountains, into Kunming. The only thing that could be said for this operation was that the 80 tons of supplies were better than no supplies at all; everyone involved in the operation, however, was painfully aware that this limited cargo hardly made up a single drop in the capacious bucket of desperate need.

Nevertheless it *was* a beginning. During the month of June the ABC crews managed to double their cargo load to 320,000 pounds. The figures would certainly have risen higher except that the pilots were being dragged off to fly emergency missions in Burma, and transports were rushed off to Africa to help stop Rommel.

The pilots flew missions with their transport planes that, after the passage of so many years, seem more impossible now than they did during those days of urgency. One of the greats of the transport campaign was a lieutenant who laughed at the odds, juggled the word "impossible" just for fun, and defied death at almost every turn. His name was Jakey Sartz, and one day at Myitkyina he made history in his own special way. He watched Japanese troops pouring onto one end of the airfield, firing wildly, while he sat at the controls of a Gooney Bird at the other end of the field.

Normally the C-47 had a maximum load when it carried 24 passengers. But Myitkyina was a million miles away from normal, and Sartz had 73 human beings jammed into his airplane. The Japanese did their best to shoot down his unarmed and vulnerable transport, but failed to keep Sartz from a successful takeoff and flight.

Sartz landed with seventy-*four* passengers—his latest addition was born during the hectic flight over the Naga Hills!

During the month of August, despite the special missions, the enemy fighters, the violent storms, the mountains, the terrible food and horrid living conditions, the lack of spare parts, and other everyday problems, the transports carried 600 *tons* into China. The pilots dragged the C-47s far above the altitudes for which they had been designed to fly. The engineering books said that 12,000 feet was the normal top ceiling for the Gooney Bird, but the engineers had never been to India and China. So the pilots took the planes on up to 18,000 feet as a matter of course, and when they ran into the seething turbulence of storms, and heavy ice, they dragged them wearily up to 21,000 and 22,000 feet; up there the planes labored mightily and the engines screamed under the full load in the thin air. The transports were loggy at the controls and they wallowed like drunks from the combination of altitude and overload, and the crews cursed and went through hell when the Japanese fighters came dancing in nimbly, while they could only do their best to keep the wings level so they wouldn't stall out and fall helplessly like a piano tumbling through the air.

Colonel Robert L. Scott, Jr., who blazed a trail of flight from the days of biplane pursuits in the Army Air Corps long before World War II, and who flew Army mail-carrying planes in that disastrous era, served with Colonel Caleb Haynes as one of the pilots who created the ABC ferry service. Following are excerpts from the notes and reports of Colonel Scott, who tells in unexcelled fashion just what it was like early in 1942:

"On April 24, Colonel Haynes and Colonel Cooper transported a load of ammunition and aviation fuel to Lashio for the Flying Tigers, and on their way back an enemy fighter plane made an attack on their transport. Recognizing the ship as an enemy Zero, Haynes and Cooper left the flying of the plane to the co-pilot and went back into the fuselage, to ward off the attack as best they could with Tommy guns. Don Old, the co-pilot, dove the transport until they were actually skimming over the jungle trees. These evasive tactics kept the Jap ship from coming up under the vulnerable transport. Just one of the Jap tracers in that Douglas would have set it afire.

"As the Jap dived towards them, Cooper and Haynes and their crew chief, Sergeant Bonner, fired magazine after magazine at the Jap. This either discouraged him or the enemy ship lost the transport in a turn, for they got away. But even considering the bravery of these flyers in using their meager armament against a fighter ship, it is poor policy to shoot Zeros with Tommy guns; 45-caliber ammunition is not very effective against aircraft, but, as usual in a case like this, if you have only a popgun to point at the enemy, it helps the morale. . . .

"Major Joplin, whom we called 'Jop,' was another of our pilots. This man claimed that he had been born in a DC-2 and weaned in a C-47. One of the Pan-American pilots had made a forced landing with one of the transports, putting it down with the wheels up in a rice paddy near the Brahmaputra. Jop took a crew to the transport, took the bent propellers off and roughly straightened them. With his crew and some volunteer natives, he dug holes under the folded-up landing-gear and then let the gear down until it was fully extended, with the wheels down, to the bottom of the holes. Now he placed heavy timbers from the wheels to the surface of the rice paddy, putting them in at a small angle to form an inclined plane. Next he had about a hundred natives pull on ropes that were tied to the wheels, and dragged the Douglas transport up the inclined plane until it rested on the more or less level ground of the rice paddy. Then Jop demonstrated that he could justify all his claims of having been born in a Douglas transport. He gave the ship the guns, and in a flurry of mud and water and rice stalks, bounced it from the field and flew it home to base.

"All the pilots were good, and they were eager. The weather never became too bad or the trip too dangerous for men like Tex Carleton, Bob Sexton, or the others to get through. The enlisted men were the best. There in Assam they fought a constant battle against boredom, malaria, and every form of tropical disease. They ate and slept in the mud, and didn't grumble more than the average soldier gripes about the native food. The stringy buffalo meat was fairly tough; the mouthful used to get bigger and bigger as you chewed it. . . .

"Colonel Haynes and I were ordered to leave immediately for Shwebo, Burma, down on the Mandalay-Rangoon Railway, and evacuate the staff of General Stilwell. It seemed that the Japs had crossed another place on the Irrawaddy and were about to capture the entire American Military Mission to China—the Ammisca. We didn't even know whether or not there was a landing field in Shwebo, but I found it on a map and in the late afternoon we took off for lower Burma.

"We flew through black storms all the way to the Mekong; then turning south, we found better weather, even if we were getting into Japanese-controlled skies. We landed at Myitkyina [for fuel]. . . .

"Flying as low as we could without hitting the tops of the jungle trees, we followed the Myitkyina-Mandalay railroad to the South. . . .

"All the country ahead of us was marked with columns of black smoke, rising straight into the clear sky. We looked for hostile ships until our eyes ached—or for any ship at all, for we knew it would be a Jap, ours being the only Allied plane in the air. We had been flying these unarmed transports so long that both of us had become used to it. Behind us in the empty cargo space I could see the crew chief and the radio operator searching the skies on both sides, with their inadequate Tommy guns at 'ready' position. We kept the transport low to the flat country now, so that it wouldn't be silhouetted against the sky. Moreover the trees under us caused the olive-drab of the ship to blend in, making us harder to see. I thought many times that we couldn't get lower; but we kept going down until I know if the wheels had been extended we'd have been taxiing.

"I guess we were both a little bit nervous as we peered ahead for any little dot that would mean a Jap. Fly specks on the windshield—and you get lots of them when flying as low as we were—scared us many times. I could feel the palms of my hands sweating as the tension increased. . . . Colonel Haynes saw the field at Shwebo and pulled the big transport around like a fighter, slipping her in and sitting her down like a feather-bed. . . .

"Some of the loads that ferry pilots packed into those DC-3s would have curdled the blood of the aeronautical engineers who designed the ship. The C-47, or DC-3 . . . was constructed to carry a full load of twenty-four passengers or six thousand pounds. The maximum altitude was expected to be about 12,000 feet—but we later went a minimum of 18,000 across the hump, and sometimes we had to go to 21,500 to miss the storms and ice. Carrying the refugees, we broke all the rules and regulations because we had to. There were women and children, pregnant women, and women so old that they presumably couldn't have gone to the altitude that was necessary to cross into India. There were hundreds of wounded British soldiers with the most terrible gangrenous infections. At the beginning we used to load the wounded first, those who were worst off; but later, when we realized that with our few transports we'd never get them all out, we took only the able-bodied. That was a hard decision to make, but we looked at it finally from the theory that those must be saved who could some day fight again.

"But as I say, at first we carried the terribly wounded,

Douglas C-47's—military versions of the old DC-3—
operated out of crude fields and carried
loads that "would have curdled the blood of
the aeronautical engineers who designed the ship."

piling them in until the ship groaned and the door would
hardly close. I always carried out fifty or more in this
ship that had been designed for twenty-four....

"It was hot as hell flying the loaded transport off the
fields in Burma. We'd try to fly with the windows open
in the cockpit, but that created a suction that drew the
air from the cabin up to where we pilots were. With those
filthy bodies and the terrible stench of gangrenous wounds
we couldn't bear it, and would have to close the side
windows and just sweat. Sometimes the poor dev-
ils couldn't stand the trip and we'd have dead men aboard
when we landed in India...."[1]

The removal of all the heavy bombers of the Tenth Air
Force from India to North Africa wrecked the plans of
that organization to mount a bomber offensive against
the Japanese. During the three months of July, August,
and September, 1942, the only bombers remaining in the
Tenth—B-25 medium bombers—managed to drop a to-

tal of 135 tons of bombs. This was hardly enough to annoy the Japanese in their moment of triumph, and the bombing offensive that had been planned with such great hopes foundered even as it was getting under way.

Brigadier General Clayton L. Bissell, new commander of the Tenth Air Force, received an immediate new assignment—creating the China Air Task Force (CATF), which was to be made up of the 23rd Fighter Group under the lead of Colonel Scott, and the 11th Medium Bombardment Squadron under Colonel Haynes, with nearly one hundred fighters and bombers, according to the table of organization, to make up the striking force.

Bissell lost control of the CATF almost immediately, since there had been under way for some weeks a plan (on which Chiang Kai-shek and Claire Chennault were in agreement) for a renewed air offensive in China with the CATF, but under the command of Chennault.

The "new" air war was about to begin in China—but it would be crippled by the familiar old problems of shortages in just about everything needed to fight that war.

12

CHINA CASTOFFS

During the first months of its existence the China Air Task Force functioned as the bastard stepchild of the Army Air Forces—a stepchild with precious little to fight a powerful enemy arrayed across a vast battlefront. The CATF at first could mount for combat operations no more than seven B-25 medium bombers and approximately 30 P-40B and P-40E fighters; the fighter force inherited by the CATF actually amounted to 35 fighters (of which several were always grounded for repairs). There were ten additional fighter planes—the intensely distrusted P-43 Lancers—which were considered as totally unfit for flying, let alone mixing it up with Japanese fighters.

With its seven bombers and about 30 flyable fighter planes, in its early operations the CATF had to fight the Japanese along a front that stretched for approximately 5,000 miles. The battle line of the air ran from Chengtu in northwest China to Chungking, on the Yangtze, and southward to the Red River of Indo-China. It encompassed the Tibetan plateau and the Salween River to the west, and to the east spread out over the China Sea. To meet the Japanese across this distance the CATF juggled its few airplanes with typical Chennault dexterity. That old China hand used Kweilin (500 miles east of Kunming) as his main operations center, and shuttled his planes through Hengyang, Yunnanyi, Nanning, and other Chinese airfields, as well as staging some operations through Dinjan in Assam.

The men who operated in the CATF came from a bewildering variety of backgrounds, places, and former combat assignments; some of them "ordered themselves" out of stifling desk jobs and made the long trek to join Chennault in his one-sided air war. Bob Scott at least had the 23rd Fighter Group to launch into the Japanese; Caleb Haynes had only his meager handful of B-25 bombers which were flown by men whose experience had been in every type of bomber operation one might imagine, including veterans of the Doolittle raid against Japan.

The personnel complement of the CATF grew in typical ragged fashion. Its maintenance crews included survivors of the Royal Air Force evacuated with the AVG from Burma when the Japanese rushed in. They had gone on to service AVG fighters, and now were with the CATF, an adaptable group of men who worked day and night to keep Chennault's planes in the air. The CATF men were a group of wanderers and castoffs mixed with personnel assigned directly to CATF. But they all had in common the same curses and the same problems: they were poorly fed, clothed, and housed. They were ridden with Asiatic sores and diseases, they were sick to death of China, and they were desperately lacking in everything from toilet articles to sparkplugs.

The first two bombers to arrive early in June, 1942, were the survivors of six B-25 Mitchells that had departed from Dinjan under command of Major Gordon Leland. At 10,000 feet Leland was trying to break through thick clouds when his bomber smashed into a mountain and exploded. Two Mitchells followed him to the same disastrous end, with the loss of all three crews. A fourth bomber scraped by the mountain but became lost over the clouds and ran out of fuel; the crew bailed out safely. Two Mitchells survived the harrowing flight and made it to Kumming and Kweilin.

Two weeks later six more Mitchells slipped into Kweilin for the 11th Medium Bombardment Squadron, and with them came pilots who were adept in their profession. The new squadron commander, Major William E. Bayse, had handled a B-17 Flying Fortress through the ill-fated Java campaign. Seven pilots aboard the new bombers were hand-picked veterans from the Doolittle mission against Japan.

Caleb Haynes now had eight bombers with which to hit the Japanese, but immediately one of the Mitchells vanished from the CATF roster as mechanics stripped down the plane and cannibalized it for spare parts. For the next two months the skeletal frame of this one airplane was to keep the other seven Mitchells flying their

combat operations. The mechanics also performed miracles of improvisation. Getting bombs into China was a
formidable task and one way to overcome the problem
of supply was to use everything at hand. The mechanics
built "adaptable" bomb racks that carried missiles of
American, French, British, Chinese, and even Russian
manufacture—which were lying about at various airfields.

The Mitchells roared into battle with a thundering cry
that brought the Japanese straight up in surprise. On July
1 (three days before the AVG was phased out of existence), four Mitchells were escorted by five Flying Tiger
pilots in a raid against the harbor facilities of Hankow.
Although there were claims of heavy damage, intelligence
reports failed to confirm any major effects of the attack.
The next day the Mitchells struck again at Hankow, and
flames leaping through buildings along the waterfront left
no question of the effectiveness of the raid. That the Japanese were disturbed by the appearance of the swift bombers was all too evident later that same day when a heavy
Japanese bomber force plastered Hengyang airfield.

On July 3, the Mitchells made it three days in a row
by raiding Nanchang; the Japanese were caught off balance
by the attack, and promptly pounded the Hengyang base
once again. On July 4, the Japanese installations at Tien
Ho airfield near Canton took a severe beating from the
mixed force of B-25s and P-40s. The crews were delighted
with the absence of enemy opposition, and discovered
why there were no interceptions when they returned to
Kweilin. They were forced to circle their home field, while
P-40s of the new 23rd Fighter Group fought a pitched

The rugged, maneuverable B-25 Mitchell,
the *only* bomber for months available for strikes
against the Japanese. It was also flown in the
Doolittle raid against Japan, and became recognized finally
as one of the greatest aerial weapons ever built.

battle with new Japanese fighters—twin-engine, fast, and heavily armed.

As the weeks passed, the airfield scenes looked less and less like those of typical American installations—which our bases in China certainly were not. The picture of American airmen well fed and clothed was a hollow mockery. Men wore any clothes they could scrounge, and their old and worn garments were well mixed with the Chinese padded coolie coats, castoff British gear, American military issue, and a variety of civilian attire.

The airfields were, at their best, crude in design, construction, and facilities. They lacked hangars or maintenance shops, and were barren even of protective revetments for the planes. Mechanics (aided many times by the pilots and crew members) worked out-of-doors on the fighters and bombers in every type of miserable weather one might expect. Equipment for the airplanes came from an international junkheap; spare parts were of Russian, American, Italian, French, German, Chinese, and other sources. Proper tools were a laugh to the mechanics, who adapted a bewildering variety of tools to fit our airplanes. Even the belly tanks for long-range missions were a travesty of modern equipment, since many of them were made of bamboo calked with clay, and had the distressing habit of leaking fuel.

There are, unhappily, few complete official records of those days. In the early weeks of the CATF, the records were largely nonexistent because there was no means of recording—paper was as much in short supply as spare parts and tools. For months the men kept notes, combat logs, and other information on rice paper, envelopes, the backs of letters and order sheets, and even matchbox covers.

Unquestionably the worst problem was illness—many of the pilots, crewmen, and mechanics were so ill from a variety of ailments and diseases that had they been in the United States they would have been declared unfit for duty and ordered immediately into a hospital. But the CATF had to make do with men who were ailing, whose bodies revealed sores that could not heal because of the lack of medicine, whose bodies and clothes often were filthy, and who could only dimly remember what soap was like. Not only were medical supplies in critically short order, but medical personnel also were not available, and missionaries performed around the clock in the absence of army doctors and nurses.

Yellow jaundice and dysentery were so widespread (from the basic diet of filth, greasy pork, sweet potatoes, and rice) that these ailments were considered to be "normal health."

And against this pitiful assembly of American military might the Japanese had so many aircraft that the complement of fighters and bombers at a single Japanese base exceeded *all* the planes in the entire China Air Task Force.

The promise of supplies ferried over the Hump faded with the onset of winter weather; storms shrouded the peaks and lashed the air with a violent fury, and for weeks at a time no pilot in a C-47 dared to brave the terrors of weather within the Asiatic mountain country. Without tools or spare parts, few planes could be put into the air to make an effective showing against the enemy.

And yet, miraculously, the fighters continued to go up, continued to intercept the Japanese on their bombing missions, continued to strike at Japanese ground forces and to strike in strafing and bombing raids across the combat front that stretched for thousands of miles.

The CATF was still a squalling infant when it opened its campaign against the enemy with the raids of July 1 through July 4. Haynes personally made a daring follow-up raid to these initial four missions by flying in a single B-25, escorted by two P-40s, against the Japanese air headquarters of Tengchung on the Salween. To make the most of the mission, the three airplanes on their way home pounded a supply column on the Burma Road, making repeated strafing runs against the exposed Japanese force and inflicting casualties estimated in the "several hundred."

The Weary Fighters

Sixteen veterans of the AVG had promised to remain in China for approximately two weeks after the AVG on July 4, 1942, officially ceased to exist, to assist the CATF in getting combat-ready. They made certain not to overstay their temporary duty. Promptly on July 18, as Chennault was planning to increase his fighter operations against the enemy, his personnel ranks were severely and suddenly depleted. A transport slid into a landing at Kunming with several replacement fighter pilots. When the plane took off it carried with it the "we've had it!" pilots of the AVG. There were, however, only 15; one man had been killed in the brief interval of extra volunteer combat duty.

Even in mid-July the CATF was being crippled by a shortage of fighter pilots, and the 23rd Fighter Group was unable to count even one dozen experienced men. Replacements unfortunately need training, and training replacements has the distressing habit of burning up precious fuel, wearing out airplanes, and sometimes wrecking them as well.

The combination of the woes that beset the CATF made all the more incredible its feats in combat.

The Japanese closed out the month of July with a major attempt to cripple or destroy the CATF. Fighters and bombers for several weeks had made sporadic raids against the CATF fields, but on July 30 and 31 the enemy went for the knockout punch. An estimated 120 fighters and bombers, including many Army fighters (with numbers of the Oscar, a radial-engine dervish considered the most maneuverable Japanese fighter of the war), tried to inundate CATF opposition and smash the fields. For 36 hours the badly outnumbered CATF pilots hurled their fighters against the enemy. In the frantic fighting the P-40 pilots of the CATF burned and shot apart 17 Japanese fighters and bombers, while losing only three P-40s in combat (the pilots survived).

Caught by surprise at the unexpected intensity of opposition, the Japanese immediately shifted to night bombing operations, pounding Kweilin and Hengyang (100 miles to the northeast of Kweilin) in attempts to destroy CATF operational capability. In this campaign they ran into their "old friends," Flying Tiger pilots Major David Hill and Major Gil Bright. Flying night interceptions with Hill and Bright were Major John R. Alison and Captain Robert J. Baumler.

The men climbed into a dark Chinese sky to fight a heavy raid against Hengyang; no one knew just how many Japanese planes were in the air, since their number could only be estimated as "several dozens of planes." John Alison achieved fame among his fellow pilots by shooting down three bombers out of a formation of five planes, and Baumler cut down two more bombers in the shadowy combat. To complete excitement for the evening, Alison's fighter, severely damaged in the battle, overshot the landing strip and thundered beyond the field to crash deliberately into a river. Alison escaped from his plane, and later the Chinese salvaged the precious fighter by dragging it from the river with bamboo mats.

On August 5 Alison was in the thick of it again. An estimated 100 fighters and bombers roared toward Kunming, and Alison with seven other pilots tried to turn the enemy formation. In the fight the CATF pilots shot down four Japanese fighters which blocked their intercept; Lieutenant Lee Minor was killed in the crash of his P-40, for the only American loss of the battle.

Abruptly—and strangely, since they had not suffered excessive losses—the Japanese pulled back their claws, and for the month following did not make further attacks against the CATF.

A Pilot Named Scott

There is a "side story" to the tale of the CATF in the form of the 23rd Fighter Group's Commanding Officer—Colonel Robert Lee Scott, Jr. Scott pulled every trick in the book (and invented a few of his own) in order to get into combat with fighters. In April, 1942, while flying transport missions with Caleb Haynes in the struggling ABC Ferry Command, Scott managed to wangle a new P-40E Kittyhawk from Claire Chennnault. Scott's argument was that with one Kittyhawk he could raise enough hell in India and Burma to give the Japanese all sorts of problems.

"I told the General," explained Scott, "that I wanted one single P-40 to use in India and Burma. I knew they were scarce, but I would promise him that nothing would happen to it, and the instant he needed the ship I would fly it back to him in China. The General smiled. I'm sure he was thinking and wondering whether, if he were in my position, he wouldn't have begged for the same chance. He didn't give me some excuse that he well might have used—that the P-40s belonged to the Chinese Government, that it would have been against regulations, and so forth. General Chennault knew that I would use that 'shark,' as we called the P-40s, against the Japs. He made his own regulations then; what did it matter who killed the Japs and who used the P-40s so long as they were being used for China?

"By the twinkle in his eyes I knew that I had won my case. The General said, 'Some Forties are on the way from Africa now. You take the next one that comes through. Use it as long as you want to.' That's the way I got the single fighter plane that was to work out of Assam."[1]

Immediately on acquiring his new P-40E (Serial Number 41-1496) Scott had the famed shark's mouth painted on the lower nose of the airplane. Starting on May 1, 1942, Scott hurled himself into a wild month of flying that raised eyebrows through the Allied camp and threw the Japanese into consternation. Within a week the Japanese were convinced that they were facing an entire P-40 squadron rather than just one man in one airplane, and Scott went to great pains to further this belief.

He flew from the first light of day into the night, every single day that his new fighter could be taken into the air. During that one month, Bob Scott put in a total of nearly 215 combat hours in the Kittyhawk, averaging just over seven hours a day of flying for May. For a while Scott used the fighter to escort the unarmed transports across the Burma jungles, flying 3,000 feet above the Gooney Birds, hoping for Japanese fighters to go after the "sitting duck" targets, so that he could come barreling in from out of the sun after them. But four days of escort flights failed to flush a single enemy fighter. Then, on May 5, Scott drew first blood—and launched his amazing campaign against the enemy.

North of the now Japanese-held air base of Lashio he caught sight of a twin-engine bomber being serviced, gasoline drums and trucks in front of the airplane. This was his first opportunity to cut loose with the six heavy guns of the Kittyhawk; after three passes the bomber spewed forth flames and smoke and Scott turned his attention elsewhere.

He found his next targets on the Burma Road—two long columns of Japanese soldiers, marching in closely packed formation, with a dozen trucks making up part of the column. The Allison engine screamed as Scott came down in a flat dive. A thousand yards out he gripped the trigger, and streams of .50-caliber lead hosed in a devastating blast the length of the entire column. For several minutes Scott pounded the trapped Japanese force, then raced away to the south. Low over the horizon, he turned sharply and came back in again. He caught the survivors, already re-formed, completely by surprise. When he left the second time, his ammunition exhausted, four trucks blazed brightly and there were dozens of bodies sprawled along the road. (The Chinese confirmed more than 40 dead.)

Later that day Scott was out on his second mission— but went home grumbling about a lack of targets.

For the next three days he waited for news of the destruction of a huge fuel cache of 100,000 gallons—an RAF fuel dump at Myitkyina which the British were supposed to set off before abandoning the field so that the aviation gasoline would not fall into enemy hands. While he waited, Scott strafed and set aflame Japanese fuel barges on the Irrawaddy, south of Bhamo, and on the Chindwin.

Then, on May 8, came the fall of Myitkyina—and no towering plume of black smoke in the sky to mark the destruction of the valuable fuel stores. As Scott related the mission:

"When I came over the field at Myitkyina, the enemy fired at me while I was yet ten miles away; I could see the black bursts of the 37mm AA in front and below me. I started 'jinking' and moved to the northeast, so that I could come from out of the sun and be as far as I could get from the field. With my first burst the whole woods seemed to blow up—I have never seen such a flash as that which came when that veritable power-train of high octane fuel caught fire from the tracers. I also fired at two of the gun installations on the field. But the bursts from the Jap guns were so close to me that I decided to let well enough alone, and turned for home in Assam. Many times on the way home I looked over my shoulder, and the smoke from the thousands of gallons of gasoline was visible when I was sixty miles from Myitkyina."

Scott quickly discovered the severe battle discipline which held the Japanese ground forces together as a powerful fighting force. On May 9, he made four separate missions into Burma. On one of these, he returned to Lashio where he found a "choice target" waiting for him:

". . . I turned West for the field and came in right on the treetops, strafing the anti-aircraft guns in two passes.

On the second run across the field I felt and heard bullets hitting my ship, but didn't see their origin until nearly too late. Down close to the West end of the field, almost under the trees, were Japanese ground soldiers. They were grouped into two squares like the old Macedonian phalanx, and were firing rifles at me. I turned my guns on them and could see the fifty-calibre fire taking good toll from the Jap ranks. But even after I had made three runs on them, I noted that they continued to hold their positions, an excellent demonstration of perfect battle discipline. Later on one of the AVG aces, Tex Hill, told me that he had seen the same thing down in Thailand, and that after he'd strafed one of the squares of about a hundred men and there were only two or three on their feet, those few still were shooting at him when he left the field."

A fighter plane is an unbelievably deadly weapon, and under certain conditions it can seem—the men on the ground can only see it this way—to be all hell on wings coming after them with flaming death. Near Chefang, where the Burma Road is 8,000 feet above sea level, Scott caught a long Japanese troop column, and proved the lethal effectiveness of his Kittyhawk:

". . . . I turned to the side, to watch them—they were in heavy rain, and from the standpoint of their own safety they were in the worst possible place on the road. The Burma Road was cut out of red Yaunnan clay, and there were steep banks on both sides of the column—besides, I don't think they had heard me over the roar of the rain, and I know they hadn't seen my ship.

"I turned my gun switches on and dove for the kill, sighting carefully through my lighted sight. My tracers struck the target dead center, for I had held my fire until the last moment. There was no need of doing this job at high speed, for if I merely cruised I'd have longer to shoot at them and could also look out for the hills hidden in the rain and the clouds. This time there was no dust, but the red, muddy water went up like a geyser. The six Fifties seemed to cut the column to bits. As I passed over, I could see those who hadn't been hit trying desperately to crawl up the muddy bank to the safety of the trees and slipping back.

"Turning very close to the hills, I came back over. Every now and then I'd lose them, for the rain was heavy and it was dark in the clouds, so dark that my tracers burned brilliant to the ground and then ricocheted away into the air again, still burning. I think it was in my third pass, as the Japs seemed to be giving up the effort to climb off the road, that I decided my ship would be called 'Old Exterminator.' . . . I kept on cutting them to pieces until my ammunition was gone; I fired 1890 rounds into those three or four hundred Japanese, and I don't think more than a handful escaped."

The effectiveness of his strafing and bombing attacks against Japanese ground forces prompted Scott to think up ways of bedeviling the enemy as well as tearing him up with guns and bombs. Each time that Scott flew, on three or four missions a day, his fighter took on a different appearance:

". . . I'd go out early in the morning with the spinner on the 'shark's' nose painted white, and I'd attack Lashio or Mogaung from the South. Later in the morning I'd strike from the West, with the spinner painted blue. After lunch the eager painters or my drafted crewmen would have the spinner another color for my flight. By the time I made the fourth sortie, with the spinner a fourth color and my approach from a fourth direction, I'm sure the Japs didn't know where I came from—and most certainly they didn't guess that the American fighter force in Assam was composed of one single Kittyhawk. If they had, they would have been forced to do something to 'save face.' For at the moment, with me drunk with the wine of my first combat, the Jap was losing face."

Scott's repeated missions and his tactics with the "always being repainted" spinner of his Kittyhawk quickly created the reputation of the "One Man Air Force." But Bob Scott had other ideas about his fighter—he was fairly straining at the leash to meet the Japanese in the air. During May he flew to China at every opportunity to discuss combat tactics with the AVG pilots. He knew several of them—as an Army instructor he had actually checked out some of the pilots to whom he now turned for combat savvy. And he took every opportunity that came along to fly combat with the AVG veterans.

Scott's unusual role—a transport pilot flying his own shark-painted Kittyhawk fighter both in China and alongside with AVG—has in subsequent years clouded just *what* position he held in Burma and China, before the AVG was phased out and Scott took over as leader of the 23rd

Fighter Group, finally commanding several former AVG pilots assigned to his group.

Russell Whelan, who wrote a detailed history of the AVG, *The Flying Tigers*, discussed the arrival in the theater of Bob Scott as a fighter pilot:

"Col. Scott had arrived in April to learn of the technique of downing Japanese from the A.V.G. Although he had commanded the Seventy-eighth Pursuit Squadron in Panama and was a former supervisor of Army Air Corps pilot schools in Southern California, Col. Scott 'demoted' himself to the role of wing man on every A.V.G. strafing and bombing mission that came along. When the A.V.G. had no flight scheduled, Scott operated as a one man air force over Burma. He won the Army Silver Star award for destroying a Japanese plane and two [later confirmed as four] supply trucks near Myitkyina on May fifth. In quick succession thereafter he knocked out a Japanese anti-aircraft battery, bombed the Myitkyina airbase runway three times and raided Homalin. Col. Scott was learning the ropes the hard way and everyone in the A.V.G. was delighted with him."[2]

The brief phrase, "raided Homalin," obscures a wild combat day for Colonel Scott, when he attacked the target not once, but four separate times during the day. Each time he dropped a 500-pound bomb and slashed through Japanese bodies and targets with the murderous firepower of the Kittyhawk's guns. Homalin was a concentration of Japanese military forces.

From 11,000 feet on his first mission, Scott watched four barges easing from the broad Chindwin and heading for the Homalin docks. Alongside the wharf, the barges were caught by surprise as the Kittyhawk screamed down from the sky. The explosion of the heavy bomb hurled chunks of one barge 100 yards down the river, and cut two other barges free. As they drifted on the river, Scott put 200 rounds of tracers into each barge; one blazed from gasoline stores he had ignited, and the other was settling in the water. For good measure, Scott strafed the Japanese in the water.

His second strike of the day had even more devastating effect as his 500-pound bomb ripped directly into the largest building in Homalin, pinpointed by British Intelligence as the Japanese police station. Before the day was over—as reported later by British Intelligence—200 Japanese were dead in the shattered police station, and between 600 and 1,000 Japanese had been killed by Scott's four bombs and his devastating strafing passes.

By July 3, 1942—the last day of the AVG—Scott was able to tally his two months of flying with "Old Exterminator." On the day following he would take command of the 23rd Fighter Group with the CATF, and he had prepared for his new assignment with startling effectiveness. He had flown a total of 371 hours—something over 80,000 miles—destroyed a variety of enemy targets that included bridges, buildings, ships and barges, locomotives and trains, airfield installations, airplanes, gun emplacements, and other objectives; and he had killed so many Japanese that the official records show only "several thousand dead and wounded" at the guns and bombs of this one airplane and one pilot.

Scott describes his new assignment:

". . . When I took over things at Kunming there were three fighter squadrons and one headquarters squadron. Major Tex Hill had one squadron at Hengyang, China, and with him were such deputy leaders as Maj. Gil Bright, Maj. Johnny Alison, and Capt. Ajax Baumler. Maj. Ed Rector had another squadron at Kweilin with Capt. Charlie Sawyer for his assistant in leadership. These outlying stations are about five hundred miles in the direction of Japan from our headquarters on the plateau of Yannan at Kunming. The third unit was the squadron under Maj. Frank Schiel, who was very busy training the most junior members of this new fighter group in the way of fighter aviation. I got the Group headquarters to running and stood by for orders to begin leading the fighter forces in action to the East."

On July 11, 1942, the 23rd Fighter Group marked the death in battle of a pilot named Johnny Petack, and it was an occasion of unusual sadness:

". . . Hill led eight fighters, four with wing bombs, for dive-bombing Nanchang. While these four went down with their bombs, Hill was to stay aloft with the other four to act as top-cover—just in case some Zeros tried to surprise the dive-bombers. Ajax Baumler said that he was on Petack's wing for the bombing and that he saw the whole thing: Johnny Petack dove for his target, one of the gunboats on the lake, but as his bomb hit the boat the P-40 was seen to explode, evidently hit by ground-fire. Ajax followed the burning ship almost to the ground and saw it strike in a rice paddy near a Buddhist temple.

"So Petack, one of the AVG who had stayed for the extra two weeks, was killed in action. It's peculiar how a man could fight all through those last nine months and then go down from a lucky anti-aircraft shot. John Petack had remained for the purpose of training the new pilots and his job was that of airdrome defense. He was killed on this offensive mission. It was one that he could have refused with honor; instead, he had volunteered for this dive-bombing fight and had been killed in carrying it out. It was the most inspiring thing he could have done."

Colonel Robert L. Scott, Jr., carved his mark in the sky with even more effectiveness than he had against enemy targets on the ground. On July 31, 1942, he shot down a Japanese twin-engine bomber and an escorting Zero fighter—after diving alone into a large enemy formation. Before he left the combat theater in Asia, Scott had carved 12 enemy planes on his guns.

During his days of flying "Old Exterminator," Scott had received much instruction from Major Tex Hill—whom Scott was later to command in the CATF. But it was a "command" strictly on paper, as Scott had many times pointed out, for to him Tex Hill was "the greatest fighter that I ever saw, the most loyal officer, and the best friend." Scott tells a memorable story of an incident with Tex Hill:

"One day over Hengyang, after we had broken the Japanese wave with our assault and support and there were some fifteen Zeros burning around among the pagodas of this Hunan capital, I saw an odd sight down below. There was one lone Jap, doubtless of the suicide Samurai school, for though his buddies had either been shot down in their attempted strafing attack or had turned for home, this arrogant follower of the Shinto Shrine was strafing the field—alone. Two of us rolled to go get him, but from the end of the field towards the river I saw a P-40 pull out of a dive and head for the Jap. It was Tex Hill.

"As the two fighters drew together in this breath-taking, head-on attack, I saw their tracers meeting and for a second I didn't know whether the ships ran together or both exploded in the air. As the smoke thinned I saw the

P-40 flash on through and out into the clear, but the Jap crashed and burned on the field of Hengyang. Hill and the Jap had shot it out nose to nose, and once again I thought of the days of Western gunplay.

"We landed and waited for Tex to come over. As we stood around the burning enemy ship, I saw Hill striding across the field from his fighter. Hanging low on his right leg was his army forty-five. Subconsciously I looked at his other leg as if I expected to find the mate hanging there.

"Tex's blond hair was blowing in the wind, his eyes were looking with venomous hate at the Jap, his jaw was set. I had opened my mouth to congratulate him, for he had shot down two enemy ships that day, when I had a closer look at his eyes. . . . Tex strode over close to the fire and looked at the mutilated Jap where he had been thrown from the cockpit. Then, without a change of expression, he kicked the largest piece of Jap—the head and one shoulder—into the fire. I heard his slow drawl: 'All right, you sonofabitch—if that's the way you want to fight it's all right with me.'

"Tex calmly left the group and walked back to his ship and into the alert shed for his cup of tea. None of us said anything. The Chinese coolies who usually yelled 'Ding-hao—ding-hao' saw his eyes and the set of his jaw, too—and just waited until later to congratulate him."

Bob Scott (during a long fireside get-together one night) told the writer about a man he considered to be one of the greatest fighters of all time. He didn't specify fighter pilot—just a fighter. He was Lieutenant Dallas Clinger from Wyoming. "Clinger was another man who in years gone by in the West would have been a great gunman like Tex Hill," Scott told me. "Only Clinger wouldn't have cared whether he was on the side of the Law, the Mormons, the Church, or Jesse James. He just wanted to fight."

One of Clinger's brief combat reports of a fight he had over Hengyang, while flying with two other P-40s, put things right to the point:

"I was flying on my leader's wing—Lieutenant Lombard—at 23,000 feet when we saw three enemy planes down below circling. There were larger formations reported around. Just then I heard my flight leader say: 'There are three stragglers—let's attack 'em.' So we dove into them like mad. As I shot into the Zero on the right of the formation I saw that we were in the midst of twenty-four other Zeros, all shooting at us. I got mad and shot at every plane that I could get my sights on. I think I shot one down but I was so busy I didn't see it crash."

The combat report was signed: "Dallas Clinger—2nd Lieutenant—Almost Unemployed."

Bob Scott continues with his story of what Clinger *didn't* say in his combat report:

"What Clinger had really done was the greatest piece of daredevil flying that any of us had ever seen. Instead of diving away from the twenty-seven ship circus as the others had done, he had stayed and fought the old-fashioned 'dog-fight' until the Japs just about took him to pieces from sheer weight of numbers. When they straggled home they must have been the most surprised bunch of pilots in all Japan, for this crazy American with his heavy P-40 had done everything in or out of the book. He fought right side up and upside down, from 23,000 feet down to less than one thousand. As many Japs as could fill the air behind Clinger would get there and hang on while they shot; but Clinger wouldn't fight fair and stay there. In the end, he came right over the field, diving from the enemy until he had outdistanced them enough to turn; then he'd pull into an 'Immelmann' and come back shooting at them head-on.

He was last seen after the unequal fight skimming out across the rice paddies, making just about 500 miles an hour, with some ten to twelve Zeros following. For some reason they seemed reluctant, as though they didn't know whether to run after Clinger or leave him alone. He came in for lunch with his ship badly shot up by their cannon. But he had shot down one of them . . ."

Despite the brilliant flying of its fighter pilots, and their effectiveness in battle against the Japanese, the CATF never was able to emerge the victor in the ceaseless struggle of scrabbling for supplies and weapons. Major campaigns—which meant a short series of bombing raids and fighter missions, one coming quickly after the other—invariably exhausted the CATF. After such periods of combat flying virtually every plane needed extensive repair work, and many of them were in need of complete overhaul. Planes were so precious that pilots chose not to bail out of crippled fighters, but to ride them down to the ground in the hope that they could save the ship for future use. Fighters were dragged up from the bottoms of rivers, hauled across paddies, carried down mountain slopes—and more than one pilot landed his fighter plane with bombs still jammed under the wings. But not in normal landings—these were emergencies with the gear jammed or the airplane crippled. *Save the fighters*—that was the word.

At times fuel was so desperately short that victory rolls over the home field were forbidden. If the Japanese came over in strength, as they did unpredictably, one maximum-effort mission to intercept the attackers would literally drain the available fuel so that a second mission with full strength could not be flown until the transport planes ferried in additional fuel.

Mechanics had to clean spark plugs again and again when normally the plugs would have been thrown into the nearest trash bin. The men lacked even hard wire with which to safety removable parts and units of the different planes. Engine oil was long overdue; mechanics tried to strain old oil to keep it usable. On their off time the men would scour the countryside for wrecked airplanes—for the Japanese fighters and bombers that had been shot down proved to be a valuable source of parts: they contained sheet metal, wires, screws, bolts, and a variety of precious materials with which to patch and repair the P-40s of the CATF. More than once the mechanics ran out of Prestone coolant for the liquid-cooled Allison engines, and pilots flew their airplanes with temperature readings at dangerously high figures. There were no new carburetors, and even tail wheels, worn bald and thin, could not be replaced for long periods.

The month of August, 1942, ended with the CATF badly battered and reeling from all its woes. The Japanese had executed some of this punishment, but they actually inflicted only a minor portion of the problems plaguing the American force. During the month only three P-40s and no bombers had gone down in battle; the real enemies were distance, lack of supplies, disease. . . .

The CATF wearily abandoned its bases in eastern China, and the men began the disheartening move back to the long shadows of the Himalayan mountains, closer to the sources of supply. Fifty attacks against enemy targets, plus the interceptions of massed waves of Japanese planes, had drained the CATF of strength in its opening months of life.

Not until the first weeks of September did the CATF begin to stir back into life. Some of the new P-40K Warhawk fighters slipped into Chennault's hands. The Caribbean Command released some of its veteran P-40 pilots, so desperately needed as replacements. With supplies accumulating, with new men coming in, the Tomahawks, Kittyhawks, and new Warhawks—a complete lineage of P-40s—went back to striking at the Japanese on the ground.

In October, Chennault was in Kweilin (operating his headquarters from within a huge limestone cave) and preparing to send the CATF out on its biggest missions to date. October 25 proved to be one of the most memorable combat missions ever flown, when ten Mitchell bombers were escorted by seven P-40 fighters in a raid against shipping and port facilities at Hong Kong. The American planes first had to fly 500 miles to the east from Kunming to Kweilin, where they refueled, and then staged another 350 miles on to Hong Kong, where they carried out a pinpoint-accuracy strike against their targets. The American fighters and bombers shot down 19 intercepting Japanese fighters, while losing one bomber and one fighter. But the scorecard for the day rose when the results of fighting at Kunming came in. The same day that our mixed force hit Hong Kong, a large Japanese formation tried to wipe out Kunming—where the P-40s shot down eight of the enemy without loss to themselves, making the day's tally 27 Japanese fighters shot down.

Bob Scott recalls the battle over Hong Kong:

". . . 'Bandits ahead—Zerooooos! At eleven o'clock.' Fumbling again for the throttle quadrant, shoving everything as far forward as I could, I marvelled at the steepness of the climb the enemy ships were maintaining. I called: 'Zeros at twelve o'clock. . . .' I heard Tex Hill reply: 'Hell, I see 'em.' I could hear the jabber of the Japs still trying to block our frequency.

"I was diving now, aiming for the lead Zero, turning my gunsight on and off, a little nervously checking again and again to see that the gun-switch was at 'on.' I jerked the belly-tank release and felt the underslung fifty-gallon

bamboo tank drop off. We rolled to our backs to gain
speed for the attack and went hell-bent for the Zeros.
I kept the first Zero right in the lighted sight and began to
fire from over a thousand yards, for he was too close to
the bombers. Orange tracers were coming from the B-25s
too, as the turret gunners went to work.

"Five hundred yards before I got to the Zero, I saw
another P-40 bearing the number 151 speed in and take
it. That was Tex Hill. He followed the Zero down as it
tried to turn sharply into the bombers and shot it down.
Tex spun from his tight turn as the Jap burst into flames.
I took the next Zero—they seemed to be all over the sky
now. I went so close that I could see the pilot's head
through the glass canopy. . . . My tracers entered the
cockpit and smoke poured back, hiding the canopy, and I
went by.

"As I turned to take another ship below me, I saw four
airplanes falling in flames toward the waters of Victoria
Harbor. I half rolled again and skidded in my dive to
shake any Zero that might be on my tail. I saw another
P-40 shooting at a Jap, but there was a Zero right on his
tail. I dove for this one. He grew in my sights, and as
my tracers crossed in front of him he turned into me. I
shot him down as his ship seemed to stand still in the
vertical bank. The ship was three or four hundred yards
from me, and it fell towards the water for a time that
seemed ages. An explosion came, and there was only
black smoke; then I could see the ship again, falling,
turning in a slow spin, down—down—down.

"I shot at everything I saw. Sometimes it was just a
short burst as the Jap went in for our bombers. Sometimes I fired at one that was turning, and as I'd keep
reefing back on my stick, my ship would spin, and I'd
recover far below. I shot down another ship that didn't
see me. I got it with one short burst from directly astern,
a no-deflection shot. In this attack I could see the Japanese ship vibrate as my burst of six fifty-calibre guns hit
it. First it just shook, then one wing went up. I saw the
canopy shot completely off; then I went across it. Turning back in a dive to keep my speed, I watched the
enemy ship, as it dove straight down, stream flames for a
distance the length of the airplane behind.

"As I looked around now the bombers were gone, but

climbing up from the south I saw four twin-engine ships.
. . . I had plenty of altitude on the leader, and started
shooting at him from long range, concentrating on his
right engine. He turned to dive, and I followed him
straight for the water. I remember grinning, for he had
made the usual mistake of diving instead of climbing. But
as I drew up on the twin-engine ship, I began to believe
that I had hit him from the long range. His ship was
losing altitude rapidly in a power glide, but he was making no effort to turn. I came up to within fifty yards
and fired into him until he burned. I saw the ship hit
the water and continue to burn. We had been going towards the fog bank in the direction of the Philippines, and
I wondered if the Jap had been running for Manila.

"I shot at two of the other twin-engine ships from long
range but couldn't climb up to them. Then I passed over
Hong Kong Island, flying at a thousand feet; I was too
low but didn't want to waste any time climbing. . . .
Then I saw above me the criss-crossing vapor trails of an
area where fighter ships have sped through in an air attack.
They almost covered the sky in a cloud. Here and there
were darker lines that could have been smoke paths where
ships had burned and gone down to destruction.

"I was rudely jerked back to attention by a slow voice
that yet was sharp: 'If that's a P-40 in front of me, waggle
your wings.' I rocked my wings before I looked. Then I
saw the other ship, a P-40 nearly a mile away. I think
from the voice it was Tex Hill. I went over towards him
and together we dove towards home.

"The presence of the other P-40 made me feel very arrogant and egotistical, for I had shot down four enemy
ships and had damaged others. So I looped above Victoria
Harbor and dove for the Peninsular Hotel. My tracers
ripped into the shining plateglass of the penthouses on its
top, and I saw the broken windows cascade like snow
to the streets, many floors below. I laughed, for I knew
that behind those windows were Japanese high officers,
enjoying that modern hotel. When I got closer I could see
uniformed figures going down the fire escapes, and I shot
at them. In the smoke of Kowloon I could smell oil and
rubber. I turned for one more run on the packed fire
escapes filled with Jap soldiers, but my next burst ended
very suddenly. I was out of ammunition. Then, right into

the smoke and through it right down to the tree-top levels, I headed northwest to get out of Japanese territory sooner, and went as fast as I could for Kweilin."

One month later the fighters of the 23rd were over Canton on another escort mission. It was the biggest strike of the CATF to date, with 14 bombers escorted by 22 P-40 fighters.

Forty-five Japanese fighters came up to intercept the CATF strike force. When the battle ended all the P-40s were still in the air, with the pilots victors over 29 Zero fighters confirmed as shot down.

The CATF was to continue its battle against the Japanese in China until March 10, 1943, when the CATF went out of existence, replaced by the 14th Air Force.

The CATF had fought for eight months, in a ragged and weary campaign in the air and against enemy targets on the ground. In that eight-month period the CATF hammered out a tremendous record for itself. The Mitchell bombers had flown 56 missions—and lost but *one* airplane.

The P-40 fighters had their number reduced by 16 planes. They exchanged their loss for 149 enemy planes shot down—and confirmed as destroyed.

13

JUNGLE RATS

Many months before the Japanese launched their lightning strikes against Allied objectives throughout the Pacific and Asia, a young Australian fighter pilot named Gregory-Richmond Board transferred from Australia to Singapore as a member of the 453rd Squadron, Royal Air Force.[1] Their mission was to defend the powerful bastion of Singapore against the Japanese strike from the sea expected by a large percentage of Australian and British officials—but by no means all of these officials: among their number were those who sneered at the talk of powerful Japanese military thrusts against entrenched British might. Thus the young Board, along with his fellow pilots, came quickly to know the frustrations of the military when he discovered that the 453rd Squadron, charged with the aerial defense of Singapore, clearly could not fulfill its assigned mission. The reason was simple enough—the squadron lacked fighter airplanes.

After the squadron had spent many weeks chafing at the lack of flying, a ship tied up at the Singapore dock with a load of huge crates, containing within them the disassembled parts of new fighter planes—planes of a type none of the pilots had seen before. It was an American airplane known as the Brewster 339 Buffalo, a barrel-shaped chunk with wings, that had all the lines of an aerial bulldog.

The pilots hovered impatiently about the mechanics as they hauled the crates to the 453rd's airfield. The planes were not assembled quickly, not at all. The RAF mechanics closeted themselves with the detailed instruction pamphlets before starting the complicated task of converting subassemblies and parts into fighter airplanes. For their part, the pilots fairly devoured the manuals on how to fly the bulldog-cowled beasts.

Each airplane came with one of these manuals, and the procedure was simple enough for checking out. Whoever finished the manual first would be first to fly. While his fellow pilots slept the night through, Board burned the midnight oil and went through the manual without a stop. He explains that he was a "quick reader who raised the eyebrows of the commanding officer, who had never noticed this particular trait before." Nonetheless the CO gave Greg Board the signal as the first man up with the Buffalo.

In this respect the young Australian fighter pilot proved to be fortunate. As he was yet to learn, the Buffalo was a "dog" as a combat machine when eventually it would be pitted against the Japanese Zero—and those pilots with the greatest experience in the American export fighter would also have the greatest opportunity for remaining alive.

"The Buffalo wasn't exactly what the British might have planned for the air defense of Singapore and the surrounding area," states Board. "The Buffalo fighters either had no radio, or were afflicted with radios that wouldn't work. The mechanics lacked even a single page to guide them in servicing and maintenance, and for the pilots—well, the handbook stopped very far short of what was needed. We could only guess as to the limitations we were to observe in flying the airplanes. Sort of guide us to keep the wings from tearing off in the wrong maneuver. The absence of these aids certainly gave us lots of practice."

Fighter pilots are prone to look at the world with a sanguine view, but this attitude definitely was not shared by the high command of the RAF. They looked askance at the niggardly assembly of airpower under British control. By December 8, the total British force (with British, Australian, and New Zealand pilots and crews) available to meet any Japanese move included four squadrons of Buffalos—52 fighters. There were four squadrons of British Blenheim bombers and two squadrons with Australians flying American-built Lockheed Hudson bombers. Exactly three American-built Catalina flying boats, based at Seletar, near Singapore, were available for long-range reconnaissance. Completing the airpower roster were two squadrons of Vildebeeste torpedo bombers, archaic and rickety biplanes with fixed landing gear, masses of rigging wires and braces, and open cockpits. At a normal combat speed of just about 100 miles per hour, the Vildebeeste was *slower* than some British two-man ships flown during World War *I*. It was noted among the British crewmen after the war began that some Japanese casualties might have been caused when Japanese pilots caught sight of the Vildebeestes and laughed themselves to death.

All together, the British had 110 planes available in the Malayan area to meet whatever the Japanese would offer in the way of offensive operations. (This force was to be supplemented with one squadron of AVG fighters; the Dutch also rushed nine Buffalo fighters and 22 Martin B-10 bombers—which the Japanese promptly slaughtered in battle—to the aid of the British after the opening of hostilities.)

The conditions for modern airpower operations in Malaya and surrounding areas, including the islands of Sumatra and Java to the south and the southeast, left almost everything to be desired. As the official historian of the Royal New Zealand Air Force noted of this situation:

"Facilities for the repair and maintenance of these machines were sadly lacking. Such as did exist were concentrated in the workshops at Seletar on Singapore Island. These workshops, although equipped only to deal with the requirements of two squadrons at the most, were called upon to service the whole air force in Malaya; the magnitude of their task may be gauged from the fact that twenty-seven modifications had to be made in the Brewster Buffalo fighter before it could be used in battle. . . .

"Our squadrons were seriously short of trained and experienced pilots. Many of those serving in Malaya had come straight from flying training schools in Australia and New Zealand, where most of them had never flown anything more modern than a Hart and had no experience of retractable undercarriages, variable pitch propellers or flaps. Furthermore, when the Japanese attacked, the Buffalo fighter squadrons had only been formed a few months and half of them had not reached full operational efficiency.

"The situation as regards airfields was also far from satisfactory although great efforts had been made to improve matters in the year before war came. Of the airfields that had been built, fifteen possessed no concrete runways but were surfaced with grass, a serious matter in a country where tropical rains are frequent and severe. Several, such as that at Alor Star, were out-of-date, with congested buildings close to the runways and few facilities for dispersal. Very few were camouflaged. Ground defenses were inadequate or non-existent. Because of the rugged and difficult nature of the territory in Malaya many airfields had to be built on the exposed east coast, and several were sited in places where their defense proved well-nigh impossible. For example, the landing grounds at Kuantan and Kota Bharu had been built next to long and excellent sea beaches, a fact of which the Japanese were to take full advantage.

"Another serious feature, especially for the fighter defense, was the lack of radar units to detect the approach of hostile aircraft and ships. On the east coast of Malaya, where the first landings took place, only two were operational, the remaining five still being under construction. On the west coast one had been completed and two others were approaching completion. Only on Singapore Island itself were there three posts in working order. At some stations there was no more effective warning system than that provided by an aircraftsman standing on the perimeter and waving a white handkerchief on the approach of hostile aircraft. These were some of the handicaps under which our pilots and crews went into action against the Japanese invaders."[2]

The official histories of the weeks leading up to the Japanese attack, and of the events subsequent to repeated invasions, obscure the personal element of these times—which we are fortunate to have through the experiences of Greg Board. The Australian fighter pilot recounted to the writer that during the months prior to open combat, vague reports of powerful armies and air forces massing for an all-out strike filtered slowly down to the ranks of the fighter pilots. Board and his fellow pilots were provided with "intelligence briefings almost daily by the most learned of men, who came in from the other side of the Japanese bamboo curtain, and they told us the best of the Japanese fighters were old fabric-covered biplanes which wouldn't stand a chance against the Buffaloes.

"With this ringing promise of slaughtering the Japanese in the air should they get too big for their breeches, we

runways but were simply sunk in grass, a serious defect in

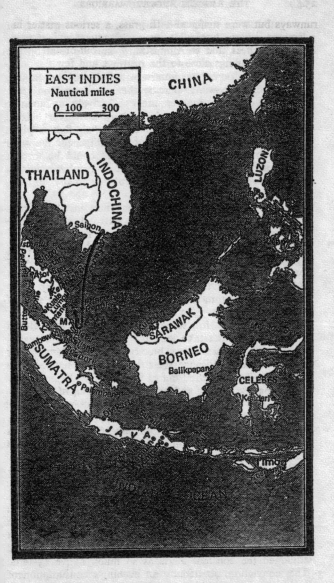

concentrated on flying and learning different methods of drinking gin and tonic. We flew with absolute confidence in our prowess, and we drank hard, and we were on top of the heap, as far as we were concerned."

Royal Air Force headquarters reassigned the Buffalo fighters to Sambawang, placing them in a position from which they might counter more effectively a Japanese thrust which now seemed more likely than ever before. "In mid-November," explained Board, "all fighter pilots were given emergency briefings by Intelligence. We were warned that a Japanese surprise attack could be thrown against us 'at any moment.' We went on combat readiness alert, with several fighter planes always ready for immediate takeoff."

At the Sambawang airfield, mechanics installed sirens and other devices with which to alert all pilots—while they were on duty at the field and when they were off duty, and in the surrounding area. Board and the other fighter pilots practiced combat intercept takeoffs—getting into the air within the shortest possible time. The practice alerts came without warning by day and night, with pilots dashing madly from their bamboo huts at the first wail of the sirens, and running to their fighters.

"This went on for some three weeks or so," Board said, "and it didn't take long for all the pilots to regard with great distaste those bloody practice alerts. They were a damned nuisance after a while. The natives were jumpy; they were scared out of their wits at the possibility of a Japanese attack, and every time a flock of birds appeared near the border, they would become hysterical and sound the alarm and set off every siren within ten miles. You couldn't get any sleep or any rest while all this commotion was going on. Things got so bad we had a tendency to ignore the alarms. . . ."

One night—as had happened on previous evenings—the alarms again shattered the quiet of sleeping men; sirens screeched, bullhorns blasted, and natives howled. Cursing, the pilots clumsily donned clothes and set out on foot and bicycle from their bamboo barracks to reach their planes. Except Greg Board; as fighter pilots are wont to do after much commotion and little action, he had adjudged the constant alerts as so much native hysteria. This conviction, abetted by an evening's consumption of gin and an overwhelming desire to sleep, left him less than eager to leap from his bed. Board cursed the pilot who shook him furiously; he rolled over and ignored the din by going back to sleep.

Until a distant *crump! crump! crump!* brought him bolt upright and wide awake. This was *not* an alert. This time the distant sounds were very real, and the sounds that knifed into his sleep were faraway antiaircraft guns blasting at some unseen enemy. He slipped into his clothes, glanced at his watch (2:30 A.M.) slapped a pith helmet on his head (he still doesn't know *why* he did that), and tore off on a bicycle to reach his fighter.

In the Stygian blackness Board pedaled furiously down the dirt road that led from his barracks shack to the airstrip. Dazzling flashes of light suddenly split wide the darkness, and Board blinked stupidly as the savage glare stabbed into his eyes. Then searchlights flashed on. Board looked up to stare at a giant V of bombers thundering in his direction.

"Then," he recalled with a wince, "I thought my ears were going to come right off my head. Every goddamned gun on that island started firing at the same time and they kept right on firing. I seemed to be in the middle of the concussion waves. On top of that I saw the bombers heading for the airstrip and I decided—very quickly —that this was no place for *me. . . .*"

Board spun around on the bicycle and pedaled wildly to reach a slit trench atop a nearby hill. It turned into a sharp race between Board on the bicycle and the Japanese planes, and the bombers had it all over the bicycle. Greg Board went clean over the handlebars and hit the ground with his feet moving in a blur. What spurred him on to such Olympic speed was a knifelike whistling sound, a keening cry in the night that heralded the bombs even at that moment pouring earthward. Board never did make the slit trench, but managed to hurl himself bodily into a ditch as the earth heaved wildly from the exploding bombs.

Later, when the earth settled back to normal and the screams of jagged steel whipping overhead were gone, an amazed pilot strode through the shambles that had been a fighter airstrip. By some miracle no one had been killed, but the field was pitted with craters and several Buffaloes remained only as smoking junk.

That was the opening play of the war for Board and his fellow pilots from England, Canada, Australia, and

New Zealand. The Japanese came over again and again in their massed waves of bombers and fighters, and the RAF planes went up again and again, but with decreasing frequency, in attempts to stem the aerial tide. The Buffalo fighters of the 453rd and 21st Squadrons did their best to hammer down the Japanese bombers—but too many Japanese fighter planes, of far greater performance than the RAF Brewsters, snuffed out hopes that the RAF might push back the Japanese from British skies. . . .

On the third day of the attacks the Zero fighters were present in great numbers. The 21st Squadron, sharing the airstrip with the 453rd (to which, it will be recalled, Board was attached), went up in force to "take on" the Japanese fighter pilots. No one yet knew what the Zero fighters were, except that they were *not* ancient, slow, fabric-covered biplanes. As it became shockingly evident that the Zero was not merely good, but a superb fighter, the RAF pilots learned to their dismay that the enemy pilots could also be quite brilliant at their work.

"The entire 21st Squadron was wiped out to a man," explained Board. "Suddenly we realized what we really had in the Buffalo—a barrel which the Zeros could outfly, outclimb, outgun, outmaneuver and outdo almost everything else that was in the book for a fighting airplane. And all this time, *I* hadn't yet fired my guns at a Japanese machine. Every time we went up, the Nips came through another sector. The boys were taking a beating almost everywhere they tangled with the Zeros. . . ."

Two Buffalo pilots who attempted to intercept a Japanese bomber formation striking at Singapore came back to their airfield in mingled rage and frustration. The Buffalo fighters heated up dangerously in the maximum-power climb. The pilots approached the Japanese bombers but were never able to close with them, and found to their dismay they could have done nothing to stop the enemy even had they made an attack—in neither aircraft would the guns fire!

Later on that same day (December 8), J. B. Hooper sighted seven twin-engine bombers 2,000 feet above him. Repeated calls to his command unit on the ground failed to bring any response (his radios proved to be dead), so the pilot rammed his throttle forward and climbed to attack position. Before Hooper realized what was happening, six Zero fighters bounced him. Hooper flipped the

Buffalo onto its back, pulled hard on the stick, and plummeted earthward. The Japanese fighter pilots broke off pursuit and returned to their escort positions, while Hooper ran gratefully for home.

Two other Buffalo pilots—Kinninmont and Chapman—near Singora, were bounced by 12 Mitsubishi Type 96 Claude fighters. The open-cockpit, fixed-gear Mitsubishis turned the fight into one of desperate attempts to escape on the part of the Buffalo pilots. Kinninmont found his Buffalo being chewed to ribbons by the Japanese fighters; he watched Chapman struggling with four Mitsubishis. Kinninmont yelled over his radio for Chapman to return to base, and slammed his own Buffalo into a vertical power dive. He caught a glimpse of Chapman streaking earthward with three fighters on his tail, snapping out bursts at the diving Buffalo. Kinninmont reported later that three Mitsubishis also followed him down and that "one stuck and he stuck like a leech. . . . As I watched him, my neck screwed around, I saw his guns smoke and whipped into a tight turn to the left. It was too late and a burst of bullets splattered into the Buffalo. . . . It was then that I felt the first real fear in my life. . . . It struck me in a flash. This Jap was out to kill me. I broke

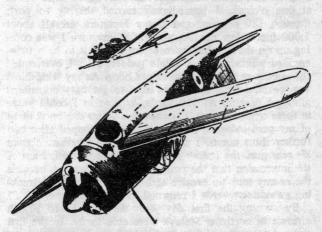

Buffalo *vs.* Zero—and with rare exception it was
the Buffalo, too heavy, too slow, too clumsy,
that went down before the guns of its opponent.

into a cold sweat and it ran down into my eyes. . . . My feet kept jumping on the pedals. My mouth was open and I was panting. . . . My feet were still jumping on the pedals. . . . I couldn't control them. Then I saw his attacks were missing me. I was watching his guns. Each time they smoked I slammed into a tight turn. And then my whole body tightened and I could think. I flew low and straight, only turning in when he attacked. The Jap couldn't hit me again. We raced down a valley to the Thai border and the Jap quit. . . ."[3]

Later that day Kinninmont, on a reconnaissance flight, was jumped again—this time by five Zeros. This time he fought it out with them, maneuvering desperately to stay alive; the Japanese failed to co-ordinate their attacks and Kinninmont escaped finally—*after* studying Japanese invasion ships massed in Singora harbor.

R. S. Shields, with one other pilot, after flying several patrol missions, made several strafing runs on Japanese troop barges on the Kelantan River and, later in the day, also participated in an attempt to intercept nine Japanese bombers. The debriefing given by Shields illustrates the frustrations of the Buffalo pilots:

"While at 9,000 feet in pursuit of nine enemy bombers, I observed a bomb burst approximately three miles ahead at one o'clock. I immediately turned sharply to port, through 180 degrees, and saw a Japanese aircraft about 1,000 feet below me. As a result of my turn I was coming up on the bomber from astern. I saw it to be a twin-engined aircraft with a single rudder. . . . I overhauled the enemy at about 25 miles per hour. As my windshield was covered with oil, I was able to get only occasional glimpses of him. At 350 yards, as near as I could judge in these circumstances, I opened fire. After one burst three of my guns stopped; the remaining gun stopped after two further short bursts. I was unable to see whether, despite his rear gun, the enemy returned my fire. Indeed, I am of the impression that the rear gun was not manned, because the enemy took no evasive action as I approached. Breaking away downwards I returned to the aerodrome. . . ."[4]

By evening the first day, only 50 out of 110 British aircraft in northern Malaya were able to fly. In the first three days of the aerial attacks the Japanese rendered untenable every airfield in northeast and northwest Malaya.

After the loss of the 21st Squadron on December 10, Greg Board's fighter unit shifted its operations to Butterworth on the west coast of Malaya. Here the squadron had its first encounter with the enemy when 13 Buffaloes took off to intercept a formation of Japanese bombers.

"It's the kind of a fight you never forget," mused Board in recounting the battle. "The Zeros shot eleven out of the thirteen Buffaloes to wreckage in the air. One other pilot and myself were the only ones to land in our airplanes."

On December 13 the 453rd Squadron was dispatched to Ipoh, just south of the Thailand border in the center of Malaya. The fighter pilots struck immediately at Japanese troops pounding the hard-pressed 11th Indian Division. The Buffaloes went in at treetop height, strafing Japanese convoys and troop forces on the roads and in open areas. The fighters did a thorough job and inflicted heavy casualties wherever they caught the enemy. But the effort failed to have the effect needed in providing relief to the Indian forces; there simply weren't enough planes with which to hit the Japanese.

Soon afterward, with only ten fighters serviceable throughout the 453rd Squadron, the pilots rose to attack an approaching force of 27 bombers with an escort of 27 Zero fighters. The Zeros were lax in their formation discipline; they were following the bombers and left a slim opening between their formation and the twin-engine planes.

That slim gap gave the Australians a rare opportunity and they made the most of it by roaring down in diving attacks against the bombers. The gap proved slimmer than they thought, for the Zeros were on them in a flash. Board had barely enough time to hammer out one long burst at a bomber, dive below his quarry, and zoom upward to close to pointblank range with a rear-quarter attack from below. Japanese bullets suddenly rocked the Buffalo; grimly Board kept firing. He watched his tracers pouring into the bomber. Without warning it disappeared in a tremendous explosion that shook the Buffalo almost out of control.

Then the Zeros were in the midst of the Australian pilots, angrily snapping out bursts at their opponents. "Fortunately, there were enough loose clouds around for us to hide in," Board admits candidly, "because if you mixed it up with a dogfight in a Zero, the outcome was very clear. Very quickly you were a dead man."

Working day and night, mechanics pieced together the wreckage of old airplanes, and rejuvenated the 21st Squadron with six ramshackle Buffalo fighters. It took the Japanese exactly one more fight to rip them down to only two fighter airplanes.

There were fewer aerial fights than ground-attack missions. On the roads alongside the airfield the fighter pilots watched streams of refugees fleeing from the approaching Japanese. The lack of anything more than token resistance in Thailand had freed the Japanese Army, and it thundered down into Malaya with all the force of a tidal wave crashing onto a beach. Again and again the surviving Buffalo pilots went out on their treetop strafing runs against the enemy forces.

Only three men were now left of the original group, and they took off one morning to hit a Japanese infantry column reported advancing on the main Ipoh highway. This time the Buffalo pilots found the road swarming with thousands of men packed tightly into close columns, and for the first time in the one-sided fighting, the Australians had the opportunity for which they had been waiting.

The fast-firing machine guns of the Buffalo fighters slashed torrents of bullets through the dense ranks of the Japanese soldiers, exacting a gruesome toll. Down the long columns went the Buffaloes, the pilots squeezing out long bursts, gently sawing rudder back and forth to encompass the full road in their fire. Their guns became red hot as they poured the scythe into the bodies of the Japanese—a devastating sweep that killed (by Japanese confirmation after the war) more than 400 men, and seriously wounded another 200.

Wings glinted in the sun as the three fighters completed their long strafing pass and swung sharply to come around for another lethal run. The Buffalo pilots were caught completely by surprise as two Japanese fighters "appeared out of nowhere and came hellbent for leather right at us."

On Greg Board's right wing was Max White, who went down almost immediately in flames, caught by a single well-aimed burst from one Zero. Board tramped down hard on rudder, skidding wildly just above the trees, and

slewed around on the tail of a Japanese fighter. It was
first blood against the Zero for Board, and he made the
most of the rare opportunity, glued to the tail of the Japanese plane, hammering out bursts. Flame mushroomed
from the wings and almost at once a huge ball of red
fire swept around the Zero; the blazing mass trailed greasy
smoke into the jungle and then disappeared in a blinding
explosion. The third pilot—Jeff Seagoe—managed to
chew pieces of metal off the second Japanese fighter, but
that airplane hauled upward into a steep climb and left
the Buffaloes far behind.

Seagoe remained in his turn, nose dropping as he came
around again to bring his guns to bear on the Japanese
troop column. Board climbed to fly top cover and prevent
any more surprise attacks. Below him, Seagoe was taking
a terrible beating. The brief respite brought on by the
appearance of the Zero fighters gave the Japanese time to
ready their weapons, and Seagoe's Buffalo was quickly
shot to ribbons; he struggled back to Ipoh with Board
flying cover off his wing.

The days melted into a nightmarish blur, and the flying
and fighting of Board was representative of what the other
British pilots went through. Japanese bombers staged
down against Burma, Malaya, Sumatra, and other areas
in round-the-clock raids until the pilots were bone-weary
from intercepts and from trying to sleep in between.
Finally only three fighters could be scraped and patched
together for the entire 453rd Squadron. The end seemed
to be at hand during one alarm; as Board rushed from a
dirt strip to climb into the air, he was shocked to see the
other two fighters streaking along an intersecting runway.
All three planes were going too fast to slow down or to
avoid collision; to save the other men, Board chopped his
throttle, yanked up his gear, and belly-whopped the Buffalo into the ground.

The barrel-shaped fighter careened off the dirt strip,
hurling up a fountain of dirt on each side. It smashed into
a tree with an ear-splitting roar, broke in half at the
cockpit, and sprayed wreckage and fluids in all directions.
Dazed and rattled from the crash, Board discovered that
he was pinned tightly into his seat—which in turn was
partly imbedded in the tree! He shook his head in wonder,
noticed with disbelief that his feet were in a creek and
that there wasn't any airplane in front of him.

At this instant he heard the thin scream from the sky that warned of bombs already falling from high altitude. An Australian ground officer dashed up to the tree, tore Board loose from his seat, and half-dragged and pushed the dazed pilot to a slit trench, where both men tumbled in desperately just as the first bombs exploded nearby.

The mechanics did the impossible by existing on starvation rations and going without sleep and patched some more of the wrecked Buffaloes into machines that would get into the air. Board and the other pilots still alive barely got their airplanes out of Ipoh even as Japanese artillery shells were falling on the field perimeter—and snipers' bullets whined dangerously close by.

"The men couldn't even bury their dead," he said coldly. "There were too many of them. They packed the living and the wounded into trucks, buried bombs in the runway, and as soon as we got into the air, they set off the bombs and tore up the airstrip. Then they drove for their lives to Kuala Lumpur, where we all began the same bloody struggle over again."

Hopes soared when British merchantmen fought their way to the Singapore area and unloaded replacement fighters, including new Buffaloes. Board and his friends hoped to be assigned to the Hawker Hurricanes, but instead—because of their experience with the Brewster airplanes—were kept in the "suicide barrels." Board and the other pilots were dismayed when they watched the Hurricanes roar into battle with the Zeros—and saw catastrophe befall them. The British pilots tore into the Japanese planes with the same tactics employed against German fighters in Europe. They expected, no doubt, that the "inferior" Japanese fighters would be swept aside by these tried-and-true tactics.

The Japanese pilots watched with delight as the Hurricanes broke up their formations to mix it up in swirling dogfights. They laughed and promptly tore the British fighters apart. The answer was, and had been, clear to Board and any other man who had experience against the nimble Mitsubishis: *never* dogfight with the Zero.

Board and ten other pilots went up in spanking-new Buffaloes to intercept a skyful of Japanese planes—108 bombers and fighters. The Australians were given one of their rare opportunities to climb to high altitude before the fight—they reached 25,000 feet (the Buffalo would fly

An excellent fighter, the Hurricane was expected to "slaughter" the Zero. Unfortunately, the Zero was faster, could outclimb and turn inside the Hawker fighter. And when the British pilots used the Hurricane to dogfight with the agile Zero, there could be only one outcome— slaughter of the British, not the Japanese, fighters.

no higher) and watched the bombers sliding along nearly two and a half miles below them. It was just the chance they had been waiting for.

Board shoved the stick forward, rammed the throttle to the firewall, and plunged from the sky in a howling vertical dive. He held the dive until a bomber appeared in his gunsights and expanded with tremendous speed; leading his target carefully he squeezed the trigger. The big Mitsubishi raider erupted in crimson flame and almost immediately afterward broke into large flaming chunks that tumbled earthward; that gave Board his third confirmed kill.

Gritting his teeth, he horsed the stick back into his stomach, sagging with the punishing g-forces as the Buffalo mushed helplessly through the pullout. Then the wings grabbed at air and the fighter screamed upward, using the momentum of the pullout to zoom swiftly back to higher altitude.

The swift plunge against the bomber and rocketing climb away from the Japanese formation put Board into the clear. Spotting a Zero fighter below him, he half-rolled onto his back and brought the stick back toward his body; the Buffalo fell out of the sky like a stone. Before Board could set up the Japanese fighter for the kill, all hell broke loose behind him. He had never seen the Zero that flashed away from its own formation and that now was clawing at his back and with cannon and guns methodically chopping the Buffalo into small pieces.

The instrument panel exploded and blew apart in Board's face, showering him with sharp pieces of metal and glass. Instinctively he hunched lower in his seat—just in time. Mighty pistons crashed into his back, sending pain ripping through his spinal column; Japanese bullets spanged off the armor plate and 20-mm. cannon shells tried to drive the plating right through him. Yet those terrible, thudding crashes into his back were saving his life as the plating held off the fatal blow. It was all like a bad dream in slow motion.

The Japanese pilot shot the top layer of the Buffalo's wings clear off the airplane, revealing naked ribs beneath; Board could see and feel the fighter coming apart beneath and all about him. Desperately, he went wild in the Buffalo, trying every trick he knew to shake the Mitsubishi. He feels that he tumbled, cartwheeled, and corkscrewed madly in his airplane in between the more conventional maneuvers.

"But whoever it was in that Zero was good, damned good," Board recalled grimly, "and he had a hell of a better airplane under his hands. He chopped that Brewster into ribbons and pieces as though he was an artist at his work. I had nothing left but to try and get out by going straight down. I was pulling all the power the airplane had and I shoved the stick forward and tried to save my life by diving vertically. . . ."

It didn't help; the Zero stayed glued to his tail like a nightmare that wouldn't go away, snapping out short, neat bursts that pumped bullets and exploding shells into the disintegrating Buffalo. Then there just wasn't anything else that Board could do, because he was sitting in the midst of a thundering, white-hot furnace as the Buffalo flamed. Brilliant fire gushed wildly from the fuel tanks, ammunition exploded in the wing racks, and the acrid, stinging fumes swirled through the cockpit and tried to choke him.

Blazing from nose to tail, Board sliced frantically into a cloud, trying to pull out of the plummeting dive. He needed to slow down to ease the tremendous air pressure about the cockpit as he slid back the hatch. Then there was only the screaming need to escape; as he flipped the stricken fighter onto its back, flames washed in a blast furnace of heat over his body. He released his belt and fell through the roaring fire, the blessed relief of cold air sweeping away the scalding touch of his airplane. For long moments he fell, hand on the D-ring of his parachute, but not pulling, keeping his wits about him, freed of the sensation of falling with his body stabilized in the long plunge, he delayed opening the parachute until he could visually separate the trees in the mountainous jungle beneath him. Convinced he was as low as he dared fall—and that there would be a minimum time swinging in the chute with the Japanese fighters still about—he hauled on the D-ring. Silk blossomed open with a loud *crraaaack!* and he was drifting gently downward.

Good fortune stayed with him. Seconds later the canopy caught in the trees. A long branch bent slowly under Board's weight, and he had the luck simply to unfasten his harness and step out. But that about used up whatever fortune was smiling on him. On his person he had a pistol —and nothing else in the way of survival equipment. The jungle about him was incredibly dense, choked with foliage and with a trap at every step in the form of gnarled roots and rotting vegetation. Following a creek, Board fought and stumbled more than an hour just to claw his way a distance of 400 yards.

Two days later he staggered into a village clearing—and into the hands of friendly natives. They slipped him through Japanese Army lines and pointed him in the direction of Singapore.

The Hapless Fighters

Many of the pilots serving with the RAF endured the same sort of adventures as Gregory Board, who was extremely fortunate to escape without any serious injuries or burns. His friends were not so lucky.

Early in the campaign, Pilots Williams and McKenny of the 21st Squadron attempted to stave off an attack by 54 bombers and fighters. As a reward for their audacity in taking on odds of 27 to one, they were bounced by a dozen Zero fighters and promptly torn to pieces. McKenny was shot down in flames, but managed to bail out and parachute into the sea. Attacked by three fighters that made a special target of his Buffalo, Williams was enraged to find his guns jammed before he could get off a single burst, and he plunged earthward in a howling dive to shake his pursuers.

The Buffalo ran away from the Zeros and Williams rushed for his airstrip; he made it ahead of the Japanese fighters but was moving so fast he was unable to land and so came around in a screaming turn, to bounce onto the runway on his second try. He hurled himself from his cockpit and dove headlong for the nearest trench—as his pursuers pounded over the strip, pouring cannon shells into his downed fighter.

Two other Buffaloes from the same squadron rushed against the Japanese force. Pilot Montefiore was the only one of the four who shot down a Zero fighter, and he had no more than a few seconds to enjoy his victory before the Japanese exploded his Buffalo into flaming wreckage. He bailed out, sailed out of the sky into a palm tree; climbing down the tree, he grabbed a native's bicycle and pedaled madly down a jungle trail until he returned to his squadron. The fourth Buffalo pilot—A. M. White, who was to die on December 14, 1941—managed this day barely to escape with his life. Zeros shot his plane into a mess, which he was able to crashland on Penang Island without injury.

Confusion was rampant at the forward bases. Although at these fields ground crews worked day and night under conditions that were considered intolerable, the proximity of the swift-moving Japanese combined with broken communications to bring on panic situations. One official report of a field abandoned in haste—after the aircraft at the field were evacuated—showed what lack of communications and direction could do. An Australian officer noted: "In half an hour that little flame of panic had spread like wild-fire. I looked out on a deserted station. . . . There were only four of us left—the C.O., the Adjutant, the Armament Officer and myself . . . myself still too numb to appreciate the sarcasm of the other men's conversation. Then I realized they were talking of Australians, that I was an Australian, and that many curious glances were being cast in my direction. . . . For the first and last time I felt ashamed of being an Australian. . . .

The next day twenty-three men returned in a couple of trucks . . ."[4]

Operational problems—especially weather—proved to be an enemy as severe as the Japanese. One mission flown by three pilots of the 453rd Squadron ended quickly in disaster. The pilots—Neale, Brown, and Livesey—were swept up in a sudden storm and lost all direction. Livesey attempted a forced landing in a paddy field; his Buffalo went through incredible gyrations, flipping and tumbling over and over, leaving the pilot injured when it finally settled as a tangled mass of wreckage. His fellow pilots fared otherwise. Neale's fighter smashed into a tree and exploded in flames, instantly killing its pilot. Brown's aircraft crashed with terrible force into the ground and exploded violently, also killing the pilot immediately.

On December 14 three other Buffalo pilots of the 453rd Squadron found their day a busy one; they started off by attacking nine Japanese bombers. Pilot Vanderfield cursed a balky landing gear that refused to retract; his airplane shuddering and groaning from the unexpected drag, he nevertheless roared into the enemy formation, and shot down two of his targets! The other pilots—Read and Collyer—shared three kills between them. These two landed, refueled and rearmed quickly, and rushed into the air to make strafing runs against Japanese soldiers and trucks north of Alor Star.

As they came back to land, a new flight of Buffaloes arrived at Ipoh, their operational strip. The new pilots were greeted with an attack by more than 40 Japanese fighters. The intercept mission by the Buffaloes turned into a mad scramble. Pilot Vigors had his Buffalo explode into huge flaming chunks; by a miracle he escaped from the careening wreckage and took to his parachute. As he dropped through the air a Japanese fighter made run after run at him with guns firing. Vigors was already in agony from severe burns on his legs, arms, and hands—and a bullet in one thigh. Each time the Japanese fighter roared in against him, the badly wounded Australian reached up to grasp his shroud lines, and deliberately collapsed his parachute so that he fell like a rock. As soon as the fighter swept by, he released the lines and reinflated his canopy. Four times he was forced to go through this terrifying experience—but survived to land on Penang Mountain (from which he was later rescued). Vigors was so badly wounded that he could not recall more than scanty details of his battle—and only the fact that men on the ground observed the crashes of three Japanese planes enabled him to receive confirmation for the kills.

The courage of the Japanese pilots was demonstrated in dramatic fashion on December 15 when three Japanese *dive bombers* attacked five Buffalo fighters! One Australian pilot was shot down immediately and killed. Another died in the crash of his fighter immediately afterward. A third pilot flew in agony with one shoulder shattered by an explosive bullet, but was escorted home by the other two pilots.

The official history notes, regarding Australian fighter operations:

"By 15th December the two fighter squadrons could put only three aircraft fit for combat into the air, a state for which enemy action was not solely responsible. The whole burden of maintenance had been placed on the already overworked and understaffed ground crews of No. 21 Squadron, who also had to cope with increased trouble with the Buffaloes' guns. For example, when three Buffaloes intercepted three unescorted enemy bombers over Ipoh, only four of the total twelve guns would fire. One bomber was shot down but there was little doubt that had all their guns been serviceable, the Buffalo pilots would have brought the score to three."[5]

It was also painfully evident that the Japanese were masters at the art of luring their enemy into old but still effective traps. On December 17 a scramble alert at Ipoh sent eight Buffaloes to 20,000 feet to intercept an approaching Japanese force. The Australian fighters ran into ten Zeros which "immediately wheeled and made off. With their superior speed the enemy pilots kept just out of range of their pursuers who followed them until it was obvious that the chase was hopeless. They then turned back to base and came over the airfield to see clouds of smoke rising from burning aircraft on the ground and ruined station buildings. Too eagerly they had taken the enemy's bait. In their absence ten bombers had flown over in complete safety to make an attack in which they destroyed three grounded Buffaloes and several buildings. It was not a new trick but it had succeeded. Even so, it had been only half played. The Buffaloes came in to land,

and just as the last of them were taxiing across the airfield a second bombing raid began. One of the fighters swerved into a deep drain and was wrecked. Another was caught by the blast of an exploding bomb and flung onto its side with one wing ripped off. A small transport plane used as a mail carrier, that had already narrowly escaped when two Buffalo pilots had mistaken it for an enemy aircraft, received a direct hit. It was blown to pieces and its crew of two and two passengers were killed.

". . . at Ipoh the next morning part two of the enemy's trick was tried again. Immediately the raid warning was received six Buffaloes took off, failed to intercept the enemy, and returned and landed. Two of the aircraft were still making their final taxi run when fifteen bombers attacked. Both aircraft were caught in the bomb line and destroyed, though both pilots had time to leap from their cockpits and tumble into slit trenches and safety. The squadron equipment officer . . . was mortally wounded when a bomb burst beside a motor car in which he had just driven onto the airfield. At midday three Zeros again swept in on a low-level gunnery attack. . . ."[6]

The New Zealand fighter squadrons fared little better than did the Australians. The official combat diary of No. 488 Squadron for January 13, 1942, is typical of operations:

"At 0630 hours Pilot Officer Hesketh led four aircraft of A Flight on a security patrol, but no contact was made with the enemy. At 1100 hours Flight Lieutenant Hutcheson took off with eight aircraft, some being from a Dutch squadron, to intercept thirty Type 96 bombers, making contact with them and attacking from astern. The speed of the bombers was such that the Buffalo aircraft could only just overhaul them but could not get into position for beam or overhead attacks. Flight Lieutenant Hutcheson was shot up by rear-gun fire and crash-landed at base. Pilot Officer Greenhalgh attacked an Army 96 bomber. Although only two guns fired, he managed to get smoke from one engine. Pilot Officer Oakden was shot down into the sea by rear-gun fire from a bomber, and was rescued by a Chinese sampan, sustaining slight injuries to his face. Sergeant Clow was shot down in the sea, swam four hundred yards to a small island, and was picked up by some Chinese in a sampan and returned to Kallang two days later. Pilot Officers Hesketh and Gifford were unable to get sufficient height to attack. Pilot Officer McAneny had to break off his attack through gun failure. Sergeant de Maus was hit before he got within range. [A] Dutch pilot went missing. Casualties: five aircraft written off and one damaged with no loss to the enemy.

"Today, although we did not meet up with the fighters because we did not attack from above, we were badly shot up from rear-gun fire. The Japanese bomber formations of twenty-seven packed aircraft throw out such an accurate and heavy rear-gun barrage that they are very difficult to attack. Some way must be found to break up these mass formations and attack bombers independently. No doubt there was fighter escort in the near vicinity, but it did not pick up our fighters owing to cloudy conditions and also because we attacked from astern.

"In the last two days 488 Squadron has lost seven aircraft and had many others damaged, with no loss to the enemy. No blame can be attached to the pilots, who have done their best with Buffaloes. Until we fly as Wings of thirty-six aircraft we will be unable to inflict heavy damage on the enemy."

One of the rare fighter victories came on January 18, when New Zealand and British pilots shot down two out of nine Zeros without loss to their own ranks. Later that day another fight resulted in one more Zero being shot down—but the loss of two Buffaloes.

The arrival of more than 50 Hurricane fighters as replacements sent spirits soaring. One squadron received nine of the Hawker fighters, but fell into the same disastrous routine as in previous action. A surprise Japanese air raid destroyed two of the Hurricanes and heavily damaged another six—before they were committed to their first battle. While the men were still clearing up the wreckage from the attack (which also smashed up several Buffaloes, burned some bombers to slag heaps, consumed fuel stores, set off a munitions dump, and incinerated most of the vehicles at the field), a second Japanese attack destroyed two more fighters "and pitted the aerodrome with craters, making it completely unserviceable."

Over Burma a New Zealander demonstrated the lengths to which the fighter pilots went in order to combat the enemy. Sergeant Bargh of No. 67 Squadron singlehandedly mixed it up in a furious dogfight with a swarm of Japanese fighters, and barely managed to escape with his life from the scrap. But he succeeded in his mission of drawing away the Japanese fighters from their bomber formations, which were hit by other Buffaloes.

Bargh dove for his life in a fighter screaming from wind rushing past hundreds of bullet holes. Safe from his pursuers, he climbed steadily until he reached 17,000 feet, where he calmly awaited the Japanese bombers—which would have to cross his path on their return from their bombing run. By now (as usual) the windscreen of his Buffalo was thickly smeared with oil.

Nothing seemed to daunt Bargh. Slowing down his airplane, he took off one of his flying boots and removed his thick woolen sock. He placed his hand within the sock, released his belt, and stood up in the howling wind. He leaned as far forward as he could against the windblast and wiped his windscreen free of oil. He had just enough time to turn and dive at the approaching Japanese formation, shooting down one bomber and a fighter in the brief but wild fight before he roared earthward to escape a hornets' nest of Japanese fighters!

The end was clearly in sight. Despite the bitter efforts to hold back the Japanese, the Zeros reigned supreme on almost all occasions. Even the Hurricane fighters, far superior to the obsolescent Buffaloes, could not stem the tide. On their first battle engagement, the Hurricanes shot down eight Japanese bombers without loss to themselves. The burst of enthusiasm that resulted was dissipated the day following when a Zero fighter escort appeared—and without losing a single fighter shot down five Hurricanes, heavily damaged an equal number, and destroyed any hopes that the newer British fighters could whip the Mitsubishis.

On February 10 the last British combat airplane evacuated Singapore; five days later the "impregnable fortress" went down to Japanese arms. Just before its surrender, RAAF headquarters ordered seven surviving pilots without planes—among them Gregory Board—to the Singapore dock area. The men drove through streets splashed with bodies and stained with drying and caked blood, through which scurried human scavengers as well as huge rats which feasted boldly in the open on the shattered bodies. The pilots were to board an Australian cruiser; the warship's captain, realizing the danger of imminent bomber attack, slid neatly against the dock, never stopping. The pilots leaped in mad dashes onto the deck and the warship immediately picked up speed. All about the cruiser, ships burned brightly on the water, and hundreds of corpses bobbed in the oily waves. Engines driving at maximum speed, the cruiser raced for Java, where American, Dutch, British, Australian, and New Zealand aircrews were putting up a desperate but hopeless attempt to stem the Japanese advance.

"It didn't last long," Board recalled. "The Zeros just tore us apart. Everything sort of melts into a blur after that. We got out of Java one step ahead of the Japanese and made it to India. Here we tried to get back into fighters, but there weren't any. We managed to get aboard another Australian cruiser, and we were on our way back home. We weren't too happy about things. No one knew where or when we would stop the Japanese. . . ."

14

DISASTER IN JAVA

The aerial campaign of the British forces throughout Malaya and Sumatra, which was to be repeated in Java, as well as along the northern coastline of Australia, followed a pattern that was all too distressingly familiar to the one man who had consistently whipped the Japanese —and had done this with numerically inferior forces. Claire L. Chennault could do little more than groan at the insistence of the Allied forces upon fighting the Zero fighter on conventional terms. On almost every occasion when Allied fighters tangled in wild dogfights with the nimble Mitsubishis, the outcome was decided before the battle—the Japanese were almost certain to win.

When Japanese fighters caught unescorted British bombers—the Blenheims, Hudsons, the Vildebeestes—almost always they tore apart the British ranks and inflicted severe casualties among the bombers. Fighter escort properly handled—as it frequently was—enabled the bombers both to hit their targets and return home without their ranks being decimated. On occasion the Hudsons would emerge from a bitter fight with the Japanese, perhaps not the victors, but nevertheless unexpected survivors who managed to drag their bullet-lashed airplanes home. This happened when the Hudson pilots were skilled and daring men who used the great structural strength and maneuverability of the Lockheed bomber to best advantage—by turning tightly into the Japanese fighters and bringing the Hudson's fixed guns to bear. Such incidents did take place, but they were rare, and the Japanese made the skies over their operations areas essentially a Japanese domain.

The extent to which Chennault had to struggle to overcome the entrenched ideas of fighter pilots and air forces had been nowhere more evident than in Burma, where he

worked closely with the Royal Air Force in the defense
of Rangoon. There the AVG and the British fighter pilots
fought side by side. Chennault has pointed out in speeches
and elsewhere that the AVG and the RAF were comparable in their equipment, numbers, and courage in facing the enemy—although prior to combat, AVG pilots
were bitter that the RAF had been given the Buffalo,
which they had considered to be a superior aircraft to
the Tomahawk!

In that combat, Chennault has made it clear, the British
barely broke even in terms of losses with the Japanese,
including bombers that were attacked as well as fighters.
Flying the much-abused P-40B, the Americans went on
to rack up the astounding kill ratio of *15 to one*, often
wrecking entire Japanese formations.

Then came February, 1942, and a massive increase in
Japanese air operations, when they mounted heavy raids
simultaneously against Rangoon and Port Darwin, Australia. It took such attacks to prove the validity of Chennault's tactics. During the same week there were two separate battles to clear away the clouds of controversy.

Over Rangoon five AVG pilots in Tomahawks plunged
into enemy formations totaling 70 planes; when the battle
ended the Tigers had shot down 17 Japanese planes without a loss to themselves. Over Darwin, 12 P-40s raced
against a Japanese force of the same numerical strength—
and only one P-40 survived the melee.

As Chennault has stressed, the weakness lay in attitude
and in tactics. The Tigers' tactics of diving into the enemy,
shooting, and diving away had become the butt of much
ridicule. At Rangoon, Chennault emphasizes, the RAF had
gone so far as to post notice to the effect that "any R. A. F.
pilot seen diving away from a fight would be subject to
court-martial." Obviously, that notice was torn down and
quietly forgotten. In the Chinese Air Force, Chennault recalls, "the penalty for the same offense was a firing
squad."[1]

In March, 1942, the British decided to put an end once
and for all to the obvious superiority of the Japanese fighters in combat. Still ignoring the astounding success of
Chennault's men, the RAF rushed a crack Spitfire squadron from Europe to Australia to teach the Japanese a
thing or two. The Spitfire, acclaimed as perhaps the finest
close-in fighter plane of the war, came over with pilots

well experienced against the German Messerschmitt Me-109 and Focke-Wulf FW-190. And there was no question, even from Chennault, that the "Spitfire was far superior to the P-40 as a combat plane."[2]

In *two raids* the British lost 17 out of 27 Spitfire pilots at the hands of the Zero fighters!

"It was simply a matter of tactics," Chennault said later. "The R.A.F. pilots were trained in methods that were excellent against German and Italian equipment but suicide against the acrobatic Japs."[3]

When the Japanese swept down into and through the territories and island groups of Asia and the far Pacific, they carried out a series of thrusts simultaneously along a front that extended for thousands of miles. Thus by December 11 Japanese troops were pouring ashore on the northern coastline of Borneo, and rushing swiftly to take control of the riches that were their objective—oil wells, rubber, spices, tin, and sugar, for which the East Indies were justly renowned. Seven days after they raced ashore, the Japanese troops were solidly entrenched in Kuching, capital of Sarawak.

The aerial defenses of the Dutch comprised a weird variety of aircraft; the fighters included P-40B Tomahawks, CW-21 Demons, Curtiss P-36 Mohawks, and Brewster Buffaloes as the main force. Martin B-10 bombers, sadly outdated for World War II, made up the backbone of the bombardment strength. Trainers and liaison planes were pressed into service, with a few flying boats, the latter mostly of American and German manufacture, to complete the force with which the Dutch would resist the Japanese. Before the East Indies fell to the enemy, more makes and types of planes were in service there—Douglas A-24s (AAF version of the SBD Dauntless in service with the U.S. Navy) as dive bombers; Douglas DB-7 Bostons and their AAF counterparts, the A-20s; old-model and new B-17E Flying Fortresses; Consolidated LB-30 Liberators; British Blenheim and Vildebeeste bombers; Beaufort night fighters; and Buffalo and Hurricane day fighters. The Japanese took them all on with devastating losses to the defenders.

The Dutch Air Force at the outbreak of hostilities amounted to some 200 airplanes. Within a week of the Japanese push into Malaya and Sumatra, the Dutch shifted

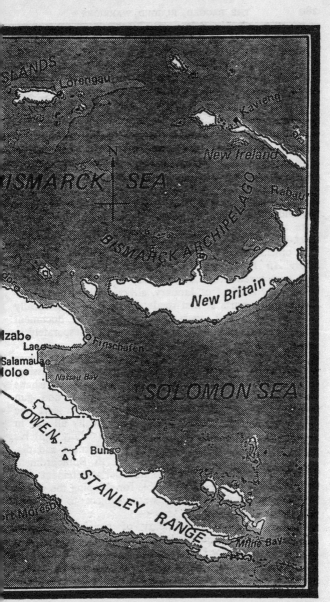

their entire bomber force to Sumatra to aid the British—
who unhappily were forced to send most of the Dutch
bombers back to their home bases so the crews could be
trained in night flying, which they had never done in
combat formations. By the beginning of 1942, Borneo
was left seriously exposed to air attack, with only 158
planes of all types (including trainers and liaison planes)
left to defend all of Borneo and its sea approaches.

The defense of the Netherlands East Indies had been
predicated on extensive aerial reinforcements staging
northward from Australia. Unfortunately, rampant confusion riddled the program for reinforcements from the
start, and proved of inestimable aid to the Japanese.

Many of the airplanes which were assembled by the
day-and-night labor of mechanics and technicians never
were able to get into combat in time even to stave off
what was clearly eventual defeat through the East Indies.
The official combat document, *The AAF in Australia,
Army Air Forces Historical Studies*, No. 9, notes that
"the men assembled enough planes to begin training operations by the first of January, although the lack of certain essential parts at first rendered the planes practically
useless for combat operations." The official document
notes, in reference to dive bombers needed desperately in
the East Indies:

". . . after the fifty-two A-24s were assembled, it was
discovered that certain pieces of armament were missing.
A thorough search of the cargo unloaded at Brisbane
disclosed no trace of the triggers, solenoids, and gun
mounts. This exasperating situation caused at least one
harassed lieutenant to rush around 'frantically all day in
his jeep trying to collect spare parts, and wildly beat his
head when none were available.' The bitterness and dis-
appointment of those pilots of the 27th Bombardment
Group is reflected in their commander's statement that
the persons in America responsible for shipping the planes
without the necessary parts were 'subject to trial for
criminal negligence.' "[4]

No clearly defined boundary of operations existed
through Malaya, Sumatra, Borneo, Java, Timor, Celebes,
the Philippines, New Guinea, and intermediate points during this time. Reaction to the pounding drives of the
Japanese took place in scattered thrusts wherever the most
likely targets seemed to appear, and the campaign carried

out from Australia was one that encompassed strikes extending from New Ireland and the Bismarck Archipelago on the west all the way northwest to the Philippines.

Some veteran groups arrived in Australia during February, for example, and were immediately sent out on missions covering the area just described. Men of the 88th Reconnaissance and 22nd Bombardment Squadrons of the 7th Bombardment Group had flown 168 patrol missions out of Hawaii for two months preceding their departure from that area. Pieced together into a squadron of 12 Fortresses, they flew from Hawaii in late February, moving south to protect the supply lines to Australia. They stopped in the Fiji Islands for five days to fly another 12 missions, arriving in Townesville, Australia, on February 18 and 19. Then for the next month the bomber crews flew reconnaissance and bombing missions without benefit of ground crews.

It is all too easy to wax eloquent over the violent actions of combat, but much more difficult to grasp the feeling of utter weariness experienced by men such as these. After flying long missions at high altitude during the day, their strength sapped by the roar and vibration of the airplanes, and breathing thin air at operational heights, the combat personnel worked almost the night through to maintain and repair, refuel, rearm, and bomb up their large airplanes. Because there was no fighter protection available and antiaircraft facilities were a mockery of the term, it was necessary to disperse the B-17s into the Australian interior. Thus it became necessary for the crews to fly two separate flights—one from the interior to the Australian coast, and one from the coast to an advanced base—before they could take off on an actual mission.

Despite these crippling obstacles, the crews kept their airplanes in battle condition and flew their missions. Six full crews of this squadron assembled above Magnetic Island on the morning of February 23 and began the long flight to carry out the first American bombardment of Rabaul, New Britain. The weather turned bad during the mission but did not deter the Fortresses from pressing home their attack. One large cargo vessel went to the bottom, another was damaged, and several Zero fighters were either destroyed or damaged. The large bombers fought off their attackers, sustaining wounds to three crew mem-

bers. On the flight home, one Fortress exhausted its fuel
and made a wheels-up belly landing 220 miles from Port
Moresby, New Guinea; its exhausted and malaria-ridden
crew did not return to their squadron until April 1.

The official history of the AAF in Australia notes of
these actions:

"This American 'offensive' strike from the east coast of
Australia, though modest in scale, was nevertheless a 'shot
in the arm' for the tired and outnumbered members of
the Royal Australian Air Force who were attempting to
oppose the Japanese advance through New Guinea and
New Britain. To provide for the defense of New Guinea,
New Britain, and the whole of Australia except Darwin
[where defenses were provided by the British, Australians,
New Zealanders, and Americans] the RAAF in January
had a total of only forty-three operational aircraft—
twenty-nine Hudsons, fourteen Catalinas, and *no* fighter
airplanes. In addition, it had eighty Wirraways—advanced
training planes—which, of course, were ineffective in operations against the enemy. With heavy losses being sustained daily in the New Guinea area, this small force was
rapidly depleted, but by the end of January the members
of the RAAF had already distinguished themselves in
making the most of the little at their disposal.

"The heavy Japanese attack on Rabaul on 20 January
had seen five slow Wirraways rise to defend the Australian
garrison against more than one hundred enemy planes.
Although the Wirraways were lost after exacting their
toll of five enemy aircraft, this action set the pattern for
Australian air resistance during the first few months of
1942. Likewise, the action at Rabaul was typical of the
enemy assaults on practically defenseless Australian positions throughout the Bismarck Archipelago. Following
closely upon the heavy aerial bombardment, the Japanese
on 22 and 23 January landed strong invasion forces at
Rabaul and drove the Australian garrison of 1,400 men
from their positions. At the same time, landings were
made in the northern Solomons, and the bombardment
of northern New Guinea continued. On 21 January enemy
cruisers had shelled undefended Kavieng, New Ireland,
while bombs were being dropped on Lorengau [capital of
the Admiralty Islands] and on Madang and Salamaua,
New Guinea. Lae, undefended capital of Northeast New
Guinea, was subjected to forty-five minutes of heavy

bombing and strafing by over sixty enemy aircraft on 22 January. . . .

"Extending the range of their attacks still farther, the Japanese on 3 February bombed Port Moresby, capital of Papua, only 334 miles from the northern tip of Australia. For the defense of this strategic point in New Guinea the Australians had only one anti-aircraft battery and a dwindling handful of Hudson and Catalina planes. With this new penetration to the south by an enemy which was superior in numbers and in equipment, it was obvious that the northern coast, and perhaps even the whole, of New

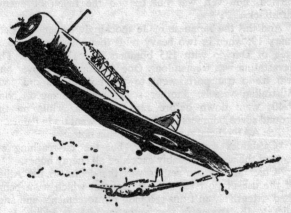

A "scout-fighter" version of the Harvard training
airplane, the Australian Wirraway, flown by
courageous crews, attacked Japanese forces vastly
superior in both quality and quantity. Some Wirraways—
to the astonishment of both adversaries—
actually shot down their opponents!

Guinea would be untenable. Mining prospectors who had pioneered in the gold fields of New Guinea and other civilians living on New Britain and islands of the northern Solomons had to leave their holdings and possessions in a hurried flight to safer territory on the Australian mainland. Throughout January and February every airplane in the area—both civilian and military—was pressed into service, with the result that more than two thousand men,

women and children were rescued without the loss of a
single life. 'All the laws of civil aviation were flouted.
Planes built to carry sixteen carried thirty-five. . . .' Day
after day the crazy rescue fleet of battered old transport
planes that had freighted the mining dredges up to Edie
Creek and Bulolo; of unwieldy old Ford monoplanes; of
sleek, modern airliners; of two-seater Moths, and shabby,
fabric-covered biplanes, joined with camouflaged bombers
of the Royal Australian Air Force in ferrying backward
and forward between Australia and the newest battle zone
of the Pacific.

"The continent to which these evacuated civilians were
carried, however, was not beyond the reach of enemy
air attacks. . . ."5

And this the Japanese made shockingly evident on February 19, when in two heavy raids they plastered the port
area of Darwin with 125 bombers and 18 fighters. The
devastation was tremendous. One American destroyer and
two troop transports went to the bottom, as did four
Australian vessels; another seven were damaged. Nine
P-40s went down before Japanese guns, while on the
ground seven bombers and two fighters went up in flames.

The AAF official report on Australia notes:

"Casualties were not heavy, but the far-reaching effects of the attack probably exceeded all enemy hopes.

"Chief among the results was the denial to the Allies
of the use of port facilities at Darwin, which were being
used extensively in trans-shipping reinforcements and supplies to the troops in the Netherlands East Indies. In a
broader sense, these two raids gave tangible proof of the
enemy's capability and intention of bringing the war to
the continent of Australia. Because of the proximity of
the newest enemy gains in the Netherlands East Indies
the northwestern coast of Australia was no longer safe for
military concentrations. Immediately following the Darwin
attacks, therefore, the Australian army authorities ordered
the demolition of Keats Airdrome, 130 miles southwest
of Darwin, and ordered certain other west coast airdromes prepared for demolition.

"These two enemy attacks had a dark foreboding about
them which started the hurried movement of civilians
from the west coast to the interior of Australia. Likewise,
the attacks were portentous of the trend of events in the

Netherlands East Indies, for it was becoming increasingly evident that Allied resistance could no longer continue . . ."[3]

The "dark foreboding" became reality with the swift movement of the Japanese forces. By February 14 crack parachute troops dropping from Japanese bombers and transports were in control of Palembang, the center of the rich Sumatran oil fields. Six days later Japanese troops splashed ashore on Bali, the island east of Java, and on Timor, the island lying between Java and the Australian mainland.

Throughout the repeated invasion thrusts of the Japanese, the Fortresses operating out of Australia continued their desperate strikes at the enemy. Throughout January they attacked a wide variety of targets, from enemy warships to airfields. Japanese resistance on rare occasions was light or absent; most of the time the Zeros swarmed up to rip into the big bombers. The latter enjoyed a new defense against their opponents—the B-17E not only carried up to 13 .50-caliber machine guns, but it came equipped with an upper power turret, a power ball turret in the belly, and a tail position with two heavy guns. Two Fortresses in January, during attack against Japanese troopships in Menado Bay, were intercepted by 15 fighters; as usual, the Japanese in their attacks against the four-engine bombers made their attacks from the rear. This time the reaction of the American planes was not usual, and during the fight that lasted for more than an hour, the two Fortresses shot down six of the fighters.

"During the engagement," reported Vern Haugland, "Private Arvid B. Hegdahl, tail gunner on Major Conrad F. Necrason's plane, was wounded severely in the leg. Master Sergeant Louis T. Silva, a forty-seven year old line chief of the 9th Squadron who asked to go along with his squadron commander on this first mission as a gunner, helped carry the wounded tail gunner forward for first aid, and himself was credited with shooting down three planes with a side gun. Silva was killed in an airplane accident in Australia five months later.

"Necrason's plane escaped major damage, but Lt. J. L. Dufrane's had one engine shot out. The two Fortresses were refueling at Kendari when five Japanese fighters attacked the field, at 2:15 A.M. Major Necrason took off fought off three attackers, and reached Malang six hours later. Dufrane's plane, which had not yet been serviced, was caught on the ground and destroyed."

Haugland describes a "particularly costly mission" carried out February 8, 1942, against Kendari installations. "Enemy aircraft set the B-17 piloted by Lieutenant Dufrane afire. Six men bailed out before the plane exploded.

"Another B-17 exploded under heavy fire from enemy planes. Only one man parachuted from it. In another plane, a gunner was killed, while still another was so badly shot up about the tail section that it took two men to hold the controls. When the plane went into a spin, the copilot, navigator and tail gunner bailed out. The pilot brought the plane under control and landed safely with a wounded gunner aboard. Another plane was set afire but escaped destruction by jettisoning its burning bomb-bay tank. The B-17s shot down five enemy aircraft."

As the attrition of planes continued, Haugland reports, the "first Japanese bombers were not long in putting in their appearance over Java. There were heavy raids upon Malang, Madioen and Soerabaja, February 3. Thirty-one Allied aircraft, including four B-17s, were destroyed. Nine B-17s had left Malang shortly before to raid Balikpapan, but some of those still on the ground were loaded with bombs. Two of these were blown up. Another B-17 on a test flight failed to return, and was believed to have encountered the enemy formation of nine dive bombers and twenty high-level bombers. Another B-17 caught fire in the air. Five members of the crew bailed out, but the pilot managed to land the big ship on Arenda Island. A B-18 was shot down near Soerabaja and a B-17 shot down near Malang, with all seven members of the crew killed.

"Reinforcements continued to trickle in. A new B-17E arrived from Africa February 10. Two more came on February 11. An LB-30 arrived via Africa February 12, and another came in from the Pacific February 15. A B-17 coming in from the Pacific overshot Singosari airdrome near Malang and smashed into another new B-17 which was stuck in the mud at the end of the runway. New pilots were continually having trouble with the muddy, rain-slick airstrips of Java, and the number of operational losses was high."[7]

Allied fighter strength in the Netherlands East Indies took a fearful beating at the hands of Japanese fighter pilots; many raids early in February helped to start the destruction of fighter strength by destroying dozens of fighters at Soerabaja. On February 3, American P-40s participated in their first intercept of the campaign. But the story of the P-40s in this theater left much to be desired.

Forty of the desperately needed P-40 fighters in mid-January were ordered north from Australia by staging through Darwin and Koepang, their destination a secret airfield southeast of Djombang, near Soerabaja. Losses were heavy on the ferry mission. Japanese bombs destroyed two P-40s at Koepang during a surprise air raid. At Bali, off Java's eastern tip, another five P-40s went up in flames on the ground. Several others were shot out of the air by Japanese fighters or were lost through engine failure. When the force reached Soerabaja, 13 out of the 40 P-40s were already stricken from the provisional fighter squadron. The fighters were attempting to land when the Japanese came over in a heavy air raid, causing the loss of still another P-40 fighter and reducing the arrival group to only 26 airplanes.

Fighters and bombers made desperate attempts to hit the enemy invasion forces that kept pouring ashore at widely separated landing points throughout the many islands and extended shorelines. Throughout February 19 and 20, for example, heavy bombers, 16 P-40 fighters, and seven A-24 dive bombers hammered at the invasion force off Bali. Their efforts were courageous, but their effect negligible—the Japanese smashed their way swiftly through resistance to occupy Bali and its vital airstrips. That night a news broadcast from London boasted that the American planes had sent 15 Japanese warships and troop transports to the bottom, virtually wrecking the invasion fleet. The comment of the fliers who were involved is not printable.

Japanese fighters and bombers staged into newly occupied airstrips throughout Sumatra, Malaya, Borneo, Celebes, Timor, and Bali; as quickly as they were readied for additional missions they thundered against every Allied airfield in Java. It did not take long for the Japanese to smash Allied resistance and the morale of the defenders. On February 22 Japanese planes caught a force of Fortresses on the ground at Malang and quickly destroyed five of the heavy bombers. One pilot noted that the raid "just about cleans that field out and reduces our air force by one-third. Our bombers have accomplished little since Major Robinson was shot down a month ago. Too much caution and fear of what a Jap Zero can do to a B-17."

A last-ditch, desperate attempt to bring heavy fighter reinforcements to Java ended in disaster. Japanese bombers pounded the aircraft carrier *Langley*, with 32 P-40 fighters on deck, into blazing wreckage and sent her to the bottom. In the same convoy was the *Seawitch*, carrying 27 P-40s in crates. On February 28 the *Seawitch* reached Tjilatjap, on the south coast of Java. But the next day the Japanese landed on Java, and the Dutch destroyed the precious fighters in their crates to prevent them from falling into enemy hands.

In one blow we had lost 59 fighters, not one of which ever got into the air.

Dutch pilots counted heavily on the performance of the Curtiss-Wright CW-21 Demon, an American export fighter renowned for rapid climb and agility in dog-fighting. But the Zero proved faster, even more maneuverable and much more heavily armed; the combat-proven Japanese pilots easily crushed their opposition.

The Japanese lost no time in destroying what Allied air-power was left. At Jogjakarta four B-17s disappeared in flames from enemy bombs. All the remaining P-40 fighters, along with six Brewster Buffaloes and five Hawker Hurricanes, were concentrated on what had been their secret airfield. Japanese bombers waited until the planes were on the ground, then swept in with a low-level attack and destroyed *every* fighter.

On March 3 the Japanese caught Allied planes attempting a final mass aerial evacuation from Broome, Java. The harbor was crowded with flying boats and the airstrip crammed with American, British, and Dutch planes. It took only 12 Zero fighters to wreak terrible destruction. They caught the flying boats heavily overloaded with passengers, most of them women and children refugees, just as the flying boats were trying to take off. Almost all the big airplanes were shot into sinking, flaming wreckage—killing some 200 aboard. A B-24 in the air with 20 men aboard was blown out of the sky with the loss of all 20. On the ground, the strafing Zeros burned and destroyed two B-24s, two B-17s, six Dutch planes, three British, and one Australian aircraft.

There was no opposition in the air to the Zeros.

Saburo Sakai,* the Japanese fighter ace whom we have met earlier in these pages, has provided us with details of the air fighting in the Netherlands East Indies campaign which shed much light on the confused aerial combats of that area. Despite the effect upon our heavy bombers of the Zero fighters, the Japanese pilots found the big Flying Fortresses formidable opponents—as Sakai relates in this report of a battle against a B-17 formation late in January:

"Late in the morning, several specks appeared in the sky, approaching from the general direction of Java. They came in fast, swelling in size until two formations of four planes each became clear. Fortresses, in close flights . . . The rear flight flew slightly above the lead group and, as we approached, the second group of planes moved closer to form a defensive box.

"The B-17's passed about a half mile beneath me. I

---

*Read *Samurai!*, Saburo Sakai's own story as told to Martin Caidin, another volume in the Bantam War Book series.

rolled, Uehara glued to my wing tip, and dove against the formations. I was still out of gun range, but flicked a burst as I passed them. I saw the bombs falling as I flashed by the planes. We rolled back and climbed steeply. . . . I moved into position again, a half mile above the rear of the formations. . . . I shoved the stick forward and rolled as I dove. The fighter picked up speed quickly; I kept the stick hard over, in a long rolling dive, firing with both guns and cannon. No results. Everywhere around me the Fortresses seemed to be filling the sky, and tracers arced through the air as we flashed through the formation. We slipped through without damage, and I climbed again for another dive.

"Again. Dive, roll, concentrate on one bomber! This time I caught one! I saw the shells exploding, a series of red and black eruptions moving across the fuselage. Surely he would go down now! Chunks of metal—big chunks —exploded outward from the B-17 and flashed away in the slip stream. The waist and top guns went silent as the shells hammered home.

"Nothing! No fire, no telltale sign of smoke trailing back . . . the B-17 continued on in formation.

"We swung around and up, and rolled back in for the third run. The enemy formation continued on, seemingly impregnable, as if nothing had happened. The third time down I went after the bomber I had hit before, and again I caught him flush. Through the sight I watched the shells exploding, ripping metal from the wings and fuselage, ripping the inside of the fuselage apart. Then I was past the plane, pulling out into a wide, sweeping turn, going for height.

"The plane was still in formation! No fire, no smoke. Each time we dove against the B-17's their gunners opened up with heavy defensive fire which, fortunately, seemed to have been impaired by the tightness of the formation. So far I felt no damage to the Zero. I made two more passes, each time swinging down in a dive, rolling as I dropped, Uehara right with me, each of us snapping out bursts with the machine guns and cannon. And every time we saw the bullets and shells slamming into the bombers, seemingly without effect.

"We had just completed the sixth firing run when the eight B-17's split into two flights. Four banked to the right and the other four wheeled away to the left. Uehara pointed excitedly to the flight bearing to the right; a thin, black film trailed the left engine of the third B-17.

"We *had* gotten through, after all. I turned to follow the four bombers and pushed the throttle all the way forward, closing in rapidly behind the damaged plane. He was hurt, all right, dropping behind the other three planes. As I moved in I saw tangled wreckage instead of the tail turret; the guns remained silent. At maximum speed I approached to fifty yards' distance, and held the gun triggers down. Every last round poured from my guns and cannon into the cripple. Abruptly a cloud of black smoke burst from the bomber, and he nosed down steadily, to disappear into a solid cloud layer below. . . . Two days later a Japanese reconnaissance plane reported that a B-17 had crash-landed on a small island between Balikpapan and Surabaya."[8]

On February 19, a force of 23 Zero fighters of the Tainan and Kaohsiung wings took off from Balikpapan, on the east coast of Borneo, on a fighter sweep against Soerabaja. A fast reconnaissance plane acted as pathfinder for the Zeros during the 430-mile flight; the main Japanese force reached Soerabaja at 11:30 A.M., cruising at 16,000 feet. As Sakai tells the story of one of the wildest battles of the entire campaign in the Netherlands East Indies:

"The enemy force anticipating our arrival was unprecedented. At least fifty Allied fighters, flying at about 10,000 feet, maintained a large, counterclockwise sweep over the city. The enemy planes extended in a long line, composed of three waves of V groups which outnumbered us by more than two to one.

"Upon sighting the enemy fighters, we jettisoned our tanks and climbed for altitude. Sighting our force, the Allied fighters broke off their circular movement and at full speed closed toward us. They were prepared and eager for a fight—unlike the American fighters we had encountered over Clark Field on December 8.

"Less than a minute later the orderly formations disintegrated into a wild, swirling dogfight.

"I watched a P-36 scream toward me, then flicked into a swift left roll, waiting for the enemy's reaction. Foolishly, he maintained his course. That was all for me, and I snapped around into a sharp right turn, standing the Zero on her wing, and came out directly on the tail of the startled P-36 pilot.

"A look behind me showed my own plane clear, and I closed the distance to the enemy fighter. He rolled to the right, but slight control movements kept the Zero glued to his tail. Fifty yards away I opened up with the guns and cannon. Almost immediately the right wing broke off and snapped away in the air stream; then the left wing tore loose. Spinning wildly, the P-36 broke up into wreckage as it plummeted. The pilot failed to get out.

"Swinging into a wide, climbing turn I headed back for the main flight. At least six planes were falling in flames. Fighters swirled crazily about in the air and abruptly the olive drab of a P-36 rolled toward my own fighter. I turned to meet his rush, but in the next moment another Zero whipped upward in a steep climb, caught the P-36 in a long cannon burst, then snapped away as the Dutch plane exploded.

"To my left a P-40 closed in on the tail of a fleeing Zero, and I turned desperately to draw the enemy fighter off. There was no need to do so; the Zero whipped up and around in a tight loop which ended exactly above and behind the P-40. The guns and cannon hammered and the P-40 burst into flames.

"Another P-40 flashed by, trailing a streamer of flame fully three times as long as the fighter. A P-36 flipped crazily through the air, its pilot dead at the controls.

"Below me, our unarmed pathfinder plane flashed by, caught by three Dutch fighters. The Japanese pilot was corkscrewing violently to evade the enemy tracers which flashed all about his plane.

"Again I arrived too late. A Zero plummeted down in a power dive, and his cannon shells exploded the top Dutch fighter's fuel tanks. Pulling out of the dive, the Zero flashed upward in a steep zoom, catching the second P-36 from beneath. It fell off on one wing even as the third pilot whipped around to meet the Zero. Too late; his cockpit erupted in a shower of glass.

"The other Zero pulled alongside my plane, the pilot waving and grinning broadly, then dropped away as he escorted the reconnaissance plane out of the area.

"A P-36, apparently fleeing the fight, passed over me. I slammed the throttle on overboost and yanked the stick back, looping to come out close to the Dutchman. Still climbing, I opened up with the cannon. Too soon; the pressure of the turn threw my aim off.

"The cannon gave me away; the P-36 jerked hard over in a left roll and dove vertically for the ground. I cut inside his turn and went into a dive as the Curtiss flashed by less than fifty yards away. My finger snapped down on the button, and the shells exploded in the fuselage. Thick black smoke belched back. I fired two more bursts, then pulled out as a sheet of flame enveloped the Dutch fighter."[9]

The finale to the Java campaign is contained in the official AAF report of that operation—which came to a close on March 7, 1942. Even in the cold and analytical expressions of this document, the feeling of despair and defeat for the moment comes through:

"Air Corps men who survived the Java campaign and the attacks on western Australia gradually made their way to southeast Australia, but they were unorganized and without equipment. They were the remnants of units which—along with the units already in Australia—were to be welded into a new force, but in the first week of March the prospects seemed dismal. The Allies in Australia had their backs to the wall and were faced with the threat of increasing enemy pressure, not only from the northwest but also from the northeast.

". . . it was clear that Australia now had to be the main base for operations against the enemy in the Southwest Pacific—not simply the supply base for forward units. Three months of war had resulted in a radical change of Allied plans, and for the moment the Air Corps units in Australia were not at all certain of their future. In this period of uncertainty the Secretary of War could well state that 'circumstances will determine the extent and nature of the future United States air operations in the Southwest Pacific area,' but the American airmen and their commanding officers in Australia wondered just what those circumstances would be."

15

INTERLUDE

Even amidst a sea of defeat it is possible, and certainly
it is urgently sought, to strike a hard and unexpected offensive blow at the enemy. After the fall of Java, accompanied by defeats along the long front of combat established by the Japanese, the United States military leaders in
the Southwest Pacific were aware that they had two great
needs. The first, of course, was for fighters—fighters to
stop the enemy air in its tracks, and to open the way
back for our bombers. Second, and equally imperative
(but without the strategic profit of a major campaign),
was the need to show the ranks of the Allies that we
were not so beaten that we could not strike back. Thus
while preparations were made to bring in fighter reinforcements, the first aerial combat assistance for the beleaguered American and Filipino troops 3,000 miles to
the north of MacArthur's new headquarters in Melbourne,
Australia, was being planned. This would take place in
April, 1942.

The flights of the B-17 Fortresses in the emergency
evacuation of personnel from the Philippines to Australia
had demonstrated the possibility—precarious though it
might be—of getting bombers through Japanese-infested
skies up to Mindanao, where the Japanese were in large
numbers on the ground as well, and back safely to the
Australian continent. Early in April rumors of a combat
strike into the Philippines began to spread among the
crews of the 40th Reconnaissance Squadron operating
from Townesville, on the northeastern coast of Australia,
and the 3rd Bombardment Group at Charters Towers,
southwest of Townesville. The rumors stuck hard, and
the crews learned quickly enough that they had substance
to them. It was essential that plans for such a strike be

made in the shortest possible time, for the position of the American and Filipino troops was growing more insecure every day as Japanese pressure increased in Luzon.

By April 9 the debacle loomed on the horizon; the defenders at Bataan went down before the tidal wave of Japanese troops. The defense was continued by the fortress of Corregidor (which would continue to hold out for approximately one more month). What cast a pall on even the plans for the strike into the Philippines was that regardless of the critical need for air reinforcements in these islands, the planned aid from Australia could be only on a small scale. On April 4 there were only six Fortress and eight B-25 Mitchell bombers in commission; mechanics worked day and night to get six more B-25s into flying condition.

No doubt existed among the crews preparing for the strike to the north that their mission into Japanese-held and Japanese-controlled territory approximated a suicide flight. There could hardly be any question of this unhappy fact of life. Yet every man volunteered, and early on the morning of April 11, the crews of three B-17s and 11 B-25s assembled at Darwin. They ate a hurried breakfast while ground crews fueled the planes for the long ocean hop to Mindanao.

"To those members of the 27th Bombardment Group (at that time a part of the 3rd Group)," notes the official history of the operation, "who had been bouncing around the skies for several months in A-24s, the B-25 felt 'like a ball of fire' until they could become accustomed to the extra speed and power. The eleven B-25s had flown to Brisbane two days before in order to pick up bomb bay tanks for the long flight northward. The entire mission was under the personal leadership of General Ralph Royce, who flew in the lead B-17, piloted by Captain Frank P. Bostrom of the 40th Reconnaissance Squadron. The first flight of five B-25s was led by Colonel John H. Davies and the second flight by Captain Herman F. Lowery."[1]

One B-25 aborted its takeoff from Darwin because of mechanical difficulties. The 13 bombers assembled over Darwin and in formation roared northward; they managed to keep their formation positions until they reached the coast of Mindanao late in the afternoon, when severe weather scattered the planes. The heavy black rain clouds, with poor visibility and severe turbulence, forced the pilots to struggle separately to Del Monte airfield.

"Battle-scarred veterans of the Philippines, from colonels down to privates," notes the official report, "rushed out to meet the first planes and clustered around them 'with tears of appreciation in their eyes, viewing the new arrivals as saviors and conquering heroes.' The last plane landed after dark, twelve hours after taking off from Darwin. The flight of B-25s led by Captain Lowery flew forty miles to Valencia, a dispersal strip cut out of the jungle, and the remaining planes were dispersed at Del Monte for the night."

The hours of darkness were spent in removing the bomb-bay tanks from the Mitchells, loading bombs into the planes, and refueling for the first mission which was to start at dawn. The crews received their briefings during the night, and then, weary after their long flights, rolled up in blankets beneath the wings of their planes to snatch several hours' rest. As dawn broke, the two flights of Mitchells raced from their fields and headed for Cebu.

They shot over the Japanese-held town, with almost complete surprise. The swift medium bombers attacked the town area, and at pointblank range sent their bombs directly into several ships in the harbor, swiftly setting them aflame and leaving them sinking rapidly. The dock installations were left in sheets of flame.

One of the Fortresses also participated in this action; the bomber droned carefully on its runs, cascading its bombs directly into several merchant ships. Another B-17, piloted by Captain Bostrom, made a solo reconnaissance over the open seas for any concentrations of enemy ships; finding none, it flew over Corregidor, and flew on to attack Nichols Field near Manila. The third Fortress was left on the ground, crippled with a balky engine. It was still at Del Monte field undergoing emergency repairs when Japanese planes came over; bomb explosions severely damaged the grounded Fortress.

Soon after the Japanese attack the two B-17s in the air landed; the crews rushed to prepare the planes for a second strike. But the Japanese were not idle; before the big bombers could get off the ground the enemy bombers were back. A direct hit shattered one Fortress and other bombs damaged the other two bombers.

The ground and bomber crews now had the unhappy

task of trying to repair the two damaged planes just so they might limp back to Australia; further combat operations with the B-17s seemed out of the question, and survival now was their main goal. While the salvage work went on, however, the Mitchells carried out further bomb strikes against Japanese installations. Following the inital raid at Cebu, one Mitchell flight returned to Valencia, and the other slipped into a well-concealed jungle airstrip near Del Monte. The crews helped to ready the planes for another immediate mission, and at 1:30 P.M. the same day, April 12, they were in the air and searching for a Japanese carrier reported in the vicinity. The big warship having failed to materialize, the Mitchells swept in against their former target of Cebu and caught the Japanese unawares, wreaking great havoc amidst shipping and dock installations.

The next day, April 13, each flight carried out another two missions. They were in the air at six A.M., winging toward Cebu and Davao to strike various targets, including a Japanese air base. Later this day, at 5:45 P.M., the Mitchells swept with complete surprise effect over the Davao dock area. Their bombs sent one boat to the bottom, spread large fires through the dock installations, and set off either a fuel dump or a munitions store—quite evident in the form of a terrific explosion along the docks.

As soon as the planes were back on the ground at Del Monte, with darkness closing in, mechanics and the crews rushed to install bomb-bay tanks for the long return flight to Australia.

Earlier this day the two surviving B-17s had taken to the air, no longer fit for combat without extensive repairs. They barely made it away from the Japanese; the first bomber had hardly cleared the fence at the end of the airstrip, and the other was bringing up its wheels, when the shriek of falling Japanese bombs was heard. Jammed with as many men as could clamber into them, the two Fortresses without further mishap—to the immense relief of all aboard—managed to complete the trip to Australia. One plane was so badly in need of repairs that its landing gear collapsed as it settled to the runway, but no one aboard was injured.

Shortly before midnight on April 13 the ten B-25s, heavily loaded with men who had crawled into every space and corner of the small bombers, pounded their way into the skies from Del Monte. Darkness was much in their favor, for the Japanese were looking with rage for the airplanes. They made the flight without incident to Batchelor Field, 40 miles south of Darwin, Australia, landing after daylight on April 14. The planes refueled and continued on the last leg of the flight to Charters Towers, arriving late the same day.

"Thus, the four-day mission was completed," states the official report. "Without the loss of a single man and with the loss of only one B-17 on the ground, the ten B-25s and two B-17s had sunk or badly damaged four enemy transports (one large, one small, and two medium), and scored direct hits on two others and near misses on eight others; in addition, they had succeeded in badly damaging the warehouses and docks at Davao and Cebu, and in damaging Nichols Field and buildings in the city of Davao. General MacArthur's promise to send aid to the Philippines had seen its initial fulfillment. . . . But this remarkable aerial feat, which had given new hope to the Filipinos and Americans on the islands, could not be repeated. The Japanese immediately tightened their hold on Mindanao. The alternate base which the fliers from Australia had planned to use was taken on the day of their arrival in Mindanao, and the main field was taken only one week later."

The official opinion that the raid was worth while because it had renewed faith and hope in the Filipinos and Americans on the islands was not shared by the men who carried out the mission. One of the pilots who flew a B-25 in the attacks summed up the opinion of the men who were there:

"The trip was not worth while. We never got to Bataan on time. The flight was conceived to show the boys on Bataan that they hadn't been forgotten—to bring them medicine, cigarettes and hope. As usual, it was too late. It only caused the Nips to invade Mindanao earlier. Back at Melbourne, General Royce called in the reporters. If the news had been withheld, the Japs might still be guessing."

16

THE LONG NOSES

The invasion of Guadalcanal on August 7, 1942, marked one of the pivotal points of the war in the Pacific—the first major offensive against the Japanese carried out by air, sea, and ground forces, and a story of incredible valor and skill carved out by the pilots of the U.S. Navy and Marines, and the AAF. The saga of the fight on Guadalcanal is not a part of this book; notwithstanding the terrible conditions under which men fought and the savage fighting against the enemy, it *was* the beginning of the road back, in which we were the attackers and the Japanese the defenders.

Part of the preparations for the Guadalcanal struggle, however, are very important to our story—for it is of another battle carried on without guns. This was the fight to prepare for the beginning offensive—a fight of logistics, supplies, and readiness for combat. The 67th Fighter Squadron of the Army Air Forces, which fought alongside the Marines, Navy, and other AAF units on Guadalcanal, went through a thousand kinds of misery getting ready for its combat test. The 67th flew the Bell P-400 Airacobra, the export version of the P-39; they were stuck with the P-400 because these models had been snatched from foreign shipments and rushed to American fighter pilots who needed planes with which to fight. Finally, the squadron ended up with a polyglot mixture of both the P-400 and P-39 models—airplanes that became well known for their long noses, and for a deficiency in performance that has contributed much to the guidebook of American military profanity. Much of this chapter is directly as it was written during the war by anonymous members of the 67th and preserved in its official but unpublished history, which was found in manuscript form in 1956.[1] It is a story that has long needed telling.

One unknown historian of the 67th noted, six months after the invasion of Guadalcanal:

"How the squadron helped [on Guadalcanal] . . . is a story of ingenuity and perseverance and stamina. The 67th had lived and flown alongside a total of eight Marine and Navy squadrons which had arrived, fought like wild men in their Wildcats, and gone home to re-form, to re-equip and recuperate, and perhaps come back to fight another day. But the 67th, by flying skill and the grace of a special providence who takes care of pilots, is still there plugging away. It has been in the hell of Guadalcanal for six months so far and has now been given to understand that it will be there 'for the duration plus six months.' So it is high time the story of the 67th was told.

"But first there is another story of how it prepared for combat. There is the chronicle of a bunch of pilots and mechanics who were dumped in the mud and mosquitoes of a tropical island in the rainy season with some air-planes—in crates—which most of them had never seen except in magazine illustrations, who hauled them over torturous mountain roads and assembled them without instruction books; who built their own flying fields in cow pastures nestled in the mountains and operated under hazards which would have horrified peacetime pilots; who alone for months were the sole aerial protection for the important South Pacific base of New Caledonia, and who at the same time taught themselves combat tactics and gunnery and prepared themselves to fly into their baptism klunkers called P-400s—without the oxygen to keep them alert and alive at combat altitudes."

When the squadrons arrived at New Caledonia, their new "island paradise," they discovered that they had 45 P-400s and two P-39s with which to prepare themselves for combat. The pilots groaned in a chorus of dismay—in volume exceeded only by the mechanics—when first they examined their new machines. "The P-400 was a cheap version of the early P-39s, manufactured for export to the British," sourly noted a pilot. "Only two of the 67th pilots had ever flown a P-39, and not a single one of the mechanics who were faced with the task of not only assembling, but maintaining a strange airplane [had ever seen the P-400]. And, when they pried the crates open, they found that the Handbook of Instructions for the P-400 type aircraft was missing."

The unpublished squadron history continues with this description of life and work at the squadron's base:

"With trucks and drivers mostly finagled from other outfits, the squadron hauled its equipment to a spot in the woods two miles from the field. Due to the invasion scare [the fear that the Japanese would invade New Caledonia], no large tentage was allowed during the months of March, April and part of May—until the Coral Sea victory. Everything had to be camouflaged and invisible from the air, so the men slept under shelter halves rigged as lean-to's under the tree branches. The officers slept in a farm-house. There were forty-four of them crammed in the parlor, the bedroom, and on the dirt floor of the base-ment. The tropical rains were frequent and unpredictable. The clothing and bedding consistently became soaked, mildewed, fly-blown and ruined. Many nights were spent in soaked clothes under sopping blankets while rain dripped through the shelter halves and trickled in rivulets underneath. Trucks crunched the camp site into a mush of miasmic mud.

"But the most agonizing were the mosquitos [sic]—the damned mosquitos. They were so thick, one swipe of the hand over any part of the body could be made to kill at least three. Customary dress was a headnet to pro-tect the face and neck, gloves for the hands, and boots or trousers tucked into heavy sox for the ankles. But they bit through shirts and pants and switches of tree leaves were used to slap them off the back. When they got under the headnet you were really busy.

"Several men in nearby outfits went out of their heads due to the intolerable, agonizing worry from the stinging and had to be hospitalized. Then there was the long epidemic of diarrhea [sic] and cramps which caused suf-fering and enervation of much of the personnel. A wad of paper—for emergency use—was carried at all times. The combination of diarrhea and mosquitos was intolerable, since the former made tender parts of the body especially vulnerable many times a day, to the latter. The phrase then was, 'my mother told me there would be days like this but she didn't tell me there would be so many of them.' ..."

There Were Days Like This

"But the squadron knew its job and started to work. The airplane crates were scheduled to be the first equipment unloaded from the first deck. The squadron lacked the rank to press its demands and it turned out that the airplanes were the last crates to be unloaded from the last ship.

"Then came the wearing job of hauling airplanes. Only one combination truck and trailer was available. It took eight hours to jockey the airplane crate on the trailer at the dock, to wrestle the big truck around the narrow, twisting, mountainous 'little Burma Road,' 35 miles from Noumea to Tontouta, unload the crate, then return. Eight hours round trip! That meant three trips each day and night. So the big truck ran continuously 24 hours a day, seven days a week, until the 47 airplanes were delivered. It was accomplished without serious accident.

"Pilots rode the truck and a jeep which preceded it, riding 24 and 36 hours [at] a stretch. The ones in the jeep carried a red flag and shooed all traffic out of the way. They spoke softly to the command cars—'Sir, would you mind pulling off the road a minute?' They hollered Brooklynese to the dogface driver—'Hey, we've got a big semi coming; pull over!' To the native cars, they spoke a sort of pidgin French. . . . Day after day, night after night, the big prime mover whined and groaned as it crept up the mountains, and roared as it highballed down the other side and the natives and the Frenchmen and the American soldiers cheered as it passed because that meant one more airplane was on the way.

"Unloading the huge 10,000-pound crates at Tontouta was an engineering feat itself. They were slid gently to the ground without any crane or hoist equipment except the truck's winch.

"The job of putting a strange and complicated bunch of parts together into an airplane in which a pilot would risk his life test-hopping was one long nightmare of tedious work in mosquitoes and mud and rain. Inside the crates were instructions for P-39s—D, F, and K models —but none for this type, the P-400. One day, the engineering officer hopefully opened a big batch of handbooks which had just come, only to find they were the Hand-

book of Instruction and Maintenance of the Automatic
Pilot...."

During this period the line-chief of the 67th Fighter
Squadron was veteran Army Master Sergeant Robert
Foye (later promoted to major); as the work went on
Foye scribbled notes to keep a record of what was going
on:

"Assemblying rig built from old timbers picked up
around Tontouta. Mechanics had only the simple 1st
Echelon maintenance tools and only about ten kits of
these for the entire squadron. No special tools of any
kind. Even the truck tools were at a premium.

"No replacement parts. Every fifth crate was designated
'spare parts' before it was uncrated.

"Rain, mud and mosquitos [sic]. Mechanics worked
sopping wet. Pvt. Jones worked on tail assembly sitting
in six inches of water, so wet from rain he never knew
the difference. Rain poured down their faces and necks
—still they worked on, passing the scanty wrenches from
one to another. Not a growl from any man.

"Work day from five A.M. until dark. Cold (sometimes
hot) chow at noon, and back to work right away. No
transportation during the first five days and men had to
walk two miles to work and home again through the
mud.

"No Technical Order or Manuals of Instruction but
started producing airplanes at the rate of 1.5 a day after
the first week.

"Frequent troubles. One prop was missing from crate.
Sometimes vital fuel and pressure lines found to be mysteriously plugged with scotch tape. One airplane had elec-
trical circuits hooked up at the factory evidently by a
maniac. Press, and wheels would retract. Press wheel
switch, flap switch, and guns would fire. Took days to
straighten things out. Promptly named plane 'Rube'
Goldberg Special.'

"Mechanics became production-conscious and still section chiefs would urge them on. Assembly run like a
factory—all in the open and in the mud. Would put any
depot to shame, with Initial Assembly, Empennage Section, Wing Section, Engine Run-In Section, Rigging Section, Radio Installation Depot, Armament Installation Department, then Field Inspection Department, and Test
Flight Section. Every man to his job, and never a growl

except when one section chief would hold up another: 'Come on! This is war—keep 'em rolling!'

"From crate to flying in one day. Thirty airplanes assembled by the 67th—which was not equipped or required to do the work—and eleven by the 65th Materiel Squadron. All in twenty-nine days, and in twenty years in the Army, I have never seen it done before.

"One mechanic (Hartfield) improvised tools by cutting wrenches and welding on extensions. Servicing funnels made from gallon cans with makeshift spouts soldered to the corners. (Incidentally, 67th should have patent on the gas drum washing rack—one drum split in half and resting on a V-shaped cut in the other. Door cut in bottom half for the fire. Result: A practical G.I. messkit wash stand.)

"During the second week of assembly, officers and men began to come down with dysentery. *Men literally dropped on their knees with cramps at the rig before they would ask for relief.* Had to be ordered home, sometimes even threatened with trial for disobedience of orders to leave their place on the line. Why hasn't Washington designed a decoration for men in the Air Corps who, far above and beyond the call of duty, perform feats on the ground?

"It would be impossible to pick out outstanding men during this period—when they worked from five A.M. until dark in the mud and rain and then volunteered to go back at night. The whole damn outfit was outstanding. An outfit like this could be the nucleus for six Air Corps groups and with recruit fill-ins could start operating tomorrow. . . ."

One week after the squadron disembarked from its troopship the men received their first crate. Six days after receiving the first crate, Lieutenant Dale D. Brannon took the first P-400 into the air for a successful test flight. Everyone sighed with relief, and redoubled his efforts. Then, notes the squadron history, "Such was the rush that on two nights they rigged up field floodlights for an attempt at twenty-four-hour assembly. But mosquitos were driving the men insane and it had to be stopped. Once there was an air raid scare and pilots and men spent all night dragging uncrated planes around with trucks to dispersal points."

Then there were the unique problems—without spare parts, instruction or maintenance books, or proper tools—of keeping the 67th's klunkers in the air. The historian of the 67th was quick to notice that "every airplane in commission soon became an example of the ground crew's ingenuity and resourcefulness."

Ignition harnesses, normally in good supply, were scarce items, and those in use quickly became frayed and developed short circuits. Since there were no replacements, mechanics had to take harnesses from wrecked airplanes, which were already in a poor state of repair, and try to bring these back into usable shape. The crew chiefs violated every imaginable rule in the book just to keep the airplanes flyable. Among them—it "would have given the experts at Chanute Field the holy horrors," notes the squadron history—was the habit of patching up high-voltage spark plugs with ordinary friction tape. The P-400 pilots were often to report a "sudden stoppage of the heart" when their Allison engines sputtered and cut in and out (especially at takeoff), "but that was part of the excitement of a day's flying."

The Long Noses in Battle

Months before the P-400s of the 67th Fighter Squadron went into battle at Guadalcanal, a mixture of P-400s and later-model P-39s were thrown into the air fighting over New Guinea. The 35th and 36th Fighter Squadrons of the 8th Fighter Group moved into Port Moresby at the end of April, 1942, to relieve Australian units (flying P-40s) which were down to a handful of exhausted and ailing pilots flying patched-up wrecks for fighter airplanes.

In the first mission for the P-39 Airacobras, 13 fighters took off from Moresby to strafe the Japanese airstrip at Lae, 180 miles to the north. Within a very few minutes, approximately a dozen Zero fighters were mixing it up with the Airacobras in a wild, scrambling dogfight extending from 50 to 1,000 feet, which ran for 30 miles along the northern coast of New Guinea, and then reversed itself to continue the same distance back toward Lae. In the wild melee, the American pilots claimed four Zeros shot down—three of them to one man—at a cost of three P-39s.

What made the fight even more significant was the quality of the pilot who led the Airacobras into battle. The leader was none other than Lieutenant Colonel Boyd D. ("Buzz") Wagner, who had distinguished himself brilliantly in combat during the early days of the war in the Philippines. Wagner, of course, was not only a sensational pilot, but also a man with extensive experience in fighting the Zero—explaining in great part why three of the four fighters shot down dropped before his guns.

Although there were characteristics of the Airacobra which brought some pilots to prefer them to the P-40 (such as greater level speed and the heavy punch of the 37-mm. cannon in the nose), there was still little doubt about the fighter-to-fighter superiority of the Zero. The official histories of the AAF in Australia and New Guinea note of the pilots who engaged the Zero in April and May that all thoroughly respected and admired the flying qualities of the Zero.

Late in May, 1942, Colonel Wagner submitted a report that stated in part:

". . . there has seldom been an even fight between Japanese Zero type fighters and our own. Only by virtue of armor plate protection, leak-proof fuel tanks, and ruggedness of construction of our fighters, has there not been a great many more of our pilots killed and airplanes destroyed. Our fighter pilots have proven their courage and ability to fight continuously against superior odds and still maintain a very high morale. This high morale, however, has been with fighter pilots a forced one, with the knowledge that Japanese fighters would be just as high above tomorrow as they were today, and that the first enemy combat would be an attack from above out of the sun."

Many of the fighter combat missions flown against the Japanese Zero with the P-39 and P-400 airplanes went badly for the same reason—inability to meet the enemy on his own terms. But the most damning indictment of the Airacobras quite possibly came from the Japanese themselves (unknown at the time to our pilots, of course): of all the American fighter planes to be encountered in battle, the Japanese most *preferred* to meet the Airacobras!

During the Guadalcanal campaign, in which the 67th Fighter Squadron fought with eight Marine and Navy fighter units, the P-400s of the 67th quickly became identified as perhaps the worst fighters in the Pacific (although the British might have argued that *they* had the worst machine ever put together in the Brewster Buffalo).

In the first combat action over the island, two P-400s

scrambled into the air with a pack of Grumman F4F Wildcats flown by the Marines. The chunky Grummans clawed swiftly for altitude, got above the Japanese bombers, and howled earthward—while the P-400s were still

Bell P-39 Airacobras with heavy machine guns
and a single 37-mm. cannon proved effective in attacks
against ground forces and shipping of the Japanese—
but in the air they were regarded by Zero pilots
as "meat on the table."

struggling to gain height. Well above them, the Marines shot down eight of the nine Japanese bombers.

The two P-400s were delighted to find a stray Zero fighter wandering about in a stupor, and they bounced him with everything they had. The Zero exploded to make it first blood for the 67th—but the Japanese almost as quickly returned the favor. As the combat report of the fight states:

"Then the wingman discovered tracers passing his cockpit and a Zero on his tail. He had heard that 'the Zero is so flimsily constructed, its wings will come off in a dive,' so he put his P-400 in a dive, making right aileron rolls on the way down. When he pulled out he looked back to see the pieces of the Zero floating down, but found that the Zero, defying all the intelligence reports to date, was still intact, and furthermore was still on his tail, shooting. It was another one of those things the 67th learned the hard way.

"He screamed over his radio for help, but his leader, in the haste of takeoff, hadn't time to plug in his earphones (or fasten his parachute harness or safety belt either). Finally the P-400s got together and the Zero broke away."

The principal missions assigned to the P-400 fighters were patrols—scheduled for cruising flights at 14,000 feet. It was an altitude particularly dangerous for the pilots—for two specific reasons. At this height the Zero fighter was in its prime and the P-400s reacted in sluggish fashion; they could struggle up a few thousand feet more, but that was all, and they were sitting ducks for the agile Mitsubishis. Even if the planes could go higher, the pilots were at their limit. Their fighters lacked oxygen. Since the P-400 was an export model intended for English use, it was equipped with the British high-pressure oxygen system—worthless for the systems used in American fighters. The 67th had screamed for months to get its oxygen equipment changed, but to no avail. The official report notes, "Oxygen should be used above 10,000 feet. Here, these pilots were flying two-hour patrols at 14,000 feet. They found that after twenty minutes they became groggy and punch drunk and had spots before their eyes.

"Often, they flew two or three of these two-hour patrols a day. Once one of the pilots, who had lost sleep due to a bombing during the night and had no breakfast because the kitchen had been hit, flew three of these missions in succession, being sleepy, hungry, groggy and had to handcrank his landing gear up and down each time because there was no interval for repairs."

There is no document more eloquent—and damning—than the official combat record of the 67th Fighter Squadron. The following excerpts tell "how it was" at Guadalcanal during the late summer of 1942, with the 67th's outmoded fighter airplanes. No other record ever seen by this writer tells the story better.

"On August 29, the pilots' morale, which had held up through six months of continuous toil and trouble in New Caledonia, took a set-back. The P-400s were scrambled with the Grummans at noon to meet an expected wave of bombers. The Army formation climbed up to 14,000 feet and staggered around, looking closely at all spots within their vision to make sure they were just spots and not enemy formations. Then, they saw the enemy—3,000 feet above and *out of reach*. They saw his bombs hit, sending up geysers of smoke and debris and they saw the Marine Grummans hit the bombers. All the 67th could do was fly around, helpless. Discouraged, they went back to land. The whole field seemed to be afire. Grass was burning, two hangars built by the Japs were afire, several airplanes were burning and ammunition was exploding in every direction. The runway was swarming with men and strangely, seemed to have sprouted bushes. They found out why. The bushes were held by ground crews to mark bomb craters. The men would hold the bushes as long as they dared when a plane came in, then duck as it zig-zagged crazily down the pitted strip.

"The field was in a chaos of activity. Truck crews were hauling dirt to fill up the holes in the runway. Men were beating out grass fires with their only blankets. Litter bearers were hunting for the wounded. Men were shoveling dirt on the burning airplanes, about to explode any minute. Ground crews were rolling gas and oil drums around to the landed airplanes to refuel them by handcrank. Ammunition was exploding everywhere, and the snipers were in trees across the river. All worked in a silent fury at the enemy.

"But what could the 67th do in its damned P-400s?

"The next day, August 30th, it was to have its chance, it thought.

"The day's activity began, routinely enough, at midnight. Four enemy destroyers were reported standing off the beach preparing to shell the field. All the pilots were aroused from their straw mats. The Navy dive bombers took off and the fighter pilots went down to their hangars to stand by. They sat around on ammunition boxes, chilly and sleepless, until dawn and nothing happened. Then they began to take off on their regular patrols. They flew the two-hour patrols until 11:30 A.M., when all planes were called in for reservicing. An enemy raid was expected at noon. The 'coast watchers' up the way had reported 'twenty or more single-engine planes' headed for Henderson Field [on Guadalcanal].

"This was the 67th's chance! When the Grummans went up, the 67th scrambled all the planes it had in commis-

sion. Six of them were to cruise around the towering
cumulus clouds at 14,000 feet and catch the dive bombers
before they started down. Four more were to patrol over
the boats at Tulagi at 1,500 feet and catch the Japs as
they pulled out of their dives. Then P-400s were all the
67th had in flying condition.

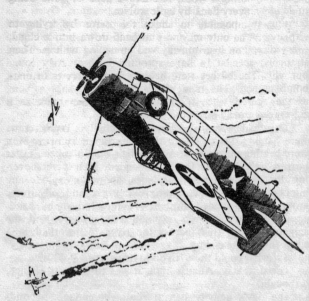

Marine F4F Wildcat whistles up and over in
climbing attack against Zero fighter. Airacobras with
inferior performance were used as either "bait"
or "cover" in Wildcat-Airacobra sandwich combats
against the Japanese—but the poor performance of the
Airacobra destroyed most attempts to "box in" the enemy.

"The six-plane formation had been searching for about
half an hour at 14,000 feet and was already feeling
oxygen-lack when the action began. The 67th didn't attack; it was attacked, with Zeros and not the expected
dive bombers. The Zeros dived down around a cloud and
then zoomed up into the six P-400s from behind and
below. There were about twenty of them.

"The P-400s started turning into a Lufberry but there were more Zeros in the Lufberry than there were P-400s. Then the Grumman Wildcats came down from above and hit the Zeros. The mixup began. Zeros were everywhere, zipping, darting and twisting, climbing straight up, and practically making square turns. The 67th pilots, in their heavy, lumbering P-400s, felt like a herd of cows being attacked on every flank by agile wolves.

"It was impossible to shake the Zeros by trying to maneuver. The only way was to head down into a cloud, make a turn on instruments, and come out on top. Then try to get a burst at a Zero before three others jumped you. All over the sky P-400s were running for the clouds with two or three Zeros on their tails. . . .

"The next day only three of the original fourteen P-400s were in commission.

"When the regular Jap aerial armada was reported on the way, the remaining P-400s were ordered by operations to take off and fly down around the island on a reconnaissance flight.

"The morale of the 67th had scraped the bottom.

"They could not help thinking: 'We can't climb high enough to reach the bombers. We have already lost two pilots and half our planes proving what we already knew —that we can't maneuver and dogfight with the Zero. What good are we? Our enlisted men are risking their lives every day trying to get the planes patched up—for what? We're just eating up food—and there's not enough to go around anyway—and using up valuable gasoline, and the gas supply is getting lower every day. Hell, we can't fight. When the Japs come we're told to "go on reconnaissance." What good are we?'

". . . the 67th was willing. It wanted to fight. *But how?*"

They found out soon enough.

Operations at Guadalcanal assigned the fighter of the 67th Fighter Squadron to ground-attack missions—strafing and bombing the Japanese on the ground and at sea. They did a hell of a job, too.

But there was always the reminder that they couldn't fight the enemy in the air, and that the Marines could— and did.

"DUCEMUS"—"WE LEAD"

"We Lead."

That was the war cry—with meaning—of the 22nd Bombardment Group, a hellbent-for-leather organization of men who flew a tough, fast bomber called the Marauder. They flew from Australia and Seven-Mile Drome at Port Moresby to strike at Japanese targets from Portuguese Timor to Lae and Salamaua, at Rabaul and other hornets' nests of Japanese fighters and antiaircraft. Flying in early 1942, and through the summer of that painful year, they were the first airmen to start hitting the enemy on a consistent basis in his most strongly defended centers. While the Allies all about them foundered in the choppy sea of defeat, the 22nd's Marauders acted like a bombing group that never accepted the fact that we were losing a war. Sometimes their losses were frightful, and certainly they were as crippled within their organization through lack of parts, supplies, and manpower as any other organization. But they kept on hitting the enemy, again and again, until the Japanese came to marvel at the grim courage of these pilots and their crews.

And the 22nd did it all in a bomber that was considered so dangerous to fly that—while the 22nd pounded into Japanese targets—*that same bomber was grounded in the United States as a killer!* When Air Force headquarters finally got around to asking the men of the 22nd if they were having any serious difficulties with the Martin B-26 Marauder, they received their response in an enthusiastic chorus that amounted to "Hell, yes, we got problems. Send us *more* of the damned airplanes!"

The sleek twin-engine Marauder was quickly earning a reputation in the States as the "widow maker." The wags called the airplane the "Incredible Prostitute," by virtue of the fact that its wings were so short the Marauder had no visible means of support. But the sleek lines, huge engines and propellers, and short wingspan also gave the Marauder the greatest speed of any medium bomber in the business—making firing passes more than difficult for the Zero fighters. The B-26 had a landing speed on its final approach that was almost as great as the combat cruising speed of other bombers.

"There were a lot of pilots who called the Marauder a bitch and a killer," remarked General Samuel E. Anderson (who commanded the Marauders in Europe during World War II). "But you could never prove it with guys like Walt Krell or Jerry Crosson [pilots with the 22nd]. They were wild about the B-26; they loved that airplane. They could just about make the B-26 sit up and sing songs to them. There were pilots in the States who dreaded flying in the B-26 under normal conditions. Krell, Crosson and the other pilots in the 22nd Bomb Group could fly that thing better on one engine—which Stateside pilots often said was impossible—than most fliers could with both fans going."[2]

Gerald J. Crosson was one of the old B-26 pilots who had ferried the third production airplane from its Baltimore factory before the war (and later flew it in combat), and became one of the outstanding bomber pilots of the war.

The 22nd made its headquarters at Garbutt Field near Townesville, Australia, dispersing its squadrons to Antill Plains and Reid River in the surrounding countryside. But this was strictly the home base; to fly combat missions the men had to stage on from Australia to Seven-Mile at Port Moresby in New Guinea, refuel, and then go after the Japanese still farther to the north. On April 5, 1942, the 22nd launched its first combat strike. This was a mission against the heavily defended bastion of Rabaul on distant New Britain Island. It was the first combat mission for the B-26 in any theater of the war, and also the first medium bomber attack against Rabual, which had been officially listed as a target to be reserved for long-range heavy bombers. Top command didn't have enough B-17s, so they tore up their official listings of targets and planes and gave the assignment to the 22nd.

Seven-Mile as an advance base was a crude, rough, miserable forward outpost, which the Japanese found delightful as a place for target practice by day and by night all through the week. It was worse than bad for the men who flew from Seven-Mile, and it was hell for the men who patched and fixed and worked to keep the planes going. The white-hot summer sun scorched the grass into dirty brown straw, blistered the air, and produced a savage combination of huge mosquitoes and the choking dust of the airstrip, and at the same time the dank and oppressive humidity of the nearby jungle and the sea.

A good example of what the ground crews went through came one day with the sight, to crewmen returning from a raid, of two Buddhalike figures in the burned grass on one side of the airstrip. The figures were mechanics Charles Fuqua and Bill Spiker, sitting perfectly upright, legs crossed beneath their bodies, and sound asleep from exhaustion.

If luck were with the ground crews (and the Zeros and bombers were busy elsewhere for a respite) they could get five or six hours' sleep; more often they averaged three hours' sleep a night. The men used to say that you didn't live at Seven-Mile; you existed. Bodies became caked with dirt, hair matted with grease, hands and faces packed with grime. Cuts and bruises along the body were common because the men used makeshift tools and often slipped and fell from their precarious working mounts.

"I'll never forget the men who worked on my plane and those of the squadron whenever we got to Moresby," Crosson asserted. "You see and experience a lot of things in a shooting war, and ours consisted of a lot of pretty wild shooting. But it was those men on the ground who really got to me.

"In the early days especially we didn't have any facilities for the mechanics and ground crews at Seven-Mile. The sun was pure hell. It came down with an intensity that is just about impossible to describe. New Guinea under the best of conditions is only one step short of something for which you can develop a violent dislike, and these weren't the best of conditions.

"I've seen these men so battered by the sun that they couldn't work on the planes during daylight. We were even lacking the proper clothes for them to wear. More than a few had broken out in huge, painful blisters on the necks, across their backs, and on other parts of their bodies.

"Back in the States, they'd put a man into a hospital for something like that. Out here, they just kept right on working. But even the best of them couldn't remain in the blistering sun in that condition. So they'd knock off work and try to sleep during the day, in order to work the night through without that sun tearing them up."

Walt Gaylor of 22nd B.G. Headquarters, on conditions at Port Moresby: "What Jerry describes is bad enough, but it doesn't tell how insidious this became for them. When the sun hammered down, it was just too hot to sleep. They had to lie on their stomachs, face-down, because of their burned backs and necks. And the sweat just poured off them.

"By night, with the sun down, they'd start to work. It was almost as hot, but at least they weren't being burned. But then came the mosquitoes. . . . And those poor guys couldn't wear shirts because of their blistered and raw skin, and there just wasn't any salve or medicine for them, and so the whole night through they'd fair go out of their minds—but they worked and they put those planes in shape. Sometimes they broke off work at night. That's when the Japanese hit us with bombers, and most everyone would run for the ditches and trenches. But not all. Some of those guys were so tired—the mechanics working on the airplanes—they said to hell with it and kept working. We had to *order* them under cover.

"If they wanted to pick the real heroes of the 22nd, for my money, those are the people."

Through all this the men of the 22nd not only kept on working and fighting, but through some incredible strength shared by them all, they kept throwing themselves at the Japanese. General Anderson, who spent several weeks in 1942 with the 22nd, refers to their spirit as "the incredible morale of the men of the 22nd Bomb Group. And this was despite something that didn't reflect credit on the Army Air Forces, or on the whole general military organization. These boys felt as though they had been written off by the United States. They were convinced that hardly anybody knew anything about them. I hate to say this, but it was largely the truth as far as the public was concerned. And despite all this, their morale was simply marvelous.

"The more we saw of the wretched conditions, the more amazed we became at the evidence of this high morale. It didn't seem possible that men could endure their privations, their terrible losses against the Japanese, their feelings of being abandoned by the United States, and still throw everything they had into the war against an enemy who outnumbered them, and against whom they fought without even a pretense at escort protection. There were also the so-called 'little things' that can sap the morale of a fighting outfit, which they endured.

"For example, the shortage of supplies was so bad, the men even had to scrounge their clothing. They were a motley-looking group, with patched clothes and odd combinations of attire. Some of the men flew their missions with Australian shirts, cowboy boots, and sport shirts, simply because there wasn't anything else to wear and they were glad to get this.

"This was the outfit that got a hot emergency call to go to war. On the morning of December 8, 1941, they were ordered out with such a critical call they didn't even have time to pack. As an indication of their dedication to duty, when they were told to get along and *at once*, they took their orders literally. They didn't stop to talk it over or question what was happening. Some of these pilots just ran out to their planes and even took off in their bedroom slippers. They never had the chance to return home to get their gear; they stayed on the move, and they ended up by having to scrounge for the clothes to wear on their backs. . . . It was difficult—but wonderful—to reconcile the sights we ran across, in terms of their clothing, with their fabulous fighting record and their wonderful morale. Instead of looking shaggy, with their Australian bush hats and boots, and their wide grins, they even had a jaunty air about them."[3]

The Marauders had to make their bombing runs over the cream of Japanese fighter opposition—the Zeros flown by the top aces of Japan, operating out of Lae, Salamaua, and Rabaul. Lieutenant Louis W. Ford[*] stressed the fact that, in spite of the appalling losses suffered in combat against the Japanese, the group had no

---

[*]Shot down on April 11, 1942, by Zero fighters during a raid against Rabaul. Six weeks later Ford and his crew, after an incredible saga of survival, walked out of the jungle and returned to their group.

choice but to continue driving deeply—*without* fighter escort—into skies controlled by the enemy.

"The Japanese at that time," he explained, "enjoyed a solid air superiority over New Guinea. . . . I hesitate to be specific [today], of course, but it's completely accurate to say that our average losses approximated between fifteen and twenty-five percent per mission. [Ten percent losses per mission are considered 'prohibitive.']

"Some of our men were incredible. It was during this period that Carl King of the 33rd Squadron gained quite a reputation for carrying along his toothbrush and brushing his teeth under attack. Jay Zeamer had quite a reputation also. He was in the 19th Squadron. He used to wear an old-fashioned helmet, the tin-hat kind. He would go to sleep—literally—while under fighter attack. One of the pilots once had Jay for a copilot and as the Zeros were blasting in and shooting them up, this pilot had to keep punching Zeamer on the chest to keep him awake as the Zeros were pouring bullets and cannon shells into the airplane. Jay Zeamer was later shifted over to the 43rd Bomb Group and his total lack of nerves earned him the Congressional Medal of Honor during a rough mission in the Solomons."[4]

Whereas combat missions always have their obvious dangers—of the fatal variety—even flying over New Guinea proved to be a dangerous adventure, for the mountain range jutted to well above 10,000 feet. The passes through which the heavily loaded planes sometimes tried to slide were rarely below 7,000 feet and thick, turbulent clouds often covered the area.

At Moresby itself, the only strip, among several, that could handle the Marauders was Seven-Mile. "Everything there was primitive," related John Richardson, 22nd Bomb Group Operations Officer. "All about the field were the mountains, matted over with a pestilent jungle growth. The hills and mountains were inhabited by treacherous natives, and there was always a ruthless enemy to contend with. Moresby proper was a malaria-infested hole at the time. The crews had to bring their own bedding and mosquito bars. Since no adequate living quarters of *any* kind were available, the men slept—or tried to sleep—the night through beneath the wings of their planes. Since the Japanese would hit us without warning at night, two men always slept in their plane—ready to kick over the engines and rush to dispersal points. The food consisted of emergency rations. There was no radar, and there were no sirens, and our air raid warning consisted of an alarmed sentry firing three shots rapidly into the air. If you didn't hear the shots, the next sound you usually heard were the bombs whistling down toward you.

"During daylight, the air raid warning signal was a bit different. Someone frantically hoisted a red flag atop the rickety operations tower (it was made of logs and was a laugh) and if you saw the tower guys themselves come tumbling down and scooting off in all directions, why— you might even have two or three minutes to run and throw yourself into a deep ditch or any hole around. We were pretty fond of some of the old bomb craters.

"There were no revetments for the dispersed planes, and to save them, pilots often took off with cold motors and with bombs raining down as they went along the runways. And then there were the Zeros, which could always be counted upon to come right down to the runway and strafe everything and anything."[5]

There were aerial charts and maps that drifted in every now and then to the pilots, but they were a rarity rather than a normal part of operations. When the men finally did receive the charts they needed so badly, they soon threw them away in disgust because the information was so inaccurate.

Weather forecasting was almost nonexistent, and more than once entire formations were turned back from their targets because of violent—and unpredicted—storms.

Over the Owen Stanley Range particularly the weather was treacherous. Frequent storms, vicious downdrafts, and often impenetrable mists claimed planes and their entire crews.

The crews remember one takeoff at three o'clock in the morning from Seven-Mile Drome. No one liked to try to get off Seven-Mile at night; it was bad enough racking a B-26 into the air from that field during the day. The strip was what the pilots called an "uphill-downhill thing and there were times when it could get pretty hairy." Above all, the pilots wanted no part of the uphill take-offs, because of the load to be carried and the condition of the runway. At one end of the runway there was a small hill, and if the temperature was high they needed a lot more speed and distance than usual to get safely into the air.

But sometimes they did not have the speed, and maybe the wind was blowing from the wrong direction—or maybe it shifted just after a Marauder began its takeoff roll. Along the runway were dull, small ground flares—barely enough to keep a man going in the right direction. Every flare had someone standing by to douse it immediately if the Japanese came over suddenly.

That particular takeoff made the other pilots wish they could forget they had ever seen it. The Marauder sailed into the darkness, her exhausts spitting dull flame. Just as she was over the grove of trees at the end of the runway, pulling hard for altitude and speed, something happened. No one knows what, of course. But the darkness vanished before a mushrooming ball of orange flame.

Then a vicious blast ripped through the trees, giving the body of each man on the strip a squeeze as the pressure wave enveloped him. The sharp, roaring sound brought signs of relief to the faces of the waiting, watching men. The roar meant that the bombs in the Marauder had exploded and that any survivors in the wreckage had been mercifully released in that shattering instant. That was a blessing, the men said; burning alive was every kind of known hell.

Walt Krell—one of the greatest bomber pilots who ever lived—had some memorable comments to make on Seven-Mile Drome. Krell's notes taken during this phase of the war show starkly the nature of conditions at the time: "Seven-Mile used to get laced by the Japs two or three times every few days, and the bomb craters would get refilled with gravel, sand and earth, uncompacted. This would allow the heavily laden wheels of the B-26 to rut and sink. With about nine inches of propeller clearance from the ground even on a hard surface, you can well imagine the amount of pebbles with which we nicked the props as we wallowed around trying to get lined up in this soft dry mush, with landing struts compressed under a full load of bombs, ammo, fuel and crew. A number of times we had to take off downwind and we'd clip grass for a mile or more getting the wheels up and bleeding up the flaps before we really could figure we were flying.

Nothing like a good thrill first thing—why wait to get to the target?

"The B-17 and B-25 pilots didn't quite have this problem of the tremendously high wing-load factor of the B-26 and they couldn't seem to understand why we griped so much about the runway. After I explained that we were running short of pilots and having to borrow Aussies, and that arrangements undoubtedly could be made to have some of the B-17 and B-25 pilots transferred to the 22nd Group and B-26s, we heard no more queries about why the B-26s didn't clear the runway as easily as the other types of aircraft."

The reputation of the Marauder as a pilot-killer—and the charge that she was unable to fly on one engine—deserve comment by the men of the 22nd Bomb Group. Jerry Crosson noted that "the plane met with mixed reactions at first. People who loved to fly a good airplane were wildly enthusiastic about it. It demanded a lot of its pilots, but it also gave them more in return than any other airplane flying. . . . It was like a big pursuit plane. . . . She was absolutely responsive to the controls. If you knew what you were doing, she never gave you any sudden or unexpected surprises. I've flown about every hot ship the Air Force ever had and the B-26 is right at the top of the list as one of the finest I've ever flown. . . .

"The B-26 was incredibly strong, and packed into a long, beautiful shape. I've seen holes as big as beer barrels in the wings and it didn't bother that bird a bit. It was a real military machine—a *weapon*.

"Whoever said the '26 couldn't fly with only one fan going is clear out of his mind. I flew one home all the way back from Lae with one engine shot up and dead. Hell, I've made dozens of flights with one of those props feathered—and I'm talking about the original '26 with the short wings. Arkie Greer and John Richardson dragged over the mountains one day with only one engine going. And they weren't the only guys in our outfit to climb out with a full load, including bombs, with one engine dead. . . ."

John Richardson: "Everything seemed to fall apart on us that day. We lost an engine right after takeoff. We were really loaded with fuel, bombs, and everything else. We were marginal all the way, of course, but on only one engine we dragged ourselves over the hills until we got out over the water—beyond Seven-Mile at Moresby—and we could salvo our bombs safely. So even if things got real bad for you, that Marauder was enough of a brute to drag you on out of trouble."

"But of all the things we liked best about the B-26," added Crosson, "the nicest was its speed. We would get up to three hundred miles per hour indicated, right on the deck, and that is true speed. It was just about as fast as most fighters flying at the time. Many times in combat we shoved over into long dives—a very steep gliding angle would be closer to it—and we would indicate three hundred and sixty miles per hour, and that was enough to give the Zeros a real hard time trying to stay with us.

"Some of the guys, of course, when they were being shot to ribbons, would pound toward the ocean, trying to get to the water with everything in the cockpit shoved all the way forward, and in their dives they would indicate over four hundred miles per hour. The airplane is supposed to start coming apart at the seams when you do things like that, but ours never did, even when they were all shot up with holes all over them. The Zeros couldn't turn to make their pursuit passes at us. The moment they turned when we were hellbent for leather we'd pull ahead of them."

John Richardson expanded on this point: "I was on one mission when it seemed that the Zeros picked us out as their particular target. They shot us to ribbons. They hit us at their leisure until we completed our bombing run. Not until then were we able to start running downhill, to run for home and build up our speed. I don't know how we ever got back.

"That B-26 was a flying wreck. It shook and buffeted from all the gaping holes and the jagged pieces of metal sticking out into the wind. We were really pouring the coal to the airplane and we were way over the maximum permissible speed, and we were still doing our very best to squeeze even more speed out of the machine. If we had been in any other airplane, we would never have made it."

John N. Ewbank, Jr. (today Brigadier General, Deputy Assistant Director of Operations, Tactical Air Command,

USAF): ". . . we would fly the pants off a B-25. We had that short-winged B-26 and except for a few fighters we could outrun anything in the air. We could carry a bomb load about as big as that for a B-17 and a lot faster, although not as high or as far, of course.

"But in terms of the medium bombers, every one of us preferred the B-26 to anything else ever built. It was unbelievably rugged. We brought them home smashed and battered, we bellied them in when our gear systems were shot away, and three days later or sooner they were back in combat, slugging it out and taking everything dished out to us.

"For my money, it was the finest weapon we had. It's too bad we didn't have more of them. And, as well, the spare parts and mechanics and the crews really to give us a chance to concentrate more on the enemy, rather than spending so much time scrounging parts and jury-rigging repairs so that we could get back into the air and fly our missions. . . ."

"Who was the nut who told everybody back in the States that the Japanese were no match for us in the air? Those Japanese we met over New Guinea and up at Rabaul weren't just *good*—they were hell on wheels. They were real good. We never had a doubt in the world that we were slugging it out with the cream of the crop. And Lae was about the worst of all. You were raked over the hot coals just about every single time you made *that* haul over the mountains. Remember those missions, John?"

John Richardson waved a hand at General John Ewbank. Ewbank leaned back in his seat; he did not have to try hard to remember the missions over New Guinea and New Britain. He had said more than once that you *never* forgot what it was like in the skies of the Southwest Pacific. . . .

"Yeah, Rabaul was really something. There was only one way to think of that target. Rabaul would really shake you up whenever you went up there to try your luck. It was rugged, real rugged. Those Japanese were some damned fine flying people, let me tell you.

"There was a run against Lae when I was convinced we would never make it back home. The mission called for us to make the flight to the target right on top of a cloud deck, and then to break through and go busting over Lae. Hit them with complete surprise.

"I led that mission. Everything was going fine; we thought we really had it made. But all of a sudden we had company. Those pilots at Lae [this was the base to which Saburo Sakai was attached] were always hungry for bear, it seemed. Call them—well—'exceptionally aggressive' is as good a term as any, I suppose. Far as I was concerned, they were out to tear us to pieces.

"This was the first mission I was ever making when the Zeros ringed me in. I thought we had full surprise, and the funny thing is, we *did*. But the moment we were in sight we could see activity ahead of us. We were really moving, too. By the time we got to the end of the runway I was staring at those Zeros scrambling into the air like a swarm of gnats. They just hauled those planes right up at us, and they came running for us straight out of their takeoff runs. I'd never seen anything like it.

"We went low over that field, bombs cascading down from us, and our gunners not knowing whether to shoot up the targets on the field or to try to track those Zeros that were clawing at us. Soon as we got the bombs out, I turned sharply and led the formation down low over the water. But the Zero pilots acted like they were pretty mad because they hadn't been able to stop the attack. When we turned to head for home they cut inside real tight and fast and then they were all over us.

"They stayed with us and gave us hell. That was also the first time I brought my airplane home a flying wreck, we were so full of gashes and holes. They really gave us a going-over. They came in to pointblank range as though our gunners weren't even there, and then they hosed everything they had at us. And they had plenty."

On May 24, the men of the 22nd Bomb Group had even more cause to be grateful to the planes by which they swore; May 24 was also a day to remember as the grimmest kind of evidence of the quality of the fighter opposition. Six B-25 Mitchells of the 13th Squadron, 3rd Bomb Group, were led by Captain Herman F. Lowery against Lae. There was no fighter escort.

Lowery took his bombers through a pass in the Owen Stanley Range, swept wide of the Salamaua air-base substation, and then swung in from the east to attack Lae. The six B-25s settled down for their bomb run.

Eleven Zero fighters met them head-on. They included some of the best pilots at Lae, and they slaughtered the American planes.

Lowery's B-25 was jumped almost at once by a Zero piloted by Hiroyoshi Nishizawa. Under a short burst of cannon shells the B-25 exploded and smashed into the ocean as a ball of fire. Toshio Ota shot down the second Mitchell. Moments later, Saburo Sakai tore the third American bomber into disintegrating wreckage. Junichi Sasai's guns blew up the fourth B-25. Saburo Sakai came into pointblank range of the fifth plane to rip into burning wreckage his second kill of the fight.

The pilots then crowded against the last B-25, cutting it to ribbons before they finally broke off their attack and went back to Lae. Somehow, with their airplane almost falling apart about them, the crew managed to get back to Moresby, where the pilot crashed his airplane on the strip.

Five out of six . . . and the sixth almost a complete wreck.

There came about a strange postscript to the disastrous mission of May 24, told by Walter A. Krell, at the time a lieutenant with the 22nd. War Correspondent Pat Robinson said of him: "If ever a man subordinated himself to his crew, it was Krell. To him, leadership was more than a responsibility; it was a consecration to those who served with him."[6]

Walt Krell made a meticulous examination of the combat records of the Lae fighter wing, especially the reports by Saburo Sakai. And then (in a meeting with the writer) he recalled the past—"much too vividly," as he said.

He had compared his own flight log with those of the Japanese pilot. "As I go back through all this," he said, "a thousand and one incidents flash through my mind. As I thumb through Sakai's records covering this period of the war, almost every page comes to life with episodes with which we were so terribly familiar. For example, Sakai details the great day they had when they knocked down five out of six B-25s.

"I was worried that the Japs had come up with some sort of a new gimmick that gave them some kind of tremendous odds. I was particularly concerned because I was scheduled to take the next group flight over Lae, where this had happened. After some effort, I got next to some 3rd Group pilots, but they couldn't seem to do a thing but lament what they thought was in store for them on their next trip over the target.

"Weeks later, a very thin little blond pilot wearing dark glasses came to Woodstock, seeking a ride south. He was going blind, and was on his way to a General Hospital in Melbourne. Combat was over for him.

"He was Don Mitchel, an old friend and classmate of mine, *the sole survivor of the five bombers shot down on May 24.* He told a fantastic tale, too long to go into now, except that he was riding in the co-pilot's seat, the formation got split, his ship was being shot up—both engines out and burning, the cockpit full of smoke, everybody yelling, nothing working—when somebody hollers, 'Bail out!'

"Don remembered that somebody jerked the emergency release panel over his head. He stood up on his seat, getting ready to leave, when somebody gave him a powerful boost on the fanny, and shoved him clear of the ship. He jerked madly on the D-ring of his parachute; the silk banged open with a terrific jerk. Don must have been right on the deck when he went out. He was still in mid-air when his ship hit the water with a roaring explosion. His body then made only one swing and he was in the water himself. He looked toward his plane, but all he could see was that little cloud of steam the planes would leave when they went down.

"Now for the payoff. His legs were useless, having been injured somehow. He was several miles offshore, and a few of the Zeros came down after him. They strafed him repeatedly while he kept pushing himself underwater to duck. Finally they got tired of the game or figured he was dead, and flew away.

"Don was in the water for a long time before some natives picked him up. How he got back over the Owen Stanley Range to Port Moresby without the use of his legs is a fantastic story all in itself.

"You know, it's particularly interesting for me to get Sakai's point of view, since it's nice to know that we weren't the only people in the air to be worried over New Guinea. Sakai tells of a Zero pilot who was determined to get a B-26 by ramming; he even gives his name—Suitsu.

"Don't question what Sakai says about this because, believe me, *I know.*

"I remember this guy coming in from the right front. There was a flight of four B-26s on me, and another flight of four right behind. I kept waiting and waiting for this guy to fire so I could kick the formation down and spoil his aim. I'll be hanged if this Zero didn't slide right over the left wing of my airplane. He was nearly inverted, and still trying to pull down. Had he been a little more on center, he might have clipped our tail, but he missed us and slammed into Moe Johnson's ship.

"Joe Morningstar and I went over the full report by Saburo Sakai. He tells how the Zero, after the collision, went through a series of slow rolls and went into the sea at full speed. Then he describes how the B-26, without its vertical fin, yawed and rolled crazily, flipped over on its back, and plunged into the water with what Sakai called a blinding explosion.

"Well, he's right. Every single detail checks out; there isn't a shred of conflict about that episode as the Japanese pilot told it—and as we saw it.

"Not until I saw Sakai's story did I know why I wasn't killed myself on that mission."

Several days after the loss of the five B-25 bombers, Lieutenant Colonel Dwight Divine, commander of the 22nd Bomb Group, wrote in his diary:

"The lads had some tough luck today. Five went over Lae—two from 18th Sq. were Ellis and O'Donnell, two from 33rd were Coleman and Lanford, and there was Burnside from the 19th. Ellis' ship was riddled, the navigator (Kallina) killed. O'Donnell lost an engine, came all around the tip of New Guinea to get back and landed two hours late. Coleman's ship made emergency landing at Moresby. Lanford crashed into the ocean on fire near Lae. Bad show, and for several reasons. Moresby must not have given them any definite plan, and no one was in charge. Bad."

There was this entry for the day following:

"May 28th, 1942. ——— came back today, and gave me some dope on his mission. He said he doesn't want to go over Lae again without fighter cover, and I certainly don't blame him. . . ."[7]

Walt Krell, more than any other one man—so state the members of the 22nd Bomb Group—had a deep and intimate sense of identification with the job that he, the other pilots, and the crewmen were expected to carry out in the war against the Japanese. The sense of identification, an unflinching devotion to the uniform he wore, enabled Krell to record, through the years, the words that best describe what the angry skies over New Guinea were like:

"There were many struggles in that war," Krell said. "And it's still amazing to me, after all the years have gone by, how many of them had to be fought just to get the airplanes off the ground and on their way to the target. At the end of a long line of obstacles, of which more than a few were maddening to people who were overworked and overtired, and who saw no way out of the maw of continuous missions . . . well, at the end of it all waited the Japanese. There were moments when they seemed to be only part of that great over-all picture so glibly described as 'the enemy.'

"For the lads hanging around under the wings of the B-26s, waiting for the word to go, a lot went on in the Operations Shack they never knew about. For example, time and again I would be ordered to depart Townesville with a flight of six, eight, or ten ships, having been told by the Group Powers that *no specific targets were known.* All we were told was to hit some enemy point like Lae or Rabaul. Nothing else! What kind of a way was that to fight a war?

"Once in Port Moresby, I would again check with Aussie Intelligence, only to find that their reconnaissance planes had picked up nothing new in the way of targets. Time and time again our missions resolved themselves into nothing more than raids to expose ourselves to ground fire and the engagement of Zeros, with no specific ground targets. And no matter what size bombs we used, we were never able, it seemed, to tear up their runways enough to prevent the Zeros from getting off the ground.

"In the absence of specific targets and because the Japanese on the 90-mm. antiaircraft guns were awfully good, I sometimes decided to take the flights through the target area flying defensively instead of holding a straight and level course. Our aircraft losses were far exceeding our replacements as it was and from the standpoint of pursuing the war, I couldn't reconcile the deliberate and prolonged exposure of a standard bombing run on nothing but a strip of dirt with 100-pound bombs.

"We had been told that most of the enemy installations

and stores were concealed some distance back from the runways—just where, no aerial photograph ever seemed to show. I reasoned that anywhere that our bombs might hit within working distance of the runway might do good and, at the same time, obviate the straight and level flying.

"One time at Lae we set off an ammo dump that nobody seemed to know was there—except the Japs. Often the boys on my wing couldn't see this philosophy, and I was criticized for not following the standard, textbook, Emily Post procedure for delivering bombs. The facts were that, when we did have something to go after, we did follow the instruction book on the Norden bombsight.

"Because of this lead policy of mine, there were certain crews and craft on hand to fly another day, when our purpose was of greater import than 'Douglas MacArthur's Smashing Raids' headlines. The low-level attacks really came into their own a little later, when ordnance came out with the delayed fuse. Often our sheet-metal people had more work to do patching up holes from our own bomb shrapnel than from enemy ground fire.

"All the foregoing is background for the idea that as combat airmen we didn't think we were doing any good because of the obscure and elusive targets. We felt like misfits and stepchildren. In fact, it wasn't until George Kenney came over to command the new Fifth Air Force later in 1942—that guy was a real cock-of-the-walk—that we started to get some true indication that people really knew we were even in the Southwest Pacific and fighting pretty much of a wild war down there.

"Any semblance of organization or leadership from the group level on up to Air Force level was pure fiction. At one time our own group even received orders, in the middle of all that miserable way of life and the staggering losses we were taking, that commissioned officers would carry swagger sticks and grow mustaches and that squadron commanders would not fly combat. We'd heard all kinds of weird things, but this really topped it off. I leave to your imagination just how much attention we paid to *that*.

"General Brett was barely on speaking terms with MacArthur. There was a host of old Air Corps brass dumped into our combat area who negated, confused, and compounded problems by the score. It took several months of operation to weed this latter group out, away from the forward combat areas.

"In the final analysis, it was the persistence of the individual pilot and his crew to get to the target that kept the war alive and the enemy engaged. We were, very simply, doing our best. It wasn't a matter of being gung-ho; it was a lousy war and things were rough no matter how you looked at it.

"Time gives you perspective. But one truth hasn't changed a bit. The determination and resourcefulness of the flight crews and the ground crews was the greatest single deciding factor in relation to the number of times a plane got out on a mission."

A vivid picture of combat tactics is given in crew reports on the mission flown by the 22nd Bomb Group on June 9, 1942, against Lae and Salamaua. On this mission Lieutenant Commander Lyndon B. Johnson, U.S.N.R., then on a fact-finding assignment for President Roosevelt, flew with the crew of the B-25 *Heckling Hare,* commanded by Captain Walter H. Greer. During the mission the plane in which the future President of the United States rode was hit by generator trouble. Heavily attacked, while in this condition, by no fewer than eight Zeros, the *Heckling Hare* survived only by dint of a stubborn defensive fire and brilliant evasive tactics. Excerpts from reports by pilots of other planes on this mission follow:

Johnny Ewbank: "Those Zeros coming in is the most vivid thing I've remembered. . . . You know right away when you're in trouble, and we were in it up to our necks. . . . They hit Krell's formation like a ton of bricks. They were all over them and coming in from the side and the front and whipping through the formation and then they were coming wide open for us.

"Right there I switched from Lae to Salamaua for our target. Krell's formation just bored right on through the Zeros to the primary. We started going downhill now because we had not only the bombing to worry about but getting out of there as well. My objective was to get the formation down *low*. To hell with the precision-bombing run at ten thousand feet. Up there, we were sitting ducks for the Zeros. I wanted to get our bombs out and get low, real low, right down on the deck, just as soon as possible. Down there, we had real speed with this B-26, and we could close off our blind spot which is our belly, and our turret and tail guns could really work on the Zeros.

"So we pulled out the plug and went downstairs for everything we had. Man, we were really picking up airspeed with a tremendous clip, really unwinding the altimeter needle and bringing our airspeed to the *Do Not Exceed* limit—and then going right on past. . . ."

Jerry Crosson: "They were up at eighteen thousand feet . . . and then they came straight for us, coming down to where we were at fourteen thousand feet. We were just starting to pick up some speed, but nothing like those Zeros in their dives. They were accelerating so fast you could really see them getting up steam. We got the yokes forward in the cockpit and we all started going downhill. We were real anxious to let the old '26 really unwind and pick up her head to run.

"About five miles out from Lae they plowed in a wild, loose mass right into and through Krell's flight directly ahead.

"I watched them really start chewing at Krell's formation. In the lead position of my flight, Johnny Ewbank saw all this, of course. Suddenly he ordered a change of course. We veered off to the right, away from the attack, and now I knew we were going to try to hit Salamaua. We actually passed right over Lae and the airfield, but we were going downhill like a bunch of locomotives dropping down a mountainside, and there wasn't a chance of our own flight hitting the primary target. We went all-out for Salamaua and the bombardiers were working frantically to set up for the final run, because with a sky full of two dozen or more Zeros there wouldn't be any second chance for us.

"They were all over us and around us and trying to get under us where we were blind, and we were really whipping up the steam and getting up our speed. They were making passes at us from the sides. Towards the field at Lae, they started coming in with some pretty wild frontal passes, their wings and noses blazing, guns and cannon hammering away at us.

"On our actual bombing run the Zeros broke away suddenly and gave the flak crews a chance to get in a few licks at us. It was like leaping from one bed of hot coals into another, with everyone just itching for their turn to work you over. The moment we came out of the bombing run, the Zeros came slicing back in with those frontal and side passes at us, and all this time we were doing our utmost—with all our bombs gone now—to let the B-26s grab for all possible speed.

"When the guns fired . . . from the cockpit you could hear a steady rumble. The whole plane was shaking from the recoil. The rumble came at you from the nose and then up and behind or directly behind, and they merged in and out, and there was all the noise of the engines and propellers and, of course, the kind of noise you always hear and *never* forget. That was the sound of the 20-mm. cannon shells from the Zeros as they exploded against us. They sounded like a shotgun blast going off in a bucket of sand that was being held right next to your head.

"You could *smell* the fight. You could smell the guns when they were firing, the powder, and I tried for years to compare just what it smelled like. But the closest thing to it is that it smells just like a subway station in New York; I swear that's just what it smelled like up there.

"There was one particular Zero that spelled trouble. I had watched him lead the attack into Krell's flight, and he flew—that pilot in that Japanese fighter—as if we didn't have a gun that could bother him. We were moving off to the right from the northeast coast of New Guinea when again I saw that one particular Zero boring in. . . .

"He kept coming in from three o'clock out of a shallow diving turn. He stayed in this turn, really coming in fast, and suddenly he screamed over us with tremendous speed. I'd guess he was maybe a hundred feet or so right over us, no more than that, but perspectives are rough to judge under these conditions. He was a pro; he wasn't wasting any ammunition in that long curve, and he was just a hairsbreadth away from a skid; not skidding, but squeezing all the performance out of that airplane. A real master; he waited for just the right moment. You can spot the master at this sort of thing right away. A lot of the rookies would splash their ammo all over the sky, but the pros who'd been around for a while knew just what they were doing. And then in a blur he was gone.

"My top turret gunner—Johnston—had been tracking this same Zero, and he called on the intercom that the Zero had suddenly flashed up and down, . . . twisting like a dervish so that he couldn't track him with his guns. . . ."

Walt Krell: ". . . there were the Zeros. It was a flying

circus and there must have been twenty or twenty-five of them—the most enemy planes I had ever seen all at once up to that time. They were like a swarm of mosquitos. . . .

"We went over Lae, pouring the coal to the airplanes, our noses down and grabbing for all the speed there was to squeeze out of the engines. We went across the target at about six or seven thousand feet and dropped our eggs, and the tail gunner—John Engleman—said we were getting some pretty good strikes on the runway. A few bombs had geysered in the water, but most of them were right where they were intended.

"We were going downhill now for everything that we were worth, really unwinding, going for that speed that now was so precious. There was one particular point when you made your run against Lae that let you know it was time to head for the deck. First you had to pass 'Rapid Roberts'; you had to get past him. He was a Japanese anti-aircraft gunner at the end of the Lae airdrome. He was *good;* he could play an unbelievable tune of fast and accurate shooting with his flak guns, and it was always a matter of holding your breath until you got past him. The Zeros would swing off for those seconds that you had to run the flak gauntlet, and the moment you did, then everything got even wilder.

"We hit out for the water just as fast as we could get those planes to move, and thank God they were the fastest kinds of airplanes of their class on wings anywhere in the world—or there would have been a great many people who would never have gotten home. We were going downhill with everything we had and—well, I know it violated all the structural limitations and everything else we had on the airplanes that was forbidden, but we were indicating over four hundred miles per hour, the nose of the airplane way down and the Marauder pounding along like there wasn't any tomorrow.

"We couldn't outdive the Zeros, but we were now going so fast that in order to stay with us they couldn't go into their long, wide pursuit curves to set up the best gunnery angles. This threw off their aim and gave us the opportunity to throw some good lead in their direction.

"All the other B-26s had only those little .30-caliber popguns in the waist positions, but ours was a bit mongrelized in the rear. Pat Norton, our radio operator, had thrown away those little .30s and he'd cut a large hatch in the bottom of the side fuselage so that he could have a good field of fire, and he was really cutting into those Zeros with that big gun of his.

"It's too bad we had to turn our planes after making the bomb run, because if we could have kept on going, with everything wide open, no bombs, and much of our fuel gone, the Zeros would have been really hard-pressed to keep up with us. But we had to get home, and anytime we turned, those Zeros would cut in after the advantage with those 'square turns' of theirs.

"They came after us after we got down to the deck . . . ran with and after us like a pack of howling wolves, snapping and slashing. . . ."

There's a certain military medal that few men in uniform wear. It is known as the Soldier's Medal, and it is one of the most universally respected awards any man may hold. It is the medal awarded to those men "who distinguish themselves by heroism not involving actual conflict with the enemy . . . for the performance of an act of heroism involving voluntary risk of life under conditions other than those of conflict with the enemy."

One day at Seven-Mile Drome a Marauder came back to the strip, almost staggering through the air. It was badly shot up—more a flying wreck than a sleek bomber. It lurched dangerously as it came down from the sky toward the runway. And then it did stagger, and smashed helplessly against the unyielding earth, sliding down the runway with a terrifying screech of flame-engulfed metal.

Almost all the crew got out. But the co-pilot was trapped, and the flames tore at his flesh. His pilot stood in the fire, struggling madly to get his friend out of the airplane. It was too late; the co-pilot died, but not before the pilot himself suffered agonizing third-degree burns across his body from the hips down.

They gave the pilot the Soldier's Medal.

His name was Walter A. Krell.

THE OTHER MIDWAY

The first light of dawn of June 4, 1942, broke swiftly over the eastern Pacific. On tiny Midway Island, hundreds of men standing by their planes shifted their bodies, an instinctive movement as the spray of light washed over the metal forms. This moment of a new dawn held the promise of what was to become, in the brief hours ahead, perhaps the single most vital battle of all World War II in the Pacific.

The light glistened on four short-winged killers, beneath which hung the ominous shapes of long torpedoes. The bombers were four Marauders of the 22nd and 38th Bomb Groups, assigned to Navy control on Midway to be used in strikes against the most powerful naval armada ever assembled. The Marauders were the only bombers in the AAF to mount the sleek torpedoes, and this was to be the morning of their baptism of fire.

The war was now six months old, and the Japanese were pressing for a single tremendous fight on the sea in which they might break the back of the Pacific fleet of the United States. Our losses had been so severe that the outcome of the fighting for years to come—perhaps the very war itself, so the Japanese believed—might be decided by this one final, smashing blow.

Admiral Isoroku Yamamoto—remembered in Washington, D.C., as one of the toughest and shrewdest poker players ever to serve as a naval attaché in the capital—commanded the Imperial Fleet. He was also one of the few Japanese who could make an intrinsic evaluation of American strength and resources; not even the early overwhelming gains of Japan could blind Yamamoto to the towering industrial strength of the United States, and its strategic role in the Pacific. Time was on the side of the

Americans; Yamamoto desired fervently to deny the United States that time.

Annihilate the U.S. fleet: that was his driving goal, and he was determined to force the issue. To draw the American fleet into battle, he planned to attack and occupy Midway Island. The U.S. Navy must defend Midway because of its proximity to Hawaii and its vital role in the supply lines to the Southwest Pacific. This, then, was Yamamoto's bait, and he began to draw together his pincers in the form of a tremendous naval force.

He moved Admiral Nagumo into position from the northwest. Nagumo, the man who had wrecked Pearl Harbor, cruised the Pacific with four large aircraft carriers, two battleships, three cruisers, and 12 destroyers. From Saipan, to the southwest, came Vice Admiral Kondo with 12 troop transports, screened by two battleships, ten cruisers, the carrier *Zuiho*, and 20 destroyers. To the west of Midway was Isoroku Yamamoto himself, aboard the monster battleship *Yamato* (68,000 tons); in this same fleet there were another two super battleships, the carrier *Shoho*, three cruisers, and 13 destroyers.

The United States Pacific Fleet was ill equipped to combat the Japanese armada of six carriers, seven battleships, 16 cruisers, 45 destroyers, 12 transports, and several hundred fighters and bombers. The enemy enjoyed the superior performance of the Zero fighters, outstanding torpedo and dive bombers, and airmen trained to the highest skill.

But we enjoyed a critical advantage in Intelligence: we had cracked the Japanese secret naval code and we were thus able to utilize to the best possible advantage our limited forces. No one doubted that we would need every ounce of that advantage.

The big carrier *Lexington* had gone to the bottom in the Battle of the Coral Sea. The *Yorktown* was crippled and had been refloated from drydock only on May 29. The *Saratoga* had not been able to leave San Diego until June 1. The *Wasp* was in the Atlantic. The *Hornet*'s air group lacked battle experience, but the men were ready. *Enterprise* was our main strength; it was fully equipped and its men were skilled combat veterans.

But the inescapable fact was that we could deploy only three carriers against the six of the Japanese.

The value of our aircraft on Midway and in the Hawaiian Islands was questionable. Thirty Catalina flying boats on Midway were useful for reconnaissance, but could hardly be used against well-defended warships; they were also sitting ducks for the Zeros. We had 17 Flying Fortresses, but the crews had not yet completed training and their effectiveness was considered to be gravely in doubt (they failed to score a single strike on a warship during the early part of the battle). The Marines had ready for the fight some Vought SB2U Vindicator dive bombers, which the pilots considered to be fine antiques for a Stateside aeronautical museum. The Marine fighters were made up of a small force of Grumman F4F Wildcats, plus a larger group of Brewster F2A Buffaloes—but the reader is already aware of the value of *this* airplane against the Japanese Zero.

There were ten land-based torpedo bombers for which great hopes were held. Six of Grumman's new TBF Avengers, single-engine bombers, were about to make their combat debut along with the four torpedo-carrying Marauders of the 22nd Bomb Group.

On June 3, a lumbering PBY sighted a Japanese force some 700 miles from Midway—almost precisely where Intelligence had pinpointed the enemy. That afternoon nine Fortresses attacked the Japanese; they returned with reports of "terrific damage to the enemy." In reality the heavy bombers had managed to hit but a single ship—a transport—and that vessel with only one bomb. The attack started a small fire aboard the troopship which the Japanese quickly extinguished.

Shortly after midnight on June 4, four Catalinas used their radar to pick up the Japanese. Immediately afterward the Catalinas changed a lot of ideas about their "lumbering uselessness" as weapons. Engines howling, they roared in at wave-top level, sliced a torpedo neatly into the tanker *Akebono Maru,* strafed the decks of transports, and by a miracle clattered away safely into the darkness.

But these were only preliminary movements, cautious probes and stabs; the real battle was to begin a few hours later. The moment of action went down on the official combat log of the Battle of Midway as 5:34 A.M., when another Catalina proved its value by sounding the alarm: *"Many enemy planes heading for Midway."*

The Marine Buffaloes and Wildcats raced into the air,

climbing steadily to the altitude of the approaching enemy planes. The Marines made a desperate attempt to stave off the initial air strike against the island fortress; while gallantry was evident in their actions, success was not. The Marines were promptly slaughtered by the swift Zero fighters, which shot down 14 of the 24 Marines and, more important, kept them from blocking the attack of the Japanese bombers.

In the meantime, the ten torpedo bombers roared away from Midway's airstrip and headed for the Japanese fleet. Exactly at five minutes past seven o'clock on the morning of June 4, the Marauders and Avengers caught sight of their enemy. And at approximately the same moment the cordon of Zero fighters protecting the fleet sounded the alarm for the approaching American bombers, and slashed in to attack.

What ensued was a violent, sustained bloody mess. The story of the Battle of Midway is a well-known page of our World War II history, of course. But this story—as seen through the actions of one Marauder crew—is *not* well known, and it has waited until now to be told for the first time.[1] This is the story of the "other" Midway. . . .

In the lead position of the Marauder formation was Captain James F. Collins, Jr., of the 69th Squadron, 38th Bomb Group. To his right was First Lieutenant Watson of the same squadron and group.

Flying the left wing position was First Lieutenant Herbert C. Mayes, of the 18th Reconnaissance Squadron, 22nd Bomb Group. In the slot position of the diamond formation was First Lieutenant James P. Muri, also of the 18th Squadron. The last two planes, of the 22nd Bomb Group, had been detained in Hawaii when the main force of Marauders continued on to the Southwest Pacific during the overseas transfer of the group. They had been trained by the Navy in torpedo attacks—and now were to try their skill for the first time against the enemy.

Fifteen minutes out of Midway, the four Marauders pounded over the Pacific at a height of only 800 feet. Ahead of them across the entire horizon were silhouetted the warships of the Japanese fleet. The bombardiers in each of the Marauders checked their sights, their arming devices, and called their pilots. This was a task to be carried

out, actually, by the man at the controls, for to sight the
Marauder along its torpedo run was a matter of aiming
the airplane and flying "into" the enemy warship to be attacked.

Almost as quickly as the Marauder crews called to each
other by radio about the enemy fleet, making swift decisions as to their targets, gunners broke in over the
bomber intercoms with excited shouts. Dead ahead of the
four Marauders were two large formations of Japanese
fighters. They cruised in wide circles about 20 miles before
the American planes, maintaining an aerial defensive wall
between the approaching torpedo bombers and their own
ships.

The sight was enough to chill a man to the bone. The
Marauders were fast, and the pilots hammered the throttles to the firewall to squeeze all the speed out of their
bombers that the planes could give. But they were at a
serious disadvantage. The torpedoes slung beneath the
Marauders' rounded bellies slowed them down. The Japanese fighters cruised between the attacking planes and
their objectives, and the Zeros were high—circling in two
formations at 12,000 to 15,000 feet. Height was a tremendous advantage to the Japanese pilots, who could trade
it off for diving speed and perfect positioning for attack.
The gunners in the Marauders called off at least 18 Zeros
as the Japanese pilots peeled off in precision maneuvers
and swarmed down for the kill.

By now the men were able to distinguish clearly the
shape and the disposition of the Japanese fleet. The warships were deployed miles deep, arranged in a loose box
formation, with the enemy carriers moving swiftly, with
plenty of maneuvering room about them, in the midst of
the other warships. The carriers thus were protected by
thousands of antiaircraft guns of varied calibers, by defending fighters, by their own massed guns, and—as important as any other factor—by more than sufficient
room within this bristling defensive array to maneuver and
avoid even those torpedoes which might be successfully
launched.

The Zero fighters hit the American planes in a devastating blow that was the opening move in the one-two
defensive punch. Hundreds of big and medium guns in the
enemy fleet were depressed and aimed—in plenty of time
for the moves—at the approaching Marauders and Aven-

gers. The big rifles included the enemy's main 16-inch bat-teries of the battleships, and these hurled salvos of shells at their maximum range. The bomber pilots and crewmen watched the flanks of the battleships and cruisers suddenly flash with the rippling fire of the big guns, with new flame appearing swiftly through the roiling smoke from the initial salvos. Long seconds later the water in front of the racing bombers erupted in towering geysers where the shells struck. Running into one of those huge spouts of water that leaped from the ocean surface would have all the effect of smashing into a brick smokestack.

The bombers immediately began to dodge defensively, flying around and between the great plumes of water erupting steadily along their line of flight. What hopes they had held for a tight formation for defensive cross-fire to protect them against the Zero fighters vanished at first sight of the spouting water.

Jim Muri, in the slot position, said later that as they closed the distance between their own planes and the Japanese warships, it "seemed as though every ship ahead of us had burst into flames, they were throwing up that much flak." As quickly as they could manage the maneuver, the four Marauders skidded and slipped together to return to their diamond formation. Most of the water towers were now behind them, and formation meant everything to the bombers, for the Zeros were almost in firing position with their line-abreast head-on attacks.

The battle opened with six fighters speeding in against the four Marauders. Each Zero flashed and sparkled along its nose as the enemy pilots opened fire with their nose guns; when the wings of the Zeros suddenly showed darker flame and black smoke the men in the Marauders knew that the Japanese had the range. The black smoke tes-tified all too clearly to the bursts from the 20-mm. wing cannon of the Mitsubishis, and a burst from those cannon in the right place could break a Marauder in half.

With the erupting waterspouts and swiftly blossoming clouds of flak preceding their own attack, the Zero pilots might well have assumed that their massed head-on at-tack would destroy the Marauders on the first firing pass. The American bombers were trapped; they couldn't climb, and if they dove, they would have to run the gauntlet close to the water where the heavy guns were churning the sea into a spouting maelstrom.

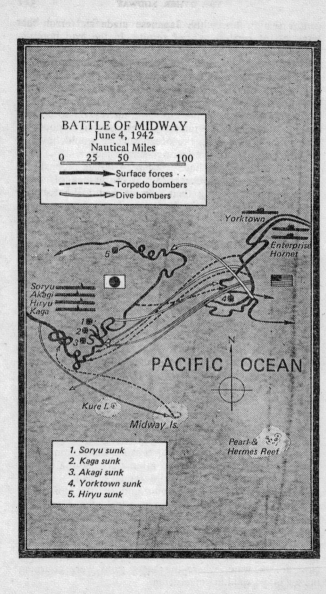

BATTLE OF MIDWAY
June 4, 1942
Nautical Miles
0   25   50   100

→ Surface forces
--→ Torpedo bombers
▷ Dive bombers

Yorktown

Enterprise
Hornet

Soryu
Akagi
Hiryu
Kaga

5

1
2
3

4

N

PACIFIC | OCEAN

Kure I.

Midway Is.

Pearl &
Hermes Reef

1. Soryu sunk
2. Kaga sunk
3. Akagi sunk
4. Yorktown sunk
5. Hiryu sunk

But this is where the Japanese made the error that gave the Marauders a brief respite. In the lead bomber, Collins had tried to anticipate the Japanese line of thought. The moment he sighted the telltale black smoke streaming back over the wings of the Zero fighters, Collins rammed forward on the control yoke of his airplane. The bomber plunged seaward in a sudden dive, three Marauders following him in perfect formation. This disrupted the aim of the Zero fighters and it also gave the top turret gunners the opportunity to rake the bellies of the Zeros as they flashed overhead. But the big gamble—to evade that first head-on firing sweep that could have ended the battle right then and there—had paid off. The Marauders swept right past the Zeros, running faster and faster as they picked up speed in the brief dive.

What worked for the swift Martin bombers didn't work for the slower Grummans. In short, the Avengers didn't make it. Much slower than the twin-engine Marauders, the TBFs were armed only with a single gun in the nose and one in the ball turret aft of the pilot (the belly gun was useless at this height). Under the head-on attack of the Zeros, the Avengers turned out to be cold turkey for the Japanese pilots.

An explosive spray of bullets and cannon shells hammered into the helpless Navy bombers. Almost at once two of the Avengers exploded into brilliant fireballs and smashed into the sea. A third bomber shed part of a wing and instantly cartwheeled wildly through the air, exploding in a spray of disintegrating metal as it sliced into the boiling water. The remaining three Grummans plowed resolutely forward but they never stood a chance.

A tremendous geyser of water lifted suddenly from the ocean, leaping into the sky like a live creature in search of aerial prey; it stood unbelievably before a speeding Avenger. Then it was over; the impact destroyed the Grumman as though a giant hand had slapped it angrily out of the air.

The momentary respite gained by the Marauders vanished as the Zeros snarled back with renewed fury. Pulling well ahead of the shattered Avenger formation, the Marauders, against all the odds, were closing in swiftly on the Japanese warships, fighting their way in toward the carriers. The Japanese pilots hurled themselves wildly at the American planes.

"They hit us first, and *hard*," Muri related. "We were flying through a storm of bullets and shells. We were right on the water going for everything we were worth, with bullets rattling off our skin like hail blasting against a tin roof. . . ."[2]

The Marauders dropped down to ten feet above the ocean, skidding and weaving madly to throw off the aim of the tenacious Japanese fighters. All hope of maintaining formation was now permanently gone as they slewed from left to right, pilots tramping rudder and banging the yoke around. The bombers rose and fell suddenly, precariously, skidding and yawing as the Japanese pilots closed in to pointblank range, firing in steady, sharp bursts.

Grumman TBF Avenger . . . its first combat debut
was the Battle of Midway in June of 1942. Six of
the new torpedo bombers went out against the
Japanese . . . one Avenger returned from the mission.

The Marauder in the slot position, flown by Jim Muri, staggered as though struck with a hard physical blow. Three Zeros came winging in hard and fast, determined to close to ramming distance. The Japanese pilots were better than good; they were seasoned combat veterans. They got the range and they glued themselves into the firing groove, and the next thing that Muri's crew knew was that they were right in the midst of thousands of maddened, whining hornets as the bullets and shells slammed into and through the bomber. It seemed impossible that the plane could survive.

Technical Sergeant Gogoj, in the upper turret, near the tail of the bomber, never had the chance even to recoil as a barrage smashed into his turret. A sudden screaming roar assailed his ears as bullets tore the Plexiglas cover of the turret into a blurred spray of shattered plastic; the Plexiglas seemed to dissolve right before his eyes.

In the same instant that the flying shards, whipped by a wind of more than 300 miles per hour, slashed his face into a mass of gory flesh, gashes, and blood-spraying wounds, the physical impact of the shattered Plexiglas blasted the gunner clear out of his turret seat. His face spurting blood, slivers of skin hanging from his cheeks, nose, chin, and forehead, Gogoj tumbled onto the floor of the wildly careening airplane. He was stunned from the terrible blow and the sudden agony of his face wounds; for a long moment he could not determine where he was. He struggled to regain his senses. He was banged back and forth against the sharp edges of his turret mechanism as Muri kept slamming the airplane through its evasive maneuvers.

Even as Gogoj fought to regain control of his senses and his body, the Zeros increased the fury of their attack. The formation was now hopelessly scattered as the four bombers hugged the waves, jinking desperately, gunners snapping out bursts as they tried to stave off the Zeros.

Suddenly, a tongue of flame leaped into existence behind one Marauder. Brilliant scarlet flashed from a wing tank that sprayed a thin streamer of gasoline, issuing from a self-sealing tank that had been chewed into ragged rubber. The Zeros rushed after the stricken plane like wolves incensed by blood.

And then the tongue of flame was a bright, glaring sheet. The roaring flames spread steadily, blazing into the cockpit to the left and mushrooming through the wing tank and the engine on the right. For one terrible, timeless second, a huge crimson eye writhed in the air as the Marauder's tanks exploded. Pieces of wreckage whirled insanely through the air and smacked, steaming, into the water.

The three remaining Marauders pressed on, the crews unaware that almost at the same instant that the Marauder exploded, the fifth Avenger also was cut down from the sky and pounded into the ocean.

In Muri's plane the carnage continued unabated. In the rear of the fuselage, the stunned and cursing Gogoj, blood streaming onto his clothes, shouted imprecations at the Japanese and forced his way painfully back into his turret seat. He pushed his head and shoulders into firing position and grasped the triggers. A faint strawberry-pink spray leaped into being about his face. Without the Plexiglas shroud around the turret the wind was steadily plucking with steel fingers pieces of skin and more blood from his gashed and mangled face.

Gogoj ignored the wind as much as it was humanly possible to do so; tramping on the power controls and swinging the twin .50-caliber guns around, he tried to draw a bead on an incoming Zero. He never had the chance to fire. Other Zeros clawed in from left to right in beautifully concerted attacks, and once again the turret caught a terrible blow of enemy fire.

A cannon shell exploded almost in his face; his ears rang shrilly from the blast, and the world seemed to go crazy with buzzing hornets all about him as a burst from a Zero at close range shot the charging handle clear off his left machine gun, right out from under his closed hand. The Japanese fighter held the range and fired another long burst; in the wild fury of the spray of bullets Gogoj watched the turret control handle and triggers shatter before his blood-stained eyes. At the same time the firing attack smashed the turret wiring to a pulp and ripped the power units to shreds, burning them out instantly. The turret was without power, useless.

Still the indomitable Sergeant Gogoj refused to leave his post! Bleeding profusely from a dozen or more serious wounds, he waved off help from his fellow crewmen and "stayed put." If nothing else, he could at least bluff the Zeros that his guns were still hot and that his turret was dangerous.

But the Japanese pilots weren't buying it. They weren't being bluffed and they didn't seem to care if the turret was operating or not. Another fighter group howled in, engines screaming, and once again the Marauder rocked wildly beneath the onslaught of heavy firepower.

A machine-gun bullet sliced through metal, ricocheted with a shrill whine through the airplane, and smashed into Gogoj's face. The slug pierced the skin over the sergeant's left eye and lodged there like a white-hot poker; it struck with all the force of a hammer blow against his forehead.

There was a sudden inarticulate cry; a mass of roaring black and red pummeled Gogoj and he tumbled in redoubled pain to the floor of the airplane as bullets whined and shrieked through the metal all about him.

And still this incredible man refused to quit. On his knees in the rocking, violently maneuvering bomber, covered with blood and wracked with pain, Gogoj reached up and with his hooked fingers he clawed the slug out of his face. More blood spurted from the wound.

Trying to keep his balance in the berserk Marauder, ignoring constant death in the air about him, he ripped free the first-aid kit from his gunbelt. As his body slammed back and forth against the gun mount he matted sulfa powder into the gaping wound, and then jammed on a patch to stem the spurting blood.

And once again he hauled his battered and bloody body, inch by inch, back into the turret to bluff the Zeros—and stayed there!

While Gogoj went through his own terrifying ordeal, his fellow crewmen were going through their own hells under the Japanese onslaught. Almost at the same moment that the shattering Plexiglas slashed Gogoj's face into bloody shreds, PFC Ashley, in the tail turret, was slammed violently against the side of his turret position. The Marauder was jinking its way, with violent side-to-side movements, through a continuing swarm of Japanese bullets and shells, and in a single, long burst kept up by a determined Zero pilot, Ashley took a terrible beating. Almost simultaneously, *five* bullets crashed into his hip and knee.

The blood gushed out wildly. Crying out in agony and clutching his leg, Ashley managed deliberately to throw his body backward, far enough so that he might be able to lunge and fall free of the turret position. Despite his severe and badly bleeding wounds, Ashley's immediate thought was to get his body out of the tail position so that another man could grab the single .50-caliber gun and defend the airplane in its vulnerable area from rear attacks.

Immediately behind Ashley, Sergeant F. Melo was swinging back and forth in the narrow fuselage bottom to fire the tunnel guns. On each lower side of the fuselage the Marauder had a small hatch with a single .30-caliber gun; Melo would snap out a burst with one weapon, then fling himself across the short space to grasp and fire the other gun when the Zeros came in from that side.

Melo saw Ashley come tumbling out of the tail, his fingers crimson and blood spurting in founts from between his fingers where he clutched his shattered leg. Ashley tumbled to the floor of the bomber; his body jerked several times and then he collapsed. Melo leaped across the open hatch to grasp Ashley and prop up his body against a structural beam.

It was at this instant that yet another torrent of bullets and cannon shells came tearing into the staggering bomber. One slug ripped through the Marauder's skin and grazed Melo's forehead just above his left eye, slashing open a long and deep wound from which the blood sprayed. The bullet had cracked with terrible force against the bone beneath the skin; Melo lurched helplessly from the terrific impact. He sucked in air deeply to regain his senses; grimly he clenched his teeth and started again for that critical tail-gun position. Without that gun firing the whole thing could be over in seconds.

Melo hadn't yet completed his first step when the Zeros struck again. Another bullet slammed into Melo's right arm near the shoulder. The impact of the bullet stopped Melo where he stood. There was a moment of blinding red in his eyes; the world roared in his ears. He shook his head; blood whipped out from his head wound. And then Melo started again for the tail gun. . . .

A huge sledgehammer pounded into his side. He gasped soundlessly with the pain as two more bullets ripped into his body. And still he was on his feet. And once *again* he started for that gun. . . .

Again he was stopped where he was. A white-hot claw with flaming talons raked all the way down his left leg as pieces of smoking steel from an exploding cannon shell slashed the whole of the leg.

By all the laws of medical science, Melo should have been a crumpled, bleeding heap on the floor of the airplane. He was covered from head to foot with blood, and still the scarlet flow spread down his body.

Melo kept moving. He made it to the tail, and staggered painfully to his knees in the turret position to grasp the heavy machine gun. Gritting his teeth and aiming through one eye—blood had poured into the other—he

Shot to ribbons, gashed and cut from Zeros
and antiaircraft fire ... Marauder with torpedo
slung beneath its belly pounds in toward its target
in the Battle of Midway. Four Maurauders went
out ... two returned from the mission.

led an oncoming Zero fighter in the sights, and squeezed
the trigger. There was a single shot—and the gun
jammed. Cursing, Melo tore at the stoppage and cleared
the jam. Again he took aim and began snapping out short
bursts at the oncoming fighters. He watched his tracers
arcing their way toward the Mitsubishis, watched several
Zeros skid from the unexpected fire, noted that he had
thrown off their aim.

Without warning, his body bent violently as a savage
flame creased his back. Japanese tracer bullets had torn
into the gun position even as he was firing and set aflame
the seat cushions about him.

Melo grasped a blazing cushion in his bare hands and
flung it wildly out of the open space of the tail-gun position. He was dismayed to see the flaming pad caught by
the wind—and hurled swiftly back into the airplane. The
returning pad caught him completely unawares, and he
was unable to stop it from slapping hard against his body.
Once again he hurled the flaming mass away from the airplane, and now, with his bare hands, beat out the flames
on his clothes and another cushion.

Melo shouted into the bomber's intercom, trying to tell
Muri what was happening in the tail. The phones were
useless; Japanese bullets had torn and shredded the wiring.

Suddenly more flames leaped up around Melo.

Ignoring the pain of his multiple wounds, Melo worked his way forward through the bucking, rolling, slewing Marauder; somehow he managed to fight his way along the fuselage, along the catwalk of the bomb bay, through a small circular hatch, down into the radio compartment and then up two steps to the cockpit. His bloody hand grasped Muri's shoulder, and he shouted to his pilot that everyone in the rear of the airplane was badly wounded and that they were on fire.

That was all that Melo had left in him; he had exhausted his strength. Overcome with shock and the constant flow of blood, Melo collapsed even as he shouted his report to the pilot. The co-pilot, Lieutenant P. L. Moore, shoved back his seat and released his belt. Moving as quickly as possible, he clambered over Melo's body and worked his way to the tail where the fire leaped higher. He rushed to the turret and flung the blazing cushions out a hatch, and squeezed his body into the turret position to man the gun. He had no sooner fired than his eyes went wide. Directly before his gaze, a Marauder took a devastating barrage of cannon shells, exploded violently into flames, and hurtled with terrible impact into the ocean.

In the violence of the battle, spurred on by his determination to reach the target no matter what the opposition, Jim Muri ignored the already severe and still mounting damage to his airplane; he ignored the flames; he kept the throttles jammed forward for maximum power and he worked the control yoke and stamped on the rudder pedals as if the Marauder were a thing alive.

And still they hadn't reached their target....

But they *were* through the several defending rings of the enemy fighter planes. With a swift rush a Japanese carrier loomed up before the bomber. The entire side of the huge warship and the sides of the escorting vessels blazed with the concentrated fire of hundreds of antiaircraft guns. Because the range was so close the smaller cannon and the machine guns also were firing, and the air literally seethed with the sparkling, glowing blobs of tracers that snaked and spun toward, over, under, about, and into the Marauder.

The first Rising Sun flag they had ever seen appeared before them, fluttering stiffly from the carrier's mast. Muri leveled the battered bomber and set up his run—flying

straight and level in the face of violent fire—to release
the torpedo. Countless guns blazed terrifyingly in their
faces.

The great bulk of the carrier was already heeling over
as her bridge ordered a turn into the path of the American bomber. Muri held the Marauder straight and true;
the bombardier—Lieutenant R. H. Johnson—yanked the
release to spring the torpedo free. The deadly fish dropped
away, splashed into the foaming water, and began its run
toward the starboard bow of the carrier.

Almost as quickly as the long torpedo fell away, the
Marauder rushed headlong at the warship in front of
them. Jim Muri hauled desperately on the yoke—they
were so low he had to *climb* to get over the flat carrier
deck. As the Marauder skimmed with a howl across the
carrier, Johnson grabbed the single .50-caliber gun in the
nose. It was a unique opportunity and he took advantage
of it, spraying a long burst directly into the island of the
carrier. Dozens of Japanese stared open-mouthed at the
sight of the American bomber only scant feet away,
mushrooming in size. Johnson watched his tracers pouring
into their bodies and ricocheting wildly about the island.

There had been a blessed, brief respite from the fighters. But with the carrier now falling astern the Japanese
pilots swarmed back in fury. The Marauder was picking
up speed; without the drag and weight of the torpedo,
with much of their fuel gone, the bomber was light. Muri
was beating the engines of the plane, banging on the
throttles and propeller controls to squeeze all the power
he could from the thundering engines, and the battered
airplane responded with even more speed. Muri stayed low
on the water, hugging the waves to protect the vulnerable
belly position, restricting the diving attacks of the Zeros,
and gaining the maximum possible speed from the airplane. At more than 300 miles per hour the now-lightened
Marauder actually began to pull away from her pursuers.
The speed of the bomber could save their lives.

Johnson clambered out of the nose position and moved
into the co-pilot's seat to help Muri with the controls of
the airplane. It shook and vibrated badly and Muri's arms
were almost numb from the pummeling they had been
taking. Sergeant Melo regained consciousness; he stumbled back to the radio compartment and attempted to
pick up a homing signal from Midway. But the radio had

taken several direct hits and the vital antenna had been blown clear off the airplane. They were lost.

Yet, at that moment, the men in the Marauder couldn't have cared less. There were other American planes racing in toward the enemy fleet, and the Zeros suddenly weren't interested in chasing a crippled bomber.

There was still a long way to go for this crew, still a long pull to survive this mission. Muri eased back on the yoke and gained some altitude; he eased off on the power to lessen the wild vibrations and severe buffeting of the bomber. Lieutenant W. W. Moore, the navigator, clambered onto a stool and shoved his head into the small Plexiglas dome atop the fuselage, "shooting the sun" to get their bearings and head them back toward Midway.

Despite the relief from fighter attacks, every man knew the Marauder was a potential bomb that could detonate at any second. Fuel sprayed from the ripped and torn fuel tanks; a spark could turn them into a blazing torch. Gogoj came up front—"looking like a blood-soaked rag," Muri said—and began transferring fuel into two tanks that were yet whole and sealed.

With infinite care Muri nursed the battered airplane carefully toward the short airstrip at Midway Island. The airplane was literally a flying wreck, and the men on the return flight kept finding more damage than they had noticed during the battle or in the relief of watching the Zeros turning away from them.

Muri came in to Midway as though he were flying on a razor's edge of survival (which he was). He came in holding right aileron and left rudder, sliding down from the sky at a drunken angle. The maneuver was deliberate, for he knew he would have to ease down the weight of the bomber on the right wheel. As it turned out, he was right. The left tire was a mass of chewed and mangled rubber, and any sudden impact on that wheel would have snapped the gear and sent the airplane cartwheeling down the strip.

The Marauder touched on her right gear, still heeled over sharply. Muri played her like a master; as long as he could do so with the controls he kept her cocked over. As the speed fell the bomber lurched over onto the left gear. Swiftly Muri and Johnson together stamped on the brakes. The effort was wasted—they had been shot away.

The impact of hitting the shattered left gear, and rumbling on the wreckage at nearly 100 miles per hour, was "unbelievably violent." There was a terrific, rattling roar; the Marauder buffeted so wildly that the entire instrument panel in the cockpit ripped completely out of its fastenings and collapsed onto the startled pilots. In the back of the airplane the men were flung about and battered severely.

At long, weary last, *Old 1391* clumped and groaned her way to a stop. Men came running to the scene, and stopped to stare in disbelief first at the torn and riddled airplane, and then at the bloody men who climbed painfully down through her hatches.

Before they left to receive the medical attention they needed so urgently, the crew of the Marauder walked around their airplane. It was hard to believe what they saw.

The left gear was a mangled ruin. Fuel dripped from the tanks; hydraulic fluid and oil spattered steadily onto the ground. Every propeller blade was riddled and chewed. The entire top edge of one wing had been blown off. The radio antenna was shot away. The engines were filled with holes. The rear turret was a blood-sprayed shambles. Blood had sprayed the entire interior of the airplane. The navigator's compartment showed daylight brightly through what had become a sieve.

They counted more than 500 holes, tears, rips, gashes, and other damage to the Marauder. Then they quit counting, because they still had more than half the airplane to cover. They called it a day and clambered into jeeps for the ride to the hospital.

It wasn't until the shooting was all over and a careful survey was taken that we realized the terrible sacrifice of the initial attacks against the mighty Japanese fleet at Midway.

The toll was grisly.

Out of the six Avengers, five were shot down.

Two out of four Marauders were lost.

Twenty-eight Marine Vindicators and Dauntlesses attacked; 12 went down in flames.

Fourteen out of 24 Marine fighters had been smashed from the sky by the Zero fighters.

In the first wave of fighting, we lost 33 planes and their crews—and failed to hit a single Japanese ship.

Fifteen Devastators of Torpedo Squadron 8 from the *Hornet* went in low and slow. The Japanese blew *every* bomber out of the sky. Hits: *none*.

Twenty-six more torpedo planes went in. The Japanese shot down 20 of them. Hits: *none*.

But the sacrifice—in the full meaning of the term—was not in vain. The Japanese committed a grievous error. Every gun in their fleet was depressed to the maximum to lash out at the low-flying torpedo planes. Every Zero fighter had come down low to the water, tearing apart our planes and men. *The sky overhead was undefended.*

The shrill scream from the sky was heard after it was too late. The Dauntless dive bombers from *Enterprise* and *Yorktown* came down from 17,000 feet in near-vertical dives. For three miles they plunged—and the carriers lay naked and exposed before them.

It was all over in minutes.

Soryu took three 1,000-pound bombs in her vitals.

Akagi took two devastating strikes that shattered her.

Kaga took four big bombs in her belly and vomited gigantic sheets of flame.

Within minutes, all three carriers were wracked with explosions and swept from bow to stern by huge blazes that could not be quenched.

By the next day, four of Japan's biggest and most powerful aircraft carriers had slid to the bottom of the Pacific. With them went 234 planes and more than 2,500 men. The greatest disaster lay in the loss of life—not in numbers, but in quality. Among those men who had died were the finest pilots and aircrews of the Japanese nation. They were never to be replaced in time.

When the shooting ended they celebrated the victory at Midway. They had good cause to stand proud—the Navy dive bombers had broken the back of the Japanese Navy and crippled her airpower.

On the side of the Midway airstrip, several men, swathed in bandages, went out for a long look at *Old 1391*. The Marauder stood at an ungainly angle, her skin punctured and blackened. She was a wreck. They say it is possible for an airplane to look tired. This one looked it.

EPILOGUE

The new planes soon would come. They would be fast and deadly. Men would come to know them well—the Lightnings, Thunderbolts, Mustangs, Hellcats, and Corsairs that would sweep the enemy skies before them. There would be new bombers—Helldivers and Invaders among the many. They would smash the Japanese on the ground and pursue him to the last corner of the seas. And then, finally, would come the mighty Superfortress bombers that would put the torch to the cities of Japan, that would burn out the cities and the factories and kill more people in six months than the Japanese Army had lost in eight years of war.

The long road back began in the latter part of 1942. It is easy enough to remember the smashing victories over the enemy, and it is understandable for us to do so.

It is less easy to remember the defeats, and this too is understandable.

This is the way it was. . . .

NOTES AND SOURCES

Chapter 1

[1]Saburo Sakai with Martin Caidin and Fred Saito, *Samurai!* (New York: E. P. Dutton & Co., Inc., 1958), pp. 176–77.

[2]Robert S. Johnson with Martin Caidin, *Thunderbolt!* (New York: Rinehart & Company, Inc., 1958), pp. 280–81.

[3]Masatake Okumiya and Jiro Horikoshi with Martin Caidin, *Zero!* (New York: E. P. Dutton & Co., Inc., 1956), p. 238.

Chapter 3

[1]Okumiya and Horikoshi, *Zero!*, pp. 22–23.
[2]*Ibid.*, pp. 24–25.
[3]*Ibid.*, pp. 26–27.

Chapter 5

[1]Sakai, *op. cit.*, p. 46.
[2]*Ibid.*, p. 47.
[3]Olga S. Greenlaw, *The Lady and the Tigers* (New York: E. P. Dutton & Co., Inc., 1943), pp. 20–21.
[4]Sakai, *op. cit.*, pp. 48–50, 51.
[5]Okumiya and Horikoshi, *Zero!*, p. 33.
[6]Sakai, *op. cit.*, pp. 61–62.
[7]Okumiya and Horikoshi, *op. cit.*, p. 38.
[8]*Ibid.*, pp. 44–45.

Chapter 6

[1]Okumiya and Horikoshi, p. 70.
[2]*Ibid.*, p. 70.

Chapter 7

[1]Okumiya and Horikoshi, *op. cit.*, p. 70.
[2]*Ibid.*, pp. 71–74.
[3]*Ibid.*, p. 76.
[4]Vern Haugland, *The AAF Against Japan* (New York: Harper & Brothers, 1948).

⁶United States Air Force, History Office, *The Army Air Forces in World War II*, Wesley Frank Craven [and] James Lea Cate (eds.) (Chicago: University of Chicago Press, 1948–58), Vol. I, p. 201.

Chapter 8

¹Haugland, *op. cit.*
²Okumiya and Horikoshi, *op. cit.*, pp. 84–85.
³Sakai, *op. cit.*, pp. 70–71.
⁴Statement appeared in *The New York Times*, September 28, 1946, p. 6.
⁵Okumiya and Horikoshi, *op. cit.*, pp. 87, 88–89.
⁶*Ibid.*, pp. 110–12, 113–16, 118.
⁷*Ibid.*, p. 121.
⁸United States Air Force, History Office, *op. cit.*, Vol. I, p. 214.

Chapter 9

¹Diary of Lieutenant David L. Obert. Made available to the author through the kindness of Vern Haugland.

Chapter 10

¹All quotations in this chapter are from Greenlaw, *The Lady and the Tigers*, pp. 32, 87, 91, 94, 112, 118, and 127, unless otherwise indicated.
²United States Air Force, History Office, *op. cit.*, Vol. I, p. 490.
³*Ibid.*
⁴*Ibid.*, Vol. I, p. 506.
⁵*Ibid.*

Chapter 11

¹Colonel Robert L. Scott, Jr., *God Is My Co-Pilot* (New York: Charles Scribner's Sons, 1944), pp. 86–88, 102–103, 104, 112–13.

Chapter 12

¹All quotations in this chapter are from Scott, *God Is My Co-Pilot*, pp. 124, 134–35, 137, 138, 159, 160–61, 175–76, 194, and 194–95, unless otherwise indicated.
²Russell Whelan, *The Flying Tigers* (New York: The Viking Press, Inc., 1942), pp. 194–196.

Chapter 13

¹Statements in this chapter quoted from or attributed to Gregory-Richmond Board are from personal interviews with

him held at length by the author at Tucson, Arizona, and Guadalajara, Mexico, in 1962.

[2] *New Zealanders with the Royal Air Force*, Vol. III (Wellington, New Zealand: War History Branch, Department of Internal Affairs, 1953).

[3] Douglas Gillison, *Royal Australian Air Force, 1939–1942* (Canberra: Australian War Memorial, 1962), p. 222.

[4] Gillison, *op. cit.*, p. 249.

[5] *Ibid.*, pp. 257–58.

[6] *Ibid.*, pp. 277–78.

Chapter 14

[1] Claire Lee Chennault, *Way of a Fighter*, Robert Hotz (ed.) (New York: G. P. Putnam's Sons [1949]), p. 114.

[2] *Ibid.*, p. 114.

[3] *Ibid.*, p. 114.

[4] *AAF Historical Study No. 9: The AAF in Australia to the Summer of 1942* (United States Air Force Document No. 3-2674-1C, Washington, D.C., Declassified, 1958).

[5] *Ibid.*

[6] *Ibid.*

[7] Haugland, *op. cit.*

[8] Sakai, *op. cit.*, pp. 85–86, 87.

[9] *Ibid.*, pp. 91–93.

Chapter 15

[1] Quotations in this chapter are from *AAF Historical Study No. 9* (see above) or from personal material from the 22nd Bomb Group.

Chapter 16

[1] *History of the 67th Fighter Squadron (Single Engine)— Activation to Early 1944*. These records, lost for many years, were discovered in late 1956 "in a very worn out and badly decomposed condition." Their restoration was carried out by Richard A. Long, Base Historian, 18th Air Base Group. Until recently they have not been available to the general public. Quoted matter in this chapter is mainly from these historical records.

Chapter 17

[1] Much of the material in this chapter is reprinted by permission from *The Mission*, by Martin Caidin and Edward Hymoff (Philadelphia and New York: J. B. Lippincott Company, 1964).

[2] This and all other references that pertain to General Samuel E. Anderson, USAF (Ret.), stem from conferences with

General Anderson in Washington, D.C., on December 12, 13, 18, and 30, 1963, and January 10, 1964, or from extensive source materials, including personal diary and official logs and reports, studied during these conferences.

[3]Discussions, tape-recorded by the author and Edward Hymoff, with officers and men of the 22nd Bomb Group, December, 1963, and January, 1964.

[4]Statements by Lieutenant Ford were made during interviews with the author and Edward Hymoff in December, 1963.

[5]Material in the remainder of this chapter from John Richardson, Gerald J. Crosson, Walter A. Krell, and Brigadier General John N. Ewbank, Jr., is from personal interviews by the author and Edward Hymoff in December, 1963, and January, 1964, or from diaries and group records supplied by them at the time.

[6]Pat Robinson, *The Fight for New Guinea* (New York: Random House, 1943).

[7]Diary made available by Lieutenant Colonel Dwight Divine, II.

Chapter 18

[1]The facts related in this chapter are based upon the written records of the 22nd Bomb Group.

[2]*Ibid.*

INDEX

ABOUT THE AUTHOR

MARTIN CAIDIN, a prolific and versatile writer with more than eighty books to his credit, is also a commercial and military pilot, a stunt flyer, parachutist and a recognized authority in the field of aviation and astronautics. From 1950 to 1954 Martin Caidin served as nuclear warfare specialist for the state of New York. He analyzed the effects of nuclear and other weapons on potential targets in the United States. As a commercial multi-engine pilot, Mr. Caidin flies his own plane all over the country. He has flown two-engine and four-engine bombers in Europe. For a time he flew his own World War II Messerschmitt in Europe and the United States. Martin Caidin's first novel, *Marooned,* a thrilling account of a space rescue, became a major motion picture, and *Devil Take All, No Man's World* and *Almost Midnight* were all bought for films. *Cyborg,* published in 1972, is now the highly popular ABC-TV series "The Six Millon Dollar Man." Mr. Caidin is the author of an impressive list of authoritative books on military air history. Many of them, including *Samurai!, Zero!* and *The Ragged, Rugged Warriors,* are considered classics in their field. Martin Caidin is a charter member of the Aviation Hall of Fame, a Fellow of the British Interplanetary Society and a founder of the American Astronautical Society. Although he and his wife, Isobel, live within sight of the launching towers at Cape Kennedy, Martin Caidin is giving much of his attention these days to the problems we have fashioned for ourselves with nuclear weapons. His most recent books are *Aquarius Mission* and *Wingborn.*

Coming in June of 1985 . . .

THE
HAJ

LEON URIS

From one of the consummate storytellers of our era, here is the sweeping saga of Palestine, filled with all the memorable characters and meticulous detail that are Leon Uris's trademark. After such landmark novels as EXODUS and TRINITY, he has written a still more mature and committed work.

THE HAJ will be available June 1, 1985, wherever Bantam Books are sold.

Join the Allies on the Road to Victory
BANTAM WAR BOOKS